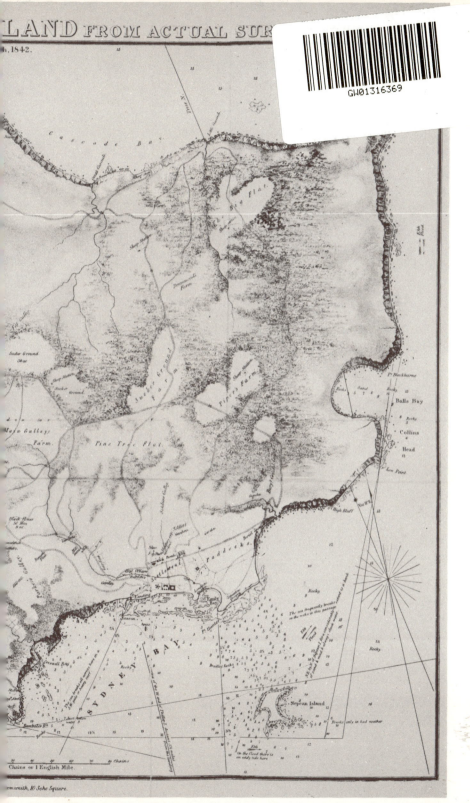

Map and Survey of Norfolk Island 1840. Published J. Arrowsmith, 1842. (British Library, London)

Punishment Short Of Death

A History of
the Penal Settlement
at Norfolk Island

MARGARET HAZZARD

HYLAND HOUSE   MELBOURNE

First published in 1984 by
Hyland House Publishing Pty Limited
10 Hyland Street
South Yarra
Melbourne
Victoria 3141

This book was published with the assistance of
the Literature Board of the Australia Council.

National Library of Australia
cataloguing-in-publication data:

Hazzard, Margaret.
   Punishment short of death.

   Bibliography.
   Includes index.
   ISBN 0 908090 64 1.

   1. Norfolk Island—History. I. Title.

994'.82

Jacket and plates by Crosstown Graphics, Melbourne
Typeset by ProComp Productions Pty Ltd, South Australia
Printed by Brown Prior Anderson, Melbourne

Foreword

IT WAS A PARADISE TURNED INTO HELL. SUCH IS ONE SUMMARY OF THE HISTORY OF NORFOLK ISLAND FROM ITS DISCOVERY BY CAPTAIN COOK in 1774 until its evacuation by the government of Van Diemen's Land eighty-one years later. Into that period of time Margaret Hazzard, in this History which relies so impressively upon the primary sources, describes the two eras of Norfolk Island.

The first is that which was marked by the settlement of convicts and their masters transferred from Port Jackson as a result of instructions to Governor Phillip. This period lasted till 1814 by which time other directions from the colonising authority had led Macquarie to remove the ex-convicts to Van Diemen's Land, where they gave the name of their erstwhile home to Norfolk Plains (later Longford) and New Norfolk.

This early period stars many famous actors in the story of early Norfolk Island and Australia. There is Phillip Gidley King, Robert Ross, D'Arcy Wentworth, Joseph Foveaux, 'General' Holt and John Piper. Perhaps for the first time Margaret Hazzard, as a result of her assiduous work in the Mitchell Library, the La Trobe Library and elsewhere, is now able to offer us more than glimpses of the usually inarticulate and illiterate convict-settlers, notably through the out-pourings of the mysterious 'Buckey' Jones, said to have been transported on the First Fleet.

It is through both the immediacy of these sometimes semi-coherent memoirs and through the formal language laid out in official reports that the author leads us to begin to understand the nature of existence in one part of colonial Australia. Here are the wild fluctuations of kaleidoscopic fortune—human and natural—which lead one prisoner on to fame and fortune, another to the gibbett and yet another to monstrous punishment short of death.

Life goes on. Women's treatment is described by the author when it is recorded and significant. Female prisoners are maltreated and then cosseted. Children are born, including William Charles Wentworth, famous son of the retired highwayman D'Arcy and the mysterious convict woman Catherine Crowley. The earth is tilled.

First and last the society and landscape of Norfolk Island is dominated by the military and their works, in their fearsome authority and in their buildings. John Grant, transported for shooting a man in the course of a love affair, was able to write home from Norfolk Island, 'We have no venomous animals here except the Military', not that Grant was exactly an amiable and collected individual himself, as the reader will discover.

Norfolk Island's second phase began in 1825 and lasted for thirty years. It was during this period of its turbulent history that the island became infamous throughout the world as a place of secondary punishment as severe as the human frame could stand—and could not stand, as Margaret Hazzard affectingly describes.

Again skilfully deploying and citing substantial bodies of primary records, the author takes the reader through the regimes of such commandants as Morisset, Alexander Maconochie and Joseph Childs. The terrors such as those recounted by Bishop Willson of Hobart Town led to exposure of sadism but little effective remedy. Ms Hazzard is enabled to describe the notorious 'Ring' of hardened convicts, the final upheaval of the July 1846 mutiny and its macabre aftermath, and the regime of John Price. We read the agonising reports of such as the Reverend Rogers as he comforts as best he can the 2000 wretches confined on Norfolk Island in the mid-1840s, when it came under the control of Van Diemen's Land.

It is no wonder that such writers as Price Warung and Marcus Clarke fastened upon Norfolk Island and its convict population as scene for stories of artistic accuracy. Here was a place of perverted values where evil was reckoned to be good and where the unbelievable became the norm. It was a surreal world.

Norfolk Island was broken up as a penal establishment in 1855 and its human contents, such as they were, transferred to Van Diemen's Land. Left behind were the formidable remnants of the convict system in the shape of a sharply altered landscape and introduced animals running wild. The descendants of Bligh's mutineers of the *Bounty* appeared, their grandparents men who ironically enough could well have been transported to Norfolk Island had they been apprehended.

Now peace and tranquillity characterise the Island. It is difficult to begin to imagine its history but Ms Hazzard's lengthy and carefully-constructed account enables us to come to terms with one aspect of the enormous violence of Australia's origins, and the systematic inhumanity which so characterised the life of the first generations of Australians.

The ghost of our past remains always present, and grim as some of Margaret Hazzard's History is, yet it is necessary for our education, no matter what our age, that we come to terms with it. If we sweep our history under the carpet, then our perceptions of the present are dislocated; a false image comes to distort the prism of the past through which we come to terms with the present and ourselves. One of the tasks of the historian is to set the record straight without fear or favour, another is to understand the continuity between past and present. Margaret Hazzard's study of Norfolk Island may confidently be recommended as a component in the education of Australia. No student of Australian history should disregard this sobering and yet enlivening work.

L. L. ROBSON
Reader in History
University of Melbourne
April 1984

Contents

List of Illustrations

Preface and Acknowledgements

THE STORY OF NORFOLK ISLAND'S FIRST AND SECOND PENAL SETTLEMENTS HAS NEVER BEEN TOLD IN ITS ENTIRETY; IT IS DOUBTFUL IT EVER WILL be. History is made from the lives of people and the written words of their time, but so many who were instrumental in shaping the history of Norfolk Island's early days, were unable to write even their names.

In this book I have endeavoured to set down not only the major figures, all of them literate to some degree, but those others who left no record of their lives except as names on a muster-list or in a punishment-book. These names make up the mass of men who lived on Norfolk Island in its first 68 years of occupation. It is remarkable that so many of the 'human dregs' condemned to spend years, or a lifetime, on the dreaded Hell of the Pacific, lived through those years and emerged to become, in larger measure than they have been credited with, part of the rugged core of the Australian nation. Their defiance and endurance of the worst brutalities forced upon them, eventually brought to the authorities the recognition that men's souls could not be won by the lash or the chain or any other of the refinements of torture. It was a brutal period, tempered only during the time of the prison-reformer Alexander Maconochie whose efforts during his years as Superintendent on Norfolk Island, was the forerunner of today's open-prison system. In his term of office men were recognised as fellow-beings rather than outcasts fit for nothing other than the chain and the prison cell, but his method was not approved by the authorities, and brutality returned with renewed force after Maconochie was removed. During his lifetime his work was considered experimental, and only those men to whom he had given hope and a new way of life, and his friends who staunchly supported him and his efforts, believed that his theories of Reform by Moral Persuasion pointed the way to Prison Reform. That one small beautiful island could hold so much misery and degradation gathered in the short space of sixty years or so, speaks sadly for mankind. That it could have been largely forgotten or ignored, speaks badly for historians of the time. These scars on history can never be erased, but they need to be seen. They prove that man's resilience, along with his capacity for both good and evil, is an awesome thing and that reason is, in the long run, stronger than brute force.

Many of the men not mentioned by name in this book—for to the authorities they had no name, only a number—are buried in the Old Cemetery on Norfolk Island though few of the first settlement graves are marked, and none now know where they lie. Alongside their graves are those of others, wives and children of their soldier guards, officers and men from the Old Country. At times their restless spirits seem to wander through the place they had cause to know so well, as if still seeking peace.

*   *   *

I record with gratitude the great debt I owe to the staffs of the Mitchell Library, Sydney, and the La Trobe Library, Melbourne, without whose untiring assistance I could not have completed this work. Also my sincere thanks are due to the Dixson Library, Sydney, the Archives Office of New South Wales, the Trustees of the State Library, Sydney, the National Library, Canberra, the Archives Office of Tasmania, the Alexander Turnbull Library, Wellington, New Zealand, The Royal Commonwealth Library, London, the Public Records Office, Kew, England, The Australian High Commission Library, London, The British Library, the London Museum and the Guildhall Library, London, for pictures and maps and information supplied. To Dr Charles Craig, historian and good friend, of Launceston Tasmania, my grateful thanks for his help freely given and for his good wishes when the going was rough. To the writers, long dead, of the many manuscripts I have quoted from, I give special thanks for the light they have shed on the sombre whole of the text. To Mr Patrick Singleton, Senior Research Librarian, Bailleau Library, Melbourne University, special thanks for his kind help and advice, and to my editor Tim Bass for his patience throughout the years. Heartfelt thanks are due to my family who have borne with me during the sometimes harrassed years just passed.

Sir John Barry, author of *Alexander Maconochie of Norfolk Island*, and *The Life and Death of John Price*, wrote, in 1964, 'No complete history of Norfolk Island as a penal settlement has been written, and he who undertakes the task will need a strong stomach . . . for the story of the island is consistently one of appalling inhumanity'. In this he writes no less than the truth, and I am greatly indebted to him for his two works that bring the period of penal settlement appalling though it was, into perspective for comparison with prison systems of today.

Margaret Hazzard
June 1984

A Paradise Discovered 1

NORFOLK ISLAND LIES LIKE A GREEN GEM ON THE VAST BOSOM OF THE SOUTH PACIFIC OCEAN. 'A SPECK UNDER THE FINGER OF GOD', WROTE the novelist James Michener, and indeed it is, yet this speck has a history as terrible as that of any place on earth. Its early years as a penal settlement were a period of degradation and inhumanity unparalleled in the annals of human suffering. Men chose death rather than go to this Island which Captain James Cook had called a Paradise.

Cook was the first white man to set foot on the Island. He discovered it on the morning of 10 October 1774 while on his way from New Caledonia to Queen Charlotte Sound in the *Resolution*, during his second round-the-world voyage of 1772 to 1775. He wrote in his log: 'At daybreak we were standing to the West, an Island was discovered bearing SWBS'[1] and noted the soundings, remarked on the coral and the sandy bottom, the shoals of submerged rocks, and gave it as his opinion that the isle was part of a ridge extending from New Caledonia to the northernmost tip of New Zealand.[2]

Norfolk Island is indeed (with its smaller neighbour, Philip Island, a few kilometres to the south) the only remaining peak of that 1770-kilometre chain of mountains which had slid beneath the grey swirling waters three million or so years before, during a violent eruption. Then it had been a spitting volcanic monster, bare of everything but white-hot rock and lava, but over uncounted centuries the peak grew green and the rich volcanic soil harboured trees, creepers, plants of many species, and brilliant birds and insects. The seas around it teemed with fish, seabirds nested on the monolithic rocks; it was truly a Paradise.

Cook, impatient to reach Queen Charlotte Sound, where he hoped to 'refresh his crew' and gather flax from the plants indigenous to the place, stopped to take a look at this new Island and take possession if it should prove to be uninhabited. On 11 October he sailed around its thirty-kilometre coastline and after dinner hoisted out two boats:

... in which myself, some of the officers and gentlemen went to take a view of the island and its produce. We found no difficulty in landing behind some rocks which lined part of the coast and defended it from the surf. We found the island uninhabited and near akin to New Zealand, the flax plant and many other plants common to that country was found, but the chief produce . . . is Spruce Pines which grow here in great abundance and to a vast size . . . We cut down one of the smallest trees we could find to cut a length of its end to make a topg't mast or yard. My carpenter tells me the wood is of exactly the same nature as the Quebeck [*sic*] Pines. Here then is another isle where Masts and Yards for the largest ships may be had . . . It is in the latitude of 29° 00′, Longit. 168° 16′ East. It is about 5 leagues in circuit and its shores are steep and rocky . . . I took possession of this isle as I had done of all the others we had found and named it Norfolk Isle in Honour of that Noble Family. [the Howards, Dukes of Norfolk] The approach of night brought us all on board, when we hoisted in the boats and stretched to the ENE with the wind at the south-east.[3]

To Cook, superb master-mariner and navigator, whose life was the sea, the little island 'five leagues in circuit', with steep and rocky shores, was yet another place to mark on his chart as a possession of His Majesty King George III. In his report *Voyage in the Southern Hemisphere*, published in 1778 after his untimely death, he described it as 'a Paradise'. Had he lived to return to it it might not have become the sad and dreaded place it did.

Among his 'officers and gentlemen' were a few who left graphic descriptions of the island. Although these men have largely been forgotten in the onrush of history, their written reports give clear pictures of that afternoon of 11 October 1774. William Wales, astronomer of the voyage, was 40 years old, a dour, slightly corpulent little Yorkshireman, well liked by Cook. In his report, the birds and trees on the Island get far more detailed descriptions than do the few flowers, though he did remark on the wood-sorrel and sow-thistle which he 'took back to the ship in a bag', doubtless to feed to the penned stock on board, an endearing touch.

I found the shores exceeding steep and rocky and in most places inaccessible on that account. Near the shores the ground is covered so thick with New Zealand flax it is scarcely possible to get through it . . . but a little way inland the woods are perfectly clear and easy to walk in. The soil seemed to be exceeding rich and deep . . . probably formed by the decay of its vegetable production . . . I saw many trees which were, breast high, as thick as two men could fathom and at the same time exceeding straight and high. I believe much larger ships than the *Resolution* might on occasion furnish themselves with Main-masts. The greatest rarity we met here was the Cabbage Tree . . . those trees are of the same genus as the cocoanut . . . what they call

Trial in progress at the Old Bailey, London. Rowlandson, 18th or early 19th century. (The Museum of London)

PRISON-SHIP IN PORTSMOUTH HARBOUR.

Prison ship (hulk) in Portsmouth Harbour; convicts being taken on board. Drawn by W. Cooke, 1828. (Guildhall Library, London)

Engraved for the Newgate Calendar.

Representation of the Transports going from Newgate to take water at Blackfriars

Transportees being taken to Blackfriars, artist unknown, possibly Rowlandson. (Guildhall Library, London)

Model of a prison cell at the Neptune Street prison, London, 1700. Note the hand fetters. (The Museum of London)

the Cabbage is properly speaking the Bud of the tree . . . situate at the
Crown where the leaves spring out. The Island we have just left, the
Captain calls Norfolk Island after the Duchess of Norfolk. It abounds
with rails, parrots and pigeons, the latter are the largest in the
world . . . We saw no inhabitants nor the least reason to believe it had
ever been trod by human feet before . . .[4]

The naturalists Johannes and George Forster, father and son, were in the
shore party as a matter of course. They had been recruited after the influential
Sir Joseph Banks, scientist, naturalist, patron of the arts and wealthy
benefactor, had withdrawn from the voyage. He did this because of Cook's
refusal to allow the top-heavy superstructure Banks insisted was necessary to
house his entourage, his collection of plants, and the 'round-house' he had
had erected for Cook after taking over Cook's 'great cabin' for himself. The
extra deck made the 462-ton *Resolution* unseaworthy, said Cook, and the
Admiralty ordered its removal. Banks removed himself, his servants, friends,
and presumably his patronage. The Forsters were brought on instead.

Johannes Forster, 45, was a Prussian who had lived in England for seven
years. He was appointed to Banks's post as 'Naturalist', with his son George
as assistant. George was then 20. Both were dedicated naturalists; neither of
them had any money. George taught languages, translated books into English,
and studied Natural History. He was later to make his mark in many fields.
Both men wrote accounts of their short stay at Norfolk Island, Johannes's
filled with Latin names of birds and plants with descriptions of the colour and
form of each species. They shot some of the birds and George made drawings
of them, noting the colours in his sketchbook. He later wrote *A Voyage
Round the World Performed in His Brittanic Majesty's Ships the Resolution
and Adventure in the Years 1772 1773 1774 1775.* There he writes:

We found a little rill which descended in a cleft between two hills, and
following the course of it we penetrated into the woods with great
difficulty through a tissue of bindweeds and climbers. However as
soon as we had passed through this outward fence we found the
forests tolerably clear of underwood and had not the least difficulty to
walk forwards . . . the parrots and parroquets were infinitely brighter
than those of New Zealand and the pigeon was exactly the same. We
found besides these, a number of small birds peculiar to this spot,
some of which were very beautiful . . . The melody of the birds was
very pleasing in this deserted spot, which if it had been of greater size
would have been unexceptionable for a European settlement. While
we examined the woods some of the boats crew had been no less busy
in catching fish . . . The tops of the Cabbage Palm, these fish, and the
birds . . . we had shot afforded us an excellent refreshment for a day
or two . . .[5]

Cook sailed on, having marked the Island named for the Duchess, not the Duke, in his charts. It was to be another fourteen years before foot was again set on that place of 'near inaccessible beaches' where the delicate-flavoured Cabbage Palm grew in such abundance and the birds were so much more brilliant than in New Zealand. It would also be a very different landing-party that came to stay. As well as the 'officers and gentlemen' there would be men and women condemned to spend years or a lifetime in labour as servants of the Crown.

Norfolk Isle, the lonely peak of that great submerged mountain chain was indeed to become a place of European settlement, as George Forster had written, but not the elegant centre he envisaged. It was to become the Hell of the Pacific, and its music not 'the pleasing melody of the birds', but the whistle of the lash, the clanking of heavy iron chains and the screams of tortured men and women.

In the last weeks of August 1786 Lord Sydney, the Home Secretary, wrote instructing their Lordships of the Treasury:

> . . . that you do forthwith take such measures as may be necessary for providing a proper number of vessels for the conveyance of seven hundred and fifty convicts to Botany Bay together with such provisions, necessaries and implements for agriculture as may be necessary for their use after arrival.[6]

So the ships were gathered into dockyards to be fitted out as transports, store ships and naval vessels. His Majesty King George III had commanded that the land Captain Cook discovered in 1770 during his first voyage of discovery around the world, should be occupied if not settled, by the felons in Britain's crowded gaols.

On 12 October 1786 a Commission was given to Captain Arthur Phillip R.N. appointing him the first Governor of the territory to be called New South Wales:

> . . . and you are to observe and follow such orders and directions from time to time as you shall receive from us . . . and likewise such orders and directions as we shall send you under our signet or sign manual . . . in pursuance of the trust we hereby repose in you . . . Given at our Court at St. James, the 12th day of October 1786 in the twenty-sixth year of our reign.
>
> By His Majesty's Command,
> *Sydney*[7]

Within his letter of instructions from His Majesty, Captain Phillip received an enclosure which read, in part:

Norfolk Island . . . being represented as a spot which may hereafter become useful you are, as soon as circumstances will admit of it, to send a small establishment thither and to secure the same to us to prevent it being occupied by the subjects of any other European Power.[8]

The first entry in *An Historical Journal of the Transactions at Port Jackson and Norfolk Island*, the journal by Captain John Hunter of his first four years in the new colony, reads:

It being the intention of government to remove the inconvenience which this country suffered from the gaols being so exceedingly overcrowded with criminals who had been by the Law condemned to transportation, the east coast of New Holland was the place determined upon to form a settlement for this salutary purpose.[9]

Hunter was a keen observer and no mean artist; he left a number of neat watercolours and detailed pencil sketches in his *Journal* which serve as a vivid record. He was appointed second-in-command on the flagship *Sirius* which carried no convicts, and while Captain Arthur Phillip was engaged on the many duties so necessary for a voyage such as the First Fleet's was to be, Hunter's duty was to take the *Sirius* down the Thames to Long Reach and the Mother-Bank at Portsmouth. On 30 January 1787 he wrote:

Two transports, one having male the other female convicts on board, dropt down to Long Reach, but they having business to transact with the owners of the ships . . . were permitted to proceed as low as Gravesend where the *Sirius* joined them next day and proceeded immediately to the Nore where we anchored . . . and were joined by His Majesty's armed tender *Supply*. On 4th February we anchored in the Downs and were detained there by bad weather and contrary winds until the 19th. when we put to sea in company with the *Supply* and transports, and arrived on the Mother Bank on the 21st. At this anchorage all the transports and store ships were directed to rendezvous; the latter were already arrived and while we lay here, the other transports joined us from the westwards.[10]

The transports, with their cargo of human wretchedness, were not Hunter's immediate concern. In 1787 Hunter was an ageing man, nearing 50 years—this voyage would probably be his last opportunity for promotion. Bred to naval discipline, to him the convicts were no more than miscreants deserving of punishment; many of them had escaped the death penalty and were being carried to the new land under His Majesty George III's merciful dispensation. Yet on those two ships that 'dropt down to Long Reach' were 195 men (*Alexander*) and 101 women (*Lady Penrhyn*), most of them direct from gaol, or from the hulks at Woolwich. Few of them had clothing fit for the bitter winter weather; many of them were sick with gaol fever or venereal disease or other ills. Some had been on board the transports for weeks; they still had months to wait before the fleet set sail.

At the Mother-Bank, where the supply ships *Golden Grove*, *Borrowdale* and *Fishburn* were already arrived, confusion reigned on the wharves, where provisions were being loaded and prisoners in chains waited to be embarked on the *Scarborough* and the *Prince of Wales*. Two more transports, *Charlotte* and *Friendship* were to arrive, each of them loaded with convicts from the hulks moored in Portsmouth harbour.

Convicts under sentence of transportation had been gathered from gaols all over England. Many of them had been rotting in prison for three years, some longer. In the eighteenth century Capital Offences numbered more than 200, ranging from stealing goods valued at one shilling or more, pick-pocketing, cattle-stealing, forgery and counterfeiting to highway robbery, rape, armed burglary, assault and murder.

Some of the women were sentenced for prostitution; it was a profession at which they could earn enough to keep themselves, and perhaps a child, alive. For many it was better than working for the owners of sweat-shops which handed out a dozen fine linen shirts to be frilled and button-holed—the woman to supply the thread for sewing out of the sum of threepence, the price paid for the dozen. Almost the only 'respectable' job for poor girls was 'service'. This often meant a sixteen-hour day of near-slavery and the constant temptation to steal pretty clothes, trinkets belonging to an employer, or unguarded money. One Scottish girl, transported for seven years for a petty theft, brooded herself to death before the departure of the First Fleet.

After many frustrating delays, the fleet finally sailed for Botany Bay on 13 May 1787. It presented a pretty sight as the wide sails filled and the sun sparkled on the water, and for some of the prisoners a faint hope of a better chance cheered them in spite of bitter grief at leaving their homeland for ever.

Of course, there were some who were prepared to make a bid for freedom. Some of the convicts on the *Scarborough* hatched a plot to take over the ship and sail her away in the dark of the night—imprisoning or murdering the officers and others on board.[11] Their irons had been struck off on Captain Phillip's orders, that 'they might have it in their power to strip off their clothes at night when they went to rest, and have the advantage of being more at their ease during the day, and be able to wash and keep themselves clean' but his leniency led to nothing other than a severe lashing for the two ringleaders and their transfer to another transport.[12]

The voyage took eight months and some days, with calls at several ports in Spain, Portugal, Rio de Janeiro, and Cape Town, where fresh supplies of food were taken on board along with wine, spirits and water, and ceremonial visits were paid to Governors and Viceroys. In Cape Town the ships anchored in Table Bay for some weeks, while repairs were made and livestock bought after much bargaining. Some of the officers lived ashore; many of them bought stock for themselves, sheep, cattle and horses, and at every port seeds or plants were sought, lemons, oranges, Indian corn—provender for the unknown new colony.

During much of the voyage the convicts were confined below-deck, with brief interludes when they were allowed up in small batches, under the watchful eyes of armed sentries. Their quarters were cleaned and disinfected regularly, their food was adequate, they were visited by the ship's surgeon when necessary, but they had no employment other than brooding on the past, on the families left behind and perhaps never to be seen again. Arguments and fights were common, as were the punishments that followed. There was plenty of time for hate to fester, alliances to be made and plans to be hatched for future crimes. No first-hand record or diary written by a First Fleet convict during the voyage has so far been found, though there are a number of eye-witness accounts written by officers who were on board, and one of these is the diary of Lieutenant Ralph Clark, who was on the *Friendship*.

He reports the occasion when Elizabeth Dudgeon had been impertinent to the ship's Captain and had been ordered a flogging for it: 'The corporal did not play with her but laid it home, which I was very glad to see'.[13] A flogging, especially of a woman, seemed to please this somewhat sadistic young man, for he entered each and every one in his diary.

The First Fleet dropped anchor in Botany Bay on 19 January 1788, but only a few convicts were sent ashore, and those only to fell timber or turn the soil, so that Phillip might decide whether the place was suitable for a settlement. It was, he said, too open and too swampy, and, with a few officers he set off around the coast northwards, in search of a more likely situation. He found the place Captain Cook had named Port Jackson. Later, in a despatch to Lord Sydney, he wrote:

> We got into Port Jackson early in the afternoon and had the
> satisfaction of finding the finest harbour in the world, in which a
> thousand sail of the line may ride in the most perfect security.[14]

The Fleet finally dropped anchor in the little bay Phillip named Sydney Cove, on the 26th of January. By the 28th most of the male convicts, except those too sick to walk, were put ashore. Lieutenant King of the *Sirius* wrote:

> The stock was also landed on this day on the eastern point of the
> cove. I should have mentioned before that, from the time of our
> sailing from England to our arriving here, we have lost only 32 people
> including marines, seamen and convicts, but were so unfortunate as
> to lose part of our stock. We landed only 4 mares and 2 stallions,
> 4 cows, 1 bull and 1 bull calf, ewes, a good stock of poultry and 3
> goats with hogs which are the property of the Governor and the
> Government.[15]

The weather was hot and threatened storms, but on the day most of the women convicts were landed, nothing, neither work, punishments nor fierce lightning and lashing rain could prevent what chronicler Captain Watkin Tench described as scenes of 'licentiousness' and 'depravity':

> While they [the convicts] were aboard, the two sexes had been kept rigorously apart; but when landed, their separation became impracticable and would have been perhaps, wrong. Licentiousness was the unavoidable consequence and their old habits of depravity were beginning to recur. To prevent their intercourse was impossible; and to palliate its evils only, remained. Marriage was recommended and such advantages held out to those who aimed at reformation, as have greatly contributed to the tranquillity of the settlement.[16]

The tranquillity was not to last for long. The marriage rate fell drastically once the convicts discovered it did not bring the immediate benefits of increased rations and reduced hours of government labour, as they had hoped.

On 30 January Governor Phillip informed Lieutenant King he was to be the Superintendent and Commandant of a new settlement at Norfolk Island. Lord Sydney had given the Governor a despatch in which he stated the Government's intention to '. . . settle a small band of people on Norfolk Isle to prevent it falling into the hands of His Majesty's enemies and to secure the same to us.'[17]

An Assembly was called, and the Commission read aloud by the Judge-Advocate, Lieutenant David Collins:

> By virtue of the power and authority invested in me I do hereby constitute and appoint you, Philip Gidley King, Superintendent and Commandant of Norfolk Island and of the settlement to be made thereon . . . Given under my hand and seal at Head-quarters in Port Jackson, New South Wales . . .[18]

An enclosure was also read. It gave King explicit instructions as to his duties, which included sending minutely detailed despatches regarding the Island's produce, the flax plant in particular, and its potential for crops—cotton, corn and other grains:

> . . . with the seeds of which you will be furnished . . . that I may know what quantity may be drawn from the island for the public use or what supply it may be necessary to send hereafter . . . The convicts being Servants of the Crown till the time for which their sentence is expired, their labour is to be for the public and you are to take

particular notice of their general good or bad behaviour that they may hereafter be employed or rewarded according to their different merits . . .[19]

No boats were to be built on the Island that were more than 20 feet (6 metres) long, and none might be decked over. Services were to be held on Sundays and ships in passing were to be allowed to pass, unless in distress.

Fourteen years after its discovery, Norfolk Island was at last to be settled.

Philip Gidley King and the First Settlement

2

I N THE EIGHTEENTH CENTURY, BRITISH ARISTOCRACY HAD A STRANGLE-
HOLD ON THE PLUMS OF OFFICE, BOTH IN THE SERVICES AND IN POLITICS,
and what a man knew was seldom as important as who he knew or who his
richest relations were. A young man with brains and little money would do
best if he found himself a patron who had the ear of those in authority.

But Philip Gidley King, born at Launceston, Cornwall, in April 1754, was
the son of a draper, grandson of a small-town attorney, and his family,
although 'comfortable' had no claims to wealth. When he was 12½ years old,
he entered the Navy as Captain's servant on H.M.S. *Swallow*, the usual entry
for boys with ambition who wished to make the Navy their career. After
five years in Royal Navy ships he was made a midshipman during the British–
American war and commissioned a lieutenant three years later, passing his
examinations brilliantly. The examiner told King's mother: 'He is one of the
most promising young men I have ever met.'[1]

After gaining his commission, King served under Captain Arthur Phillip
and was with him for five years or so. It was natural that Phillip, who liked the
young lieutenant very well, should remember him and choose him to sail on
the *Sirius* as Second Lieutenant in 1787.[2]

King had been accustomed to observe the strict discipline of the Navy, but
one is left with the impression from his many despatches, that he flinched
from punishing too readily, and preferred other approaches, at least in his
first years as an administrator. He had a paternalistic attitude to the people
under him, perhaps from his ambition to be the best, to have the best
settlement under his leadership, or perhaps because he knew, as some of the
sprigs of the New South Wales Corps later had never known, the sting of
servitude.

After receiving his Commission as Commandant of Norfolk Island he set
about choosing the people who were to accompany him, seven freemen and
fifteen convicts.[3] The choice would, he knew, make the difference between
success and failure, for this new settlement was to be more than just another

place where convicts could be sent. It was in its first inception to be a place where flax could be obtained for sails so much needed by the Fleet, and a source of timber for the masts and yards necessary for ships of the line. The Island discovered fourteen years earlier by Captain Cook was to be a source of supply for the English Navy, at a time when these vital commodities, flax and timber, were cut off by the war in the Baltic and the breakaway war of the American colonies: it was the reason for the Enclosure in Governor Phillip's instructions from Lord Sydney, in which he had written 'Norfolk Island . . . being represented as a spot which may hereafter become useful you are, as soon as circumstances admit of it, to send a small establishment thither and to secure the same to us to prevent it being occupied by the subjects of any other European power.'[4]

Two French ships, the *Astrolabe* and the *Boussole* were already in Botany Bay, and but for the difficulty of landing, the *Boussole*'s captain Jean la Perouse would have gone ashore on Norfolk Island to gather samples of the much-valued flax plant for his employers, the French Government. It was not surprising that this tiny island, so far from the main settlement, was considered a prize to be taken as soon as practicable.[5]

King consulted Surgeon Bowes who had been aboard the *Lady Penrhyn* on the voyage out, regarding the women he should take. Bowes kept those he considered 'stood the fairest' in character; they were not allowed to land along with the rest of the women but kept separate, once they had agreed to go with King. Bowes wrote in his *journal*:

> He had made choice of such of both sexes whose behaviour on board has been the least exceptional and has held out such encouragement to them, on their behaving properly, as must render their situation much more comfortable than it could have been at Port Jackson.
>
> At the same time he assured them that he should not take it upon himself to punish them in case of misbehaviour, that as the greatest punishment he could inflict upon them would be that he should send them back again to Port Jackson there to be dealt with according to their demerits. He also assured them that they would not be hard worked and would be conveyed home to England if they chose it upon the expiration of their term of transportation. He also informed them that it was the Governor's pleasure that if any partiality or reciprocal affection should take place between male and female convicts going there, or after their arrival at Norfolk they might marry and he had authorised the surgeon Mr. Jamison to perform that office and after a time the clergyman would be sent there to re-marry them.[6]

For his seven free men, who were to be the 'staff' of the settlement, King chose Surgeon's mate, Thomas Jamison, a well-liked man of 43, as Surgeon; John Turnpenny Altree, who had acted as Surgeon's mate on board the *Lady Penrhyn* with Bowes, as Jamison's assistant; James Cunningham, an energetic young man who had been master's mate of the *Sirius*; Roger Morley, weaver, and William Westbrook, sawyer, both seamen; and John Batchelor and Charles Kerridge as marine guards.[7]

The names of his nine male and six female convicts are not given in King's account of his journey to Norfolk Island, but they and the crimes for which they were transported can be ascertained by dint of much searching of records. They were men from 15 to 72 years old and women in their 20s, with one just 30. Apart from the women, whose choice he had left to Surgeon Bowes, King chose the men for the skills they might possess. Britain's prisons were, in the main, crowded with men born and bred in the cities, pickpockets, petty thieves or vagrants and drunkards doomed to nothing better than the terrible degradation of a crowded cell. Men with a trade were scarcer, and of those in prison many had been driven by the desperation of hunger, to steal or commit some crime which brought them before their Lordships at the Assizes, to be sentenced to transportation. It was this kind of man that King looked for among those who could be spared out of the First Fleet few.[8]

Nathaniel Lucas, carpenter and joiner was a young man from London, transported for theft of articles of clothing. John and Noah Mortimore, with Edward Westlake were men of middle age, from the west of England. Together they had been brought before the court accused of 'stealing a wether sheep valued 12s and forty pounds of mutton value 10s'. Each was given seven years' transportation.

Edward Garth, tried at the Old Bailey, was indicted 'for Feloniously stealing 2 live cows value *l.* 17' and was sentenced to death, but reprieved and given seven years' transportation. John Rice from Exeter in Devon, had also been sentenced to death 'for burglariously breaking and entering' but was reprieved for seven years' transportation. He was a rope-maker, and King later called him 'my right hand man'.

Williams is difficult to pinpoint, for there were three of the same name in the First Fleet. Quite likely he was the one from Bodmin in Cornwall who had been in prison since 1783 and had been sentenced to death 'for stealing one cotton gown, value 10s and other goods value 3s 6d'. A life was cheaply held in the hanging days of the eighteenth century. Williams was drowned within months of reaching Norfolk Island.

The youngest of the chosen settlers was Charles McLellan, who was listed as being 14 years old when he was sentenced in 1785. He came from 'the Parish of Sunderland by the Sea' and had been given seven years' transportation for 'stealing 1 Bladder purse, value one penny, a gold half-guinea, one half-crown, one silver shilling and six pennies in halfpence, the contents of the purse'.

The oldest was Richard Widdicombe, 72 when he reached Botany Bay. With Henry Humphreys, he had been sentenced to seven years' transportation in 1786 for 'stealing 1 wooden winch value 2s and other goods value fortyone shillings and four pence, the property of Vincente Juanez y Echelar'.

None of the nine men had committed a crime of violence, most had a trade either on the land or a craft useful to a new settlement. They were in King's judgement, the best he could do.

The women convicts were an interesting bunch, some of them London girls, one at least a prostitute and they were all young, the oldest of them, Ann Inett, just thirty. Ann Inett was a 'mantua maker' or qualified dress-maker, who came from the mid-country town of Worcester. She had been indicted for stealing from 'the dwelling house of Susannah Brookes, 1 dimity petticoat, 1 muslin apron, 1 pair stuff shoes, 3 muslin handker-chiefs' and sundry other pieces of wearing apparel, 'the property of Jane Brookes'. She was sentenced to death by hanging, but reprieved and given seven years' transportation. It is not difficult to picture her, a quiet young woman, possibly living in her own cottage, keeping herself to herself (she was listed as a 'spinster') stitching, stitching every day on other women's fripperies. Maybe young Jane Brookes was about to be married, and Ann Inett employed to make the trousseau. The clothes she stole, the dimity petticoat and muslin apron were perhaps pretty things she herself had made for the younger girl, clothes she may have coveted for herself. She was convicted in 1785 so had already spent two years in gaol before the First Fleet sailed, and was one of the shivering women on the *Lady Penrhyn* when Captain Hunter 'permitted them to proceed to Gravesend where the *Sirius* joined them next day' on that bitter January morning in the Thames river in 1787.

King took Ann Inett as his mistress during that first early settlement, and it was on Norfolk Island that his two sons, Norfolk and Sydney, were born. These boys he acknowledged, and had them brought up as his own, sent them to school in England and later, taught a profession. Ann married Joseph Robinson, a lifer whom King pardoned when he became Governor of New South Wales, and they had five children.

Elizabeth Hipsley was also a needlewoman, a London girl. She had stolen a silver watch and chain, 1 guinea and five shillings and a pair of worsted garters. She too, was in prison for some time before the Fleet sailed, and during the long voyage south probably filled her time in sewing garments for the officers, who took advantage of such opportunities to replenish their supply of 'small clothes'. Lieutenant Ralph Clark on the *Friendship*, frequently handed out pieces of cloth he had brought with him with just such ideas in mind, for among the convicts there were at least one or two tailors, as well as seamstresses among the women.

Olivia Gasgoign (sometimes spelt Gaskin), came from Worcester also and had been in the gaol since 1784. She was 25 and had been in service. She was indicted for stealing 'with force and arms 13 guineas and 1 foreign coin called a dollar' and was sentenced to hang, but reprieved for seven years' transportation. On Norfolk Island she married Nathaniel Lucas, the carpenter, and they had a string of children. They stayed on the Island until the early 1800s and Nathaniel and she later lived in Parramatta where he became a successful stonemason and builder for a time.

Elizabeth Colley, another London girl 'in service' was 22 and had been given the savage sentence of fourteen years for 'feloniously receiving at the hour of 10 in the night, 1 linen gown and 1 silk cloak knowing them to have been stolen'. Elizabeth had three or four children in Norfolk, but each one bore her name only.

Susannah Gough, aged 25 had been indicted for stealing, in London, with another girl whom Lieutenant Clark roundly condemned as a 'damned whore'. The latter girl, Elizabeth Dudgeon, was the one who gave the Captain the 'length of her spicy tongue' and he jubilantly reported the flogging she received for it. Susannah had behaved well on the voyage and was described as 'one of the best laundresses on board' by Clark. She was not Surgeon Bowes's first choice to go to Norfolk however, and had only been picked after Ann Yates, 'an eminently suitable girl', had said that she would rather stay as she was, in Port Jackson.

The last of the six women had committed by far the most intriguing crime, Elizabeth Lee, aged 24, and 'a cook in the employ of Thomas King Esq.' obviously had her eye on greater things than cooking. At the Old Bailey on a cold February morning in 1785 she was indicted for stealing:

30 gallons of Port. value *l.* 10
3 gallons of White Port value *l.* 20
12 gallons of Malmsey Madeira value *l.* 12
3 gallons of Malmsey wine value 40s
3 gallons of claret value 40s
3 gallons raisin wine value 6s
3 gallons orange wine value 6s
3 gallons brandy value 36s
3 gallons rum value 36s
3 gallons Geneva value 20s
1 gallon arak value 16s
424 glass bottles value *l.* 3 10s
1 cwt tallow candles value 50s
2 linen stocks, 1 gold ring set with garnets
and 2 Crown pieces. Property of Thomas King esq.

There must have been gasps of astonishment and disbelief as the list was read aloud. Even their stout and lethargic Lordships, snoring on the Bench would have jerked themselves awake as the interminable recital went on . . . and on. But Elizabeth (one can imagine her perky, dark haired, cheeky as a London sparrow), got only a seven-year transportation sentence for her mobile liquor-shop attempt. It is warming to find that King obtained her pardon in 1793 and she returned to England, a young woman still, and no doubt full of memories of whoever it was that should have stood beside her in the dock.

These were the men and women who accompanied King to the totally unknown Island; who were chosen to help build what he hoped would be a prosperous new settlement, of much use to the Mother Country. He was full of enthusiasm and good resolutions, keen to make his mark, mindful of the opportunities this assignment gave him, an ambitious man almost 34 years old.

At seven on the morning of 14 February 1788 the *Supply* weighed anchor and sailed down the harbour from Sydney Cove, and out to sea. A fine hurricane wind began to blow, setting the ship rolling and bucking so that King commented in his *Journal* 'I often thought it in a critical situation'.

But the little *Supply* was seaworthy, nothing went wrong, and two days later an island was sighted to the eastward. This when they landed on it, proved to be a wonderful place for turtle. Lieutenant Ball named the island 'Lord Howe', after the First Lord of the Admiralty, and took about eighteen turtle back to Port Jackson with him as food for the Governor and his officers.

By 29 February, Norfolk Island was in sight and by the evening they hove to, off the place later called Cascade, named after the stream of pure water that terminated in a small waterfall crashing to the shore.

For five days King and Lieutenant Ball, sometimes alone, sometimes with James Cunningham, searched for a safe landing place. They put out in the boat, rowed to what looked like a suitable landing place, only to find that rocks barred the shore, or that the current precluded setting foot on shore, or that even if they managed to scramble over the enormous boulders lashed continually by surf, there was nowhere to land stores and provisions, stock, or the people on board the *Supply*. 'During this excursion' writes King 'we did not see a leaf of flax, or any herb whatever! . . . which is quite extraordinary as Captain Cook says that the flax plant is more luxuriant here than in New Zealand'.[9]

At noon on 5 March, the Master of the *Supply*, David Blackburn, went out himself to find a passageway to the shore. He came back triumphant, having found the only place on the whole Island where a landing of both stores and people could take place in safety.

At sunrise the next morning the landing began. The shore close to the beach was 'covered with a long kind of iris, within which was an impenetrable forest', wrote King, but he set his men to work clearing a space where the tents might be set up and men and stores sheltered. The colours were hoisted, and before sunset everything and everybody belonging to the settlement was on shore.

> Before the colours were hauled down, I assembled my small colony
> under them, Lieutenant Ball and some of his officers being present,
> and drank the healths of His Majesty, the Queen, the Prince of Wales,
> and success to the settlement, and as we had no other way of
> testifying our loyalty we gave three cheers on the occasion.[10]

To the twenty-three settlers it must have seemed like the start of a great adventure. For them all, life would present a complete change. For King, a sailor since he was 12, it would mean a new routine, with new rules and different outlook. Only the doctor and his assistant would follow, in some measure, the kind of work they were accustomed to and even they were called upon to do their share of tree-felling, cultivating and planting. For the convicts it must, indeed, have seemed the start of a new life where their situation would be rendered more comfortable than it could have been at Port Jackson.

Here there was freedom of a sort. There was beauty, the wild beauty of a Paradise long waiting to be discovered. There were singing birds like the birds in the English countryside, there were brilliant parrots flashing across the sky, whistling as they flew in small flocks. The forest was everywhere, majestic pines with trunks thicker through than many a convict hut in New South Wales, flowering trees and trees festooned with creeper, streams of pure water trickling down the tree-covered hillsides—and all around, the sea.

That the sea was the enemy they knew well, for it prevented escape. It lashed the coast, thundered against the cliffs, foamed and swirled through narrow passageways in the great rocks standing off shore, but it, too, was part of the Paradise; the fish it held in such abundance were large and sweet, fresh food when salt provisions were wearisome. Yes, there was freedom of a sort, and wild beauty in plenty. Here, everyone could make a new beginning.

Work began in earnest the day after landing. In his despatch to Governor Phillip, King wrote:

> This day I began to clear a piece of ground for sowing some seeds, the spot which I fixed on is on the east side of a hill which has a tolerably easy ascent and the soil is rich and deep . . . we found a very fine rivulet of water which ran close at the back of the settlement . . . On the spaces of ground unoccupied by roots there grew a kind of supple-jack which in general was as thick as a man's leg . . . it ran up the trees and formed an impenetrable kind of net-work. As I had only 12 men, (one of whom was seventy two years old, the other a boy of fifteen), exclusive of the mate and surgeon, my progress for some time must of course be slow.[11]

The sawyer, with a convict or two as assistants, began felling and trimming trees and the women lumped the grain bags and other provisions into the store tent until such time as a better shelter should be built. Some of them had already paired off—Olivia Gasgoign with Nat Lucas, Susannah Gough with Edward Garth, and King himself with Ann Inett the mantua maker. Dr Jamison had little time to wait before reading the makeshift marriage service on the Island.

In March the weather was still kind and the sun warm. Until the wooden huts were built it was easy to sleep out. There were no snakes, centipedes, scorpions or indeed any biting insects at all, except those that the people might have brought with them. Strange noises penetrated the night. Whistles and a kind of long drawn-out moan came from the sea, shrill calls from the wooded valley behind the beach, and some of the people woke in terror; but the calls were only those of the small owl, and the moans from the sea were not long-lost sailors come to haunt the new arrivals but sea sounds made by the tides as they ebbed and flowed through narrow gaps in the rocks.

To keep his settlement orderly King drew up a set of rules and declared them on 18 April:

I. No person is to absent himself from public worship which will begin every Sunday morning at eleven o'clock, in the commandant's house, when every one will come clean and orderly, and behave themselves devoutly.

II. The hours of work are as follows: until further orders, to begin work at day-light, and work till half past seven; at half past eight, to work again until half past eleven; and then to work again at two until sun-set.

III. In order to encourage the cultivation of gardens, every one will have the Saturdays to clear away and cultivate gardens for themselves; and those who are industrious will be encouraged, but those who mis-apply that indulgence will be deprived of it.

IV. On application, at the proper time of the year, seeds will be distributed to those who have cleared away garden ground; and those who raise the greatest quantity of seeds and vegetables will be encouraged and rewarded.

V. The women are to sweep round the houses or tents every morning, and to cook the victuals for the men; and every person is strictly forbid cleaning any fish or fowls in or near the houses, but to go to the sea-side for that purpose.

VI. Every person is strictly forbid going near Turtle Bay, and those who are found in it, or going there, will be instantly and severely punished.

VII. The women are to collect the dirty linen belonging to the men every Friday, and to return each man his proper linen, washed and mended, on the Sunday morning.

VIII. No person is to cut down or destroy any banana tree.

IX. Exchanging or selling cloaths by the convicts is strictly forbid. As their cloathing is the property of the crown, they are not to dispose of it. A disobedience of this order will be deemed a theft, and meet with a suitable punishment. It is recommended to every one to be careful of their cloathing and bedding, as accidents may happen which may prevent a speedy supply.

X. Great care is to be taken of all the tools; each man taking his axe or hoe to his tent, or delivering them to the store-keeper, that they may not be injured by the weather.

XI. As the future welfare of every person on this island depends on their good behaviour, it is recommended to them to persevere in that

The stone marks the place where Lieutenant P. G. King landed with his first settlers, March 1788. (Photograph by the author)

Drawing of the landing-place on Norfolk Island in 1846. The jetty is convict-built. All supplies and all persons were ferried from ship (far left background) to shore. Artist unknown, but probably a civil officer stationed on Norfolk Island. (Courtesy Trustees, Dixson Library)

Drawing of Philip Island viewed from Norfolk Island. Artist unknown, 1846. (Courtesy Trustees, Dixson Library)

The Settlement at Cascade in 1846. All these buildings have gone, only a few ruins remain. (Courtesy Trustees, Dixson Library)

Kingston prison settlement in 1846, shown with pentagonal prison (uncompleted). The drawing is dated October 13, 1846, the day the twelve convicts were hanged for the 1 July 1846 mutiny. (Courtesy Trustees, Dixson Library)

willing disposition to work which they have hitherto shewn; and
above all, to be honest and obliging towards each other, which will
recommend them to those who may have it in their power, and who
have a wish and inclination to serve them: but the dishonest or idle
may not only assure themselves of being totally excluded from any
present or future indulgences, but also that they will be chastised,
either by corporal punishment on the island, or be sent to Port
Jackson, to be tried by a criminal court there.[12]

It was almost an 'Israelite' community at first, with King promulgating the
laws, determining punishment, and generally taking responsibility for them
all. He had ideals as well as ambition and possibly envisaged a settlement
where reformation rather than retribution would be the norm. He had yet to
learn about men familiar with crime and its punishments; so far he had been
familiar only with Navy men, sailors used to discipline as a matter of routine.

He had also to learn about sowing crops. In England, March was planting
time, so therefore, on Norfolk Island, seeds were sown into the deep rich soil
and by 14 March were up and flourishing. Within a couple of weeks the
burning south-west wind blew and overnight the tender plants were salt-
burned beyond recovery. Grain was sown, but the rats cleaned it up even
faster than the wind. Plants that lived through wind and rats were attacked
by caterpillars and grubs. They dealt with the rats by having empty casks
fitted as rat traps, and caught 'upwards of 1000', then when the traps
were avoided, they laid baits of oatmeal mixed with ground glass, which
slaughtered considerably more. Grubs and caterpillars had to be handpicked
by the women, nothing else having the least effect, and even though the
women picked by the million 'within two hours they were as thick as ever'.

On Sundays everyone was expected to attend church service which King
held in his own tent. After the first Sunday morning service his Commission
was read to the assembled group, then, looking towards the convicts standing
together, he earnestly assured them that 'as Servants of the Crown' his first
duty was to his sovereign King George III and after 'to all those who were on
the island'. If they behaved well, he said, all encouragements would be held
out to them, but if not, those who were idle or dishonest could not escape
punishment.

Then, Sunday being a free day (except for attendance at church and, for
the women, the return of the men's laundry washed and mended by Sunday
morning) each person was able to attend to his own wants, go fishing or just
wander along the rocky shores.

How many of them stood on the cliff-top staring out at this vast 'foreign'
sea, longing for home?

Before they had been on the Island more than a week or so, Surgeon
Jamison discovered, during his explorations, that what King had described as
a large kind of iris, was really the most-desired flax plant and it was all around
them, especially on the steep sides of the cliffs.[13] They had already cleared the

c

flat piece of land at Sydney Bay of hundreds of plants and King hastened to put two or three bundles of the long wide leaves into the stream to soak. The weaver, Roger Morley, knew little or nothing of this type of flax and was at a loss how to 'cure' it, but soaking brought away the fibre which he declared to be of good quality. Now, what they wanted was tools to prepare it for manufacturing, as well as someone knowledgeable in the manner of weaving it. King found his path beset by minor worries such as these, but was full of enthusiasm and confident that his little settlement would be successful.

Surgeon Jamison's first patients were the timber cutters, when some of the men, blinded by sap from one of the trees, were in terrible pain. All he could do was to treat the eyes with Florence oil (a sweet olive oil), but King wrote 'one man was totally blinded by it for want of making timely application to the surgeon'.[14]

Inevitably the first flush of newness wore off before many weeks passed. On 17 April King detected John Batchelor, the marine, stealing rum from his tent. 'In the afternoon I assembled the settlement and punished the offender with 36 lashes, causing him to be led by a halter to the place of punishment.'[15] He also stopped the rum from Batchelor's allowance, which was a more telling deterrent.

This display was not enough to prevent young Charles McLellan from robbing Surgeon Jamison's tent of rum three days later. 'This boy is not more than 15 years old,' wrote King, though possibly he was mistaken there, for McLellan was convicted in 1785 'when he was 14,' which would make him 17 or 18 when he arrived on Norfolk Island. 'I ordered him to be punished with 100 lashes which I hope will have a good effect.'[16]

In May, a convict was punished with 40 lashes for uttering 'seditious speeches'. He told the other convicts 'they were fools for suffering their rations to be stopped when fish was issued instead of salt pork. 'The convicts will soon be the strongest, and then it will be seen who is the Master,' he is reported to have said.[17] King, never a coward, outfaced the dissenting ones, and assured them all that he 'should invariably attend to his orders and put them in execution, and that a very severe punishment will be inflicted on anyone who presumed to excite sedition or behave improperly on that account'.

His punishments may seem tough but they were in fact mild by comparison with those given on the mainland for similar crimes. In New South Wales, Governor Phillip stated that death would most certainly follow the theft of provisions—and rum, surely, was a very necessary part of the provisions. For minor infringements of the law 150 lashes was the usual order, and sedition the quick way to hanging.

In June, John Batchelor was drowned 'when returning in a small boat after going fishing', and the settlement buried its first dead.[18] A worse accident happened in August when the *Supply* came up with provisions and stores. Young James Cunningham, the midshipman, with William Westbrook the sawyer, John Williams, a convict, and Tomlinson, a seaman from the

Supply, were all drowned when their boat, going out to the ship, was suddenly swamped by a heavy wave and driven by succeeding waves on to the rocks where it was stove in. Only one man of the five in the boat was saved.[19]

This was a heavy blow for King. Two of his free men gone and the first of the convicts drowned. Four deaths out of twenty-three persons was a high toll and sadly diminished the workforce at a time when every man had a heavy load each day. But within a week or two the *Golden Grove* arrived and on her, the twenty men and women convicts King had asked for some time earlier.[20] He wrote in a later despatch:

> We shall be able to maintain this number in 2 years' time. Everyone is satisfied and no-one wishes to be relieved. There are fish in great quantities and of delicious flavour and large size, about half a mile from land. Streams contain a number of eels, larger and finer than any I saw in England . . . we have caught over a 1000 rats in traps, on moderate calculations.[21]

Through the mild winter and spring, gardens began yielding well, root-crops and grain, and King sent glowing reports back to Phillip who sent more convicts to help with the clearing and cultivating. With them came 1 midshipman, 1 sergeant of marines, 1 corporal, 5 privates and 2 gardeners, 2 small boats and 1 cutter. One of the new arrivals among the convicts was Joseph Robinson, the 'lifer', who later married Ann Inett, King's mistress.

Despite the plagues of groundworms and caterpillars, and the burning winds, more ground was cultivated, more crops planted and gathered, and the settlement expanded into a township.

In January 1789 Ann Inett gave birth to King's first son, whom he christened Norfolk. The christening ceremony took place in his own house, and King himself sprinkled the water on his baby son's head. Later the child was entered in his Letter-book as the first child born on Norfolk Island.[22] The name of the father was not given, though King acknowledged him, as he did his second son born the following year.

Quite a number of births followed. In March 1789 Olivia Gaskin's daughter Anne; in April, Elizabeth Colley's Maria, followed by Mary Ann Gough in October, Sydney King in February 1790 and Thomas Colley in March 1790, Gaskin twin girls in August 1791 and another Gough in October.[23] Besides these infants of the first band of settlers, there were a number born to the later arrivals. King began to think of setting up a school.

Not all the new arrivals shared King's enthusiasm for tilling the soil and making the Island into a supply depot for the main colony as well as themselves. Some were old lags, trouble-makers Governor Phillip was pleased to be rid of, and for them King's more humane approach to punishment served only to make the hardened ones look for ways of avoiding work. The first insurrection on Norfolk Island was planned at the end of January 1789. It was an ingenious plot which, if it had worked, would have taken the convicts to Tahiti at the time Captain William Bligh's ship *Bounty* was preparing its cargo of breadfruit, and the subsequent mutiny had still not been planned in the mind of Fletcher Christian.

Every Saturday it was King's custom to walk through the forest to a little farm he had established some distance from the settlement in Arthur's Vale, and on Saturdays also the marines went into the forest to gather cabbage-palm. It would be a simple matter to seize the Commandant on his way through the forest and bind and gag him. Then a man would be sent post-haste to the surgeon's house and bid him and Mr Altree come at once on the Commandant's orders. When they came running, they too would be seized and securely tied. Then with the principals taken care of, some of the convicts were to lie in wait for the marines to come from collecting cabbage-palm, surprise them on the path, tie them securely and make off with their weapons. After that a party of men would signal the ship to send her boat ashore. As the crew landed they, too, were to be made prisoner. After that, two or three convicts would go out to the ship, tell the commanding officer that his boat was stove in on the landing and another would be sent to bring off the crew. When the second boat arrived its crew would also be captured. With three boats and enough men, the insurgents could row to the ship, seize the Commanding Officer and anyone else on board, and sail away to Otaheite and the delights of love and freedom.

The plan came to nothing; it was 'blown' to King by a gardener, Robert Webb, who had no wish to go to Otaheite. He had been told by his mistress, Elizabeth Anderson, a convict woman who desperately wanted to go with the others and wanted Webb to go too. King was deeply upset and refused at first to believe it without proof, but it was only too true as he found when another convict swore 'on the Holy Cross' that it was just as Webb had said. 'Of 29 male convicts on the island, 26 were involved,' he wrote, 'the exception being the rope-maker (Rice) and 2 carpenters (Widdicombe and Lucas).'[24]

The ringleader was William Francis. In King's words he was

> a troublesome wretch. All he can do for the convicts is to give advice
> of which he seems inordinately free, most of it of the villainous kind.
> I have no doubt but that it is my indulgences which have helped bring
> about this trouble . . . but I shall, notwithstanding, continue my good
> offices to those whose future is good.

Some of the men King was up against were incorrigible rogues who took his 'goodwill' for weakness. Francis was sent back to Port Jackson in 'light irons' to be tried and sentenced. 'If he is to be executed, I would be obliged if your Excellency could send him back to the Island,' wrote King, 'so that an example may be made.'

Francis was not executed though he received severe punishment and wore heavy irons instead of the light chains he had been sent over in. The ruling was, that as no actual insurrection had taken place, no trial and sentence for such a crime could be made.

One of King's first acts after the discovery of the plot, was to order the felling of all trees in and around the camp, so reducing the cover that might be taken advantage of in any further plans of insurrection by the convicts. This was to prove the saving of many lives in quite a different way, for on the night of 26 February 1789 a cyclone hit Norfolk Island, roaring in on the little settlement at midnight while all persons slept. Great pines on the hillsides came crashing down, some of them almost sixty metres high. Rain fell in torrents, washing away crops and the granary was flattened when a large oak tree fell on it; destruction was everywhere, yet no hut was damaged except by rain. Had the trees still stood throughout the camp it was inevitable that at least some of the settlers would have been killed.[25]

Of the planned insurrection, Lieutenant Collins wrote in his *An Account of the English Colony in New South Wales:*

Mr. King had hitherto from the peculiarity of his situation, secluded from society and confined to a small speck in the vast ocean with but a handful of people, drawn them round him and treated them with kind attentions which a good family meets with at the hands of a humane master; but he now saw them in their true colours, and one of his first steps when peace was restored was to clear the grounds as far as possible around the settlement, that future villainry might not find a shelter in the woods for its transactions. To this truly providential circumstance perhaps, many of the colonists were afterwards indebted for their lives.[26]

In June 1789 Governor Phillip sent a small party of marines to the island under the command of Lieutenant Cresswell, who was to act as King's deputy and in case of the Commandant's absence or death, 'the command of the island was to devolve on him'.

By this time a considerable influx of convicts had taken place, both men, women and children. The earliest plan for founding a settlement which could, in a short time, become a Supply Depot for His Majesty's ships was now, it was clear, changed into the simpler one of a penal settlement which, at the same time as it rid the major colony of some of its troublesome felons, might also become a source of food supplies for New South Wales. Governor Phillip's letter to King after the threatened insurrection included these instructions:

. . . I repeat it, No confidence can be placed in the convicts whatever, but it is with great satisfaction that I assure you every part of your conduct meets my warmest approbation and I feel myself happy in having at Norfolk Island an officer who makes the Public Interest his own and who will, I trust, meet a just reward.[27]

These words must have been comforting to King, who realised as well as any other officer, that the plums of promotion lay with the Governor, and depended largely on his opinion as expressed in his letters to their Lordships in London.

So the daily work went on on the Island. A road was cleared from the settlement across to Cascade, and a landing stage was planned for that rocky shore so ships could discharge their supplies when adverse winds blew in Sydney Bay. At Cascade a beautiful stream ran through forest and upland, tumbling down into the rich, fertile valley where plantain trees grew in abundance long before Cook came to the Island. Here, sheltered from the westerly winds, early settlers took up their few acres, planted crops and fruit trees, made gardens, caught enormous eels in the deep pools, and fished from rocks at the end of the valley where the stream cascaded into the sea.

The convict population grew by natural increase and more convicts arrived from New South Wales. King built a schoolhouse but there was no teacher except among the few convicts who could read and write. He became ill with the gout and applied for leave to return to England. As well, he was requested to go to London to report to the Parliament on the state of the Island, and to give an account of its development. His enthusiastic despatches had excited great interest, for in one he had called Norfolk Island 'The Madeira of the Pacific' and their Lordships wished to hear more.

Governor Phillip arranged to send Major Ross of the marines, who was also Lieutenant-Governor of New South Wales, to take over in King's absence. Ross was a difficult and contentious man; many in New South Wales breathed sighs of relief at the news that he was to be sent so far away. Judge-Advocate Collins found him 'impossible to get on with' and said he had an 'inexpressible hatred' for him.[28]

In March 1790 the *Sirius*, under Captain John Hunter, made ready to sail to Norfolk Island with Major Ross, two companies of marines and a large number of convicts, with supplies and provisions for them all. From Norfolk the *Sirius* was to go on to China to bring back supplies for the colony at Port Jackson, where times were hard and crops below what had been anticipated. Only by halving the rations there, could enough be spared for Norfolk Island where the crops had also been poor that year. Governor Phillip decided that by sending 300 souls, convict and marine, from the main settlement two purposes would be served: one, the gardens left by those people would be available to others; two, the new arrivals could be put to work to cultivate more ground to grow more crops and thus feed more people. It was sound reasoning; the outcome was to prove very different.

Major Robert Ross

3

MAJOR ROSS, BORN ABOUT 1740 (DATE OF BIRTH HAS NOT BEEN RECORDED), HAS BEEN DESCRIBED AS A TURBULENT QUARRELSOME Scot; he seems to have had few friends, and very little has been written about him other than his military record. He joined the marines in 1756, was promoted to first Lieutenant in 1759 while serving in North America from 1757 to 1760, was made captain in 1773 and brevet-major in 1783. He saw action at the Battle of Bunkers Hill, and was taken prisoner-of-war in 1779, when the ship in which he was returning to England, the *Ardente*, was captured by the French.[1]

In October 1786 he was appointed Lieutenant-Governor under Captain Arthur Phillip, of the newly-formed colony of New South Wales, and sailed in the *Scarborough* with the First Fleet in 1788.[2] His austere nature could not adapt to the utter confusion which reigned for a time after the arrival, his sternly disciplined outlook could not accept the rough convict material he saw around him, or the patience with which Governor Phillip tolerated the many difficulties that beset the early settlement.

He upheld his officers' early refusal to sit as members of a Criminal Court, despite the fact—of which he was, or should have been, aware—that such a provision had been made at the time of Phillip's Commission, authorising him:

> . . . to constitute and appoint justices of the peace, coroners
> constables and other necessary officers and ministers in our said
> territory . . . for the better administration of justice . . .[3]

This refusal the officers later handsomely retracted in a letter to the Governor. Ross complained volubly when a 'night-watch' composed of reliable convicts was formed by Phillip despite having earlier agreed to it.[4] Twelve men, orderly and in a recognisable form of dress, were to patrol each night. The men had been cautioned against disputing with either soldiers or sailors,

25

though they had power to stop them if suspicious of their movements. One night a soldier was stopped by the watch after being found in the convicts' camp, and delivered, as had been ruled, to the marine guard. Major Ross sent a strong protest to Judge-Advocate Collins who had accepted authority for the watch, a protest which Collins sent on to the Governor; Ross considered it 'an insult offered to the corps'.

At this, Phillip sent for Major Ross, to explain to him the necessity for the night-watch to have power to stop unwarranted persons entering the convicts' camp during the night, but Ross countered by repeating his allegation that

> . . . it was an insult to the corps; if I wished to say anything further on that subject he would wait on me the next day with two of his officers, giving me at the same time to understand that by the 5th Article in the Regulations given to the watch I had put the soldiers under the command of the convicts, and which Article, he hoped, would be withdrawn.[5]

Phillip pointed out to Ross that since the watch had been established robberies had ceased, and some of those robberies had been committed by soldiers, which was a known fact. Ross persisted that it was an insult to the corps to have his men stopped by convict watchmen, and for the sake of peace, Governor Phillip withdrew his order that soldiers might be stopped under suspicious circumstances. Yet no other means of controlling robberies was given by Ross, which left Phillip in an unenviable position which not only seemed to undermine his authority, but gave licence to such men of the military as were inclined to make trouble and disturbances when opportunity offered.

He pointed out these difficulties in his despatch to Lord Sydney, but there was little hope of a solution from that quarter for months, if not years. Collins expressed his 'inexpressible hatred' for his Commanding Officer; Lieutenant Ralph Clark wrote that he was '. . . without exception the most disagreeable commanding officer I ever knew' (an opinion he was to change later).[6]

It was with relief from dissension in mind, quite possibly, that Governor Phillip asked Lord Sydney for his assent regarding the transfer of the Lieutenant-Governor from Port Jackson to Norfolk Island. He wrote, in his despatch of 11 April 1790:

> As I wished to send an officer to England who could give such information as cannot be conveyed by letters, and the detachment was now divided, I replaced the officer who was superintendent and commanding Norfolk Island by Major Ross. The officer I recalled having been two years on the island is very capable of pointing out the advantages which may be expected of it, and I think it promises very fully the end proposed by making the settlement . . .[7]

On 3 March 1790 the *Sirius* and *Supply* sailed from Port Jackson with two companies of marines and a large number of convicts. They arrived at Norfolk Island on 13 March, when strong winds and currents rendered it impossible to land anyone ashore and no boats could be sent out from the Island. Captain Hunter had never been to Norfolk Island though he was aware of the treacherous seas and surf which made landings difficult; accordingly he took the precaution of following the smaller *Supply*, commanded by Lieutenant Ball, who was familiar with the vagaries of wind and weather.

Supply sailed around to the northside and the Cascade landing, *Sirius* following. Most of the officers and convicts were disembarked there, and in his diary that night Ralph Clarke noted 'Got on shore, not without getting my feet wet!'[8] There was no safe landing place there, only huge boulders which were very slippery when wet and made getting ashore a splashy job for those less agile than a mountain goat.

After landing the people, Hunter moved out to sea again, and it was two or three days before he judged it safe to come close in at Sydney Bay to land the rest of the convicts and the provisions sent from Sydney. The people were ferried across by boats manned by *Sirius*'s boatmen. King, who watched the landing from the shore, realised that at that moment there were nearly 300 more people to feed, and as yet he had no knowledge of the amount of provisions the *Sirius* had brought. He had only received Governor Phillip's despatch (giving him instructions for leaving Norfolk Island and proceeding to England), when it had been handed to him by Major Ross a day or so previously. His orders included the handing over of papers detailing the amount of stores in hand; the work commenced, or finished; the copies made by his clerk of the correspondence with the authorities, so that Ross might know how things were in the administration of the Island; and a multitude of other matters that would need to be attended to before he could embark on the *Sirius* for Port Jackson. He waited, rigid with impatience, his gout probably troubling him as well as his anxiety to meet his old friend Hunter, and with all this, the realisation that unless the *Sirius* had brought abundant provisions for this great influx of soldiers and convicts, much hardship was in store for them all. Governor Phillip, when he had ordered this large number of men and women to the Island so that he might conserve his own scanty supplies of food, already dangerously low at Port Jackson, had considered the Report King wrote in an earlier despatch from the Island, noting that 'they had vegetables in great abundance . . . and fish was caught in such quantities that it was served to the people in lieu of salt provisions'.[9]

But since that time of plenty, drought had struck, crops had been destroyed by grubs, south-east and south-west winds had burned the young growing plants; even for the small community on Norfolk Island, hard rationing was a possibility.

Out in Sydney Bay Captain Hunter edged the *Sirius* in as far as he judged was safe, put out the boats, had them loaded with provisions and sent them in. As he did so, he noted with dismay that the reef was suddenly a mass of breaking surf—the wind had changed even as he watched, and ahead he saw the *Supply* had already made sail and was safely over the reef to seaward.

The *Sirius*, a much bigger vessel than the *Supply*, had little room to manoeuvre in the shallow waters over the black coral reef, and as orders from Captain and Master were bawled to the crew, the south-east wind gusts blew the ship relentlessly to its death.

> . . . she came up almost head to wind, and there hung for some time;
> but her sails being all a back, had fresh stern way: the anchor was
> therefore cutaway, and all the haulyards, sheets, and tacks let go, but
> before the cable could be brought to check her, she struck upon a reef
> of coral rocks which lies parallel to the shore, and in a few strokes was
> bulged; when the carpenter reported to me that the water flowed fast
> into the hold; I ordered the masts to be cut away, which was
> immediately done.'[10]

The whole community waiting on shore stood horror-stricken, watching the struggle between men and the sea. It was eleven o'clock in the morning, and it had been Hunter's intention to have landed those persons intended for the Island by that night. Now, not only convicts and the marines would be put ashore, but—God willing—all the crew of the *Sirius* as well.

On board the stricken ship, Hunter ordered to get up such stores as could be brought to the gun-deck, from where they might be thrown into the sea to float to shore, and as the day wore on and the wind freshened, King signalled that everyone remaining in the ship should be brought ashore:

> . . . for this purpose the end of a small rope was floated through the
> surf and over the reef to the shore, by an empty cask, and by that rope
> a seven-inch hawser was hauled on shore, with a wooden heart on it
> for a traveller, and the end was made fast to a large tree. By this
> traveller I corresponded with those on shore and received their
> opinions.[11]

It was two hours before this task was done, but by four in the afternoon the hawser was made safe, an iron grater fixed over the 'traveller' and the surgeon's mate, first man off the *Sirius* came ashore. King writes:

> I thought there was the utmost danger of the ship parting at the
> flowing tide, the consequences of which must have been the
> destruction of every person on board. I therefore made the signal for
> the wreck to be quitted.[12]

By dark, most of the sailors had been brought ashore in twos and threes, dragged through the surf by the labouring convicts who pulled at the hawser hour after hour. Captain Hunter, and Mr Waterhouse, the Master, came ashore together 'the Captain so much exhausted that he nearly quitted his hold at the last'. A few sailors were left aboard, as darkness fell before all could be brought from the ship, but next morning, by which time the weather had moderated, the men on board were able to swim ashore.

It was five days before any of the stores on board could be brought off, and all the while apprehension mounted that a sea could crash through the doomed ship and destroy the much-needed supplies. There were now 500 souls on the island; all were put immediately on half-rations, and Hunter as well as King, knew that even half-rations would be for only a short while unless everything on the *Sirius* could be brought ashore. Hunter wrote:

> Providence was kind to us, for several days the weather was fine and the surf uncommon smooth for this place, and each of those days we got on shore from 20 to 30 casks of provisions . . . such articles as would swim were entrusted to the chance of being thrown on shore by the surf. All that I or any other officer saved was found waiting upon the beach . . .[13]

A line of marines was posted along the shore to take charge of whatever was washed up, until it was claimed by the owner, but in spite of this, some articles were never found, or turned up later in the possession—if not on the back—of a convict 'borrower'.

King left Norfolk Island on 24 March in the *Supply*, his melancholy duty of telling Governor Phillip the news of the *Sirius* weighing heavily. He had left a total of 498 people on Norfolk, 80 of them *Sirius* officers and crew with no chance of being taken off, for Sydney was without a transport ship and the little *Supply* would have to make what voyages were necessary, to bring back food for the colony. Hunter, Ross, and their men would have to live, as would all the others on Norfolk Island, as best they could with what provisions they had.

Before King left on the *Supply*, Martial Law was proclaimed. This was at Major Ross's suggestion, and King's approval was sought. On 22 March everyone, officers and marines, settlers, and convicts, were assembled at the flag-staff. Marines were drawn up in two lines, one either side of the flag, with their own regimental colours flying also; the crew of the *Sirius* stood to the right, convicts to the left, with the officers grouped in the centre, and settlers drawn up behind.

Major Ross, as Lieutenant-Governor, proclaimed Martial Law, then addressed the convicts, exhorting them to be honest, industrious and obedient. When his homily was finished everyone gave three cheers, and one by one, beginning with Ross himself, passed under the flying flag, each one in turn doffing his hat as a token of submission to the Law.[14]

This ceremony, impressive as it might have been, had little effect on a couple of convicts who, that afternoon, offered to go out to the *Sirius* and heave overboard whatever livestock might still be there. With Ross's permission they swam out, and on board found and threw over the side a number of pigs and fowls to find their own way to shore, but when that was done, they refused to come back, for they had found the grog and intended to make the most of it. Both were roaring drunk by evening, and in their roistering, set fire to the ship notwithstanding the volley of small arms that was fired from shore. Ross ordered the three-pounder to be fired, but the aim was bad and it had no effect. Eventually another convict, John Arscott, swam to the ship and put both men overboard on the hawser, when they were dragged to the shore dead drunk.[15] Major Ross was to find plenty of turbulence and strife in his new post, it was clear.

Lieutenant Ralph Clark kept his diary up day by day with bitter revilings against Fate, against the wreck, and against the convicts who, he alleged, stole his things as they were floated ashore. He, with some of the other *Sirius* people, waited on the reef at low tide in hopes of sighting some of his goods.

A great deal of what was thrown overboard floated on shore, but as yet nothing of mine. I was very near drowned yesterday, when I was going of [*sic*] on the Raft to assist the people that were coming on shore all most drowned on account of the convict who could not swim fell off the raft and pulled me along with him, in which case we should both have been drowned if I could not have swimmed, for the Raft went over us both and I was obliged to swim back to shore with him holding fast to me by the waistband of my trousers. When I got on shore he was almost dead but he soon recovered on which I took a stick out of the Serjeants hand and gave him a sound thrashing for pulling me of [*sic*] the Raft with him. He better have been drowned for I will give him the same every day for this month that I meet him.[16]

Clark changed his opinion of Major Ross quite soon after arriving on Norfolk Island—Ross was no longer 'without exception the most disagreeable officer I ever knew', when he made the Lieutenant Quartermaster-General and Keeper of the Public Stores.[17] Clark was then a man of some power in the hungry community, power which suited him well. At this time, the 'Birds of Providence' (so called by Captain Hunter) which King had noted at the same time of year in 1789, reappeared, and they were to form a life-saving part of the Island provisions. Of these birds, Captain Hunter wrote in his *Journal*:

When they are upon the ground the length of their wings prevents them from being able to rise, and until they can ascend an eminence they are unable to recover use of their wings . . . They were, at the end of May, as plentiful as if none had been caught, although for two months before there had been not less than from two to three thousand birds caught every night, most of them females with egg, which fills the whole cavity of the body . . . these eggs were excellent.[18]

The birds, when caught, were brought to Clark who kept a daily tally of the kill, and severely punished any convict who had, or seemed to have any intention of keeping some for themselves. His diary records:

April 18th. John Lovell, convict, taken out of his hut after Tattoo and having sack with 68 Mount Pitt birds in it. 50 lashes.

May 10th. 5 boats crew got 50 each for concealing fish. Also James Richardson got 50 for not flogging the men as he should have. All convicts.

May 11th. Punished W. Rainor, convict, for theft. Ordered 100 but only able to bear 16.

Punished Elizabeth Breeze and Phoebe Flaherty with 23 each for neglect of duty by suffering the hoggets to get into the garden. William MacNamara ordered to be punished for disobedience but when he was stripping himself he attempted to stab himself with a knife. The knife being blunt he did not effect it and instead of 50 lashes he is ordered to be chained to the grindstone.[19]

Each day the gruesome tally of punishments is written in, the number of lashes recorded, as is the number kept in store for when the culprit was able to bear them. One woman was 'put in the stocks because she was big with child, the Major considered she could not bear the lash'. Clark sounds slightly sceptical. However, before long he was recording:

I wish to be away from this place for a great many of my brother officers are jealous of me because I am greatly in favour with Major Ross. I am conscious of all along having acted like an honest man and am a man of honour to my friends. All this because Major Ross pays more attention to me than he does to them.[20]

In spite of the Birds of Providence rationing continued, for with so many mouths to feed the only way supplies could be made to last was to ration severely. At Port Jackson, Governor Phillip waited for supply ships which never came—there was nothing for him to send to the beleaguered inhabitants on Norfolk Island, where rations had been cut to less than half the normal allowance, and stood at 3 lb (1·4 kg) flour per week for every grown person, 1½ lb (700 g) salt beef per week or 17 ounces of pork; 1 lb (454 g) of rice per week for each grown person, and for children over 12 months, half-ration;

children under 12 months 1½ lb of flour and 1 lb of rice.[21] At this time, the order was given that all crimes not of a capital nature were to be punished by a further reduction of rations. This meant that those who had no garden and no source of supply, if they committed any misdemeanour meriting punishment, would starve.

As the situation showed little sign of improvement, Major Ross, a methodical man, evolved a plan whereby some of the people—convicts—could be taken 'off Stores' within a reasonable space of time and also obtain more freedom for themselves.[22] It was a good plan in essence, but he sadly over-estimated the convict capacity and will to work, and seemed to have also overlooked the fact that grinding hunger made few if any of the people eager to add yet more work to the amount they were required to do as Servants of the Crown. The plan was this: each convict who applied was to receive one acre of land (about half a hectare), a sow in farrow, or a hog and a sow, and two days each week free of Government work. In this free time they were to cultivate the land and sow crops, tend the pig, and turn themselves into small land-holders. They were to be in parties of three including women and children, and could work the one acre together. At the end of three months, the men—who until then would be fed from Stores—would have their regular ration reduced by one quarter; at six months by half, and at the end of one year they were to be self-supporting. In addition, all surplus pork turned into the Stores, would be credited and extra rations or supplies given in lieu. If the men worked at this task they would reap benefits. If not, they might well starve. The women in each group were to keep house, and help on the 'farms', and would not be called upon to do Government work except in great emergencies.

It was a good plan at first hearing, and to men unused to farming work an acre of land seemed an ample amount on which to support themselves, and to those who knew nothing of the land except their daily task of hoeing and planting Government crops it might have seemed an escape from two days of hard labour. It actually amounted to discontent and further hunger, and an upsurge in robberies from settlers' gardens. Major Ross, the austere Scot, had over-estimated the capacities of most of his charges.

Lieutenant Clark, busy at the new settlement of 'Charlottefield' (which was to be renamed 'Queenborough' and, later, 'Longridge') kept an eagle eye on the people under his charge, and punishments were regularly meted out:

Tuesday 15th (February)
Fine weather a great Surf—it has been Remarkably hott today—after Breakfast went out to Charlottefield and got about five thousand Ripe Cobbs of Indian Corn puld and Sent into Town—Returned back to Tea—Elizh. Breeze a notarious thief was Punished to day with 75 Lashes for killing and Stealing a hen belonging to Edward Goff—*

Vinry male Convict Punished with 100 Lashes for Stealing * Cobbs of Indian Corn—Jno. Hudson a Convict Boy Punished with 50 Lashes for being out of his hutt after nine o'clock.

Monday 21st. Fine weather but Remarkably hot . . . Henry Lovell Convict was Punished with * Lashes for telling a palpable Lye.

Thursday 3rd (March) Cloudy weather . . . Majr. Ross walked out to See me after dinner . . . he is very much pleased with what I have been doing Since his been out there last . . . * Hill Convict was punished with 100 Lashes for Carrying away the Kings Stores.

Thursday 17th. Fine weather Squaly the latter part of the day—L:Deyer Convict Carpenter was punished with 75 Lashes for Stricking James Rulby Marine—he ought to have received a 150 but he could not bear any more—he Richly deserved it for I told Deyer he was not to goe into the house as I had placed Rulby Centinel at the dore to prevent any body going into the house . . . I could not forgive that of a Damed Rascal of a Convict to Strick a Soldier . . . the Surgeon ordered Deyer into Town . . .[23]

Clark was not eternally bad-tempered; some of his entries regarding the convicts touch on the hardships they suffer and their lack of clothes to cover themselves. On Friday 25 February 1791 he writes:

. . . The Commissary served Cloaths out to the Women Beloning [sic] to Charlotte Field and Cascade which the poor devils they very much wanted for some of them had not So much peticoat as would cover ther commical cuck—the Slops that was issued out to them was as much of Lancaster Shirting as would make them a Shift—as much as will make each two peticoats as much as will make a Jacket—Six Skein of thread a Thimble a few needles and a pair of Scissors—now the [sic] have got two things of a Sort for the have only one Shift and one Jacket—Poor Soul the want things bad a nuf [sic] god knows.

And on the 9th of March

. . . got 30 pair of womans shoes out of the Store for the Most deserving of the woman out ther.[24]

The state of the weather seems to have been his daily concern—it is invariably the first item mentioned in his daily writing; 'Fine moderate weather' . . . 'no surf Round the Island' . . . 'Cloudy weather with a fresh Breeze' . . . 'Squaly weather no surf' . . . 'Blows very hard Still'—as if he was perpetually watching the days on which a ship might be expected and perhaps, his release from the Island and a return to Home and 'His Dearest

Betsy'. Towards the end of 1791 tempers seem to have worn thin, and a state of more than usual unrest had developed, judging by the number of punishments handed out to both convicts and marines: '500 lashes to John Howard for Selling his Slops . . . and for telling a Liy to Majr. Ross Respecting the Selling of the Slops—Thomas Brown, 200 lashes for the same crime'; each of these men '. . . to Receive the Remainder When his Back is well . . .', 100 to Robert Kingston for absenting himself from work; 75 to George Gest (Guest) for 'neglect of duty'—and a vicious 400 lashes to Thomas Lunn a private soldier, who was Court-Martialled by Captain Hill 'for Unsoldierlike behaviour by telling him a wicked and Malicious Lie of which Crime he was found guilty . . . to be Carried into Execution tomorrow morning at Phillipsburg at Seven oClock . . .'[25]

Crimes and punishments fill the later pages of the *Journal* written on Norfolk Island. It was as well that on 1 November 1791 the *Atlantic* hove in sight. Within a few days, Lieutenant-Governor King had set foot again on Norfolk Island, bringing with him his wife Anna Josepha, with young Norfolk King, elder son by Ann Inett. Captain Paterson with a detachment of the New South Wales Corps was to take over command of the garrison, thus freeing Major Ross and his detachment of marines and Captain Hill and his men of the New South Wales Corps, who had been on the Island only a comparatively short time.

On 7 November King and Ross 'had words', according to the sharp-eared Clark, who noted it in his *Journal*, but on what subject he doesn't say. It can only have been with relief that the inhabitants of Norfolk Island saw Major Ross, and his officers and men, sail away on the transport *Queen* on the 22nd.

A few days after his arrival at Port Jackson, Major Ross engaged in a duel with his former co-worker Captain Hill; neither man was hurt in the affair. Back in England he returned to his military career and served under the redoubtable Captain Bligh in the *St. Albans* for a year, 1801 to 1802, and then in the East Indies for five years, but little is known of him after that time; his death is not recorded in *The Australian Dictionary of Biography*.

Captain Hunter, who had thankfully returned to his naval career after some months on Norfolk Island, became the second Governor of New South Wales in 1794, an appointment which he took up in September 1795. Lieutenant Ralph Clark rejoined his Company at Plymouth in 1792 but died, according to records held by the Commissions and Appointments Register of 1755–1814, in 1794.

A statuette of George III, by F. Hardenberg, 1820. King George III was familiarly known as 'Farmer George'. (National Portrait Gallery, London)

Captain Arthur Phillip, R.N., first Governor of New South Wales. Portrait by F. Wheatley, 1786. (National Portrait Gallery, London)

D'Arcy Wentworth

4

D'ARCY WENTWORTH IS ONE OF THE COLOURFUL FIGURES IN NORFOLK ISLAND HISTORY, NOT FROM ANY MEMORABLE ESCAPADES OR BRUSHES with authority, but from the legend, still perpetuated by some Island-dwellers, that D'Arcy's eldest son, the famous William Charles Wentworth, was born there. The house of the Second Settlement's Colonial Surgeons is pointed out as the place where his birth took place.

The much drabber truth is that William Charles was brought to the Island as a young infant, in August 1790, and is listed in the Norfolk Island Victualling Book of that period under 'Convict children—on half-stores', an indication that he was under one year old.[1] It was D'Arcy, the second brother, who was the first Wentworth born on Norfolk Island, in June 1793.

D'Arcy Wentworth was described by his contemporaries as 'a tall handsome man with blue eyes, who was invariably popular with all classes and both sexes'.[2] He was also an incorrigibly high-spirited rascal at times, who occasionally seems to have thought the world owed him a living. He was born at Portadown, County Armagh, Ireland, in 1762. The Wentworths of Portadown were a branch of the ancient British family descended from Robert of Wentworth Woodhouse, a thirteenth-century personality of whom little is known, though he has been reputed to have been the hermit who was once famous in a part of Yorkshire for his plain speaking and defiance of the overlords who lived in luxury and impiety. King John was sufficiently impressed to grant Robert 40 acres, in 1216. He died in 1218.[3]

It was in the reign of Charles II of England that a descendant of Robert of Wentworth arrived in Ireland as agent to Wentworth Dillon, fourth earl of Roscommon, presumably a relative.[4] This Wentworth, an earlier D'Arcy, established himself as a landowner, but in succeeding generations the family fortunes seeped away. The Wentworths of Portadown had little money or land, and the family kept the village inn. Notwithstanding this rather humble occupation they were intensely proud of their aristocratic lineage, and acknowledged Rockingham, Lord Fitzwilliam Earl of Strafford as head of the

Wentworth family. Lord Fitzwilliam was a man of great political influence in England, and D'Arcy was to find him a useful ally during his lifetime.

Wentworth began his career as an ensign in the First Armagh Company of Volunteers, a Company made up of men from all walks of life, from the peerage to the peat-hut, and it was this early training which burnished the free-and-easy manner of his later life, a manner which stood him in good stead in Australia. While serving as ensign he also served his apprenticeship with the Company's doctor, Alexander Patton. He realised that to progress further, he needed medical training in a hospital, and went to London where he was enrolled in the College of Surgeons. It was his ambition to serve as Surgeon on a ship of the wealthy East India Company, and doubtless he enlisted his kinsman's help to this end.

In London his lifestyle was vastly changed from life in a small Irish town. It is likely that his influential relatives took him up, and that he found life gay — and expensive — particularly if he went occasionally to beautiful Mattersey Hall, where Lord Fitzwilliam entertained in the grand manner, and kept fine horses. Medical school would have had less allure than the life of an English gentleman of substance, and D'Arcy, never cut out to be a spectator, was ready to take risks to gain his fortune.

The quickest way was clearly the most risky — the penalty, if caught, was death by hanging. In December 1787 D'Arcy Wentworth was charged at London's Old Bailey on three counts of highway robbery. He was then 25 years old. On two of the counts he was found not guilty. He was acquitted on the third 'for lack of evidence'.[5]

This escape would have been enough to deter most young men, however high-spirited, from a repeat performance, but in December 1789 he was again charged at the Old Bailey, again for highway robbery and was indicted for 'feloniously assaulting John Pemberton Heywood Esquire, on the King's highway on 10th July last, in the Parish of Finchley and putting him in fear and danger of his life . . .'. He had taken 'a silk purse, a bass metal watch, four cornelian seals set in gold, a red morocco case, six guineas, a crown piece and a foreign copper coin called a farthing'.[6]

This time it was not going to be easy; Mr Heywood was a barrister who knew D'Arcy, and the Fitzwilliams also. Moreover, he was often in court, and had probably been in court during D'Arcy's earlier appearance at the Old Bailey. He remarked in his evidence:

> I said to the gentleman with me in the carriage at the time of the hold-up 'If I was not sure that D'Arcy Wentworth was out of the country I should be sure it was him, I thought he was out of the country, I knew that considerable pains had been taken to get him out of the country, I had some reason to think it . . .'

He went on to tell how he had recognised D'Arcy when the piece of black crepe tied around his face, blew up in a gust of wind. 'He has a pretty strong Irish accent as you will hear if you hear him speak', he added. The magistrate said 'Would the prisoner say anything?' and Mr Garrow, Counsel for Wentworth answered quickly 'No my Lord. I would not advise him to say anything on this occasion'.

The Bench deliberated, brought in a verdict of Not Guilty. Immediately after this the Prosecutor said 'My Lord, Mr Wentworth the prisoner at the Bar says he has a passage to go in the Fleet to Botany Bay and has obtained an appointment in it as Assistant-Surgeon and desires to be discharged immediately'. Which was allowed. This time Mr Heywood had made sure of D'Arcy's departure 'out of the country'.

The ship on which D'Arcy Wentworth had obtained his passage to Botany Bay was the *Neptune*, an East-Indiaman of 809 tons, the largest on the run to New South Wales. Its chief surgeon was Dr William Gray and D'Arcy was one of two assistants. The *Neptune*, *Surprize* and *Scarborough* (the latter on her second voyage as a convict ship—she had been in the First Fleet) made up what was later called the Second Fleet. All three ships were grossly over-crowded. In all, 1017 prisoners had embarked; *Neptune* carried 424 men and 78 women below-decks, and a number of cabin passengers also.[7] Among the women convicts was Catherine Crowley, a young woman of 23, who had been sentenced at the Staffordshire Assizes to seven years' transportation for stealing wearing apparel. She was Wentworth's mistress, but whether he had met her before his trial at the Old Bailey—which was probably the case—or had her 'assigned' to him on the *Neptune*, is not known. She was the mother of his three sons, William Charles, D'Arcy, and John Matthew, the latter two born on Norfolk Island in 1793 and 1795. She died in 1800 or thereabouts, in Parramatta. There is no portrait of her.

The voyage of the Second Fleet is remembered as the blackest in the maritime history of New South Wales: 158 convicts died on the *Neptune*, 36 on the *Surprize* and 73 on the *Scarborough*. Conditions were scandalous on all three, but worst on the *Neptune*. Upon the ships' arrival at Port Jackson, after a voyage of six months or so, those waiting on shore to greet dis-embarking passengers were horrified at the sight of convicts—those that were able to move—crawling on hands and knees as they came from the boats. The Reverend Richard Johnson, parish priest of Sydney, wrote, of the *Surprize*:

> . . . I beheld a sight truly shocking to the feelings of humanity, a great number of them [the prisoners] laying, some half and others nearly quite naked, without either bed or bedding, unable to turn or help themselves. I spoke to them as I passed along, but the smell was so offensive I could scarcely bear it.

Johnson was persuaded not to go down into the prison quarters of the *Scarborough*, and was told that the *Neptune* was 'still more intolerable and wretched' so he took this advice and waited at the ship's side to watch the disembarkation.

The landing of these people was truly affecting and shocking, great numbers of them were not able to walk nor to move hand or foot. Such were slung over the ship's side in the same manner they would sling a box, a cask or anything of that nature. Upon being brought up to the open air some fainted, some died upon the deck, and others in the boat before they reached the shore . . . Some crept on their hands and knees, some were carried on the backs of others and all were indescribably filthy, covered with their own nastiness, their heads, bodies, cloths, blankets all full of lice and filth.[8]

Judge-Advocate Collins described them as 'both living and dead, more horrid spectacles than had ever been witnessed in this country'. The prisoners, those who were able to tell of their sufferings, told how they had been chained together hand and leg, for days—many of them had died with the chains upon them—their entreaties to be released unheeded. It was from the prisoners in the *Neptune* that the most pitiful accounts came.

Governor Phillip's reports were a stinging rebuke on the methods used in the shipping of these 'unwilling emigrants', and on the *Neptune*'s return to England the crew and several of the marines who had been on board, were called before the Bench at the Guildhall. Donald Traill, the master, had absconded, but evidence was given that he had purposely kept the convicts short of provisions in order to open a warehouse on arrival at Port Jackson, to sell the surplus supplies to the public. Traill was eventually indicted at the Old Bailey (two years after the *Neptune*'s arrival at Port Jackson), but was acquitted after a three-hour trial. He was later posted as 'Master Attendant' at the Cape of Good Hope.[9] Incredibly, there seems to have been no mention of negligence on the part of Dr Gray, the Surgeon, or of his two assistants on the *Neptune*.

After the disembarkation, Wentworth, armed with letters of introduction to various personages at Port Jackson, was put to work in the General Hospital under Surgeon White. The sick were laid in rows, some in makeshift tents, some to die, others to struggle to recovery, some to remain permanent invalids. 267 people had died during the Second Fleet's voyage, and at least 486 sick were brought on shore, 269 of them from the *Neptune*, many of whom were to die.[10]

The *Surprize* was cleaned, loaded with a fresh batch of convicts, and despatched to Norfolk Island at the end of July, approximately one month after arrival at Port Jackson. On board was D'Arcy Wentworth, with Catherine Crowley and his baby son, William Charles. The *Surprize* reached the Island on 7 August, and on the 17th, as disembarkation was proceeding, a giant wave overturned one of the landing boats as it reached the channel to the landing-place. Seven souls were drowned, two of the boat's crew—men from the *Sirius*—three women convicts, one convict who had swum out to try to save them, and a small child, whose mother was saved.[11] It was fortunate for posterity that Catherine Crowley and her infant were not in the boat coming in to land on 17 August 1790. Had she been, Australia would not have known one of its most famous sons, the explorer William Charles Wentworth.

D'Arcy Wentworth's first assignment on Norfolk Island was as assistant to Surgeon Considine. At this time there were about 700 people on the Island, convicts, military and free settlers, and Wentworth's busiest period of the day would have been during flogging sessions. It was the duty of the Convict's Surgeon to supervise the flogging and intervene if the victim was unable to bear the number of lashes administered. In this regard he was far more humane than some of his successors were to be. In Lieutenant Ralph Clark's *Journal*, kept during his period of service on Norfolk Island, from March 1790 to November 1791, many floggings ordered by him were stopped when half- or quarter-way through, the victim 'being unable to bear more', though Clark often amends this by adding, 'the rest to follow when his back is better'.[12] There can be little doubt that this part of his duty was unwelcome to D'Arcy Wentworth.

In December 1791, King, now the Lieutenant-Governor, and promoted to Captain in the Navy, wrote in his despatch to Governor Phillip:

> The Superintendent who had charge of the Convicts at
> Queensborough [Mr Doidge] requested leave to resign his situation,
> as the term for which he has engaged with Government was expired;
> I therefore appointed D'Arcy Wentworth (who has conducted himself
> with the greatest propriety as Assistant to the Surgeon) to take that
> Charge, and to continue doing the Duty of an Assistant to the
> Surgeon, which Office I have every reason to expect, he will dutifully
> discharge.[13] [The new Colonial Surgeon who arrived with King, and
> who replaced Mr Considine, was William Balmain.]

Throughout his stay on Norfolk Island, from August 1791 to February 1796, Wentworth seems to have continued to 'conduct himself with the greatest propriety' and several times in his *Journal*, Ralph Clark refers to the building of a house for the Assistant Surgeon at Charlottefield. On Tuesday 18 February 1791 he writes '. . . got the Fraim of Mr Wentworth's House up—hope that it will be Soon finished for him to get into it as it is very disagreeable for him to be obliged to walk out ther every day to See the Sick . . .'[14] Spelling was not a strong point with Clark. By 3 March the carpenters were employed in '. . . putting the logs round Mr Wentworth's house', and on 7 April he writes '. . . got Mr Wentworths House so Fare finished that he may goe into it tomorrow if Majr. Ross thinks proper'.[15]

At Queenboro' D'Arcy Wentworth bought two of the Lots granted to two marines, paying £60 for each lot of 60 acres. Many of the marines who had at first been inclined to stay on Norfolk Island and become settlers, changed their minds for one reason or another. Some of the convicts whose sentences had expired, had also been given smaller grants of land, and a number of them worked hard and prospered while others offered their Lots for sale, a ploy which was stopped by King who had hoped, by granting land to these men, that they would be able to support themselves and their families honestly, while enjoying life as free men.[16]

Wentworth, however, for the first time a landowner in Australia, was allowed two convicts to work on his property, and was soon producing enough maize and pigs to be able to sell his surplus produce to the Stores, the pork at the going rate of five-pence a pound. He also planted sugar cane, which had been tried on the Island with some success. King writes:

> . . . The Clear Ground at Queenboro' being considerably enlarged,
> and the great utility of the Sugar Cane fences being obvious, I
> directed the Grounds at that place to be enclosed with Sugar Cane
> hedges—which will be a great Shelter to succeeding Crops, besides
> their great utility either for making Sugar, or feeding Swine: for the
> latter purpose I find it of the greatest use, and am certain that it has
> not only preserved, but been the means of the Swine multiplying very
> much . . .[17]

So it seems that D'Arcy Wentworth had adapted well to the somewhat bucolic lifestyle on Norfolk Island, and was proving to be something of a farmer, as well as being the much-respected Assistant Surgeon. He, with Catherine Crowley and his three young sons, William Charles (1790), D'Arcy (born 23 June 1793) and Matthew (John?) (born 13 June 1795), left the Island on 19 February 1796 on the *Royal Admiral*, for Sydney.[18] He was to return to Norfolk Island two years later, sent by Governor Hunter, and was again on the Island in Lieutenant-Colonel Foveaux's time between 1800 and 1804, as Colonial Surgeon, as the Irish dissident 'General' Joseph Holt mentions him in his *Memoirs*, describing his plea for help after Foveaux had ordered him out to work on a settler's farm:

> Mr Wentworth desired me to go to my unhappy lodgings . . . and told
> me not to do anything till he should bid me . . . and he went to the
> Commandant and told him he believed he was acting beyond his
> powers and if I was killed by labour he would make a note of the
> business . . .'[19]

After this period of service on Norfolk Island there is no mention of him ever returning. He was appointed Surgeon at the Sydney General Hospital, but got himself into trouble more than once over employing convicts well enough to be discharged as labourers in his garden, over various dealings in rum and tea (as most of the members of the New South Wales Corps did) and other peccadilloes. But this 'tall handsome man with blue eyes' was always popular with his fellows, easy-going and willing to acknowledge the children he sired—he had a second family by his housekeeper Ann Laws, though strangely none of his children other than William Charles, appear in the Census of New South Wales, 1828. The Census lists Ann Laws as 'Housekeeper to W. C. Wentworth, Homebush, Sydney'; it also lists—under Went-worth—two children: 'Catherine, F. 4 yrs, child of W. C. Wentworth; Charles D'Arcy, 7 months, and W. C. Wentworth, of Argyle'. The two children are listed as residing at Homebush.

When he died, in 1827, a procession longer than one kilometre followed Wentworth's cortège to the cemetery.

King Returns 5

LIEUTENANT KING'S RECUPERATIVE VISIT TO LONDON WAS HIGHLY SUCCESSFUL. ON 2 MARCH 1791 HE WAS PROMOTED LIEUTENANT-Governor and his salary increased to £250 per annum, and on 11 March he married his cousin, Anna Josepha Coombe, a bonny kind-hearted woman six years younger than he, at St. Martin's-in-the-Fields, London. Four days after the wedding King, with his wife and a young friend of the family, William Neate Chapman, 18 years old, sailed for New South Wales on H.M.S. *Gorgon* (Captain Parker) on their way to Norfolk Island.[1] Young Chapman wrote many letters to his 'Honoured Mother', his sisters and his father, letters which paint a picture of life as it was for a young, free and happy-natured man on the Island in its early years as a settlement.[2]

The *Gorgon* arrived at Sydney in early October 1791. King delivered the despatches he had brought from London to Governor Hunter and made preparations for his departure for Norfolk Island. Anna had been told about, and had accepted the fact of King's two young sons born outside the marriage; history does not record whether she saw Ann Inett during that very short stay in Sydney, but Anna's wonderfully compassionate nature is demonstrated by her acceptance of both children into the household. She herself was pregnant with her own first child expected in December, but she took Norfolk, the elder boy, to the Island when she sailed after a five-week stay in Sydney. The younger child was left with his mother, though arrangements were made for him to be taken to England later, and placed under the care of King's mother.[3] Ann Inett was at that time living with Joseph Robinson, the man she later married when King obtained him a free pardon.

The *Atlantic*, their ship to Norfolk Island, also carried Captain Paterson of the New South Wales Corps, a detachment of his men who were to take over from the marines, Mr Balmain the surgeon, and the Reverend Richard Johnson, chaplain to the colony, who was making a belated pastoral visit to Norfolk Island to marry, christen, and otherwise comfort his most distant flock. Chapman was also on board; he was to make himself very useful to

King in the coming years, and for Mrs King he was like a breath of the homeland.

The *Atlantic* arrived at Norfolk Island on 4 November 1791. Lieutenant-Governor King found a settlement very different from the one he had planned four years earlier. Then, he had had to sail around the Island for five days searching for a safe landing; now he found the beach lined with people waiting to greet him, uniformed marines lined up, the flag flying from the mast, and behind them all, cleared and cultivated hillsides terraced with vines and crops.

A few days after his arrival, however, he wrote in a private letter to Under-Secretary Nepean:

> I landed here on 4th November and found discord and strife on every
> person's countenance, which you may easily conceive would render
> this an exact replica of the infernal regions. I am pestered with
> complaints, bitter revilings, back-biting and almost everything to
> begin over again![4]

No longer could he be the hopeful, paternalistic leader of a small band of settlers. Norfolk Island had developed into nothing greater than a penal settlement where the mainland colony despatched its most difficult officers and its least-wanted felons. The aura had changed from auspicious to ominous and King was sick at heart, quite unaware that it was his own unbounded enthusiasm in his first years that had wrought the change.

His reports had been so optimistic that Governor Phillip foresaw a future of abundance, where any number of convicts could produce an unending supply of food, not only for themselves but for the mainland as well. If sails for ships of the Line, and timber for masts and yards was not procurable, then food for the colony it would have to be, and as producers of that food, the convicts were sent.

King was prudent enough to keep his resentment to himself while the contentious Major Ross was still on the Island, and on the first Sunday after his return he gathered the whole community together outside his small two-roomed house to hear his Commission read. For the second time the marines were drawn up beneath the raised flag, Major Ross and his Lieutenants in full-dress uniform, Captain Paterson and his men of the New South Wales Corps in scarlet and white. Eight hundred convicts lined up in their 'slops', settlers standing together on one side, Mrs King and the officers' ladies standing behind King in his naval uniform with gold epaulettes and cord, cocked hat and sword, and the Reverend Richard Johnson surpliced and gowned, ready to take a massed marrying and christening service after the Commission was read. About 100 children stood staring at the bright display, at colours brilliant as parrot feathers, listening to words they couldn't understand.[5]

In late November the transport *Queen* arrived to take Major Ross and his marines, with a few settlers, time-expired convicts, and the Reverend Johnson, to Port Jackson.

Several land grants were made at this time; the earliest had been made in 1789 to Richard Phillimore, a time-expired convict. Some of these grants were to the men of that first 'small band of settlers'. Edward Garth was granted 10 acres (4 hectares) in 1791, as were Nathaniel Lucas and John Rice. Edward Westlake and Susannah Gough received 10 acres in 1792, Noah and John Mortimore 10 and 12 acres in 1793, and Roger Morley 60 (24 hectares) as a free settler. Widdicombe, the 72-year-old man chose to return to England when his sentence was up, so did young Charles McLellan and Elizabeth Lee.[6] Tucked away at the end of the list is the entry 'Lot 99 of 50 acres, Granted to the first male child born on the Island'. It is signed 'P. Gidley King'. The first male child was, of course, Norfolk King but he was never in after years able to obtain equivalent land in the main colony, although at the time Norfolk Island was evacuated it was the general rule that to those who had held land on the Island, up to 4 acres (about 1½ hectares) for every acre should be granted.

Anna's first child, a son, was born on 13 December 1791 and was christened Philip Parker King. The birth occurred five weeks after her arrival. There was no place prepared for her lying-in, which took place in the little two-roomed house which was at that time fairly crowded. William Chapman was speedily despatched to Phillipsburgh as Deputy Commissary, and probably young Norfolk, too, as Chapman often mentions him in his letters to his mother. King made plans for a new and much larger house to be built and work was begun in the New Year.

Chapman found plenty to do at Phillipsburgh—accounts to keep, public stores to enter in the books, the itemising of each bushel of maize and every pound of pork delivered by the settlers against payment in kind or cash. Many of the convicts and some of the settlers were 'on Stores' with their families; these were listed with children's ages, for rations increased as they grew beyond the 'infant' stage.[7] Each day Chapman walked from Phillipsburgh to the Governor's house for dinner, a walk he spoke of to his 'Dearest Mother' as 'a very pleasant walk from here to the other side of the island where Governor King lives. I can compare it to nothing but some gentleman's park . . .'

It would have been a truly beautiful walk beneath tall pines, stately oaks, euphorbias and yellow-wood trees, with tiny ferns underfoot, small brown songbirds trilling unseen, brilliant parrots flashing noisily through the clearings and, here and there, glimpses of the encircling sea and cliffs. During his years on Norfolk Island, Chapman made a number of delicate watercolour sketches, quaint pictures with a lightness of spring about them. For William Chapman the Island was a lovely place, akin to the Paradise envisaged by Cook years before.

On Sunday mornings it was his duty to read the Lesson for the Day and to conduct prayers, perhaps to read a chapter from the Old Testament or the

New. How did he feel, this fresh-faced youth with such a happy background, a loving family, and still surrounded by good friends, as he stood before these men, some stony-faced, others with memories plainly written in their eyes? The Psalms would mean little to them; how could they relate the 'wings of the morning' to the rattle of the bell that drove them out each day to toil till sunset. The valley of the shadow of death was closer to them than the green pastures.

Chapman never wrote of his feelings at these times. He worked hard at his tasks, and wrote:

> I am storekeeper, Secretary, Superintendent, Banker and Merchant. You will hear by and by of my becoming an opulent merchant in His Majesty's Territory of New South Wales . . . £100 here will not go further than £30 in England. I have seen several places and all Beautiful, but I must confess none to equal my native country. Ah, that England. A pretty place![8]

He was extremely useful to King, he acted as his secretary and wrote many of King's despatches at times when the Governor suffered from gout. Gout was to plague him throughout his life, and became increasingly troublesome, as did his chest complaint, and always the 'fearful stomach pains'.[9]

For the next year or so things went on comparatively smoothly on the Island, with few dissensions or 'bitter revilings', though the soldiers of the New South Wales Corps were occasionally at odds with the convict-settlers. King's new house was built, it was sixty feet (18·3 metres) long, thirty feet (9·8 metres) wide and thirteen feet (4 metres) to under the eaves, with a small stockade built behind it as a precaution against attack, though from where an attack might come, King did not specify. A large storehouse eighty by twenty feet (24·4 by 6 metres) was built, two new prison buildings with surrounding walls, the walls spiked on top, for garden robberies had become common and cells were needed for those convicts who were caught at such depredations.

By 1792 Norfolk Island was producing a variety of crops besides wheat and maize, timber and flax; potatoes grew well, cabbages sometimes up to twenty-eight pounds (12 kilograms), vegetables and fruits of all kinds, bananas, plantains, apples, peaches, pears, oranges, lemons and limes, guavas and strawberries, all did well, nothing was unwilling to grow, it seemed. Even sugarcane and rice did well, though in the steep-sloped and undulating Island no suitable place for rice-planting could be found.[10] Cotton and European flax were tried but not persevered with, so King made an effort to import weaving skills to the Island by a stratagem that landed him in hot water with Grose.

He had asked Captain George Vancouver, when they were both in London and Captain Vancouver was planning his round-the-world voyage, if two Maoris could be enticed on board Vancouver's ship when it reached New

Zealand, and be brought to Norfolk Island. Vancouver agreed, and deputed a Lieutenant to deliver the Maoris to the Island.[11] The Lieutenant got the Maoris on board the *Shah Hormuzar* by a ruse in April 1793, and brought them from their own country to Norfolk Island. Toogee and Hoodoo however, were very unwilling visitors, and having discovered why they had been 'kidnapped', revealed that in New Zealand weaving was women's work; they themselves were a priest and a chief respectively. What little they knew of dressing and weaving flax could be taught in less than an hour. In his *An Account of the English Colony in New South Wales*, Judge-Advocate Collins writes 'they gave such instructions in the process of preparing the flax plant that even with very bad materials a few hands could manufacture thirty yards of good canvas in a week'.[12]

King treated the Maoris as honoured guests in his own house, but neither of them wished to stay on the Island. They drooped and became inconsolable as months went by and no ship arrived that could return them to New Zealand. In November 1793 the trader *Britannia* called at the Island for fresh supplies and water, on her way to Bengal. Her Commander, Captain Nepean, was a friend of King's, and on an impulse King decided that if it was possible, he would return the Maoris to their homes, if Nepean agreed, on *Britannia*.

> It being the master of *Britannia*'s intention to pursue his route to
> Bengal between the south end of Mindanao and Borneo, . . . I
> concluded that a fortnight's detention would make no material
> difference in her voyage. I therefore consulted with the master . . .
> and gave him directions to proceed on that service . . . The nature of
> the service I was going on did not preclude the possibility of accidents
> happening to me, and there being only three subalterns stationed
> here, no court-martial could be held or offenders punished, which was
> a principal reason for my requesting Captain Nepean to take
> command of this island during my absence, which he very readily
> complied with . . .[13]

Such was part of King's reply to the roasting Lieutenant-Governor Grose gave him when he heard of King's hasty journey to New Zealand and back again, and discovered that for ten days the Island had been under the command of a captain of a trading ship, rather than under Lieutenant Abbott, the senior subaltern of the New South Wales Corps. He had written:

> Your taking on yourself to appoint Captain Nepean, who by accident
> called at Norfolk Island, to a command you had left without
> permission, might have produced the most unpleasant effects. Lieut.
> Abbott would have been perfectly justified in resisting your appoint-
> ment of Captain Nepean, and the circumstance of your assembling
> the garrison for the purpose of reading them your commission,

intending, I suppose, thereby to show you was authorized in the step you was taking, was very irregular . . . Ready as I might be to put up with any want of attention to myself, I really do not see how this can be done, for I must for my own sake report the circumstances . . .[14]

He did this without delay. Grose was a martinet and fiercely partisan where the honour of his regiment was concerned. Lieutenant Abbott was an officer in the New South Wales Corps, and therefore, in Grose's opinion, entitled to act as Commandant during King's absence. To pass him over was a considered insult not to be borne without reprimand.

The incident of the Maoris was only one of Grose's grievances against King. A second and more infuriating occurrence took place shortly after that. The trouble arose, as did most of King's brushes with authority, from his desire to relieve the isolation he and the Island settlers felt in their situation. In May 1793 a number of settlers, soldiers and convicts had asked permission to get up a play. Surgeon Balmain undertook to see that if it was allowed, he would make sure everything was conducted in good order. King was pleased to give his assent, for as he said later:

The business of the play received my sanction from the sole view of affording a little amusement to every description of people on the island; I thought it would have been an agreeable relief to the mind in our recluse situation, I hoped it would have been received thankfully and permitted to go on quietly.[15]

Each month from May 1793 onwards, a play was performed in the little playhouse, all the parts being taken by men. On 18 January, the day kept as Queen Charlotte's birthday, a special programme was arranged, and beforehand King invited the officers and their ladies to a small party at his house. He and his party arrived at the playhouse a little late, and King noticed one of the soldiers, dressed in slovenly fashion and wearing his hat, a considered mark of disrespect, inside the theatre. He sent an officer to remonstrate with the man, who took off his hat but remained in his seat.

When the play was over and the Governor's party had left, a brawl began outside the playhouse, loud enough to be heard by King as he walked on the terrace outside his house with Mr Balmain. The granary keeper came running, and shouted 'For God's sake Sir, stop them! There'll be murder done!' King rushed out, seized the man who seemed to be the ringleader and ordered the Sergeant of the Guard to put him in the guard-house. He was the same man who had been reprimanded in the playhouse, a soldier named Bannister.[16] The ensuing hostility between Grose and King is best set out in their explanations to the Right Honourable Henry Dundas, Chief Secretary of State. The following is an excerpt from a letter by Lieutenant-Governor King, Norfolk Island, 10 March 1794:

Sir,

. . . The disagreeable situation I am in of having incurred Lieut-
Governor Grose's marked disapprobation . . . compells me, sir, to
request in the most respectful manner, your attention for the reasons
I have had for the line of conduct which I found myself obliged to
follow . . . soon after the arrival of this detachment [men of the New
South Wales Corps sent to Norfolk Island after the Toogee and
Hoodoo episode] they were observed to be very intimate with the
convicts, living in their huts, eating, drinking, and gambling with
them and perpetually enticing the women to leave the men they were
married to or those they lived with. Repeated complaints have been
made to me on this head by the settlers and convicts, in all which
complaints I have referred to the commanding officer of the detachment who, I believe, ever did his utmost to prevent it but with very
little effect. Among the many who had repeatedly complained of the
ill-treatment they had received from the soldiers in seducing their
wives . . . was a man named Dring, whose term of transportation has
been three years expired . . . Many complaints were made to me by
this man that a soldier was continually with his wife during his
absence; and to add to the injury he frequently received the grossest
abuse from the soldier who was (on complaint being made to the
commanding officer . . .) forbid going near the cockswains house or
wife; but this prohibition did not prevent an infamous wretch from
enticing the woman out to meet the soldier, of which the husband had
notice and detected them together, when he beat his wife. The soldier
interfered . . . on which he acknowledged to have struck the soldier . . .[17]

The incident led to bad blood between many of the settlers, especially the
time-expired convict settlers, and the soldiers of the New South Wales
detachment, but King in his optimistic way, hoped to have smoothed the
matter out by exhorting both sides to be circumspect in their behaviour. But
the ill-feeling smouldered, and many provocations brought things to a head
on the night of 18 January 1794.

After Bannister was confined in the guard-house a number of the detachment declared they would mutiny, and refused to lay down their arms when
ordered to do so by Lieutenant Abbott. They demanded that Bannister be
freed, a demand that Abbott refused and he also refused to relay their
demand to the Governor at that late hour. Ten of the mutineers were put in
the guard-house, and next morning King convened a meeting of the principal
officers. The Island was simmering with ill-feeling, settlers and convicts
prepared to wreak revenge on the detachment of soldiers; it was a tense
situation, for as King wrote in his letter to Dundas, 'What the consequence
of seven hundred inhabitants opposing themselves to sixty-five armed soldiers
would have been, if not timely prevented, may be easily imagined.'[18]

The situation was resolved by the stratagem of sending part of the detachment to Phillip Island on the orders of their officer, to gather feathers (presumably used in various ways, probably for bedding, etc.) and a further number of men to Queenboro', and while they were out of barracks their arms were seized, by Lieutenant Abbott, Ensign Piper and Mr Grimes, a civil officer. When the men returned late in the day, King assembled every person to hear his Proclamation, in which he explained his move, and avowed his impartiality towards soldiers, settlers, and convicts concerning the administration of justice. In his letter of explanation to Lieutenant-Governor Grose he informed him of what he had done with the impounded weapons:

> In the present exigence I have, sir, judged it advisable to embody the marine and seamen settlers as a militia. There are forty-four of them, very steady men and good soldiers . . . They are victualled from the store, which will, with some assistance from the convicts, be all the recompense I can promise them . . . a guard of two non-commission'd officers and eight privates mount dayly; but when the mutineers are gone I shall decrease the guard to one non-commissioned officer and three privates, who will mount guard at the upper flagstaff . . .[19]

This letter went by the *Francis* which conveniently arrived on 23 January, and with the letter went also the ten mutineers and one lieutenant, to Port Jackson. In reply to the letter, Lieutenant-Governor Grose unleashed his fury:

> The mutiny you state to have happened at Norfolk I have directed to be investigated by a Court of Enquiry composed of all the officers who were present at Sydney . . . Their opinion I enclose to you. The necessity of disarming the detachment I cannot discover although we all too plainly perceive that if the soldiers have been refractory the insults they have received from the convicts were sufficient to provoke the most obedient to outrage . . .
>
> The militia you have ordered to assemble are immediately to be disembodied and their arms are to be sent in the schooner for the purpose of being served out to those persons who are settled on the banks of the Hawkesbury.[20]

In the letter were three enclosures, and Enclosure No. 3 gives, by implication, Grose's opinion of convicts as a class:

> Any convict whether the term of his transportation is expired or not, who shall be accused of striking a soldier is immediately to be given up to the commanding officer of the detachment, who is himself to investigate the matter; and if it appears to him that the soldier has been struck, he will immediately order the offender to be punished with one hundred lashes by the drummers of his detachment. *No*

Captain John Hunter, R.N., artist, R. Dighton. (Mitchell Library, Sydney)

Captain James Cook, discoverer of Norfolk Island in October 1744. Portrait by J. Webber, late 18th century. (National Portrait Gallery, London)

Lieutenant P. G. King, R.N., first Commandant of Norfolk Island, 1789. (La Trobe Collection, State Library of Victoria)

D'Arcy Wentworth, probably 1808–10. This is the only known picture of him. (Permission of D'Arcy Wentworth, Norfolk Island)

provocation that a soldier can give is ever to be admitted as an excuse for the convicts striking the soldier [author's italics].[21]

King, as Lieutenant-Governor of Norfolk Island, refused to comply with these peremptory demands and wrote to the Secretary of State in London instead, his superiors accepted King's explanation, and later, trigger-tempered Grose tendered an apology for his hasty remarks. He did, however, suggest to the authorities in London that Norfolk Island should be closed as a penal settlement. It was too remote and difficult for shipping, he argued, and the expense of keeping a military establishment was in excess of the benefits it might confer on the main colony. Yet there might have been another reason Grose recommended the closure of the Island as a penal colony. That fertile spot with its equable climate had, in one of his Enclosures to King, been in some measure allocated to the men of the New South Wales Corps:

Lieut. Townson, the commanding officer of the detachment, having received a lease of twenty acres of land at Norfolk Island, he is to chuse such a situation in Charlotte Fields as he may approve of, and of which Mr Grimes will bring with him the description. He is also to chuse a spot of twenty-five acres for the use of the officers who at any time shall be on detachment at Norfolk, which are to be divided in the following proportions:—
To the commanding officer of the detachment ten acres and to the three subalterns five acres each of cleared ground . . . Lieut. Townson will allott the ten acres for the use of the soldiers of the detachment. Lieut. Townson will also apply to you for a spot whereon such soldiers as he may wish to indulge with sleeping out of barracks may build huts which are never to be visited by the constables . . .[22]

Major Grose was relieved of the Lieutenant-Governorship of New South Wales when ill-health required his return to England for treatment in December 1794, and on Norfolk Island affairs were peaceable for the next few years. Land grants or leases were given to well-behaved convicts whose sentences were expired, and those who wished to return to the mainland were sent on any available transport that called in for supplies, or on a government vessel.

By 1793 the settlement at Sydney Town (later called Kingston) had a surprisingly varied list of tradesmen and workers. Among them were:

12 sawyers, 4 carpenters, with 5 labourers to do [*ditto*]. 1 boatbuilder
3 labourers to do. 5 blacksmiths 5 shingle-makers 4 charcoal-
makers 6 boat's crew 3 masons 6 labourers to do. 2 plasterers 3
labourers to do 4 glaziers and did'g [*sic*] 7 limeburners 2 quarrymen
4 watchmen 51 cultivating ground 12 town gang, occasionally,
1 gardener 1 attending hospital 10 sick list and convalescent 12

E

overseers & M'r carpenters 9 working to do. 1 granary 87 with settlers off from the Store 2 measuring land 2 cooks 5 store 4 provost-marshal 2 bakers 2 shoemakers 3 taylors 1 barber 2 tool-helvers 1 bagmaker 1 errand-boy 8 carrying stone for building 4 mile-houses 12 servants to civil officers 11 do. to military do. and detachment. 320 total.

MARTIN TIMS, Superintendant.[23]

These were all male convicts, employed at Sydney Town, Norfolk Island, 19 May 1793.

At this time, convicts lived in huts outside the settlement for the most part—the gaol was for those who committed misdemeanours or serious crimes, but there were not many of these. The 293 female convicts had 90 children among them; and some of these must have belonged to those women who were living with the free or convict settlers. There was a school, and a proper schoolmaster, Thomas MacQueen, who had been transported from London for stealing. He had been a schoolteacher there, and it was the Reverend Richard Johnson who had recommended him to King. 'I had several conversations with this man and from what I saw and heard of him I thought him a fit and suitable person for this purpose.'[24] Sadly, after King's departure in 1796, and on obtaining his pardon, MacQueen took to the rum-bottle, and the school had eventually to be closed in 1800.

King left Norfolk Island in October 1796 with his wife Anna Josepha and his young family, a son (born in December 1791) and two daughters, Anna Maria (born 1793) and Utricia (born 1795). His eldest child, Norfolk King, born in 1789 of Ann Inett, had been sent to school in England in 1793 and the young Sydney was under the care of King's mother in Cornwall.

King's health had been giving him much concern, and by December 1795 he was sick with gout, and 'an almost fixed compression of the Lungs and Breast, with a difficulty in Breathing and a constant Pain in the Stomach'[25] as he wrote in a letter to Governor Hunter who was then Governor of New South Wales. King himself was to become Governor in his turn, but he never returned to Norfolk Island.

Foveaux

6

FOVEAUX'S BACKGROUND IS OBSCURE. HE WAS SAID TO BE THE SON OF A FRENCH COOK EMPLOYED IN THE HOUSEHOLD OF THE EARL OF UPPER Ossory whose family seat was Ampthill Park in Bedfordshire, England. His mother's name has not been revealed, but Foveaux was clearly under the patronage of some powerful personage who looked after his interests as he grew up.

He was born in 1765, and while an ensign in the 60th Regiment he purchased a commission in the New South Wales Corps in July 1789, was promoted Captain within a year, and arrived in New South Wales in 1792. In 1796 he was a Major, and as senior officer in the absence of Lieutenant-Colonel Paterson from August 1796 to November 1799, he commanded the New South Wales Corps.[1] During those years he acquired more than 2000 acres (800 hectares) of land, over 1000 sheep and a large number of cattle, making him the largest land-holder in the colony, and possibly one of the wealthiest also. The officers of the New South Wales Corps had considerable power in the colony, being able to acquire large grants of land, and free convict labour to work it. They also stood to make money from the sale of goods brought out to the colony by transport ships they commissioned; these goods, so necessary to the inhabitants, were sold at inflated prices sometimes, netting a handsome return for the men who had commissioned them.

In 1800 King returned to New South Wales as Governor. He was still deeply attached to Norfolk Island, and looked about him for a naval officer to take command. In a letter to Under-Secretary King, he wrote:

The bearer of this, Captain Kent, who takes the *Buffalo* home, has been employed in this colony as lieutenant and Commander of His Majesty's armed ships *Buffalo* and *Supply*, and has been appointed second commander of the *Buffalo* by Gov'r Hunter . . . The activity of this officer previous to my leaving Norfolk Island was very conspicuous in his voyages from this place to that island. Of his

53

professional merit . . . that is sufficiently known . . . When in England I showed you a letter from that officer to me at the Cape, where he expressed his readiness to accept of the Lieutenant-Governorship of Norfolk Island in the hope of getting the rank of commander in the navy . . . I shall only take the liberty of observing that if that Government should become vacant, that it is necessary a naval officer should command there, and I know of none so fit or deserving as Captain Kent.[2]

This letter written on 12 October 1800, three months after Foveaux's appointment as Acting Lieutenant-Governor, is difficult to understand without further reasons from King. It could well be that he was acutely aware of the power accruing to the officers of the New South Wales Corps, and a realisation that Foveaux was very much a military man whose influence on Norfolk Island would be to the advantage of his own men rather than the convicts he was to govern. He was not to realise then, if ever, the sadistic punishments, the bestiality and the terror that would occur on the Island which had been settled primarily, in those years, as a supply depot for the main colony.

Foveaux found affairs on Norfolk Island in a state of confusion on his arrival. Captain Townson had handed the command over, on his unexpected departure, to the senior officer of the New South Wales Corps detachment, Captain Rowley.[3] Rowley had been on the Island for only a short time, and he seems to have had many difficulties with the settlers. He was older than Townson and seems, from his activities while on duty in New South Wales, to have been something of a farmer as well as soldier.[4] Seventeen ninety-nine was a drought year on the Island, the maize crop failed, and maize was needed as swine feed. A number of settlers had been brewing spirits from their own stills and made it available to convicts who needed no urging to obtain it. A trader, John Turnbull, who visited the Island at this time, hoping for good trade, wrote of the drunkenness of the inhabitants: 'some were often intoxicated for a week on end. In 1799 the people suffered a period of ill-health, brought on, according to the surgeon, by drinking spirits hot from the still'.[5] Captain Rowley then ordered the stills demolished, a move which brought threats of prosecution from the owners. It was clearly time that an able administrator was appointed as Commandant on Norfolk Island, and Kent might well have been that man, had his application been approved.

Turnbull, who was on the Island at the time Foveaux was Lieutenant-Governor, arrived there in an American whaler, 'they preferring to refresh at this island'. He also describes it as 'wholly uncultivated but abundant in herbage', and gives a picture of the difficulties sustained in sending provisions on board ship there:

During my stay, short as it was [11 months] the surgeon of the island was drowned in his return visit to a ship in the bay, another officer at

the same time was dragged almost lifeless to the shore, the boat
dashed to pieces and the greater part of the crew dreadfully maimed.
Crossing the passage with a cargo of hogs another boat was swallowed
up and with the exception of one man, the whole crew to the number
of eight, were lost . . .
   Nepean Island in Foveaux's time, was used as a place of
punishment for convicts whose most abandoned profligacy might
otherwise corrupt their less vicious brethren, are here employed in
boiling salt, being only occasionally visited by the boats . . .[6]

Turnbull also mentions an incident concerning an escaped convict who was
not discovered in the bush for several years. This incident is probably the
same one written up in Lieutenant Clark's *Journal*, as Turnbull writes that it
had happened about 'eight years ago'. Clark, on Wednesday 1 June 1791,
writes:

This evening three marines whom I gave leave to go to the
Duncombe Bay to fish, returned with Thomas Stretch who has been
away these eight months past and was supposed to be dead long ago.
Says he has not seen a soul and has lived on birds, cabbage tree which
he climbed and cut with his knife. He is in great want of clothes and
has scarce a rag to cover himself with. Major Ross has forgiven him.
The truth is, he did not run away but was drove from the stores by
Mr Morrelly who said he was ordered not to give him any provisions
from the store.[7]

Here is Turnbull's version:

One of the prisoners belonging to the out-gang, being sent into camp
on Saturday, to draw the weekly allowance of provisions for his mess,
fell, unfortunately, into the company of a party of convicts who were
playing cards for their allowance, a thing very forbidden amongst
them. With as little resolution as his superiors in a similar position,
after being awhile an onlooker, he at length suffered himself to be
persuaded to take a hand, and in the event lost not only his own
portion but that of the whole mess. Being a man of a timid nature his
misfortune overcame his reason, and considering his situation
amongst the mess-mates insupportable he formed and executed the
extravagant resolution of absconding into the glens.
   Every possible inquiry was now made after him. It was known that
he had drawn the allowance . . . and almost in the same moment
discovered he had lost it at play; search upon search was made to no
purpose . . . it was believed he must shortly be taken . . . But these

expectations were in vain, for the fellow managed his business with such dexterity, keeping close within his retreat during the day and marauding for his subsistence only by night, so that despite the narrow compass of the island he eluded all search. His nocturnal depredations were solely confined to the supply of his necessities; Indian corn, potatoes pumpkins and melons. He seldom visited the same place a second time, but shifting from place to place contrived to make his escape before the theft was discovered . . . In vain a reward was offered for his apprehension, and year after year every search possible instituted; it was considered that he was dead till the revival of the old trade proved that the dexterous and invisible thief still existed.

In the search his pursuers have been so near that he frequently heard them express their desire of falling in with him. The reward being promised in spirits, a temptation to which many would have sacrificed their brother, excited almost the whole island to join in the pursuit; even those whose respectability set them above any pecuniary compensation were animated with a desire of hunting in so extra ordinary a chase . . . The unhappy fugitive indulged no hope of pardon.

Nothing of this kind however, was intended: it was humanely thought that he had already sustained sufficient punishment for his original crime and that his . . . depredations being solely confined to necessary food were venial and rendered him a subject of pity rather than criminal prosecutions . . . Chance however . . . accomplished what had baffled every fixed design. One morning about break of day, a man going to his labour observed a fellow hastily crossing the road . . . this must be the man, the object of much anxious general pursuit . . . He exerted his utmost efforts to seize him and after a vigorous opposition on the part of the poor fugitive, finally succeeded in his design . . . The news of his apprehension flew through the island and every one was . . . curious . . . to gain a sight of this phenomenon who for upwards of five years had so effectually secluded himself from all human society. On being brought to the camp and into the presence of the governor, never did a malefactor feel more acutely: he imagined that the moment of his execution approached . . .

His person was such as may well be conceived from his long seclusion . . . his beard had never been shaved from the first moment of his disappearance; he was clothed in some rags he had picked up by the way in some of his nocturnal peregrinations and even his own language was at first by him unutterable . . . After some . . . questions as to what had induced him to form such a resolution and by what means he had so long subsisted, the governor gave him his pardon and restored him to society . . . of which he afterwards became a very useful member.[8]

Foveaux arrived on Norfolk Island in July 1800 to find, as he wrote in an early despatch to Governor King 'a most disorderly state of things'.[9] In the four years since King's departure from there, little maintenance had been done on government property, and the most notable achievement during Captain Townson's period as Acting-Commandant seems to have been the building of the 25-ton sloop *Norfolk* in 1798.

With the coming of Foveaux things were to be different. The first paragraph of his 'Instructions' from King reads:

> On your arrival you are to cause your appointment, as well as the
> patent for constituting a Court of Civil Adjudicature, to be publicly
> read with all due solemnity, and after having informed yourself of the
> different descriptions of people under your command, you are to
> pursue the necessary measures for the peace and safety of the Island,
> and for the safety and preservation of the stock and public stores, and
> to fix such regulations as may appear to be best calculated for
> cultivating the public grounds and such other objects as are hereafter
> directed, by distributing the convicts who are now, or may be
> hereafter, under the sentence of the law, in such manner as to feed,
> maintain and cloath the inhabitants at the least possible expense to
> the public.[10]

These instructions seem open to wide interpretation. It would need a man of sober judgement to carry them out with complete justice. The 'tyranny of distance' could lead to abuse of power if the one to wield that power had little understanding of men and little, if any, compassion. Foveaux, like Grose, was a career military officer who considered the men of his regiment infinitely superior to the felons they were to guard. Convicts were a workforce, and a vicious one at that—men who were to be kept in subjection by whatever means were effective and to hand. His despatches to Governor King reveal little of his real self, they are largely concerned with work done, or in hand, or projected:

> Since my last letter there has been completed a new Granary at the
> back of the Provost Marshal's Barrack and the Public Bakehouse,
> erected upon a very strong foundation, and stone walls carried four
> feet from the surface of the Earth, constructed in such a manner to
> prevent either rats or mice from getting therein and calculated to hold
> 3 or 4 thousand bushels of wheat, in perfect safety. There has also
> been completed an additional Stone Building to the New Gaol, Forty
> feet in length and Twenty feet in breadth, with Stone walls ten feet in
> height around the whole . . .[11]

He had already weeded out several of the overseers in the workforce, and shown his readiness to listen to informers, who were rewarded by some slight indulgences:

Francis Wheeler the master Carpenter behaved so very improperly
and has also been detected in embezzling the Public Stores, I found it
necessary to suspend him, having no other person I could appoint in
his stead than Robert Jones. I have therefore been necessitated to do
so . . .[12]

Wheeler had arrived on Norfolk Island during King's term of office as
Lieutenant-Governor and had been 'on stores' for some years; no doubt he
had had his pickings over the last few years but he was, as King might have
described him 'a very complete carpenter'.

Informers were an insidious influence, one that spread fast among the
convicts who were both cunning, and fearful for their skins. To be an
informer might be the means of averting a lashing, or chains; better to see
another in such a situation than yourself, was the reasoning of some, while
revenge was a potent weapon for an informer with a grudge. Foveaux
encouraged informers, and in some instances it was his only means of
uncovering potential trouble, as was the case in December 1800. His
despatch to Governor King contained an abbreviated account of the
happenings; though by the time it was received, the events were long past:

On Sunday morning 14th December, Henry Gready, an Irish prisoner
came to me and informed me a number of convicts had concocted a
plan whereby they were to liberate themselves and their fellow
prisoners and no time to be lost. 100 pikes were already made to arm
them and the attempt was to be made that night. 30 pikes were
hidden. He also informed me that Peter McLean and John Wollaghan
were the two leading people and the former swore in and selected the
others . . . It appeared necessary . . . that some immediate example
should be made of Peter McLean and John Wollaghan which was
done accordingly the same evening. I have already promised to
intercede with your Excellency in favour of Henry Gready to get him
his free pardon . . . he was sent here for committing a rape and is a
life prisoner. Encouragement for such people is ever well received and
will in fact be the means of inducing others to come forward in
similar cases . . .[13]

On receipt of this letter King agreed that Foveaux had done the right thing,
and in his own despatch to the Duke of Portland, Home Secretary, he wrote,
in regard to Norfolk Island affairs:

I have the honour to enclose a copy of Major Foveaux's last letter to
me in which your Grace will observe that the insurgents sent to
Norfolk Island had nearly carried one of their wild plans into
execution. The pikes found—of which the Major sent several here—

are compleatly handled and ready to use. I trust that the particular situation that officer found himself in will be deemed an excusable reason for the steps he and the officers on the Island judged it necessary to adopt on that occasion; and I cannot pass over this subject without observing that Major Foveaux's conduct since he has been at that Island has been highly meritorious in carrying the instructions I gave him into effect . . .[14]

King's letter was written on 10 March 1801, three months after the events took place. There was no one to tell him of the actual sequence of what happened, nor to tell him that no trial of any sort had taken place.

Peter MacLean and John Wollaghan were two of a large number of Irish dissidents transported to New South Wales after political uprisings in Ireland throughout the 1790s. Both were young men, fiery and outspoken, and both had been re-transported from New South Wales to Norfolk Island after further disturbances in the colony. There were a number of Irish dissident convicts on the Island, it was easy to gain a following among them, and there was no doubt that an insurrection was planned. How men could have supposed that an uprising, with no weapons but pikes (against the muskets of the military) would have had even a remote chance of success, is hard to believe. Only desperate souls shut away from freedom (even the freedom to make disruption) could have considered it. Gready, an Irishman himself, too fearful for his skin to join the insurgents, saw his chance to win an indulgence, and took it.

Foveaux hurriedly convened all the officers, civil and military, 'for the purpose of communicating to them some very important information which had this morning been given to him . . .' to decide how best to act on this information. The officers, with the Deputy Judge-Advocate Hibbins presiding, were unanimous in their decision, as the letter written by Hibbins, made clear:

The information is as follows, vizt.: — That a number of convicts, amounting to one hundred, had entered into a plot or conspiracy to liberate themselves and their fellow prisoners, and forcibly to take possession of the island; that the plan they had formed to carry such plot into effect was to put to death the Acting Lieutenant-Governor and all the officers, and also such other persons, even women and children, who would not assist them in forwarding their wicked designs; that one hundred pikes were made with which they were to be armed on that occasion, and that a number of them would be found in a place which the informant pointed out; that J--- W--- and P--- M--- both Irishmen, were the two most active people; the first had also been seen making the pikes, and the latter in selecting and swearing in such persons as he thought most fit for their purpose;

that everything was ready and there should be no time lost if the
Major intended to put a stop to such a scene of bloodshed as was at
that time in meditation.[15]

There is a postscript to this letter, which says that Foveaux observed that he
had found thirty pikes in the place Gready had mentioned, that MacLean and
Wollaghan had arrived on Norfolk Island within the past month, both having
been concerned in conspiracies at Port Jackson, and continues:

> The Major, therefore, requested that the gentlemen assembled . . .
> would give him their opinions what steps appeared to them most
> proper to be taken . . . who being perfectly convinced of the truth of
> the information before them unanimously agreed that an immediate
> example of capital punishment Should be made of the two ringleaders
> P--- M--- and J--- W--- as well as such others whom it could
> afterwards be proved were concerned with them.[16]

The letter was signed by Hibbins, four officers of the Corps, and the
Surgeon.

In due course, Foveaux's action, relayed to the Home Secretary by King,
received approbation. It was rewarded by the promotion from Acting
Lieutenant-Governor of Norfolk Island, to full status as Lieutenant-Governor.
No mention of a trial had been made, and there was no one to tell the
authorities that no trial had taken place.

As the convicts shuffled from morning service, on that Sunday morning,
the exhortations of Pastor Fulton still with them, the two men named as
ringleaders of the planned insurrection, MacLean and Wollaghan, were
hustled away by the armed soldiers waiting outside. A gallows was erected in
the afternoon, and the whole number of the convicts were assembled to
watch as Wollaghan and MacLean were hanged. The convicts, and a small
number of soldiers who had been implicated, were flogged at intervals for the
next twenty days.

It was this peremptory and ruthless reaction that embittered every convict
who had a spark of resistance or any respect for justice left in him. Foveaux
was 'the Murderer' to many afterwards. And Foveaux's action was to have
repercussions. In 1803 Governor King, in a letter to Lord Hobart, reports
that 'Major Foveaux has applied to me for leave of absence to go to England
on some urgent business of his own',[17] and though no elucidation of what
this business is may have been forthcoming, Rusden, in his *History of
Australia* writes:

> Irish sedition at Norfolk Island had been serious and was repressed
> with an audacious resolution by Foveaux in January 1801. [*sic*] Being
> warned of it he concealed thirty pikes, 'Not feeling justification in
> taking the law entirely into my own hands . . . I convened the officers

both civil and military . . . they were unanimously of the opinion that an immediate example of capital punishment should be made of Peter MacLean and John Wollaghan, which was accordingly done on the same evening . . . I have had very strong information against four soldiers whom I have consequently discharged, and have a doubt but some of them would be hanged, was the Judge-Advocate acquainted with the late Acts of Parliament relating to such persons . . . One soldier received 500 lashes and was drummed out of the regiment for striking a sergeant in connection with the matter. Twenty-two convicts were severely punished.'[18]

Although Governor King and Lord Hobart, the Secretary of State, approved of this summary justice, Foveaux encountered opposition where he probably least expected it. When he heard of it, Colonel Paterson, commanding officer of the New South Wales Corps, called Foveaux to account (through Governor King) for dealing with soldiers without any form of trial. King advised Foveaux to transmit the written opinion of the officers he had consulted to Paterson, and, also through King, Foveaux sent a long defence of his conduct to the Secretary of State. It was probably Paterson's extreme displeasure and the reporting of the incident by others, that led to Foveaux's request 'for leave of absence to go to England on some urgent business of his own . . .' in 1803.

Foveaux's replacement during his absence on 'urgent business' was the officer next in seniority in the New South Wales Corps, Brevet-Major Johnstone, who had served on Norfolk Island as a junior officer some years before. In May 1803 Lieutenant-Colonel Paterson, Johnstone's Commanding Officer, replied to King's letter appointing Johnstone to take up his appointment:

Sir,
    I had the Honor of receiving your Excellency's Letter of Yesterday and communicated the Contents of it to Brevet Major Johnstone who declines going to Norfolk Island, not being his regular Tour of Duty, and I do not conceive myself warrantable by Ordering him on that Service, as Commanding Officer of the Regiment . . .
                I have, etc.
                Wm Paterson,
                Lt. Col. N.S.W. Corps.[19]

Captain Wilson, already serving on Norfolk Island, was given the job Major Johnstone refused. Great was the anticipation among the convicts that Foveaux was gone for good, but he was returned to the Island with no diminution of power over the prisoners. He was an able administrator, which was expected of him by his superiors, but he lacked compassion for the mass of humanity it was his task to govern. He had an acquisitive nature, as was evidenced by his speedy accumulation of land and stock when he first reached New South Wales, and it could have been with a view to acquiring land in beautiful Norfolk Island that he made application for its governorship; no man knows. But the Island was not to be owned by any but the Government— there was no profit for a wealthy man in selling stock to the Stores. Moreover, Foveaux began to suffer severe attacks of asthma, and made frequent applications for leave of absence to 'recruit his health'.

It was in the early years of the nineteenth century that the first steps towards the ending of the penal settlement on Norfolk Island were taken. Van Diemen's Land was being considered as a place of settlement, with Colonel Paterson as Lieutenant-Governor at Port Dalrymple, a plan which did not work very well after a year or so of experimentation. In a despatch of 1803 Lord Hobart said:

> Upon a mature consideration of all circumstances relating to the establishment upon Norfolk Island, its great expence [*sic*] and the disadvantages attending communication between that island and Port Jackson . . . it appears advisable that part of the establishment . . . at Norfolk Island, should be removed, together with a proportion of the settlers and convicts, to Port Dalrymple . . . upon the southern coast of Van Diemen's Land . . . The cultivated land, which would by this arrangement become the property of the Crown in Norfolk Island, would in all probability be considerably more than sufficient to raise wheat for the small establishment that may be left upon the island, and for growing maize to fatten swine for the purpose of being salted and cured for the use of other settlements.[20]

The scheme sounded good to some of the farmer-settlers, but as time passed and despatches took months or a year to bring replies, enthusiasm waned, and only a very few of the larger land-holders considered the removal of themselves and their households and stock to a new settlement where they would have to begin everything again.

Crops varied, as they had always done, from year to year; at times, drought took a firm hold, grain crops withered before harvesting and food for the stock had to be brought from Port Jackson—if any was available. Then would come good years in succession, bountiful crops and plenty of stock-feed, and the settlers one by one, asked that their names be removed from the list of those intending to leave the Island and re-settle in Van Diemen's Land.

In May 1803 H.M.S. *Buffalo* called at Norfolk Island on a voyage from Sydney to Calcutta. On board was the Captain's wife, Mrs Eliza Kent. Her letter to her mother gives a picture of the Island as it was to a free and happy woman.

> Our passage to Norfolk Island was boisterous and tedious . . . We arrived off the Island on Sunday morning May 8th and immediately

the cutter and jolly boat were hoisted out and the passengers landed at Cascade with great expedition, notwithstanding there was no vestige remaining of a wharf that was there formerly, and the surf made the landing on the rocks very unsafe. When the boats returned they brought a terrific account of a long narrow plank that was placed over a chasm in the rocks, which, if you happen to slip over you would inevitably be dashed to pieces. My desire to go on shore was not at all lessened by this account and I was in high spirits when a few hours afterwards a kind invitation was brought off to me from Captain and Mrs Wilson of the Corps . . .

The next morning several gentlemen accompanied me to see the new Government House, building under the direction of the Lieutenant-Governor. It will be a large house, pleasantly situated on a general eminence commanding a view of the town of Sydney, Turtle Bay, and the Nepean and Philip Islands. This afternoon Captain and Mrs Wilson had their infant daughter baptized by the Reverend W. Fulton, the sponsors were Ensign Piper, Mrs Wilson (proxy for Mrs Bellasis) and myself—the child was named Amelia.

When this ceremony was over I walked as far as Queenbury [*sic*] a few huts scattered in a vale deserve not the name of a village, but their situation is beautiful and romantic, the steep hills on each side of the valley affording rich pasture and yielding luxuriant crops of Indian corn, a charming shady walk between banana? Banyan? trees winds some distance round the bottom of the hills, near which is a hut belonging to Government, and a garden that produces oranges as fine as those at Rio de Janeiro . . .[21]

This is the first mention of the Government House which still survives today, though enlarged and improved to a certain extent. Foveaux, it was said, feared for his life towards the end of his period of service on Norfolk Island, and had strong iron bars fixed to all windows, a sentry-box built into the inner hall, and an armed sentry parading outside, throughout the night. Eliza Kent related how the Lieutenant-Governor escorted her back to the Cascade landing in his carriage, driving her himself, 'a gallant gentleman' was her description of him.

There is no portrait of Joseph Foveaux to show how he looked, or whether he was tall, short, or of medium height, nor whether he had strong features and a handsome exterior; no description of him has appeared anywhere. In fact he was probably well-featured, he certainly had a way with him, if Eliza Kent's impression of him is accurate.

On Norfolk Island, he took Ann Sherwin, the wife of a sergeant in the New South Wales Corps, as his mistress. The sergeant made no recorded complaint—there was actually very little he could do. Had he objected, it would have been a simple matter to inveigle him into some misdemeanour, bring him before a court-martial and so finish his career; such things were not uncommon in the New South Wales Corps. Sherwin was removed from the Island in the course of his duty and Ann Sherwin stayed with Foveaux. The remarkable thing is that they stayed together after Foveaux left the Island in 1804 and were married in England, at All Saints Church, Derby, in 1815, by which time Foveaux was a Major-General.[22]

By 1804 Foveaux was possibly a frightened as well as a sick man, the open hate almost every convict had for him must have created an almost visible net around him. He applied for and was given leave to return to England, and in September he left Norfolk Island on the *Albion*, never to return, though his influence made itself felt in later years. On his voyage home, he spent much time formulating a plan for the evacuation of the convict settlement on Norfolk Island and for the resettling of most of the long-established settlers in Van Diemen's Land and his plans were given to Lord Hobart, who approved them. Some of his suggestions were to surface in the distant future, to the untold misery of thousands of men.

Foveaux's place as Commandant was taken by Captain John Piper, who had spent some years on the Island, first in King's time, as ensign, and later in Townson's administration.[23] The civil establishment was considerably reduced after Foveaux's departure, only six officials remaining; Deputy Judge-Advocate Hibbins, the Reverend Henry Fulton (a former Irish dissident), Surgeon D'Arcy Wentworth, Mr Broughton, Storekeeper, Robert Jones, Superintendant, John Drummond, Beach-master and Pilot.

Times were to improve in the years to come, but Foveaux's four years of power had brought untold misery and terror to the powerless ones subjected to his authority. That story is best told through the eyes of Robert Jones, who, in Foveaux's time, was Chief Gaoler. Many years later he wrote, on what was probably his death-bed, 'Could we but live over again that which is past, what a lot of good we would do. It is too late now. The last day is too late.'[24]

Recollections of Robert 'Buckey' Jones

THE RECOLLECTIONS OF ROBERT 'BUCKEY' JONES IS PROBABLY THE ONLY FIRST-HAND DESCRIPTION OF MAJOR JOSEPH FOVEAUX'S PERIOD AS Lieutenant-Governor of Norfolk Island from 1800 to 1804.[1] It is written in a much-thumbed notebook, many years after the events described, and the handwriting at times grows weak, as if with fatigue. The writer, Robert Jones, was a convict who had arrived on Norfolk Island in 1789 or 1790, and remained there until 1809 or 1810. He was granted a conditional pardon in 1795 during King's time of office as Lieutenant-Governor.

A muster of Norfolk Island settlers in 1808 reveals Robert Jones as holder of 60 acres (24 hectares) of land, 6 of them under wheat, 20 under maize, 30 pasture and 11 fallow. His stock consisted of 2 oxen, 2 cows, 15 male sheep, 44 female, 7 hogs and 7 female pigs, 400 bushels of maize in hand. At this time he was allowed the labour of two convicts for his farm. His wife was Sarah Jones, and they had four children.[2]

From 1796 he had been appointed to several different supervisory jobs, from constable to overseer, master-carpenter and boat-builder. In 1798, Captain John Townson, Acting-Commandant, sent the sloop *Norfolk*, built at the Island from Norfolk pine, to Port Jackson for fitting-out. Jones, with two or three other 'trusties' had built her and then sailed her to Port Jackson, where she was received by Governor Hunter. Hunter immediately had her fitted out for the two explorers Matthew Flinders and George Bass. It was in the *Norfolk* that they succeeded in circumnavigating Van Diemen's Land, thus establishing the existence of Bass Strait.

Jones and his companions returned to Norfolk Island. In his *Recollections* Jones makes no mention of anything that happened before Foveaux's arrival on the Island; it is as if those years left little if any mark on him.

In *Recollections*, which gives indications of having been written over a long period and in very different states of mind, Jones piles horror on horror on some pages, with attempts at a balanced view on others, but nowhere does he write of Foveaux with anything but hatred, especially when he mentions the women convicts. 'His was a life never to repay for his brutal conduct towards prisoners', he writes.

It is not possible to positively identify Robert Jones from the early shipping lists, though a strong clue is given in a despatch from Lieutenant-Governor King to Governor Hunter when in 1795 he asked for a conditional Pardon for a Robert Jones who came out in the First Fleet. Jones probably had a seven-year transportation sentence, which would have been worked out by 1795, or earlier.

Only one Robert Jones arrived in the First Fleet, and he, to complicate things a little, was listed as George Abrahams, alias Robert Cox, alias Robert Jones. George Abrahams (on some lists 'Abrams'), stood trial at Chelmsford Assizes in March 1785. His age was given as 26, his occupation, labourer, his crime, three indictments for highway robbery, each indictment carrying the sentence of death by hanging. Yet he was reprieved and given seven years' transportation instead. This was at a time when sentence of death was the only one given for highway robbery, and it makes his reprieve all the more puzzling.

Perhaps the answer to this is to be found in 'General' Joseph Holt's *Memoirs*, to which I will refer in more detail later. Certainly George Abrahams, alias Robert Jones, fits the character of a highway desperado, with his toughness, his sympathy for the young women convicts, his hatred of the rich and well-dressed, and the deep sense of remorse in his writing. Holt maintains that Jones betrayed his partners in crime for the sake of an indulgent sentence. His partners, says Holt, were his father and two brothers.

Here follows the text of *Recollections* as I transcribed it from the Mitchell Library, Sydney.

*   *   *

RECOLLECTIONS OF 13 YEARS RESIDENCE IN NORFOLK ISLAND AND VAN
DIEMENS LAND
ROBERT JONES, 'BUCKEY', LATE CHEIF [*sic*] GAOLER AT NORFOLK ISLAND,
SYDNEY JUNE 15 1823.
[*The words 'and Van Diemens Land' are crossed out*]

Although my memory is at times inclined to be uncertain I can truthfully remember incidents that occurred during my appointment as chief gaoler in Norfolk Island in 1803 to 1805. During 1805 ended my services on that Island on account of the giving up of that place as a penal settlement. [Here Jones's memory is at fault. The evacuation was to have taken place at that time and did indeed begin in a small way, but it fizzled out owing to the settlers' unwillingness to leave, uncertain about what might await them in the new land; only a few settlers left Norfolk Island, though convicts were withdrawn regularly in small numbers.] In 1803 the number of persons was about 1200. Captain Foveaux was then Commandant. The convicts were usually worked in groups with an overseer. They were allowed rations of ten pounds of flour and three pounds of salted pork. They were at liberty to work for the free settlers after their work was done, and for which they were paid by an increase of rations, the men on such occasions were kept out in the open until my arrival which did not often happen until about 10 at night. Major Foveaux was one of them hard and determined men who believe in the lash more than in the Bible, his treatment of the women convicts was most brutal, they were looked upon as slaves and sold openly to the free settlers and convicts alike. The prices often being as high as £10 for young and good-looking girls. This state of affairs was the result of Governor King's treatment in regard to the method and control during transportation from Sydney. They were in most cases consigned and shipped as beasts of burden. Potter the bellman [Potter the bellman was the overseer who roused the prisoners each morning an hour before sunrise by hammering on an iron frame or cask, calling 'Turn out, you damned souls!'] was acting as salesman and in most cases reselling them for a gallon or so of rum until they were in such a condition to be of little or no further use. These statements I make from my own personal observation. Much can be said of the abuse of convict women at Norfolk Island. The Governor himself did not consider these practices at all immoral and was not above temtation [*sic*]. The state and moral conditions on the island is beyond human imagination. The general work for male convicts consisted in stone cutting and farm work. The production of the latter consisted chiefly maize-growing with little or no attempt at stock raising. They were often hard pressed for the necessities of life. We were often put on short rations. The usual punishments extended to male offenders for small defalcations consisted of twenty-five lashes on the triangle, and after receiving their punishment were sent to work in the quarries. The women were similarly treated only that their bodies were exposed to the male convicts, they being compelled to walk naked before them. It was usual for the men to be placed in a circle around the flogger and his victim with the Commandant as an eye witness. They were (the women) then sent to their homes and allowed two hours upon which to relieve the effects of their punishment. It has often been said that the prisoners were starved into submission and also that more barbarious punishments such as cutting off their hands and removing their eyes. But I can truthfully deny all such statements. Major Foveaux had a passion for witnessing punishments of that description. He would often order some poor unfortunate wretch to the triangle and laugh at his cries for mercy. They were all genuinely pleased at his retirement. The appointment of Captain Piper was looked upon with much hope of improvement nor were they mistaken. The announcement of his Governorship began a new era for the welfare and treatment of prisoners. My first instructions were to report personally any infringement or disobedience of the new rules made for the benefit of all prisoners. They consisted of no flogging for women, extra two pounds of flour, two pounds of salted pork and one measure of ground corn. All prisoners to be in their cells at sundown and no work in wet weather. The women were to receive an extra allowance of clothing with extra blankets and other minor necessities. To the general mind and reports appearing in the Govt. Dispatches Norfolk Island as a penal settlement was in every way satisfactory. Transportation from Sydney of the worst type of criminals did not occur to the public as to their future treatment for improvement. [Here Jones has wandered from Foveaux's time as Commandant to that of his successor John Piper. Piper was appointed Acting-Commandant in September 1804.] During my appointment as overseer I had the opportunity of meeting various classes and types of prisoners. Many were sent there for offences for which different methods of improvement and punishment would be more commendable. Political prisoners were treated with the same severity as the most dangerous class of vagabonds. In respect to the early or past positions of many convicts I need not dwell here. Their offences committed and sentences received could be more correctly acertained [*sic*] from the various official records. Their conditions and impressions of this place were in no way respected. It was usual upon arrival of each gang of prisoners to instruct and inform them that their positions became once and for all purposes dead to the outside world, they would be known hereafter by numbers only. The general rule was in the case of prisoners who were fortunate enough to possess an education above the average, also some outside means, received some slight consideration from the Commandant. He [the Governor] was at all times open to receive some slight recognition in return for favours extended. In fact most of them holding such minor positions as overseer, constables, doctors, were at all times willing to extend leniancy [*sic*] should there be sufficient compensation. So you will understand that Norfolk Island was not so bad as represented. Dr Redfern was one of those blunt and outspoken of men. He at all times listened attentavely [*sic*] to prisoners and others who may be unfortunate enough to require his services. He was well liked for his many kindnesses and liberal ways. We were always in a state of excitement during the appearance of any vessels. There was a fear that the French were coming and upon one occasion we were alarmed at the appearance of several vessels passing the island. Notice was at once given to the Chief Constable Edward Kimberley, to have all prisoners placed in their cells and scaffolding covered with brushwood. The soldiers were to set fire to the prisons on signal from me. There were about 60 prisoners in the cells. The alarm spread throughout the settlement and the whole population numbering about 200 advanced to the Cascade to offer a strong resistance to the enemy who proved to be some passing friendly vessels bound for Sydney. Governor Piper was ignorant of our doings. [This episode is described in Holt's *Memoirs.*] I would like to say more concerning Major Foveaux and his governorship of the Island. Shortly before his recall to England for the murder (the correct word) of two men named McLean and Wollehan [*sic*], the history of that case and trial is too well known to mention here. Sergeant Sherwin and his confinement in gaol, also the seduction of his wife by Major Foveaux leaves an unfavourable impression of that gentleman's character. It is well to mention that the influence and mercy given to prisoners will be remembered by many fortunate enough to have been noticed by her. Her word of goodwill and kindly remembrance secured her many friends. The power she excised [*sic*] over the Major it is well to mention, was in all cases for some kindly action. Sergeant Sherwin I believe, shortly afterwards left the island. He afterwards remarried and had four or five children and became a grocer in Parramatta. Doctor Wentworth although holding such a high position as Chief Surgeon was a most generous and kind hearted and considerate man. His duties were mostly confined to giving relief to prisoners after their flogging which were very frequent. One man named Joe Mansbury who received 2000 lashes cat of nine tails during his term of 3 years here, his back being quite bare of flesh and his collar bones were exposed looking very much like two polished ivory horns. It was with some difficulty we could find another place to flog him. Tony [Chandler] suggested to me that we had better try the soles of his feet next time. The prison and its surroundings resembled a square with stone walls about ten feet high. Along the outside of the wall were the cells, they numbered about 80 and about twelve feet by eight feet with eighteen-inch thick walls. The approach to the cells was a narrow passage five feet wide with no roof and paved with stone flags. The cells were damp and badly lighted and very cold. No restrictions were placed on prisoners should they return later from working on the farms of the Governor, but they all had to rise one hour before sunrise and roll up their bedding which was placed outside their cells in all weathers. Anyone making a complaint about wet bedding was immediately ordered to the triangle and given twenty lashes. A further complaint was another 50 lashes. Such punishment usually had the effect of subduing any further disturbance or complaint. The method of placing them on the triangle was very simple. The triangle was a tripod with the top joined and the legs spread about 3 feet with straps for holding the prisoners. The flogger was a County Clare man and very powerful, who took great pleasure in inflicting as much bodily punishment as possible using such expressions as 'Another half a pound of meat off the beggar's ribs!' His face and clothes usually presented the appearance of a mincemeat chopper, being covered with flesh from the victim's body. Major Foveaux delighted in such an exhibition and would show his satisfaction by smiling as an encouragement to the flogger. He would sometimes order the victim to be brought before him. 'Hullo you damned scoundrel, how do you like it?' and order him to put his coat on and immediately go to work. William Redfern, Surgeon Wentworth's assistant, would then ask the Governor's permission to administer some comfort to the victim which consisted of throwing a bucket or two of salt water upon his back. The prisoners were so hardened to such treatment that it became a saying 'You will get salted back for that'. Among the prisoners was one named Holt, a fiery-tempered and plain spoken man. He gave me more trouble than the worst class of criminals, I believe he was an Irish rebel. He was the only man among the gang who would dare answer the Major or Murderer as many called him. During his imprisonment here he did not receive any floggings. I believe as near as I can remember he left in the ship *Sydney* under the command of Captain Forrest for Van Diemen's Land to open a prison settlement there under the Governorship of Lt. Collins who was to form a settlement on the River Derwent, afterwards called Newtown. Drummond the beach overseer, Tony Chandler and Peter Walsh were always in trouble concerning this man who would do no work he being a favourite of Mrs Sherwin. He was well liked among the female prisoners and during his stay he would suffer none to be placed on the triangle. He was the only man feared by the Major. Ted Kimberley, chief constable, considered the convicts of Norfolk Island no better than heathens, unfit to grace this earth. Women in his estimation were born for the convenience of men. The amusements consisted mainly of dancing in the barrack room on Thursday evenings when all the women would join in the dances of the mermaids. Each one being naked with a number painted on her back so as to be recognised by their admirers who would then clap their hands on seeing their favourite perform some grotesque action. And with the assistance of a gallon or two of rum would end their night's amusement in a drunken state. Potter the bellman would arrange for the appearance of the women. I can well remember the fight between Mary Finders and Bridget Chandler as to who was favourite among the soldiers, which ended in Bridget receiving a broken arm. Mr Mitchell a store keeper and trader (who afterwards went to Sydney) would exchange his stores for rum. His flour was bad and his pork soft. I believe he came out here as a missioner but gave up that profession as there was more money in trading. He had a beautiful young woman named Liza McCann who was as cunning as himself who could drink more rum than most of the hardened soldiers and took every means to make herself disagreeable to the other females who would dare venture within the store. Her greatest pride was to be clothed in silk and a bonnet with feathers on them. Mr Mitchell usually wore a dark coat white trousers and vest of a bright red colour with a large black hat brought out from England for him by Captain McIntosh. The food as supplied to the prisoners being of a poor quality did not sustain them sufficiently long enough for the class of work required of them. Under such conditions the prisoners were compelled to resort to other means of obtaining sufficient to keep themselves alive, many were the devices carried out to obtain it, the usual manner of distribution left many opportunities for unfair dealings. Of course it must be remembered that there were favourites among the male and female prisoners and that every opportunity was taken by them wherewith to increase their own larder. The flour was served out in mess tins by Sergeant Sherwin who handed them to Peter Walsh and upon receiving of which he would lift a handful from each tin for his own use generally with the remark 'Is it one or two handsful for my share?' and should any of them refuse him he would look at them with a meaning well known to themselves, possibly a little extra work or punishment for their refusal. The pork supplied to the prisoners was so soft that you could put your finger through it and always rotten, the appearance of vermin among the food was always excused to the nature and quality supplied, it being said that the best of flour and meat always contained them. Upon receiving his allowance each prisoner was required to place his food in his cell and was compelled to do his own cooking when time could be spared for such work. There were several attempts to escape from the Island but none were successful, many murders, most of them were committed for the purpose of getting to Sydney, it being their only way of seeing 'heaven' again. Many were never to see the 'old hell' as Norfolk Island was called, again. Thomas Carpenter did not survive his last punishment or 'corporal' as it was called, his 250 killed him, died of heart failure they said, God forgive them and him too. For he was well liked on the Island, but feeling that he was ill and thinking his end was near, he struck his officer with the hope that he would see his friends once more. He did so but it was his last time. Two men were sent to Sydney. They have each received 800 lashes during their stay here and it was decided by the doctors that more flogging would be injurious. Their backs were quite bare of flesh and one mass of sores. It is a strange thing that the home Government did not send out some missionaries, we were badly in want of one here. The state of the settlement and the account of work done compare favourably with any other. I feel sure our farm and agriculture work was far advanced of any other Colony. We were at some time or other in a state of semi-starvation but that was when we were in trouble over the dry and wet seasons. 10 bushels of maize to the acre in a good crop. [The next page seems to be missing; the text continues] cannot see why you advise me to forward reports in reference to the work performed under my direction. Upon receiving this notice I went to the Major, his answer was 'Tell them they must come and make a report for themselves.' No person was allowed to write any information about the place or the work done here, they were only to write in reference to the state of our good conduct and friends. Many were the unspoken regrets at the return of the Major. How they must have wished they could have been at home and tell the truth. For without a doubt he was guilty and it is I who could tell them so. Murder, simply murder is what I call it. God forgets and forgives but I never can. His was a life never to repay for his brutal conduct towards prisoners. 'Goodnight and be damned to you I say, Chandler. 25 tomorrow and mark him'. Such were common expressions of the Major. Careful were we that his instructions were carried out. Prisoners were not informed of their punishment until the morning. No food was to be taken by the victim before receiving his punishment. Such cruel treatment had little effect in subduing the most hardened criminals. Thursday April 11 I well remember the date, began the most stormy weather on record here. The Cascade was partly destroyed. The flogging of Charles Maher almost brought about a mutiny. His back was quite bare of skin and flesh. Poor wretch, he received 250 lashes and on receiving 200 Kimberley refused to count meaning that the punishment was enough. Annie Kelly received 25 lashes and well deserved it, her conduct was very bad. She was a thief and a spy, the last being sufficient to condemn her to all. All ships from Sydney for Norfolk Island bearing prisoners or Government despatches had to use a private signal before dropping anchor. All the prisoners were removed to cells and upon arrival of a new batch or gang they were taken in before the other prisoners possibly as a lesson to them, they were informed of the rules and regulations and then assigned to me for their future work. The new arrivals were placed in irons for one week. They were often given 25 lashes to shew authority whether corporal punishment was needed or not. It was an easy matter to make him commit an offence which made him liable. Three women under sentence for child murder or white slaves [*sic*], one of the worst methods of punishment for such an offence. England for white slaves. Why were they sent here for crimes that required pity rather than punishment. Heaven forbid England if that is her way of populating her hell-holes. What would our noble persons think of our virgin settlement and the white slaves? In every case the women were treated as slaves, good stock to trade with, and a convict having a good chance to possess one did not want much encourage-ment to do so. January 1804 began with a new crime among the prisoners, that of stealing stores from ships visiting the Island. Many complaints had been received by the Governor. Also a very painful way of return to Sydney by way of cutting off some other prisoners hand or foot. During the first punishment prisoners were given 25 lashes. 200 lashes is considered a 'feeler', 500 'black box' meaning death to those who received them. Many were relieved at death from such treatment. It would be impossible to describe the tortures received and the methods employed by the Commandant, his servants and overseers. One of the Commandant's favourite and most frequent punishment was to make the leg irons smaller each month so they would pinch the flesh. The water pit was a cell sunk below ground and filled with salt water 18 to 20 inches high. The prisoner was stripped and placed in it and left for 2 or more days. Could we but live over again that which is past, what a lot of good we would do. It is too late now. The last day is too late.

Report of Commandant for half-year ending June 1804 Prisoners on Island 1180. Corporal punishment inflicted on prisoners 267 cases prisoners received 500 lashes each. Ten male and seven female prisoners died. Prisoners sent to Sydney for trial at cost of some £163. 12s.

On Saturday June 16th 1804 2 prisoners made an attempt to escape on a raft but had to return on account of bad weather. One man made attempt to get away on a door after boring two holes in it for his legs, but did not get more than 10 miles. One of his toes was bitten off. Two days in the water-pit and 250 lashes put a stop to further escapes. It is strange that the women did not attempt to escape. Their lot must surely have been greater than the male convicts. Several have not recovered yet from their treatment at the hands of the Major. Sixteen of them were flogged for minor offences such as using too personal remarks to the Commandant's fancy woman, a Mrs Sherwin, a good but badly-judged woman. Goodbye to the other woman. There was some hope that she would survive the 250 lashes. Upon being brought to the triangle, Richards complained of sickness and could not be able to perform the flogging. Kimberley was requested to act as flogger. When the time came for him to begin, Lt. Laycock commanded him to begin upon which Kimberley cried out that he did not flog women. This reply made the Major furious. He then asked one of the soldiers, Mick Kelly by name to take the tails and go on with the punishment which he immediately proceeded to perform in such a manner that not one mark was left on her back. This made the Major so wild that he ordered the woman to be placed in a dark cell for a fortnight, upon which Surgeon Redfern objected that the woman had received sufficient punishment as directed by the Governor himself. This was the last time women were flogged on the Island. On 27th May H.M. ship Calcutta (I think that was the name) came from Sydney for the purpose of inspection and to make a general report as to settlement and conditions of prisoners on the Island. But I believe it was for taking more prisoners to the newly-formed settlement of Van Diemen's Land. We had heard such bad reports from that place and in consequence prisoners were very much against going there. Many of the old hands would injure themselves in order that they may be taken. Some were in the habit of eating sand in the hope of being ill. Others would drink large quantities of salt water such was the impression of V.D. Land. The surgeons were always in trouble over such cases. Five prisoners died from the effects of sand eating. Work was suspended for one month on account of fever commonly called Sun-fever which was really a form of dysentery caused from eating bad pork. We had several herds of swine on the Island but the settlers demand too high a price. They were brought from Sydney by Governor King and given to settlers of ten acres or more. The general price of food as supplied by Mitchell was too much for the convicts. The money in use was mostly the Spanish dollar and English guinea. H.M. King George [III] has been pleased to grant all his subjects complete protection in out-of-the-way places, and trusts they will be faithful and loyal. What a mockery to issue such a piece of information to chained convicts. Protection, when we were the greatest enemy. As my orders were to murder all the prisoners under my care should any foreign national bear down upon us. Protection be damned.

Fish were plentiful and of good quality. Some fine large ones were caught by the prisoners. We were very thankful for our supply of game consisting of Birds of Providence, a small and salty-fleshed tribe. Hundreds were killed in a day, at other times they would leave us for weeks. Other small birds were in abundance, but too small and unfit to eat. Some were covered with feathers of a bright colour. Most of them were unknown to us. The last of the female convicts left for Van Diemen's Land in June 1806. They were some good-conduct women employed as servants to free settlers. All the inhabitants left in 1807, they having been granted free farms in that place. Many lost their lives in conflict with the blacks, the murder and the fighting became a general work in everyday life. They were cunning and needed much watching.

The 9th of June we received a visit from a London Missionary ship on her round trip of visiting the Islands. I believe it was with the intention of forming a new settlement in New Holland and Van Diemen's Land. They stayed a month and on leaving visited Batavia. Two prisoners escaped on her, one was known as Ginger Ryan and the other Paddy O'Keefe. We did not know what had become of them till some years afterwards. Orders received from Sydney about this time for the shipment of convicts to Newtown, the newly formed settlement in Van Diemen's Land. There was much excitement among the free settlers and they were informed by the Governor Captain Piper, that all free persons must leave the Island. Such arrivals and changes were so many and one and another much the same that the prisoners became hardened and indifferent to their person or calling. Each and every officer were obliged to continue the work as performed by his last officer. Captain Piper an ever watchful and careful man did his duty well and was liked and respected.

March 1804. Three French ships paid us a visit. One American ship and several from Batavia. The ship *Lady Nelson* bringing further supplies reached us from Sydney. She brought salted pork unfit for eating, some live birds which did not live long. On board were two society women from Sydney, sent out to be shut out from the world at large for a time, till a perjury case blew over in which they were both prominent figures. The kindness shewn by Mrs Sherwin to deserving female convicts, every comfort is given to any who may be fortunate to come under her notice. The last time I saw her she was looking very old and careworn. May her bones rest in peace for she was a good woman. May 1804 is well remembered, a month of corporal punishment and attempted murders, old and hardened prisoners being very troublesome. Ten yards you must cover in a day, the breaking of five loads of stone being a fair days work. The tools supplied were of a very poor kind, and men were constantly breaking them and bringing severe punishments through their supposed carelessness.

Van Diemen's Land

The Place of murder and bloodshed where we had to live work and fight for our own lives. The work of settlers was met with difficulties and opposition from the blacks and the weather. On my first arrival there we suffered greatly from want of provisions, all grains becoming exhausted. We were compelled to hunt kangaroos and other game. Kangaroo flesh was received with His Majesty's stores and sold at sixpence per pound and reaching as high as one shilling and sixpence. Over fifteen thousand pound weight of this flesh was consumed in six months. We had ofttimes to eat seaweed as a vegetable.

*   *   *

Here ends *Recollections of 13 Years Residence in Norfolk Island by Robert Jones, 'Buckey', late Cheif Gaoler at Norfolk Island.* The notebook in which his story is written, was sold at auction in 1935 in a collection of Australiana in the estate of a Dr Harris.

In Van Diemen's Land Jones was allotted almost 200 acres (80 hectares), he and his family and assigned labourers would be 'victualled and clothed for two years at Government expense' and given farming implements and help with building a house. Jones did not leave Norfolk Island until 1809 or 1810 (the actual date is not known), and from this time on his movements are unknown except for the one page of *Recollections*, and the occasional notices in the *Sydney Gazette* to notify 'Robert Jones' of a letter awaiting him at the Post Office. One notice said 'George Abrahams alias Robert Jones' but that is not conclusive proof of which 'Jones' is meant.

'General' Joseph Holt

8

JOSEPH HOLT WAS ANOTHER MAN WHO WROTE OF HIS EXPERIENCES ON NORFOLK ISLAND SOME YEARS AFTER HE LEFT IT. HE WAS A 'POLITICAL prisoner', as Robert Jones says, one of a large number of Irish dissidents sent out to New South Wales after the uprisings in Ireland of 1798. He is easily the most flamboyant character to have written of his stay, and although some of his recollections tally with the facts, others are suspect. He was well known as a rebel leader in Ireland before his transportation, and he rides through his *Memoirs* of those years somewhat larger than life.

Joseph Holt was born in 1756, one of seven children of a small farmer in Ballydaniel, County Wicklow, Ireland. The Holts were a Protestant family who arrived in Ireland during the reign of Queen Elizabeth I; they were given land forfeited by the O'Toole and O'Byrne families and had remained farmers through the years. Holt and his brothers were each apprenticed to a trade, one as a bricklayer, another a carpenter, and Joseph Holt was 'sent to be instructed by John Low, the gardener of a Mr Sweeny of Dublin'. He stayed there for five years, then went to Northern Ireland 'to improve his farming' he says.[1]

He joined the 32nd Regiment of Foot for a matter of twenty-one days, during which time he was made recruiting sergeant and brought in thirty-two recruits, according to his own account, 'but my parents prevailed on me to give up my intention of going into the army, and to please them I got my discharge and remained with them till 1780'. Two years later he married the daughter of a Protestant farmer, and took a small farm, and no doubt his parents hoped he was ready to settle down with Hester, who in time bore him two sons, Joshua and Joseph.[2]

But nothing so mundane as farming was in store for Holt. He began his swashbuckling life by going in chase of the leader of a notorious robber band who had been holding up wealthy local citizens, and captured the wanted man as he ran, naked, from the hut in which he was hiding. With this and similar exploits, he became the political and military leader of a mixed band of rebels. In his *Memoirs* he presents himself as the imperious General of his troops, leading an 'army' of insurgents who had 'no chance but to continue in the way they were going'. Matters in the Irish counties went from bad to worse between Protestant and Catholic, and Holt was warned as he sat at home one evening, that a party of soldiers were coming to get him. He dashed out just in time, taking his sword, two pistols and some money and fled into the mountains, looking back to see his house going up in flames.

This part of his *Memoirs* reads like a boy's adventure serial, one thing after another ending in breathless chases and last-minute escapes, but eventually it reached an end, his troops were 'an undisciplined mob, not a fourth of those with us were obedient to orders when fighting was necessary, but slunk off like dastardly cowards, running before the enemy'. The British soldiers were in full cry after him, and a reward of £300 was offered for his apprehension.

He considered fleeing to America but had no money to pay the fare for himself and his family, and finally he decided to surrender to Lord Powers-court, Commander-in-Chief of the British forces. He was treated with military honours by Lord Powerscourt, he says, though he was put in the watch-house overnight. The *Dublin Courier* carried the notice next day:

> At length the rebel hero of the mountains . . . the celebrated General Holt has surrendered to Lord Powerscourt. He was escorted to town in a coach, by a formidable troop of his Lordship's cavalry . . . Holt seems to be about forty years of age, has a smartness in his aspect which approaches to ferocity, he seemed perfectly at ease and in very good health, wore a scarlet coat faced with blue, and had the aspect of a military man. The terms on which he surrendered are not known but they are supposed to be transportation for life . . .[3]

On 1 January 1799 Holt was taken from the castle tower to a small transport vessel, the *Lively.* In spite of being conveyed there by a coach, he was leg-ironed and had two troopers as guards. Nine other male prisoners were also put on board. The *Lively* sailed around the coast to Cork where the men were transferred to the *Minerva,* bound for Botany Bay. Holt's wife and son Joshua were allowed to accompany him, their fares paid by a well-wisher, Mrs La Touche. Below decks were 132 male prisoners, others were to join them before the *Minerva* set sail in August. On 11 January 1800 the *Minerva* dropped anchor in Sydney Cove, where Captain William Cox came aboard to ask for six men for his farm, 'not to labour but to superintend' according to Holt, whose reply was 'Pray present my humble respects to His Excellency and let him know that I am not a convicted felon. I came here on terms, to expatriate myself . . . I will never be his man, nor yours', although later he was certainly employed by Captain Cox on his farm.

Holt was allowed comparative freedom by Governor King, so long as he refrained from seditious speeches and similar offences, but inevitably he clashed with authority soon after his arrival.[4] Despite his somewhat bombastic claims of total innocence, in his *Memoirs*, there is proof enough in the records of his involvement in Irish uprisings, though he invariably denied the truth of all the evidence given against him in court. His first account of corporal punishment is of Patrick Boyle, a totally fearless Irish rebel. Boyle was only one of many who received a flogging that day.

> Arms extended around a tree, wrists tied together with cord and the body pressed firmly against the tree. Two men were appointed to flog, one left hand the other right. Blood spouted from the first blow. Blood, skin and flesh flew in my face as I stood at least fifteen yards to leeward. After the punishment was over, Boyle walked to the cart waiting to take him to prison again. Others took his place at the tree, receiving one hundred or three hundred each. When this terrible exhibition was over, Mr Smythe and I walked to Parramatta and went to a tavern kept by James Larra, an honest Jew, where we dined on lampreys and hung beef.[5]

On 5 March 1804 the Castle Hill uprising brought things to a head for many of the Irish dissidents, Holt in particular. The uprising was of short duration but bloody. Two of the ringleaders were hanged, many others shot. Holt was firmly plucked from his little farm nearby—where he had been employing himself in distilling potent peach brandy, a strictly forbidden pastime for both free and bond—and brought before Judge Atkins on 19 March. A witness, John McKeown, swore that Holt had said the Governor and Judge Atkins should be put to death because men had died from the flogging they had ordered. King, tried beyond endurance by the troubles that beset him from many quarters, banished one of his troubles to Norfolk Island, and Holt, with others, left Port Jackson on the *Betsey*, in April 1804. In his *Memoirs* he recounts his arrival:

> When I was within twenty yards of shore I heard the villainous bloodhounds on the beach cry out 'Put him out of the boat', on which I was made to leap into the sea. They wanted to put a chest of tea on my back for me to carry on shore but I would not support it by my hand, and when they found this the chest was lifted up and dashed down with its corner against my back between my shoulders, which hurt me very much. I feel the effect of that blow to this day and shall do as long as I live.

The blow to his pride was equally hurtful, and bitterly remembered. On the voyage to the Island, Holt and the other political prisoners had been invited by Captain Eastwick to dine with him and allowed to sleep in cabins on the deck rather than be herded below-deck with the convicts. Captain Eastwick later wrote of his many voyages, and he has this to say of Holt's arrival on Norfolk Island:

The convicts were sent ashore in boats, each of which also carried a certain amount of cargo. This cargo the prisoners were ordered to carry through the surf and then land upon trucks, and wheel to the storehouse. The task was a humiliating one and I felt sorry for the poor prisoners who had suffered so much from the confinement during the voyage, that many of them were totally unfit for work. Among them was General Holt, a fine handsome gentleman both in appearance and demeanour . . . He was very finely dressed on landing, with a new blue coat with a black velvet collar, like a gentleman should be, which he was, every inch of him, and he sat in the sternsheets with dignity. On shore a large truck was waiting with fourteen prisoners to drag it who had just landed previously, and amongst them was Captain the Hon St. Leger and some others who had been men of fortune in Ireland. The jailor standing by [Robert Jones] saw General Holt and called out to ask who he was. 'General Holt' came the reply. 'Damn the General! Let Holt assist unload the boat. Put the biggest bag of sugar on his back for he appears a big man in his own estimation'. This was done, and the General, all in his fine clothes, laden like a common felon was forced to wade through the water . . . It was a sorry sight to see so gallant a gentleman submit himself to these vulgar people in authority . . . For after all he and many others of the prisoners were gentlemen by birth . . . they were persons of refinement . . .[6]

And next morning while taking breakfast with Lieutenant-Governor Foveaux, Captain Eastwick saw a letter brought in and handed over. The astounded look on Foveaux's face as he read, prompted the Captain to ask what was wrong. Holt, it appeared, had sent a petition in which he begged to be put to some less menial and degrading task than that assigned him. Little knowing his man, Eastwick added his plea to Holt's, and in front of his guest Foveaux could only listen and reply courteously.

I was put to hard labour and offered to pay a man for doing my work, but that was not allowed. [Holt] The dirtiest work was appointed for me because I wore good clothes as any man on the island . . . Two hours before daylight every man should get up and tie his bed and carry it out to leave it in the yard until night, let it rain or shine, then we would be marched before the door of Robert Jones the gaoler superintendent, tale-bearer, persecutor, planner of all evil. This Bob Jones, his name was Bobby Buckey in some part of England, and his father and two brothers was concerned in many robberies and this wretch went and prosecuted the father and two brothers and all three died and he was transported under the name of Bob Jones thinking he would not be known. I heard some of the soldiers tell him in my presence, of his transactions and that is the proof I give . . .[7]

Holt continues:

> I was kept at work let who would be idle. I was one of them chosen to
> fence a pig-run on Bobby's farm and at last between fasting and hard
> work I fell down, and I walked home when I recovered a little and I
> came in the house of George Geary the surgeon's assistant and told
> him I wanted to see Mr Wentworth the doctor . . . and when he came
> he felt my pulse and shook his head and in a very afflicted tone said
> 'Poor fellow, you are suffering'. He ordered some medicine for me
> and he went to the Commandant that tyrant Foveaux, and told him he
> believed he was acting beyond his powers and told him if I was killed
> by labour he would make a note of the business. 'Well, exempt him!'.
> So Mr Wentworth desired me to go to my unhappy lodgings and not
> to do anything till he would bid me . . .[8]

It took little longer than a couple of weeks to knock the stuffing out of the
General on terrible Norfolk Island, but it is fortunate that his keen ear picked
up information on Robert Jones that is found nowhere else. There is no Bob
Buckey in the First Fleet but Holt's information could fit George Abrahams
of Wanstead Parish in Essex, who stood in the dock indicted for crimes
which brought the death penalty; a man with no accomplices named or
recorded, and who was transported under three names, two of them aliases
one, Robert Jones. The pieces of the jigsaw picture seem to fit together, but
whether that picture portrays Robert Jones, the gaoler, will never now be
known.

Holt also tells in his *Memoirs* of Foveaux's inhuman treatment of women
convicts, though, as might be expected, he blames Governor King: 'Governor
King's proceedings respecting the women convicts on their arrival was
abominable. They were disposed of by Potter the bellman as so much
livestock. Some for a gallon of rum, others for five pounds, transferred from
one brutal fellow to another without remedy or appeal.' Later he tells of the
early morning rising:

> When the bell rang at five the order was . . . 'Turn out, you damned
> souls'. We then looked for our wet rags and if the slightest grumbling,
> the order was 'To the triangle' where the flogger was ready to give the
> unfortunate wretch twenty-five lashes on his bare back after which he
> had to work as usual. Hard labour, want of sufficient food, endurance
> of wet cold and hunger and if even a breath of complaint the flesh is
> cut from your back and you are worked with double severity. I think
> the usage I have seen men receive in Norfolk Island exceeds in cruelty
> anything that can be credited . . . I saw many fine men die in misery,
> inch by inch, from the oppression endured . . .[9]

Holt, however, escaped even a flick of the lash, but by what superhuman
control of his tongue is beyond imagining. Nowhere in his *Memoirs* does he
refer to Foveaux without detestation:

. . . if I had brought or borrowed a pistol the world should be free of a man killer. I would give him as short warning as he gave the two men he hung without a trial, for why should men be murdered and see his murderer before him and wait for a lingering death and leave a man killer alive? . . . He was called home so I have been told, to give account of the hanging of these two men that he put to death, but it is easy for a criminal to take his trial when there is no prosecutor to prove the facts, and we always have fine Counsel in England to plead for a tyrant if they get plenty of fees, for it is a Counsel's business to hang the innocent and clear the guilty. So Major Foveaux came out under the title of Colonel Foveaux— . . .[10]

Holt's Gethsemane was not to last long. Fourteen weeks after the *Betsey* landed him in his spanking new blue coat with the black velvet collar, Foveaux left the Island, racked with asthma, cursed by the prisoners, but accompanied by Ann Sherwin who remained his lifelong companion. His place was taken by Captain John Piper, and one of Piper's first acts was to free Joseph Holt from the servitude of a convict.[11] He remained as a political prisoner, confined on the Island but free to come and go where and when he pleased. 'A humane and worthy gentleman of honour', said Holt, and trundled off to a hut in the forest where he could grow vegetables in his garden, and go fishing whenever he liked.

I used to fish off the rocks by day . . . and at night I had my bob made with large worms hung on a thread, and used to go eeling; then got my torch and let it burn for some time, because eels, when they are full, play on top of the water . . . I would catch three hundred eels. I have caught eels thirty-two pounds in weight; not silver eels in a pond, and that kept me employed.[12]

Holt presumably made some money by his fishing. He was on good terms with Mitchell the store-keeper and here again he corroborates Robert Jones's comments on the man:

There was a man named James Michel [*sic*], one of the missionaries sent out by Sir Joseph Banks . . . He had thought it a better plan to follow business and he made a very handsome provision . . . he gave me a preference to supply me with money or goods. I drew my own bills . . . Mr Michel supplied me with cash during my time and having nothing to take up my time I betuck myself to angling by day and night. . . . Mr Michel got biscuits and pork, barley and flour and rum at Three Pound a gallon so I had all things needed and I settled with Mr Michel and passed my bill for eighty pounds sterling, thirty-one days after sight and payable to John MacArthur in Port Jackson . . .[13]

Admiral Bligh, R.N., (from a miniature) about the period of his Governorship of New South Wales 1806–8. (Mitchell Library, Sydney)

Sir Thomas Brisbane, Governor of New South Wales 1821–5. It was in his period of office that Norfolk Island was re-opened as a 'great hulk or Penitentiary', so called by Earl Bathurst. (Mitchell Library, Sydney)

Sir Richard Bourke, Governor of New South Wales 1831–7. (Mitchell Library, Sydney)

Sir George Gipps, Governor of New South Wales, 1838–46. (Mitchell Library, Sydney)

Monthly Return of Punishments at Newcastle with the nature of Offence &c. from the 1st to the 30th June 1823.

Ships	Names	Number of Lashes	Nature of Offence
Lord Sidmouth	William Smith	25	Leaving the Cedar Party in disobedience of Orders.
Daphne	Jas. McEntagart	50	Theft.
Hibernia	John Hooper	50	Neglect of Work, and refusing his rations at his Masters.
General Stuart	William Wall	50	Enciting his fellow servants to refuse their rations, & refusing his own at his Masters (Mr. Boughton's) Farm.
John Barry	Peter Rigling	50	} Disobedience of Orders in secreting Governmt. Tools.
Earl St. Vincent	John Becket	33	}
Lord Eldon	Robert Camels	50	} Having in his possession Cedar for which he could not account, & disobedience of Orders in secreting Governt. Tools.
3d. Guilford	David Hennessy	25	Beating and Ill-using a Fellow Prisoner.
Prince Regent	John Brennan	75	Absconding from his Masters service & taking to the Bush.
Malabar	George Maton	75	do. do. do.

To His Excellency, The Governor
&c.   &c.   &c.

J. T. Morisset
Commandant

A page from the Punishment Book at Newcastle prison settlement in 1823, during Major Morisset's period of office as Commandant there. (Archives Office of New South Wales)

Sir Ralph Darling, Governor of New South Wales 1825–31. In 1826 he said, 'My object was to hold out the settlement at Norfolk Island as a place of the extremest punishment short of Death'. (Mitchell Library, Sydney)

Sir William Denison, Lieutenant-Governor of Tasmania (Van Diemen's Land) 1847–55, Governor of New South Wales 1855–61. (La Trobe Collection, State Library of Victoria)

Holt remained on the Island sixteen months altogether, only the first fourteen weeks were spent under duress, the rest of the time in doing whatever he liked. He was, however, still regarded with animosity by Jones and the other overseers who probably went out of their way to mortify him when they had the chance. He was wily, and well accustomed to fend for himself after his years with the rebels in Ireland, and nothing in the general run of events could be done to reduce him to his earlier state on the Island. But at the time the seven strange ships loomed over the horizon, Holt was ordered into the prison along with over sixty other Irish dissidents. He describes it thus after relating how he had told Piper he had seen many ships coming towards the Island 'at a time when the French were in a conkering mood over many parts of the world':

> I went away to my lodging and shortly afterwards Edward Grimbley [Kimberley] came for me, this Grimbley was Chief Constable under Bobby Jones or otherwise Bobby Buckey. I went with him and was put in gaol and sixty-five more along with me, those creatures, I mean Foveaux's bloodhounds, these was weak enough to think that if we Irishmen was out that we would get them all killed because they knew they had so well deserved it, they got the soldiers to come all round the gaol and place scaffolds all round it and if it had been the French they were to put fire to the jail and burn us all in it. This we did not know till next day. We were kept in close locked, the soldiers all on the scaffolds and if we was able to make our escape through the fire the soldiers was to kill us by firing, so the wretches sat up all night in dread and fear, for guilty consciences need no accuser.

He goes on to relate the rest of the story, how it was the next morning, when the ships were found to be British, that he learned of the intended burning of the prison, with the men still inside.

> . . . Off I set to meet the Captain [Piper] and ask him he had any hand in planning such a death for men who had not committed any fault whatsoever. He wondered, and ask me my authority . . . he sent for Jones and Grimbley and the whole mob and then I got out the truth, the Captain declared his innocence and he broke and displaced a great number of those centipedes or toads, so my good Reader, you will see the great danger poor Joseph was in. . . . I said that if Irishmen had committed a fault in their own country they suffered for it and they was not to be murdered as Mick Clane [sic] and Wollihan [sic] was by Foveaux. I went away and never had one moment's peace of mind till I left that Island . . .[14]

Eventually Holt's release from Norfolk Island came, when the *Sydney* arrived to take some of the settlers and a number of convicts to Van Diemen's Land, but his departure was not uneventful . . .

G

> . . . I had orders to go in the first ship, this ship was commanded
> by Captain Forrest and his mate Mr Robison and the sailors
> was all from Bengal . . . I came to the beach in the morning and
> got a man to carry down my trunk and bed and I asked John
> Drummond the beach-master I wanted to put my goods in the boat.
> No he would not let me—he kept me boat after boat till near night. I
> was obliged to go to Captain Piper before he would let my things in
> the boat. I got my pork-cask, also bread and flour and all in the boat
> and then I prayed to God that I might have the pleasure of returning
> the villainy Drummond and Jones, the two worst, afflicted on me. I
> got my goods on board just as the storm began to rise and I gave the
> boatmen a glass on board when they put my things on the deck and
> sent them down to the steerage when I saw Drummond coming
> alongside for Mary Finders, the wife of William Finders; she was
> carried in a sack of cabbage aboard and stowed away. Drummond
> searched but to no purpose . . . I went over to where he was standing,
> 'Well Drummond you are not on the beach now'. 'No nor you
> neither'. I swore a big oath. I would rid the world of one tyrant. I
> catched hold of him and only for Mr Robison I would have thrown
> him overboard . . . He ran down in the boat and I saw no more of him
> for three years and then I got a little satisfaction of the wretch and of
> Bobby Buckey . . .[15]

Holt doesn't relate the 'satisfaction' he got, which leaves the underlying
reason for the enmity between himself and Jones unsolved but tantalising.

For the next few years Holt stayed out of trouble. He was given a free
pardon in June 1809, confirmed in 1810, but did not return to Ireland for a
year or so. In 1812 the *Isabella* (1) left Port Jackson, bound for England,
after her maiden voyage out, and Holt with his family were on board. On the
7th or 8th of February 1813, the *Isabella* was wrecked off the Falkland
Islands, and it was many months before the marooned passengers were taken
onward to England and home. Holt finally reached Dublin in April 1814.
Adventure, it seemed, was always part of Holt's life.

In Dublin, Holt began trading as a publican, lost a considerable amount of
money and gave that profession away. He then took up some land outside
Dublin, built some houses and lived on the rents he got from them, and to
the end of his life, repented his folly in leaving New South Wales. He died in
May 1826.

John Piper 9

JOHN PIPER WAS NO STRANGER TO NORFOLK ISLAND AT THE TIME HE WAS
MADE COMMANDANT IN 1804. HE HAD SERVED THERE FOR TWO YEARS,
from 1793 to 1795, during King's term of office as Lieutenant-Governor
and the stormy period of the abortive mutiny; and he was well aware of the
drawbacks, as well as the privileges of living on the isolated outpost.

Piper was born on 20 April 1773 at Maybole, Ayrshire, Scotland, the elder
son of Hugh Piper, a doctor. He began his army career in 1791, through the
influence of his uncle, Captain John Piper, who obtained him a commission
as ensign in the newly formed New South Wales Corps.[1] In February 1792 he
sailed in the *Pitt* for New South Wales, a vessel which had on board, as well
as the new Commander of the Corps, Major Francis Grose; large consign-
ments of goods ordered by the Corps, to be sold by them at profitable prices
to the settlers and others in the colony. This was to be a lucrative trade for
the officers of the Corps for some years to come, and was to lead to a
disastrous flare-up in the not-too-distant future.

Ensign Piper was sent on duty to Norfolk Island in 1793, apparently at his
own request. Rumour had it that an indiscreet love affair had made his
departure from Sydney necessary. A letter, written to him on the Island in
late December 1793 from a good friend of his, Captain Mackẽllar, has one or
two cryptic remarks:

> . . . I send you now fifty pounds [of sugar] . . . a piece of hair riband
> and a pair of shoes which I think I owe you; I fear they are too small . . .
> I have sent for forty pounds worth of goods for you and myself to
> Bengal by Raven as by the enclosed list; I hope you will be satisfied
> with the manner in which this money is laid out—so much for
> business—. . . You are to be relieved by the first ship, I need not say
> that I expect you here because the very idea of you staying in Norfolk
> Island would be absurd as was your wishing to go before when in your
> power to stay—but I need not refresh your memory of what I suppose
> you have seen the absurdity of long enough . . .

Here a paragraph of the letter is missing, neatly removed by an unknown hand. The letter continues:

> I am going to tell you something that will surprise you. I tell it
> because I think it will come as well from myself as from any other
> person — In the first place because I would not conceal anything from
> you that concerns . . .²

The rest of the surprising news is missing. There was however, a daughter, Sarah, whom Piper acknowledged and whose wedding, in April 1814 in Sydney to John Thrupp, a young English settler, was the most splendid affair of the year.³

In 1804 Piper returned to Norfolk Island as Acting-Commandant. Foveaux left the Island in September that year, and in March 1805 relinquished his Lieutenant-Governorship; Piper was then made Commandant with a raise in pay of five shillings a day.⁴

The inhabitants of Norfolk Island greeted the change with relief. The new Commandant was a man of equable temperament and a sense of justice towards the convicts, as was shown by his immediate increase of the daily allowance of flour and meat for them, and provision of a few of the necessaries of life for the women. At the same time, there was a considerable amount of confusion among the settlers as to the conditions for their removal from Norfolk Island to Van Diemen's Land or, in some instances, to the main colony. Foveaux had met with this uncertainty earlier — it was to plague Piper as well.

Apart from this, and the multitude of instructions sent him by Governor King regarding supplies to be sent to and despatched from the Island, the most exciting thing to happen in Piper's early years as Commandant was the arrival of the nine ships of unknown identity mentioned in Holt's *Memoirs.* Piper's despatch to Governor King explains it in detail:

> . . . On the evening of the 7th November the Island was very much
> alarmed by the appearance of Nine Sail of large ships to the South-
> West, and from the size, number, and regular manner in which they
> neared the land, we conjectured they were an enemy. I therefore
> judged it prudent that I might be the more able to make every
> resistance, to secure the disaffected Irishmen by confining them in
> the Gaol and the Gaol-yard, and posting the whole of the Constables
> over them as a guard . . . I made every preparation during the night
> and at Daylight next morning after receiving information that the Fleet
> were standing round for Cascade Bay, I ordered a Sergeant and
> Twenty men to join the Party on duty there; at the same time sent
> over one of the great Guns and immediately followed myself. At
> Seven O'Clock the Fleet were standing into the Bay; they fired a Gun
> to leeward and made a Signal for a Boat (there not being any at
> Cascade). They stood off and on for five hours before they attempted

to hoist one out, which induced us to believe that their hoisting
English Colours was used only as a decoy . . . we were not able to
form an Idea what they were. From these circumstances I judged it
necessary to draw all the Force to . . . where a landing was to be
apprehended. I . . . directed the whole of the Detachment to join the
party already at Cascade, excepting one officer and sixteen men
(including the Guard) left for the protection of the Stores and the
Town of Sydney . . . After remaining five Hours in suspense . . . a
Boat was hoisted out and Lieut. Little, the Officer who came on
shore, informed us 'they were the China Fleet under Convoy of
L'Atheniene Sixty-Four [guns], Commanded by Captain Fayerman:
. . . that notwithstanding they were much in want of refreshment,
Captn. Fayerman was determined to proceed on his Passage that
Evening . . .⁵

The Convoy was merely approaching the Island, it turned out, to discover
whether the *Taunton Castle*, another of the convoy, 'which had parted
company from them six weeks before, had made the Island'. She had not, but
three days afterwards, *Taunton Castle* touched at the Island and stayed for
two days before proceeding on her voyage.

Piper's administration seems to have been attended with good fortune—
the harvest in his first year was bountiful, especially that of the settlers,
whose wheat crops were favourable; Government crops of maize, though,
were smitten with blight two years running. One most interesting item in
Piper's letter to King, of 30 April 1805, reads:

The Cow-pox has been propagated with the greatest success without a
single instance of any bad effect. Lieutenant Davis's children, having
been inoculated at Sydney, arrived with it here when the Matter was
at its highest perfection, from which alone it has been communicated
pretty generally all over the Island, the Vaccine matter sent by the
Principal Surgeon having as usual failed.⁶

There is another item, of a totally different nature: 'On the 5th Dec'r Mr
Zach. Clark, Deputy Commissary, departed this Life after a short illness,
which it is supposed was brought on by excessive drinking'.⁷

Zachariah Clark, Deputy Commissary, arrived in the First Fleet as storekeeper and had his young daughter Ann with him. It was no doubt the easy
access Clark had to the rum stores, that began his intemperance, and his
drinking habit led to the graver one of incest. In King's letter of 9 May 1803,
he writes:

. . . As the crime Deputy-Commissary Clark is accused of was
committed at Norfolk Island I have sent him back there to be tried on
the charge of incest with his own daughter. I am sorry I can say
nothing in Mr Clark's favour.⁸

Thomas Hibbins, Judge-Advocate of Norfolk Island, heard the case. Ann Clark was the principal witness. Clark was given a sentence of one year in gaol. Hibbins, an old Etonian and uxorious by nature, wished to marry Ann when the child was born, and this he did. At the time of the trial Clark was the Commissary of the Island, but a Deputy-Commissary was appointed to take over from him, and in little over two years after the case was heard, Clark died. He lies in an unknown grave on the Island.

King had already given Piper instructions that the Civil Establishment was to be reduced. Seven of the senior Civil Establishment officers were discharged to return to Sydney or, as required, to go to Port Dalrymple, and seven were retained. They were Commandant, Deputy Judge-Advocate, Surgeon, Clergyman, Storekeeper, Superintendant, Beach Master and Pilot. So Joseph Holt's 'centipedes and toads' were still there to aggravate him for the short time he was to remain on the Island, as he relates in his *Memoirs*.

Piper had problems other than those of which settlers wished to stay on Norfolk Island and which wanted to leave, or the continually changing plans of Government and King's wish for things to remain as they were—one of his problems was the attraction he had for the girls of the Island. In a letter to a friend in Sydney he wrote '. . . the girls on the Island are too much for me, I need some help . . .', a fairly predictable situation for the handsome Commandant thirty-one years old.

He was a ladies' man, and had many friends among the wives of his seniors in the New South Wales Corps. He sent gifts of shells, seeds, cuttings, boxes of oranges, and small travelling chests made from the rare woods that grew on Norfolk Island, to his Colonel's wife, Mrs Paterson, to Mrs King, Mrs Macarthur, Mrs Marsden (wife of the colony's pastor), and no doubt to other married ladies, for he was a popular man and a welcome guest in Sydney's social circle. On the Island, help came in the person of Mary Ann Shears, fifteen-year-old daughter of James and Mary Shears, emancipated convicts who had become settlers on Norfolk. James Shears (or Shiers) was a First Fleeter who had been given Life at the Old Bailey in 1784 for 'feloniously assaulting Charles Wright on the King's Highway'. His sentence was Death, at which his prosecutor asked that he be recommended to mercy. Mary Shears, who was Mary Smith before she had married James Shears in the first rush of weddings after Governor Phillip's Proclamation of February 1788, was a mantua-maker. Aged 25, she had been convicted of 'feloniously stealing 1 pair of leather boots valued at twenty-one shillings, and sentenced to Death, remitted to seven years' transportation.[10]

James Shears had felt the sting of the lash in his early years in Sydney when he, with another convict who had been brought before Judge-Advocate Collins in 1791, accused of stealing a quantity of wheat from the Granary, pleaded guilty 'because he was hungry'. He took the blame for the theft and was sentenced to receive 300 lashes. The year of his emancipation is not clear, though it is no doubt in the records somewhere, but he and his family were certainly living as settlers on Norfolk Island when Piper arrived as Acting-Commandant.[11]

Piper and Mary Ann lived happily in Government House on Norfolk Island, where two sons were born to them, Hugh and John, during his term of office. During these years, Governor King made several attempts to change the British Government edict that Norfolk Island be evacuated of settlers and convicts; in one letter to Foveaux, before the latter finally left the Island, King wrote that Norfolk Island could be made into a calling place for 'the South Sea whalers whose valuable fisheries are carried on . . . in the immediate neighbourhood, all which I doubt not entered into Lord Hobart's contemplation in directing only a part of the establishment and settlers . . . to be removed'.[12]

It was a fluctuating situation, decisions changing with each change of Secretary for the Colonies, with Lord Hobart, on the one hand, ready to listen to King's respectful appeals that settlers be allowed to remain on Norfolk Island and Lord Camden, on the other, quite firm in his decision that all should be removed. What the underlying argument for evacuation was is not now clear. 'Expence' is the most quoted one, with failure of crops close behind. Yet the supply of salted pork to the colony increased to such an extent that ships taking on cargo at Norfolk Island were sometimes not able to carry all the casks away, and in many years the crops flourished to excess.

In spite of orders to remove settlers and convicts to Van Diemen's Land, prisoners were still being sent to Norfolk Island, many of them political prisoners of whom King had plenty, particularly Irish dissidents and firebrands. New South Wales had become the place of exile for 'difficult' prisoners, the educated misfits too vocal to be allowed to spread dissension among the workers at home. Fifteen thousand miles (24 000 kilometres) was a comfortable distance to put between such people and English society.

One such person was sent to New South Wales for Life in 1803, for an indiscretion which could not be overlooked in the rigid class-consciousness of England at that time. He, too, became a firebrand after his arrival, and was eventually classed as a dangerous criminal by Governor King. His fire was effectively quenched on Norfolk Island, and it was John Piper who quenched it. His story, written in recent years from papers discovered by chance, gives a stereoscopic view of life on the Island in Piper's time,[13] though only a small section of the book concerns that place.[14] He arrived on Norfolk Island at a time when Governor King was beset by troubles with officers of the New South Wales Corps. King was to be replaced by Bligh, although more than a year elapsed from March 1805 when Sir Joseph Banks recommended '. . . I know of no one but Captain Bligh who will suit, but whether it will meet his views is another question', to the time of Bligh's arrival in August 1806.

Piper was well out of the faction-ridden situation at Port Jackson in those years, and it was probably well for his future prospects that this was so. His friend John Macarthur wrote frequently to him, giving him the latest news:

'The Corps is galloping into a state of warfare with the Governor'—a warfare largely stirred up by himself.[15] No doubt Piper would have been entangled also, had he not been so far removed. As it was, his position as Commandant of Norfolk Island suited him well, his administration was not harsh, his family life was happy, and his job of slowly 'winding-down' the settlement was done satisfactorily. Only one failure seems to have been recorded in his dealings with the inhabitants, both convicts and settlers, and that, though not Piper's fault, was with the young firebrand, John Grant.

John Grant 10

JOHN GRANT WAS BORN IN LANGLEY, BUCKINGHAMSHIRE IN 1776.[1] HIS
FATHER'S PROFESSION IS NOT KNOWN, BUT AS THE BOY WAS SENT TO
Christ's Hospital for his education after his father's death, the latter
was most likely a clergyman. Christ's Hospital was founded as a school for
the sons of the clergy.

Grant's mother was French, and this could account for his very volatile
nature which was to keep him in and out of hot water for many years. He was
an ambitious and handsome young man but his circumstances were such
that he had little opportunity to reach the heights he felt he was entitled to
grace. Had it been a fitting occupation, he could have been an outstanding
actor, and he actually did write a play—but this was later, on Norfolk Island.

From school, he was indentured to his uncle, Edward Grant, 'Citizen and
Clockmaker of London, to learn his Art and with him to serve from the Day
of the date thereof until the Full End and Term of Seven Years . . .'[2] His
indenture fee was paid by the governors of Christ's Hospital.

He left his clock-maker uncle before his apprenticeship was out, and
worked for some years in the office of a merchant, David Duval, as clerk.
Such a slow road to advancement was as unsatisfactory to him as clock-
making was. He set himself up in business and almost predictably, failed
dismally, going deeply into debt over the matter. The world, if it was his
oyster, remained tightly closed for him, and this was something he neither
could nor would accept.

His conviction in court, and the sentence of transportation to New South
Wales were the result of an ill-advised love-affair. This handsome and attractive
young man fell in love with the daughter of a peer of the realm; a girl who
was, moreover, already betrothed to an eminently eligible young man, at that
time abroad on duty with his Regiment.

The girl, a Miss Ward, daughter of Lord Dudley and Ward, was engaged to
be married to Colonel-Major St. Paul, whose father lived in Sloane Street, a
highly fashionable part of London. Next door to the St. Paul's house, lived

Sir William Bunbury and Grant's mother, who was either housekeeper or mistress to Sir William. It was most likely in her sitting room that the young couple met, for Grant had a pretty younger sister, Matilda, and the two girls could well have been acquainted.

With the passionate ardour that characterised everything he did, Grant wooed the girl and even entertained hopes of eventual marriage, despite the absent Colonel-Major, and his own lack of money; and despite the fact that he had seduced the little serving-maid of his mother, and that she had borne him a daughter. This fact he kept to himself.

The young couple spent many hours together in the leafy gardens behind the tall houses of Sloane Street. It was a dream-time, and Grant was bound to wake sooner or later.

The awakening came when he—determined to pursue the matter to the point where he could formally offer his hand as well as his heart—endeavoured to obtain the necessary formal introduction to the girl's family. This could only be done through the family solicitor, Spencer George Townsend, who made enquiries into the young man's background, speedily dismissed the request, and considered the matter closed.

Grant, who could probably have accepted an opportunity to discuss the situation, but not a peremptory dismissal, refused to give up. He visited Townsend's office but the door was barred. He wrote letters that were not answered. Eventually he followed Townsend to his home in St. James, demanding that the solicitor give him satisfaction. He held out two pistols, Townsend refused to accept one; duelling was in any case against the law, and he had already refused Grant's written request 'for satisfaction'. At the hearing in court, after Grant's arrest, Townsend said: 'I had my stick in my hand and was going to hit his wrist, but he dropped his hands to his side. I then cried out 'Help, Help', upon which Grant lifted his right hand, cocked his pistol and I turned my back on him'.[3] It was then Grant fired at the fleeing solicitor, hit him in the buttocks with the swan-shot loaded in his pistol, and waited to be arrested by the Bow-street runner who thundered up at the sound of the shot and the cry of 'Help!'

The trial in May 1803 brought London society crowds to the Old Bailey. This trial was far more sensational than the usual petty thievery or pickpocket case, involving as it did the aristocracy, and a nobody who had the effrontery to pretend he was as good as they were. 'If I had wished to have formed a union with a monarch's daughter and she were agreeable and willing, no-one has the right to oppose it!' declared Grant from the dock after the trial was over. 'I wonder how this young man can aspire to such a connection', said the shocked Judge.[4]

The verdict was Death by hanging, and Grant was sent to Newgate prison to await his end. His family visited him in the rat-ridden and overcrowded gaol but Miss Ward, no doubt banished to the country, neither came nor wrote. Grant's young sister Matilda sent a petition to the Royal Princesses Augusta-Sophia, Elizabeth Mary, Sophia and Amelia, which prompted them to plead with their royal papa George III to spare the young man's life.[5]

Such solicitude was balm to John Grant's wounded pride. Ignominy could be borne, as long as that ignominy was noticed. His reprieve came just twelve hours before the time fixed for his execution; but before long he was to wish himself dead, for he was sent from Newgate to the hulks of Woolwich, to wait there until the time for his embarkation.

The hulks, rotting vessels no longer sea-worthy, were moored to the banks of the Thames, and from them the convicts were sent to labour on various public projects each day. These were the same hulks that had housed the First Fleet convicts: vermin-ridden, eternally damp, stinking, outworn vessels that could be smelt long before they were seen. Life in the hulks had broken many a man and was to break many more. Within a short time Grant was on the point of death; he had never known or imagined such horror, such vile conditions or such filth. Some years later, a visiting priest gave evidence before a Select Committee in the House of Commons, regarding conditions on the Hulks;[6] and in the *Times* was a letter from a correspondent which stated 'The cruelty exercised is so excessive, the medical treatment so brutal, and the manner in which the prisoners are treated when alive as well as dead, is such to be utterly disgraceful to a civilised and Christian country'.[7]

These months of horror, during which Grant came close to death, twisted his mind and his spirit. From that time on he was slightly unbalanced when confronted by what he considered a misuse of power, corporal punishment, or unfair treatment of any kind—treatment he himself considered unfair— and it was this which led to his arrival on Norfolk Island, after a period of comparative freedom in New South Wales.

From the hulks, he was shipped to New South Wales on the *Coromandel*, and was lucky in that a friend of his was also going, not as a convict but to work as Assistant Surgeon in the colony. Grant was allowed to share his friend's cabin; not an unusual indulgence for often 'educated convicts' with a skill were useful to the ship's Master, or some other job requiring book-learning. He was fortunate, and at times actually forgot he was a convict on his way to a penal colony.

He wrote to his mother to thank her for the box of 'valuables' she had sent on board for him, his satin waistcoat and nankeen trousers, expensive shirts and his fine white hat, as well as the drab greatcoat he 'didn't much care about', and the chocolates he did. He also wrote of something that weighed heavily on his mind: 'The distress I feel is silent but excessive. Your promise respecting my infant is a great comfort but I wish it and its mother could have come with me. Promise too, that you will not be unkind to Betty, because she has much contributed to my distress'd state of mind'.[8]

At San Salvador, where the *Coromandel* stayed for a while taking on fresh supplies, he asked his friend to purchase a cask of fiery spirits called 'Aqua-Dante', while he was ashore. He gave three shillings and sixpence a gallon for it, 'so you must judge the profit will be handsome', he wrote, 'the article in New South Wales sells from twelve to fifteen shillings a bottle. Sometimes it is so scarce and sales so restricted as to amount to prohibition'? He was already building himself into a successful businessman in the new colony. The pinch of prison was yet to come, and the Aqua-Dante was to speed the process.

The *Coromandel* arrived at Port Jackson on 7 May 1804. It was some days before Grant was allowed to leave the ship with his letters of introduction to important personages such as Governor King, Major Johnston and Judge Atkins. He began to realise, as he watched the passengers disembark, among them his young surgeon friend, that he was not, as he had seemed to think, a free person but a convict sentenced to life imprisonment in New South Wales, and as he watched the human cargo from below-decks ordered into the boats to be taken ashore, he must have felt bitter resentment against the unfair blows of Fate that had brought him to his present situation.

Within a day or two he was sent as an assigned servant or labourer to Mr Williamson's farm at Parramatta. He found the Williamsons to be good, hard-working people with no pretensions, and kind hearts. He took his box of valuables with him, reminders of his former life, and some of his things excited admiration and respect, especially the silver cream-jug—a strange thing to have brought from Home, unless, perhaps, it was a special heritage from the past. Such treasures were seldom seen in emigrant farmers' houses like the Williamsons' and Grant could have congratulated himself at having been sent to such a kind and understanding couple. He played his violin to them when invited to do so in the evenings, and in spite of his ignorance of farm-labouring, he might in time have become reconciled to his state had it not been for Governor King and his refusal to co-operate with Grant in his scheme to make money.

He had written to King, asking for his cask of spirits to be returned to him— it had been put in bond on the arrival of the *Coromandel* at Port Jackson. King, already beset with problems concerning the import of rum by the New South Wales Corps officers, and their near-monopoly of the market, had ordered all spirits brought into the colony to be put in bond, and refused permission to Grant to extract his one cask. All spirits were to be sold at the agreed price of nine shillings a gallon, and would be sold from bond.

Beside himself with rage, Grant wrote letter after letter to the Governor, letters which were not answered. Grant had found himself a hobby-horse and was to ride it to his near-destruction. At this time he made the acquaintance of Sir Henry Brown Hayes—'This attractive, wicked creature, gay, debonair and rich, with remarkable whiskers', as he was described by a contemporary.[10] Sir Henry, an Irishman and an aristocrat, had been transported for abducting a young woman and trying to insist she marry him, the wedding to be conducted in his own house—with a friend acting as a bogus priest. The girl, a Quaker, had spirit enough to refuse him and, at the moment of the forcing of the wedding ring on her finger, began to scream and fight in such a manner that Sir Henry and his bogus priest were only too relieved to bundle her back into her carriage and set her free.[11] Sir Henry was brought to court, charged, convicted and transported. King, who already had as many Irish firebrands in the colony as he could deal with, had him watched closely, and more than once Hayes was brought before a magistrate.

John Grant was just the sort of man Hayes could use. He was articulate, had strong convictions of the rights of all men and their right to voice an opinion. Governor King, basically a fair man with a strong feeling of responsibility for the people he governed, allowed John Grant his freedom within the colony, provided he behaved himself and did nothing counter to the laws of the land.

Grant, like a wilful child who has got his own way by persistence, did not stop there. Under Sir Henry's influence he wrote imflammatory letters to King and others on matters of Government and the treatment of convicts in particular. He finally went too far when he wrote:

> Now Sir! I ask you, (as an Independent Englishman) viewing with
> astonishment the miserable state to which thousands of unfortunate
> men are reduced in this Colony—by what right do you—make Slaves
> of Britons in this distant quarter of the globe.[12]

He was brought before Judge Atkins who had, up till then, been a good friend to him. Atkins read the letter, decided it was nothing less than seditious libel, and sentenced Grant to five years at hard labour for the Crown, 'in any part of His Majesty's territories His Excellency may choose to send you'.[13]

Grant had shot his bolt. This time he was to lose his newly-acquired freedom, his chance to wear the fine clothes in his box, his friends, and almost his life and his sanity. He was sentenced to serve his five years in the coal mines at Newcastle, but this was later changed to Norfolk Island because of its isolation. He was to be sent on the *Lady Nelson*, and during the time the ship was loading stores, was thrown into a cell in which a man, more dead than alive, lay gibbering and half-insane on the floor, his back raw and bleeding from a flogging of 200 lashes.

For the first time in close contact with this terrible punishment, Grant was shocked and revolted but gave what comfort he could, bathed the man's near-fleshless back, and hourly expected him to die. Consumed with pity he set about writing yet another letter to the Governor, which the fellow-prisoner signed with his mark:

> To His Excellency Governor King . . .
> The Petition of John Montague now in Sydney Gaol, Where he has
> just suffered a punishment of 200 lashes, sheweth that yr. prisoner in
> April 1795 was sentenced to 7 years transportation in Peterborough
> in Northamptonshire because certain clothes in his care while he was
> steward in the vessel *Marie* were not found on its arrival at the Port
> of London . . . when his exile legally expired he made many fruitless

applications when in Norfolk Island, to obtain the necessary certificate of his freedom. No certificate having been given him . . . yr. petitioner made an attempt to get away . . . Petitioner implores your interference that his heavy irons be taken off and he be suffered to earn his livelihood in an honest manner.

His

John   X   Montague

Mark[14]

For six days the two men were confined in the cell together, before Grant was taken to embark on the *Lady Nelson*. He had no chance to send the petition himself, but gave it to one of Sir Henry's friends who visited him on the ship before it sailed. Whether the petition was ever received by King is doubtful.

It was this response to injustice, or what he considered injustice, which was the root cause of all John Grant's troubles in the colony, as it was also to be, on Norfolk Island. Had he been better advised, and of a more stable temperament, he might have made a name for himself as a crusader for the oppressed; but as it was, his manner of judging every situation by his own standards of justice, was calculated to rouse the anger of the authorities, anger which invariably rebounded on himself.

The *Lady Nelson* had an adverse voyage to Norfolk Island, taking nearly a month to sail there from Port Jackson, and during that time Grant enlisted the sympathy of Lieutenant Symonds, the *Lady Nelson*'s Captain who allowed him to come on deck, write his journal, play his violin, and read the Ode he wrote on the occasion of the King's Birthday.

On Norfolk Island, he was assigned to John Foley, a marine settler who had taken up land as a free man in 1791. He had married an emancipist's daughter, and had two sons aged 13 and 10. Grant wrote of Foley as 'an old man', but he was probably in his forties at that time.

The small house in Cascade valley had four rooms, a parlour, kitchen, and two bedrooms, one of which Grant shared with the boys. Foley had built his own house and furniture from Norfolk pine and the Island's rare timber, 'I have only to walk two hundred yards through the most romantic scenery . . . to reach the shore', wrote Grant.

On his 20 acres (8 hectares) Foley grew maize, vegetables, fruit, and also kept pigs. His pleasant young wife was a good housekeeper, and Foley had saved money during his years on the Island, selling swine-flesh and maize to the Stores. The boys had attended Thomas McQueen's school before it closed, but were without teaching since then, and Grant took over some of the teaching himself.

He had the regular work of an assigned labourer, at the farm. Each day he rose before sunrise, worked with the hoe as other convicts did, and had a certain amount of ground to hoe before sunset. Constables, or a watching overseer, might come upon him without warning, and woe betide him if his work was unfinished, or if he stopped his labours. He settled in well, aware by this time that he was not a special case, aware too, that he had been more leniently treated than some. His back had not been scored by the devilish lash, he was not put in chains, though he wore the same kind of clothes as other convicts, rough canvas 'frock' and trousers. Once a week he was given a clean shirt and every second week a pair of socks. Mrs Foley gave him small luxuries, a piece of soap to wash himself with, ink to write his journal, he shared their home with them, and all in all was treated as one of the family. He wrote constantly to his mother and in one letter tells her of the Island:

> Dearest Mother,
> . . . The exquisite beauty of the interior amply repays the curiosity of
> those who visit it . . . The Norfolk Pine is of such exquisite beauty
> that in vain do I seek words to describe it . . . there are the blood tree
> and the blood vine, yellow wood and black wood all extremely
> precious for all forms of handiwork . . . You may be surprised at my
> zeal for the convicts, the scum of society they are called. Yet let me
> tell you there is more talent among many who have taken up
> residence, though many are lazy, spiritless and incapable of
> supporting themselves . . . We have no venomous animals here except
> the Military . . .[15]

But even in this remote prison settlement Grant could not refrain from doing battle with the authorities, especially Governor King for whom he had an intense dislike, almost hatred, since the Governor's refusal to allow him to sell his cask of spirits. He found that Foley was owed money by King (or, at least, Foley alleged this), for work done during King's time as Lieutenant-Governor on the Island when he had been employed in building King's house and training the two men under him, with payment of two shillings and sixpence a day.

Governor Phillip had paid the Government costs long before, but King, who had agreed to pay for extra work, had neglected to do so, according to Foley. Grant, true to form, grasped a cause with alacrity. Wiser, though not by much, he drafted a letter for Foley to send, with 'amounts owing'.

But instead of accompanying the letter with one from himself, protesting at the long delay in discharging a debt, John Grant wrote pamphlets and letters to the English press, telling of conditions in the prison settlements. He sent them to his sister, and told her to give them to Mr Pearce, the family banker so that they could be published. None of them reached the eyes of the public, instead, they were laid away by the prudent Mr Pearce, and conveniently forgotten.

Before long, Fate played a cruel trick on Grant. Within a little over a year, Sir Henry Browne Hayes and his boon companion Margarot arrived on Norfolk Island. They had been sentenced to imprisonment in Van Diemen's Land by King, who, his patience exhausted, had had them hustled from the colony in a matter of hours on to the only vessel in the harbour then ready to sail, the yacht *Venus*, a private vessel. Whether it already had passengers on board for Norfolk Island, or perhaps for China or India, is not known, but it certainly hied for the Island before carrying the two prisoners to Van Diemen's Land.

When the *Venus* arrived at Norfolk Island, John Grant heard of the two miscreants on board, and he asked the Commandant, John Piper, for leave to go and welcome his friends. By some extraordinary leniency Piper allowed this, and soon Grant was once again under the spell of Sir Henry. Piper, when he realised that the men were prisoners and not visitors, immediately recalled Grant, and had the two men taken to a small hut on the far side of the Island, to be close confined. But the mischief was done; Grant, who had regained some modicum of common-sense and balance, was caught firmly in the net of Sir Henry's charm and rebelliousness.

Foley was told to keep a close watch on his assigned labourer and prevent him from visiting Hayes and Margarot; but he was no match for the younger and sharper-witted Grant. Night after night Grant crossed the Island, through the forest, and night by night the three sat talking and hatching plots, while the guard set by Piper snoozed, or drank rum provided by Sir Henry's money, outside the hut. Passions flamed as Grant related stories of Foveaux's cruelties, and of Piper's time though he had met no victims of Piper's wrath. All prisons were cruel, for Grant, all vicious; he worked himself into a fever of indignation while the guards slept, or ignored them.

Hayes planned an escape for himself and Margarot, enlisted the help of two willing convicts, Paddy Boyle and John Montague — the same man Grant had seen writhing and half dead on the cell floor at Port Jackson. Both men had been re-transported to Norfolk Island for insurrection or sedition or some other crime; both were classed as dangerous, both were ready for yet another bid for freedom.

Grant implored Hayes to take him with them, eager to share in the escape. Inevitably, the plot was discovered, Boyles and Montague were seized and taken to gaol, to await the next lashing. Hayes and Margarot were confined to one room to await the vessel due to arrive hourly, on which they were to be transported to Van Diemen's Land; and Grant was ordered back to Foley's farm, strangely, with no extra punishment except that he be closely watched.

Again he evaded the men detailed to watch him. Again he slipped out at night, crossed the Island to the hut where Hayes was confined, dreading that his friend would be gone before he could bid him farewell. For a last time, he visited the two men. They were to leave in the morning, the ship was already waiting only on the tide, before it sailed. This time he was careless, or too full of woe to notice where he walked, and out of the shelter of the forest he was easily spotted by the constable detailed to watch for him. He was seized, but Grant beat him off with his stick, and agile and well aware of his danger, ran off and hid. Not until the next day did he return to the farm. Then, as guilelessly as if nothing was wrong, he walked with Foley to the Kingston settlement, confident that no one would accost him when in the company of his employer and, as it seemed, on a dutiful mission.

*A likeness of Captain Alexander Maconochie, R.N., from a
bust by Charles Essex, 1849.* (Mitchell Library, Sydney)

*Major Joseph Anderson, Commandant of Norfolk Island
1834–8.* (Permission of the Queen's Own Regiment, West
Kent Regiment Museum, Maidstone, England)

Major-General Lachlan Macquarie, Governor of New South Wales, 1810–21, from a watercolour by Richard Read. (Mitchell Library, Sydney)

John Price, Civil Commandant of Norfolk Island 1846–53 (January). (From a photograph owned by the Royal Society of Tasmania)

He was wrong. Two constables came up, said they had been looking for him, and took him into custody. Again he broke free, and this time, ran to the house of Judge Hibbins, who lived in the township with his young wife, Ann Clark. Ann Clark was big with child. Hibbins was not prepared to assist Grant evade the Law, though his wife begged him to hide or protect the younger man.

Grant was taken away, thrown into a cell and left for two or three days. The kind Foley visited him, brought him a blanket, food and water, and no doubt tried to comfort him. The blacksmith came to the cell and fastened irons to Grant's legs, although the cell was so small that there was scarcely room to lie down in it, let alone escape from it.

At his trial, conducted by Piper, Grant stubbornly refused to answer the questions put to him. Confronted by Piper, a man from a similar background to his own, and only a year or so older than himself, it was probably pride that kept him silent. The informer, a man named Linch, spoke softly to the Commandant, telling of the talk that had gone on in the forest hut, and retailing all that Grant had said, including his opinion of Foveaux. Piper listened, aware that Grant's opinions were shared by many others, but as Commandant such talk was sedition, and not to be countenanced. 'What do you answer to this?' he asked, 'What have you to say?' and time after time repeated his question. Grant stood silent, refused the chance to speak in his own defence, aware that by not doing so he was inviting punishment. Finally Piper, in a sudden rage at the unspoken insolence of this well-bred young man before him, shouted 'You have brought this on yourself, John Grant! You shall receive fitting and proper punishment. I'll prove to you that I can have you whipped!' and he ordered 25 lashes.[16]

Grant returned to his cell, his footsteps dragging against the chains, his heart sick, and no doubt a nagging fear of the pain to come. The triangle was erected in the gaol yard, the blacksmith came to strike off the irons on his legs, and Grant, after a wait of two or three hours, was brought out into the bright sunshine. A crowd had gathered to see this unusual prisoner take his punishment and among them Grant noticed a former acquaintance, young Captain Houston, ashore from the waiting transport in the bay. He stopped, took from his pocket a scrap of dog-eared paper, begged leave of the constable to let him hand the soiled scrap to the Captain. Houston took it, folded it away before it should be taken back, and nodded his sympathy to the dishevelled prisoner. The note, which contained the 'Ode to His Majesty King George III on his Birthday', was one Grant had written some time before, and underneath the Ode, was a message 'to all Naval Officers, begging them to rise up against His Excellency in New South Wales'.[17] This act demonstrates Grant's courage, but also suggests that his mind was slightly unhinged, perhaps helped by Hayes's influence.

Robert Jones, Chief Gaoler and Superintendent, was to be the flogger. To him Grant was no more than any other prisoner. As he was strapped to the triangle, it was clear that this was his first taste of the scourge. Jones laid it

H

on, as he did to every victim, while assistant surgeon John Connellan stood by. After a few strokes, Grant was unconscious. Later he was carried to his cell where he was thrown on the lice-ridden mattress to recover. That evening the blacksmith came to refix the chains round his ankles. As he lay stricken, Captain Houston came to see him before his ship sailed.

'I received your letter,' he said, 'and I read it too. But I'll give you one piece of advice, Grant. You should keep your mouth more shut.' It was sound advice, but useless to John Grant who had a compulsion to be heard whenever he had a cause to crusade for.[18]

Foley came to take him back to the farm, where Mrs Foley tended him and the boys treated him as a hero. By a remarkable dispensation on Piper's part, he was allowed two days in bed; the general treatment was a return to work as usual, after a 'twenty-five'. Grant had sores on his back where the tails had cut the skin, but the 'traps' were alert to make sure he was at work, and Foley had to send him out.

Before long he risked his liberty again, such as it was. This time it was for a settler, a young man who had come to Norfolk Island as an emancipist, and set himself up as a baker. Kingston (known at that time as Sydney Town) was little more than a tangle of huts close to the beach, where stalls and booths and grog-shops had been set up. Amongst these huts Ernest Prosser had fixed up a bakehouse and shop which he carried on as a 'mixed business', selling yards of cloth, sweetmeats, bread, and little things beloved of children and others too. There were plenty of settlers, their wives and children, as well as the military, and while there was money there was trade. Although the Island was to run itself down gradually, Prosser made a good living and was a popular, hard-working young man.

Robert Webb, one of the earlier settlers and now a middle-aged man, had married a young woman nearly thirty years younger than himself. He had become a good friend of Prosser's and invited him to his house, where Prosser met Julia, Webb's wife. The two fell in love, and Webb at first took little notice, regarding it as little more than an infatuation which would soon die down. One day he caught them in the act of making love. He demanded that Prosser come no more to the house and told Julia she was never to see him again. This, to the infatuated young couple, proved impossible, and when he found them again in adultery, instead of giving Julia a beating and Prosser a good whack over the head, he went to Piper, who ordered the young man off the Island immediately and confiscated his possessions.

Prosser departed on the next vessel, and an auction sale of his possessions was advertised. Julia, distraught, went to find John Grant who, since his last brush with authority, had become a strange figure. His hair had grown long and matted, his beard long and tangled and his eyes wild. He had a patriarchal look, like a prophet of old. He would surely know what was best to do, so Julia Webb visited Foley's farm to seek his advice.

When Grant heard of the auction he decided to go into Sydney Town and make a protest against the auction. It was not lawful, he said, and he would challenge Piper's authority. Crowds were already gathered on the beach-front when Grant reached it. Piper was there, and when he saw Grant, who was forbidden to leave his employer's farm, he shouted 'Put that man in gaol!' Grant was seized and unceremoniously thrust into the gaol-yard—but not in a cell—and the constables turned back to the auction.

The bell rang, and Grant, with great effort, scrambled to the top of the three-metre wall surrounding the gaol and yelled 'This sale is not lawful! All those who buy goods have no right to the property!'[19] Piper, enraged, had Grant thrown into a cell until Foley could come and take him back. The next day Grant was arrested and taken, all unprepared, down to the cove at the end of the valley where a small boat was anchored. He was then rowed out to Philip Island, less than ten kilometres offshore.

Philip Island, the only other vestige of that long-submerged mountain chain, was the ultimate banishment for intractable convicts. It was not often used except as a goat-run; there was little vegetation, no pastures, no streams, and few trees. Seabirds nested by the thousands during the breeding-time but few were left at the time Grant was put ashore there. He was left a cask of water, some food, a grindstone, and nothing else—no shelter, no life of any kind except one dog, gone wild. He was to remain there for four months.

He had been hustled away so swiftly that he had not brought his journal. Also, there was no ink to write with, and he didn't have the heart to do anything but brood. Then, one day, he noticed the large brown leaves of a wild banana tree, and with sap from a bush, concocted some kind of ink. With primitive tools such as these he set to work. He wrote to the Governor—Bligh at this time—which places it as 1806 or 1807.

Grant found the long days of loneliness the hardest to bear, and his mind, already unhinged, became more and more strange. He imagined wild happenings, at times he raged and cursed, at other times recited poetry, some of it his own, in French and Greek as he had done in his schooldays; and at times he lay in a stupor for days, exposed to the elements, for he had made no shelter, and in agony from a recurrence of an old complaint, the gravel (small stones in the kidneys).

Robert Jones visited Philip Island once a month, and brought supplies of food and water, then left with the tide. By his third visit, Jones found Grant prostrate, his water-cask putrid, although there had been rain in plenty; his food, what was left of it, was quite rotten. He had not been given orders to take the prisoner back to the mainland, but he placed a sack under Grant's head, moved him to the shade, and rowed back to report. Before leaving he asked 'was there any message for the Commandant?', but Grant only whispered a request for a fresh grindstone, 'as the one he had was all gritty'. His spirit was broken, he was abandoned, there was no one to care whether he lived or died. For John Grant, this was the worst of all. He needed an audience, and on Philip Island there was no audience, only a half-wild dog.

Grant was brought back to the settlement not long before Christmas 1807, and was taken to Foley's farm where the family welcomed him, though by this time Foley must have been wearied of his difficult young assigned labourer who was not really fitted for such work, with his education and delicate health. He soon recovered once he was back with friends, and he wrote up his journal, filling in with memories, real or imagined. He had been sixteen weeks on Philip Island and within a month, very early in 1808, he and the Foleys were evacuated to Sydney, for Norfolk Island was to be totally evacuated as soon as possible, by orders from the British Government, and Bligh was insistent that those orders should be obeyed.

Grant was sent to Newcastle. His occupation is not stated but he was asked to conduct Sunday services and act as Chaplain, probably in the prison camp. This proved a great success and no more tilts at Fate are recorded. He wrote many letters to his mother, and on the arrival of Governor Macquarie in 1810, Grant entreated him to allow him to return to England before his mother died. The Governor, who had met Mrs Grant and had, apparently, been much impressed by her, arranged for Grant's free pardon, but it was not until 1811 that he was able to get a passage home.

His journal ends with the words: 'The influence of religion has power to eradicate bitterness, even the bitterness left after irreparable injuries'.

The End of the First Settlement

W HILE JOHN GRANT WAS SUFFERING HIS BITTEREST MOMENTS ON PHILIP ISLAND, PIPER, ON NORFOLK, WAS BESET BY PROBLEMS OF HIS OWN. Governor Bligh had been given firm instructions on the necessity for removal of settlers from Norfolk Island by the Secretary of State, and long and detailed letters of information about that place had been written by Foveaux to Lord Hobart. Foveaux had marshalled the facts clearly, demolishing the argument Governor King had put forward as a reason to retain at least a small settlement at Norfolk Island:

> . . . for so long as there shall remain an establishment, however small,
> it will be necessary to keep up the courts of justice . . . This service
> will require that a sufficient number of officers should be retained. As
> to the plan proposed by Governor King of sending officers in a vessel
> annually for settling such civil or other matters as may occur during
> the year, I have to observe that, independent of the inconvenience . . .
> there will be found other difficulties and obstacles . . . From the . . .
> variety of cases, the . . . delay of a vessel off this island . . . would be
> attended with an expence more than equal to the saving . . . As to any
> advantage . . . in sending a vessel in the summer season to take . . .
> such pork as they may be enabled to salt during the winter . . . I am
> convinced . . . the difficulty and danger for the shipping . . . would
> more than counterbalance any benefit to be derived . . . I am clearly of
> opinion, from my knowledge of Port Jackson, that the inhabitants of
> that place will be able, in a short time, to supply Government with
> animal food at a much cheaper rate than could be raised and taken
> from hence, after including the necessary expence of freight etc . . .
> The success of the crops are, from various causes, equally precarious . . .
> They have . . . not been in a situation to supply the public stores for
> some time past with sufficient pork to victual those necessarily
> dependent upon the Crown . . . there is a necessity for issuing a

reduced ration . . . Should the idea once prevail that a gradual
reduction will . . . take place, and that the Government will positively
give up the settlement altogether, I have no doubt but the disposition
for removal will again become general . . .[1]

Bligh, when he assumed the Governorship of New South Wales, sent his
instructions to Piper on the necessity of removing settlers and convicts from
Norfolk Island, but transports were not freely available and communications
were slow. Dealing with claims for replacement of stock and the natural
disinclination on the part of long-time settlers to uproot themselves and their
families from the farms they had worked so hard to improve—all these
proved impediments to the speedy implementation of the scheme.

Piper found that one of the irritations of winding down the settlement was
the paucity of supplies, small things necessary for the everyday running of
the Island:

. . . I refer your Excellency to the Public Accounts for the general
wants of the Settlement. Being much in want of Iron, I was induced
to make an exchange with the Master of an American Schooner . . .
enclosed is the Receipt, which I hope you will approve of . . .[2]

and on another occasion Piper wrote that there was not any paper for the
writing of official notices or receipts; slops too, were needed. But to balance
matters, there were few disputes and plenty of sheep, goats and swine for the
stores.

The plan for resettlement of the Norfolk Island settlers was, in the main, a
good one. Van Diemen's Land was much closer to the main colony and,
moreover, it had many safe anchorages and harbours around the coast;
settlers could be granted larger holdings than those they had on Norfolk,
there were good rivers along which farms could be established, and an
abundance of native animals which could, if necessary, be used as food. That
Van Diemen's Land was already occupied by an indigenous race was a minor
matter—it could be overcome in various ways that need not concern their
Lordships in the Home Government. The despatch from Downing Street to
Governor Bligh concluded:

. . . In carrying this measure into effect it would be highly desirable
that Lieutenant-Colonel Foveaux should be employed, but as the
health of this gentleman does not admit of his proceeding to New
South Wales by the ships now under despatch, it will be advisable that
the removal of the Settlement should not on this account be delayed.
Should Lieut. Colonel Foveaux, however, arrive at Port Jackson
before final arrangements for carrying out these Instructions into
Effect shall have been completed, you will not fail to entrust him with
the Execution of the service . . .[3]

Fortunately for Piper, Foveaux chose not to return to Norfolk Island at any time. He arrived at Port Jackson 28 July 1808, found Major Johnstone of the New South Wales Corps in command of the settlement, and Governor Bligh under arrest. That was the year of the 'Rum Rebellion', sparked by Bligh's efforts to rid the colony of the trafficking in rum by the officers of the Corps, and of his running feud with John Macarthur who seems to have regarded himself as a kind of overlord of the colony, both from his large landholdings, his increasing wealth, and his overweening pride.[4]

The feud came to a head in January 1808 when Macarthur turned a claim for debt against Judge Atkins, into a threat to appeal to the English authorities unless the Governor and the Judge accommodated him in the matter. A further point of dissension was Macarthur's claim that some town land he had been refused permission to fence, was 'already in his possession' and it was his right to fence it in if he chose. Macarthur was brought to court and detained in the gaol, but his detention made little difference to his planning with the officers of the Corps and the document he wrote, addressed to Major Johnstone, the then Commander of the New South Wales Corps and Macarthur's very good friend. The document demanded the arrest of Governor Bligh, and that Johnstone assume control of the colony as Commander of the Corps. It was indeed Providence which had kept the impulsive Piper, close friend of John Macarthur, so far from Sydney at such a time; Norfolk Island was a haven of peace by comparison.

Piper's firm instructions were that he should leave the Island by mid-1809, but it was not until early in 1810 that a vessel arrived to take him, his family his goods and stock, and the last of the settlers back to the mainland.[5] There, Piper's house was built in the County of Cumberland (now the main part of Sydney) with 6 acres (2·5 hectares) of land, two floors to the house which measured thirty feet by twelve (9 × 3·6 metres), its value, £60; forage for his horses, wheat and grain for his cattle, to the value of £827 2s 6d.[6] The New South Wales Corps had been disbanded at this time, to be re-formed as the 102nd Regiment, but Piper resigned his Captaincy and decided to throw in his lot with the colony, where there would be many more opportunities for advancement than he could have had in a military career. He had land, and many friends in New South Wales, and a life he loved.

In 1811 Piper, with Mary Ann and their two young sons, sailed for England where he was to settle his affairs, renew his wardrobe, and cast about for a suitable offer of employment in New South Wales.

He returned to the colony in 1814, bringing with him his daughter Sarah, who had probably been sent to England some years earlier, for her education.[7] She was a lovely and lively young woman by then, and on the voyage back, she met and fell in love with John Thrupp, an intending settler. Their marriage took place soon after arrival at Sydney. It is an anomaly that the daughter should be married before her father was, but so it happened; John Piper and his Mary Ann were married in St. Philip's Church in February 1816 by special licence, and their next child, Eliza, was christened in August of that year.[8]

Piper had secured the lucrative job of Naval Officer at Port Jackson, at a salary of £400 per annum, a sum which increased to £4000 before many years elapsed.[9] He became Sydney's most sought-after host, his beautiful Naval Pavilion, which he called Henrietta Villa, was the centre of truly lavish entertainments, and his title of 'Prince of Australia' was well deserved for his large-hearted hospitality. His family grew to eleven children, and though in his later years his financial affairs did not thrive, he still managed to live comfortably on his 500-acre (200-hectare) property, 'Westbourne' on the Macquarie River, with Mary Ann and the younger members of his family.[10] He died in June 1851, a well-loved and popular man. It was true when he said, about 1821:

> I have resided about 28 years in this Colony and Norfolk Island,
> which settlement I commanded from September 1804 until April
> 1810 during which period I never had occasion to bring a soldier to
> Court-Martial or an inhabitant to a Criminal Tribunal.[11]

John Grant, however, might not entirely agree with the assessment.

After Captain Piper left Norfolk Island there remained a few of the older settlers, a few convicts, and a small detachment of the military, the whole number less than 100. Macquarie had become Governor of New South Wales in 1810 and Foveaux had been Acting-Governor in the interim between Major Johnstone's removal from his assumed post as Governor, and the arrival of Macquarie in 1810. Lieutenant Thomas Crane of the 73rd Regiment was appointed 'caretaker' Commandant of Norfolk Island during its last year or two.[12] Before his departure from England, Macquarie had been left in no doubt that the Island was to be completely evacuated, and as quickly as possible.

Many old settlers wished to remain on the Island rather than face a new start in a harsher climate. Some, like Robert Webb, had spent twenty years on Norfolk, it was their home, and to be uprooted for what seemed to them to be no reason at all, was hard in their later years. In a modest way they were prosperous, and content to be forgotten by all but the men on passing ships who might wish to call in for fresh water or supplies.

But the Government was adamant. Evacuation was to be total, and by 15 February 1813, when the *Minstrel* and the *Lady Nelson* called to take settlers, stock, and the military, with all their personal possessions to Sydney or Van Diemen's Land, only a few persons remained.[13] The Chief Superintendent William Hutchinson, who had lived on Norfolk Island for many years as convict, emancipist and later, Superintendent, and a party of the best-behaved convicts, with one of the old shepherd-settlers, were to slaughter and salt down all the stock that remained, and ship it to the Stores in Sydney. Nothing was to be left that might attract passing ships to the Island or provide food for ships' crew who might wish to stay on shore—or, for that matter, provide a hideaway for absconding convicts from any of the colony's prison settlements.

Twelve of the fiercest dogs were to be left behind to kill those animals which escaped the slaughter, for, as Hutchinson said 'they'll kill when they're hungry enough'. All the buildings were to be destroyed: houses, stores, watermills, the dam, all were to be burned. Destruction was the only weapon the Government had to ensure the protection of the once-lovely Island which had suffered such destruction already, destruction of lives, forests, and fertility of the soil.

The caretaker party set about their task with speed, the Government vessel could appear at any time. Cattle, sheep, pigs and goats were slaughtered, salted, packed in casks; wooden buildings were put to the torch and stone buildings torn down stone by stone. On 15 February 1814 the Government brig *Kangaroo* anchored in the bay and all was ready. For the last time the beach resounded with shouts and curses, curses which changed to cheers as the last heavy cask was loaded and the men took the oars to sweep the boat across from the jetty to the waiting vessels. It was a last goodbye to the fortress from which some of them had for so long wished to be free. Only the aged shepherd settler mourned the leaving.

The *Kangaroo* and *Minstrel* reached Sydney on 10 March, and in April, Governor Macquarie wrote in his report to Earl Bathurst:

> I have now much satisfaction in reporting to your Lordship that the Evacuation and Abandonment of Norfolk Island has been at length completely effected, with the additional happy circumstances of no accident whatever having attended it . . . The execution of this duty I entrusted to Mr Wm. Hutchinson . . . who has conducted this important service with great zeal, diligence and integrity . . . and very advantageously for this Government . . . As some acknowledgement for these services I have lately appointed him Principal Superintendant of Convicts and Public Works in Sydney, in room of Mr Isaac Nichols, resigned . . .[14]

There were pardons or tickets-of-leave for those convicts who had earned them, and care was given to the old settlers who had been forced from their homes and had neither money nor strength to begin life over again in another place. Norfolk Island, scarred from years of spoliation, eroded, denuded of its finest trees, was left to renew itself; the blood-soaked ground of the flogging-yard was washed by rains and little remained in that spot where men and women had screamed for mercy under the scourger's lash in Foveaux's time.

William Hutchinson, on his return to Sydney, wrote to Governor Macquarie:

> Sir, I have the honour of acquainting your Excellency of my arrival, in His Majesty's brig *Kangaroo*, from Norfolk Island, with the whole of

the people left under my charge and the provisions of every kind
which we were enabled to salt down . . .

The *Kangaroo* arrived . . . on the 15th February last, where she
remained Twelve days . . . every possible exertion was made to
dispatch the Vessel; to effect which the people wrought hard day and
night . . . I received every Support and Assistance from Corporal
McGillicuddy and the Three privates of the 73rd Regiment under his
orders . . . I beg leave also to recommend the following Free people to
Your Excellency's favourable consideration . . . Vizt. John Brown, a
shepherd and Overseer of Government stock, who had been in that
situation for more than twenty years . . . for such pecuniary and other
Assistance for himself and Wife as they may appear deserving; these
poor people having nothing to depend upon, and are now past labour
from their great Age. I also beg leave to recommend John Hatcher, a
very old man, the Master Miller . . . and George Kempney, and
Joseph Dunstan, the former a Coxswain . . . the latter a shepherd . . .
for such remuneration as Your Excellency may judge they are
deserving . . . Mr Thomas Ransome, the Master Carpenter . . . is
desirous of settling at the Derwent, I beg leave to recommend him for
such an extension of Land as Your Excellency may Judge him
deserving of.

The Prisoners in general behaved themselves extremely well
throughout the Whole of the Service, and if any distinction in
rewarding their good Conduct Could be made, I beg leave to
recommend the Old Inhabitants of Norfolk Island who from their
long Servitude have the Stronger Claims to Your Excellency's favor.

I have now the honor of acquainting Your Excellency that Your
Instructions have been carried into the fullest effect; the Whole of the
Stock that could not be taken for Slaughter have been Shot and
Otherways destroyed, except for a few Hogs and Goats . . . having left
about a Dozen of Dogs, Male and Female, there can be no doubt
when the latter Animals become pressed with Hunger the Whole of
the former will be destroyed.

The buildings of every description were Set fire to, and so
Completely destroyed that I have much pleasure in assuring Your
Excellency that there remains no inducement for human beings of any
kind to visit that place . . . and hope my Conduct has been such as to
Merit Your Excellency's Approbation.[15]

Norfolk Island, the little 'speck under the finger of God' was to revert for a
time to the peaceful Paradise it had been in 1774, though it would never
again be as perfect. It was to remain peaceful for eleven years, before men
returned to it.

The Second Settlement 1825 to 1855: 'Forever excluded from all hope of return'

12

IN HIS DESPATCH OF 22 JULY 1824 THE SECRETARY OF STATE, EARL BATHURST, SENT THE FOLLOWING INSTRUCTIONS TO SIR THOMAS Brisbane, Governor of New South Wales:

> I have to desire that you will immediately carry into effect the occupation of Norfolk Island upon the principle of a great Hulk or Penitentiary according to the enclosed plan. If the representations of the extraordinary fertility of that Island be correct, there can be little doubt that the Convicts may be made to produce a great part if not the whole of their food, and even perhaps to supply exports, especially of Coffee, the proceeds of which may be applied in diminution of the general expence of the Establishment. To this Island the worst description of Convicts in New South Wales and Van Diemen's Land must progressively be sent . . . at once establishing a secondary punishment which will not admit of Mitigation . . .[1]

In his reply Sir Thomas Brisbane wrote:

> It will readily occur to your Lordship that . . . Norfolk Island is confined, the access difficult, consequently it is not suited to receive many prisoners or frequent transportations. I have therefore thought it advisable to reserve that place as one for Capital Respites and other higher class of offences. I could wish it to be understood that the felon who is sent there is forever excluded from all hope of return.[2]

He had previously given it as his opinion that Norfolk Island should be made 'the *ne plus ultra* of Convict degradation' and recommended that it should, if the laws of England allowed, be 'completely under Martial Law . . . I cannot see that Felons, who have forfeited all claim to protection from the Law, should complain of being in a worse state than our Soldiers are in a Campaign'.[3]

So the Island which had for eleven years been left to regenerate itself was again to be inhabited, this time by men without hope of any future but the inexorable one of Death. Foveaux had been part-architect of Norfolk Island's planned Second Settlement. He had presented the British Government with a detailed outline of the necessity for evacuation of the Island in 1805 and had stressed the possibilities of food crops which could be grown there, especially of coffee — which he himself had caused to be planted and harvested — as well as wheat and maize. In 1825 Foveaux was a Major-General, had been married to Ann Sherwin for ten years, and was apparently able to advise the policy-makers in the Government at this time, on the matter of re-opening Norfolk Island. He well knew the potential of the rich, deep soil, knew the crops that could be wrested from it with an unlimited supply of free labour and a Commandant who could wring the last ounce of work from such labour.

The re-occupation went ahead with little delay. In May 1825 Brisbane chartered the *Brutus*, a privately owned brig trading between Port Jackson and India, to carry convicts and stores to Norfolk Island as the voyage would 'take her only a short distance off her planned course'. *Brutus* was to be accompanied by the Colonial Cutter *Mermaid* with a detachment of troops.

> Captain Turton of the 40th Regiment, the Commandant at Norfolk
> Island, reports very favourably of its present state, as to live stock,
> which is in great abundance; particularly pigs which he states to be
> beyond all calculations; Goats are also very numerous . . . the former
> Town of Buildings are in a state of perfect ruin but from the
> remaining walls he will be enabled to form a temporary Gaol and
> Store . . .[4]

The landing of the Detachment, which consisted of 1 Captain, 1 Subaltern, 3 Sergeants, 30 privates, 6 women and 6 children took place on 6 June. There were 57 convicts, 'mostly Mechanics to prepare Buildings and erect a Treadmill which accompanied it'. The Treadmill, which had possibly been requested by Foveaux, was not erected, and more than likely had not been sent.

More than ten years' growth in Norfolk Island's warm climate would have created plenty of hard labour for the convicts whose job it was to clear the former Settlement at Kingston. Young pines, growing to near six metres high in ten years, thrust skywards through the roofless ruins; tough creepers, coarse tussock grasses, flax plants as tall as a man, and wind-blown weeds by the million, infested the swampy area. The tiny cemetery near the shore had been washed by heavy seas at times, unnamed mounds had been obliterated and only a few rough-hewn gravestones still stood to mark the place where free men and women lay alongside the bondsmen buried there.

A stockade and huts for the military were quickly erected; the officers made do with tents, the convicts found what shelter they could, a sleeping-place against a ruined stone wall or in a hollow tree until such time as they could build their own strong stockade. The small ruined gaol close to the place where a boatshed formerly stood, was soon readied, and a storehouse built, with rooms for the Commissary attached. The working hours were long, from sun-up to sunset, a matter of twelve hours or more in the cold winter months of June and July, when winds blew incessantly and un-predictably from every quarter. Captain Turton kept the men at work with stone-cutting, lime-burning, timber-felling, ground-clearing, as he had been ordered to do. It was to be, as Lord Bathurst wrote, 'unrequited toil', with no indulgences. Within the convict stockade two 80-gallon (360-litre) boilers were placed, and two convicts appointed to attend them and keep the water boiling and the fires stoked throughout the day, against the men's return after labour, when they were required to cook their own food.

According to the Reverend Thomas Sharpe, the Anglican chaplain of the Settlement who, although he did not arrive until 1835, wrote from hearsay of many happenings of earlier days of the Second Settlement:

> . . . the men's ration of salt meat was boiled in the water, each man's ration being 1 lb salt beef or pork, with 1 lb of maize-meal. Some of the men chose to eat their meat raw, first washing the salt out in the nearby creek, then pounding it with a billet of wood to make it tender. In that way he could be sure it was his own portion that he had, and not some other man's shrunken portion that was boiled to a rag. The maize-meal was softened into a dough, and the loaf thus formed was then thrust into the ashes of the boiler to cook, though often the men were late in returning by which time the fires had gone cold. Often the chunk of meat was a man's only food in twenty-four hours.[5]

On 17 December that year the brig *Amity* arrived with thirty-one more prisoners, writes Sharpe, one copper-bottomed boat, and despatches, among which was one that gave Captain Turton his promotion to the rank of Major. It is possible that the *Amity* brought more wives, as he mentions the number of women on Norfolk Island was thirty at the time Captain Vance Donaldson and a detachment of the 57th Regiment arrived in March 1826. Donaldson brought with him the news that all women, bond or free, were to be ready to leave by the next vessel, at the Governor's orders. General Sir Ralph Darling had replaced Sir Thomas Brisbane in December 1825, and he strongly dis-approved of women being allowed on Norfolk Island, as he wrote in his despatch to Under-Secretary Hay:

> I laid it down, as a rule on my arrival here, that women should not be sent to that Settlement, and the few free women who had accompanied their husbands, belonging to the troops and the people employed there, were withdrawn. My object was to hold out that Settlement as a place of the extremest punishment short of Death . . .

Norfolk Island will soon have within it . . . the most depraved and dissolute characters. At present there are 115, and there are several others at this moment to be forwarded by the first opportunity.[6]

On hearing this order, one woman, with her three children, took to the bush, hoping to avoid being sent away. When she returned three days later, bedraggled and wan, her three children crying with hunger, she implored Captain Donaldson to allow her to remain. But he had his orders, neither she nor any other woman could stay.

Captain Vance Donaldson was born at Tyrone in 1791. He entered the Army when only 13 years old, and proved to be a good soldier, for he was rapidly promoted, attaining the rank of Captain in 1813 while serving in the 57th under Wellington. No doubt he was sympathetic to the woman's plea to stay on Norfolk Island, few Irishmen would not have been, but he had his orders and no exceptions were allowed, however pitiful.

The convicts sent to the Island from 1825 onwards were all, or nearly all, Capital Respites—their death sentences having been commuted to life imprisonment or a number of years in chains, with hard labour. Most were men in their twenties or thirties, some younger, all of them doubly convicted. For them the Island was Purgatory, no matter how picturesque the scenery. Escape was virtually impossible by sea; and the forest, laced by thorny creepers that tore flesh and clothes equally, offered only temporary refuge. But small, waterless Philip Island a few kilometres south of Norfolk, beckoned the enterprising ones. It was inevitable that one day an attempt would be made to use Philip Island as a springboard to freedom. In his journal of happenings on Norfolk Island, Reverend Thomas Sharpe describes the beginnings of one such attempt. He recounts how, early on the morning of 25 September 1826, two prisoners, Patrick Clynch and Robert Storey absconded into the forest with a great hullabaloo. Alerted by the yelling of the gaol-gang going out to their day's work, thirty soldiers were sent in full cry to catch them, and this, he says, was just what the rest of the convict conspirators wanted.[7]

Patrick Clynch was a 'lifer', transported from Ireland in 1823 for 'presenting a Pistol with intent to rob'. He arrived in the colony in 1824 and in December 1825 was convicted of two daring burglaries and sentenced to death. He and three other criminals were ordered for execution by the Acting-Governor, but Governor Darling arrived in the colony the day before the execution was to take place, the condemned men were respited and subsequently sent to Norfolk Island and hard labour in chains for life.[8]

Governor Darling, in his despatch to Earl Bathurst of April 1827, gives a short account of the mutiny; Sharpe gives a more descriptive one that still tallies with the facts while filling in the details.[9] He says the mutiny was carried out by 'Black John' Goff, who had planned a mass escape from the gaol. Goff told the others that 'within a hundred miles' was an island where they could safely hide and never be found. Clynch and Storey were to be the decoys, thus tying up most of the military while the rest of the prisoners gained time to get away. With the soldiers in full cry after Clynch and Storey, Black Goff and about thirty prisoners seized the overseers, tied them securely, robbed the Stores for provisions and weapons, broke open the boat-shed and had three boats in the water before Wilson, Corporal of the Guard, came rushing up with two of his men, to demand they leave the boats at once, on pain of being shot.

Black John raised his musket and shot Wilson dead, wounded the two soldiers, then stove in the one boat remaining in the boat-shed. By this time two of the boats were already on their way, the crews rowing for dear life. Goff leapt into the third boat, leaving only the one with planks stove-in, as Captain Donaldson alerted by the shots, arrived at the boat-shed. There was no fear of a chase, no way the escapees could be recaptured with only one broken boat in the shed.

By dawn next morning Donaldson had had the boat repaired. He set off with a number of armed soldiers, reached Philip Island at daybreak and silently secured the boats lying moored and waiting for the delayed dash to freedom by the convicts. An armed guard was left in each boat, moved silently to the place where some of the prisoners lay still asleep, and in the surprise attack captured twenty-one, with one man shot and one drowned. The rest of the convicts rushed to the high peak of the Island, Goff among them, and hid in caves which made capture difficult. Donaldson, assured that none of the escapees could get away, with all the boats now in the soldiers' possession, took his prisoners back to the settlement, well pleased with his foray. Within two days Donaldson paid a second visit, took four more prisoners, but John Goff was still at large with the last few, who were by this time quite familiar with all the bolt-holes on Philip Island. They all knew that in any case they had no hope of escape, no boats, and soon no food or water.

At his third visit Donaldson had worked out his strategy. He deployed his men to cut off access to the high peak and so drive the men towards the centre of the Island, where they might easily be surrounded. Black John Goff, badly wounded, fought to the last. He was prepared to kill his captors, and he knew it was the end for himself if he was captured alive. Donaldson, however, brought him back and on Norfolk Island he, with the other escapees, was put in irons and left to await a vessel to take them to Sydney for trial. This could be a matter of weeks or months, for there was no way of communicating other than by despatches and prisoners might be held in close confinement indefinitely. At the trial, Goff and one other man were sentenced to death, the rest were returned to Norfolk Island in chains for life. Clynch, whose escape had been the signal for the mutiny, remained at large in the forest.

Captain Donaldson returned to his regiment in August 1827 and his successor was Captain Thomas Wright of the 39th Regiment. Wright was a determined individual, as was shown at the time he embarked in England to go to New South Wales. He asked the Master of the *Boyne*, the convict ship, for permission to bring on board the woman with whom he had been living. This was refused, but when the *Boyne* was at Deptford for several days, taking on Stores, he smuggled her aboard and, 24 hours later, Wright disclosed that she was in his cabin. He had three children by this woman, but she did not accompany him to Norfolk Island on his appointment as Commandant there.[10]

In the Dixson Library, Sydney, is a diary kept by Aaron Price, a long-time resident on the Island, a man who arrived as a convict, served his sentence and behaved well, and was in turn promoted to Constable, Overseer, then Principal Overseer, living virtually as a free man, and leaving Norfolk Island in 1854, having seen many Commandants come and go. Of Captain Wright he says:

> On Donaldson's departure Wright released the whole of the chain-gang from heavy irons, which were replaced with light irons. He examined the soil, and chose 300 acres to be broken, supervising it himself. 220 prisoners at that time. Wright selected 200 and arranged gangs for agriculture, visiting them regularly. If the ground was not broken to eighteen inches, he gave them fifty to one hundred lashes. The land was known as Wright's Farm, Bennet's Farm, and Longridge. He then examined the interior of the Island and found old settlers' gardens with borders of strawberries, roses, bulbs, sweet briars, grape vines fig trees orange trees oak trees and a quantity of tobacco plants and planted two acres which produced a good crop in nine months. A second crop was planted but the Government forbade it to be brought to perfection and it was destroyed . . . there were excellent woods, ironwood and a species of teak with beautiful grain. Scarcely a piece of level ground more than one hundred acres, all is hill and dale . . . Haze and salt breeze are the chief obstacles to wheat production, maize, potatoes and all kinds of vegetables and fruits grow in abundance . . . Tobacco, sugar and wine might be produced were it not for the penal description of the Island. Livestock is bred in small quantities for use of Government officers, and an immense number of young pines are planted for use as masts for vessels.[11]

Wright was to find a great deal more trouble on Norfolk Island than the convicts who were unwilling to hoe to eighteen inches (45 centimetres), and much of it came through Patrick Clynch the absconder. The events are recorded in *Historical Records of Australia* as follows:

> About the time the mutineers were released from Imprisonment [this refers to the 'Black John Goff mutiny in September 1826] Captain Wright of the 39th Regiment assumed the Command of the Island; and in about two months afterwards he ascertained that the Prisoners contemplated a second Mutiny. On the evening of 16th of October

1827 after all the gangs had returned to Camp . . . Captain Wright, who was walking home quite defenceless from a Farm in the Interior of the Island, was furiously assaulted by Patrick Clynch who rushed from his concealment in some high grass near the road, armed with an immense Club . . . with a hideous yell he aimed a blow at Captain Wright's head . . . but the Captain fortunately warded it off and it only disabled his hand for a time . . . This was . . . to have been an organised attack for the purpose of killing Captain Wright as the signal for a general Insurrection . . . Three days after the attack . . . Clynch attacked the Principal Overseer . . . and attempted to murder him with a pole having a dagger fixed at its end. On . . . 20th October about 10 o'clock at night it being very dark, the Garrison was alarmed and turned out and Captain Wright proceeded with a Serjeant and twelve men to reinforce the Guard and attack the Prisoner's camp. On reaching the camp he heard the cries of 'It's Clynch', 'It's Clynch' 'there he goes' 'Stop him!' . . . Captain Wright despatched a Sergeant with two men into a neighbouring Swamp . . . 'You know your duty, and do it!' . . . Shouts were raised in every direction that Clynch was making for the bush . . . he was intercepted and shot, while . . . attacking a Constable and one of the Soldiers with a spear . . .[12]

Aaron Price, in his diary, says Clynch was captured near the Civil hospital and shot while attempting to escape from custody. His body was dragged to the gaol and placed on the scourger's stage and exhibited to all prisoners as a warning. The Reverend Thomas Sharpe has another slightly different version of the affair, but he wrote of this time from hearsay.

Clynch's death drew even more attention than his life had done, for although an examination of the affair took place next morning before Captain Wright and his Second-in-Command, Lieutenant Cox, and both Justices of the Peace, the whole matter flared up more than a year later, when Lieutenant Cox was Court-Martialled on certain charges made against him by Wright. This took place in Sydney and necessitated bringing witnesses from Norfolk Island. One, a convict named McCabe, gave information to Mr Hall, editor of the *Sydney Monitor* that Captain Wright knew Clynch was in custody before he ordered him shot.[13] On this, Mr Hall printed an accusation against Wright and the two soldiers, accusing them of murder. He had them brought before the Police Magistrate, when Captain Wright was discharged and the two soldiers charged with manslaughter. At this, Wright offered to stand trial in their stead, and be charged with murder. In his Report of the trial, Governor Darling says:

. . . a long Trial ensued, when Captain Wright, standing in the Dock from ten in the Morning till near 8 at night, was acquitted, Mr Wentworth, the Counsel for the Prosecution having frankly acknowledged that the case had broken down under him and stated that he would not press Captain Wright to a defence![14]

In a separate letter he wrote:

> . . . the Trial of Captain Wright was the result of as foul a conspiracy
> as was ever engendered. Messrs Wentworth Hall and Robison (lately
> dismissed the Service) hoping by means of Lieutt. Cox of the 39th
> Regt. (who had been brought to a General Court Martial by Captain
> Wright and was sentenced to be Cashiered, but pardoned) and some
> Convicts who were brought from Norfolk Island as Witnesses, that
> they would have been enabled to have effected their purpose . . . after
> Lieut. Cox's Court Martial had closed, the Party turned round on
> Captain Wright, and with the Assistance of Lieutt. Cox and the
> Convicts alluded to, endeavoured to Convict him of the Murder of
> Clynch . . . Every advantage they could desire, and more than they
> could possibly have expected, was afforded them: notwithstanding
> which the case, as Mr Wentworth was obliged to admit, had 'broken
> under him' though . . . supported by the most palpable perjury on the
> part of one witness and the most extraordinary Evidence, to say the
> least of it, on the part of Lieutt. Cox that was ever given in a Court of
> Justice.[15]

By his death Clynch had disrupted more lives than he could have hoped to
do had he lived out his time in chains on Norfolk Island. Captain Wright had
been recalled from his Command in November 1828, his actions and those
of Governor Darling vilified in Mr Hall's newspaper; McCabe had been
severely punished for perjury, Civil Courts had been convened to deal with
the manner of his death, and reputations were tarnished.

It is quite likely at this time that the legend of Barney Duffy took shape.
'Barney Duffy's Gulley' appears on maps of Norfolk Island made in the time
of the Second Settlement, and the Gulley is not far from the Commandant's
Garden, Longridge Farm and Wright's Farm. 'Duffy' could have been the
name by which Clynch was known among those convicts who knew his hide-
out. The time and place fit, but the elusive character has never been pinned
down to one particular man, a fact which adds to the legend's survival in
Norfolk Island folk-lore.

The story is as follows: Barney Duffy was a giant of a man, an Irish convict
who absconded and remained hidden in the forest for seven years. He was
finally captured by two soldiers, who brought him in though he pleaded with
them to let him go. When his pleas were ignored, and he knew that execution
awaited him, he uttered a fearful curse, 'So surely as you take me to be
hanged on the gallows so, before my corpse has hung a week, both of you will
meet Death!' Duffy was tried, and executed. And as he foretold, within the
week the bodies of the two soldiers were found floating in the sea, near the
Point known today as 'Headstone'. As a legend it is interesting; as fact, it has
never been proven, and no mention of such a man is made in any official
record; but as a word-of-mouth story handed down through the years, it gains

some credence from Patrick Clynch's thirteen months of violent freedom on Norfolk Island, and his violent death, coupled with the disappearance of the two soldiers who were taken to Sydney to stand trial for murder.

After Captain Wright's recall to Sydney, Captain Hunt of the 57th Regiment was appointed Commandant of Norfolk Island. Hunt had little time to establish himself before he, too, was recalled and Captain Wakefield of the 39th Regiment took over command as Acting-Commandant. At this time there were about 200 prisoners on the Island, and others arrived at regular intervals, all of them 'out and outers' as Captain Wright had called them. By 1829 a prisoners' barracks had been built, a three-storey barracks for the troops, quarters for the civil officers and a military hospital. Timber, stone, shingles and lime were all produced on the Island with convict labour, leaving only a small proportion for agriculture. With a rising number of people to feed, and more land to clear for planting, there was little chance that enough food could be grown on the Island, let alone coffee produced for export, as Earl Bathurst had suggested. The cost of maintenance was rising, not falling.

Agriculture was the most hated form of all hard labour. There was day after day of breaking ground with hoe or mattock; weed-infested soil was tangled with roots that seemed to burrow down to the centre of the earth; hillsides had to be terraced so that maize could be planted (or it would be washed away overnight in a sudden torrential rainstorm); the heat in summer was intense; the hours spent chained together seemed eternal; few men could stand such unremitting toil. Most of the prisoners were men from towns and cities, men who had started out in crime by petty thieving and had graduated to greater crime; few knew the daily life of a farm labourer at home. On Norfolk Island, under the withering eye of the Overseer, himself not long removed from similar torment, it is small wonder that they hated their allotted daily task of so many roods (each about 100 metres) to be hoed.

It was in the field-gang that a man, quiet and inoffensive hitherto, suddenly raised his hoe and split the head of the man walking in front of him, not from hate or revenge, but to get free of the eternal grinding toil. Better to be hanged, and finish for ever, was his only reason. The field-gang worked in irons, some weighing from seven to sixteen pounds (three to eight kilograms) and were chained at night with irons still on if they had been so sentenced. Their daily rations were '1 lb of salt beef or pork, 1 lb of maize-meal', and the luxury of vegetables if they had a friend among the best-behaved men who were allowed small gardens of their own, to work in in what free time they had.[16] For the men in the chain-gangs Norfolk Island was indeed a 'place of extremest punishment short of Death'. Death itself was to many a welcome visitor.

James Thomas Morisset

13

THE FREQUENT CHANGES OF COMMANDANT ON NORFOLK ISLAND STEMMED, PRIMARILY, FROM GOVERNOR DARLING'S RELUCTANCE TO appoint Lieutenant-Colonel Morisset to the post he had requested in August 1825, and for which permission had been given by Earl Bathurst later that same month. Darling's reluctance sprang from two main reasons: first, the high salary Morisset was to have and, secondly, that he was a married man and insisted on taking his wife and two young children to Norfolk Island. It was not until May 1829 that Morisset arrived on Norfolk Island as Lieutenant-Governor with powers to apply Martial Law—his military authority to be strictly limited to the Island and to the detachment of troops stationed there.

James Thomas Morisset began his military career at 16, in 1798. He served in India and Egypt where he was honoured by the Sultan of Egypt by the presentation of a magnificent gold medal, one of only twenty presented to officers who had distinguished themselves in the Egyptian war against Napoleon Bonaparte.[1] In 1805 he purchased a Captain's commission in the 48th Regiment, then engaged in the Peninsula Wars under Wellington, and it was in one of those battles he received the dreadful facial wound that disfigured him for the rest of his life. It was described by Captain Foster Fyans, his second-in-command on Norfolk Island: 'His jaw is much diseased, hanging slack below a stationary eye and a mouth slewed at an angle' and this is probably the reason no portrait of him has been found, other than a miniature painted when he was an ensign.[2]

Morisset's regiment arrived in New South Wales in 1817; in December 1818 he relieved Captain Wallis of the 46th, at Newcastle, one of the penal out-stations of the colony. He was at Newcastle until 1823, during which time he continued with the building of roads, erection of public buildings, barracks, and a breakwater across the narrow inlet separating the mainland from Nobby's Island.[3] Commissioner Bigge, the man sent by the British Government to conduct a commission of inquiry into the system of administration in New South Wales in 1819 and 1820, wrote in his Report of his visit to Newcastle during Morisset's term of office as Commandant:

The residence of the Commandant, Major Morisset, is placed on an elevated position at the end of the principal street and commands a view of the whole town. The houses of the prisoners are . . . at irregular distances . . . but preserve an even line towards the streets . . . which are kept in good order . . . are seven in number, and contain thirteen houses that belong to Government and seventy-one that belong to the prisoners . . . Major Morisset has recently built a barrack containing four apartments for sleeping and two for feeding the prisoners . . . the hours of labour are from 5 a.m. to 8 a.m., 9 a.m. till noon, and 2 p.m. till sunset. The labour at Newcastle consists of the common and coarser mechanical operations . . . and in cutting and procuring logs, which are brought from a place seventy miles distant . . .[4]

There was also the labour of the men who worked on the breakwater, where they stood often up to the waist in water while digging for limestone. Commissioner Bigge, who had approved of Morisset's method of discipline in the Newcastle settlement, had some doubts about it when he saw the results of such discipline on the backs of the labourers at the breakwater, the men whose backs were raw from recent floggings yet still had bags of unslaked lime loaded on them. That Morisset was a severe disciplinarian is borne out by references to his rule at Newcastle, given by residents there some years later. It was said that:

. . . even when Morisset was proceeding on a pleasure trip to visit outlying farms along the Hunter and Williams Rivers, he always carried in the stern of his gig a triangle and two scourgers. Lashings were ordered on the least provocation, and the settlement at Limeburners Bay was notorious for the bestial treatment of prisoners stationed there. Major Morisset took charge; and being a stern disciplinarian the ordinarily hard lot of the prisoners was made doubly so by reason of his drastic regulations. The cat-o'-nine-tails and the triangle . . . were in daily and almost hourly service.[5]

Governor Macquarie, while on an extended tour of the colony in 1820, visited Newcastle and was very much pleased with what he saw, 'I was . . . highly gratified . . . and expressed my unqualified approbation to Major Morisset of the manner in which he conducts his arduous duties here, and the excellence of the system he has laid down and pursues so successfully', he wrote in his Journal.[6] He was also delighted by Morisset's thoughtfulness in having built a little cottage along the route to be taken by Governor and Mrs Macquarie during their tour so that Mrs Macquarie might rest in private, if she so wished.

At this time, the plains around Newcastle were becoming settled, and the prisoners were removed to the more isolated Port Macquarie; Morisset was appointed to command at Bathurst district in 1823, at a time when feelings ran high between the white settlers and the Aboriginals there, and martial law was proclaimed.[7] Here again, Morisset made a good impression by his firm control of the situation, and Governor Darling, who had assumed the Government of New South Wales, wrote to Earl Bathurst:

> . . . from private sources of information I can state with some
> confidence that only seven Europeans have lost their lives in the
> conflict, which has taken place between the Natives and the Settlers.
> The number of the former who have been killed can only be gathered
> from conjecture, but in all probability they do not much exceed the
> number of Europeans.[8]

He sent a letter of thanks to Morisset, and a letter to Bathurst commending 'the judgement, prudence and moderation of Major Morisset, Commandant at Bathurst . . .'

Morisset took leave of absence in 1825 to go to England, and during his leave he married Louisa Emily Vaux; he was then 43 years old. He was asked by the Secretary to Lord Bathurst, R. W. Hay, to write a report on convict control in New South Wales, and it was at this time Morisset requested Lord Bathurst to do him the honour of appointing him to the Governorship of Norfolk Island, a request which was granted. That place, which Sir Thomas Brisbane had called 'the *ne plus ultra*' of prisons, was to be disciplined into submission and order by Morisset and his 'excellent system'.

Morisset, with his wife and one baby daughter, arrived in New South Wales in September 1827, prepared to go immediately to Norfolk Island. But Governor Darling had other views, and presented them to Bathurst as follows:

> . . . Should your Lordship concur in the view I have taken with
> respect to the Settlement at Norfolk Island, the circumstance of
> Lieutenant-Colonel Morisset being married would prevent his being
> stationed there. But it appears to me there is another reason against
> his employment as *Commandant* . . . the rate of his salary being £600
> would be a cause of dissatisfaction to the other Commandants, who
> are occasionally officers of equal rank and receive only £182 10s. In
> this Government, the Officers in the Military Service derive no
> advantage from their Regimental situation, and Lieut. Colonel
> Morisset is on full pay, the same as the other Commandants . . .[9]

This logical argument was, however, overruled by the fact that Morisset had, before leaving London, applied to the authorities to be made Civil Commandant, at the pay of £600 a year, for his period of office on Norfolk Island, and Military Commandant there 'without Staff pay or any emolument being attached to the Situation, nor the command to extend beyond the detachment doing duty at Norfolk Island'. His application had been sent to H.R.H. the Commander in Chief, who agreed to the appointment of Morisset as Commandant of Norfolk Island 'with all the Military Authority he can possibly require in that Colony'.[10]

Governor Darling, however, was a man with very strong views, and a reluctance to be outwitted. He appointed Morisset to the vacant post of Superintendent of Police at Sydney, still at the unheard-of salary of £600 a year. For two years the two men locked horns, but eventually there came the final order that Morisset should proceed to Norfolk Island as Lieutenant-Governor in February 1829. In a despatch to Sir George Murray, Darling wrote, '. . . that Settlement will no longer bear the highly penal character which has hitherto rendered it so obnoxious to the Convict population. Lieutenant-Colonel Morisset being a married man, women must of course be permitted to reside there as at other penal Settlements . . .'[11] Morisset was denied one of his requests however, when Under Secretary Hay, in his despatch to Governor Darling, said:

> Previously to the departure of Major Morisset to assume the duties of
> the Situation to which he has been appointed at Norfolk Island, he
> suggested the great utility which would result from the employment
> of the Prisoners there at the Treadmill. The Agent, however, having
> been desired to furnish an Estimate of the expense of providing such a
> Machine, has reported that the Cost of the same, if made capable of
> employing thirty men and twenty women, would be Two thousand
> two hundred and fifty Pounds. Under the circumstances, Lord
> Goderich has not deemed it advisable to authorize so great an expense
> . . . and has therefore, desired me to request that you will take such
> measures as you may consider necessary . . . by substituting some
> other description of punishment for that which the Treadmill was
> intended to afford.[12]

Morisset had found a treadmill good discipline at Newcastle, where refractory prisoners had been put to days and weeks of grinding labour which left them unfit for any kind of work afterwards. A treadmill was part of 'the excellence of the system he has laid down, and pursues so successfully' as Macquarie had noted. On Norfolk Island he would have to work out a different system to bring his miscreants to heel.

Morisset, with his wife and two baby daughters arrived on Norfolk Island in February 1829, and his first act was to give the convicts a half-holiday. There were over two hundred prisoners at that time, and the half-holiday was perhaps the only time they had any cause to celebrate his appointment as Commandant. A few days later, Morisset issued orders that Prayers would be read every Sunday morning at eleven o'clock, and the work-gangs would be mustered half an hour before that time. At Newcastle he had often read the Lessons in Christ Church, and it was with some dismay he found that no chaplain had been sent to the Island as part of the Civil Establishment. This omission was, it seems, more the fault of the Home Government than that of the Colonial Governor, for both Governor King and Governor Darling had asked many times for more ministers of religion to be sent to the colony; only a few had arrived. Norfolk Island, in particular, had suffered from this lack, and in 1832 Governor Bourke, in a despatch to Lord Goderich, stated:

> My Lord,
>   In forwarding the accompanying duplicate, the Report of the Venble. the Archdeacon of New South Wales (the original having been taken charge of by Lieut-General Darling on his leaving the Colony), I have no observation to make on its Contents, further than that I entirely concur in opinion with the Archdeacon, as to the Absolute necessity of Stationing a Minister of Religion at Norfolk Island. It is in truth a place where the Zeal and Devotion of an Active Missionary would find ample room for employment. It is filled with the worst Criminals, sent from hence, and as yet nothing but Severity has been attempted to effect their reformation. The same observations apply to Moreton Bay but I do not press an appointment there so strongly . . .[13]

This was not the first time an appeal had been made for a chaplain to be sent to the Island. In 1829 the Anglican Archdeacon of Sydney had written, in a letter to Governor Darling:

> The penal settlement of Norfolk Island . . . demands attention. There are not only troops and their children, but upwards of 200 convicts of the most depraved habits, most of whom have been without spiritual assistance . . . since the establishment in 1825 . . .[14]

There was, it seems, a shortage of suitable clerics who could be sent by the Home Governments to Penal Settlements, and a shortage of clerics who were willing to work in such perilous places, for often a minister was engaged to go to New South Wales and then, as his time of arrival came—and passed—it was revealed that he had not left and was not indeed intending to leave, his homeland. So for Norfolk Island, it was to be the Lesson reading and the Prayers of Colonel Morisset.

The daily list of prisoners brought on charges of one kind or another, grew daily, and the list of punishments grew longer. The same names were inscribed on the punishment lists, the number of lashes increasing with the frequency of punishment, from 10 lashes to 25, from 25 to 50 and more in some cases. Morisset must have regretted the lack of a treadmill which would have speedily brought a recalcitrant convict into submission. These defiant ones remained quite untouched by the Sunday Prayers or the infliction of the lash; it was true, as Governor Darling had written, that 'nothing but

Severity has been attempted, to effect their reformation', and severity of the kind they were undergoing was unavailing as a cure. In other circumstances or in other walks of life, many of these men might have achieved great things in the new colony, their daring and total disregard of consequences were the essence of which explorers and soldiers were made; as it was, they were chained and in the powerful grip of the Law. Defiance was their only weapon, and defiance of Morisset was met with the lash, or worse.

In his diary for 18 November 1829, Aaron Price wrote:

> The Commandant has power to visit crimes with 300 lashes and could sentence to any time he thinks proper, in cells on bread and water. Prisoner being visited by the surgeon, Morisset could sentence him to gaol in heavy irons or add 3 years to his original Colonial sentence. All were at different times inflicted.[15]

Revolt was in the air and men met cruelty with cruelty. A chain-gang returning from the day's labour turned on their Overseer as they reached the gates of the gaol, and, beating him with picks and shovels, left him for dead. Then they gleefully knocked off each other's irons and took the keys from the Overseer's body. With the keys they opened all the cells and called out the rest of the prisoners, preparatory to making a 'rush' on the Stores and the Magazine. The Overseer, however, was not dead. He managed to crawl to the military barracks and alert the garrison. Captain Charles Sturt (of later fame as an explorer of the Australian hinterland) was Officer Commanding. He immediately ordered all the exits from the gaol to be locked, and detailed men to guard the arsenal, the landing-place and the gaol. By this time it was dark, and the prisoners inside the gaol decided to wait until morning, when they would spring on the guard who was to escort the gaol-gang to work. In the morning, when the 'rush' did come, the men found themselves locked in, the guards well prepared and ready to fire. They gave themselves up and were put in close confinement after being heavily ironed. One convict shouted to Captain Sturt that he would give the names of the ringleaders to him or any other officer who would stand close under the barred window of the barrack dormitory so the men involved would not hear. Sturt crossed the gaol-yard to the window, and was promptly sloshed with the contents of a tub of water— clean, dirty, or urine, was not defined—and soaked through. In a fury he rushed up the stairs where the seventy men were confined, and with the help of the gaoler and turnkey, he had them all flogged.[16]

Not long afterwards, Captain Sturt's tour of duty on Norfolk Island finished. He could have been relieved to go, news travels fast, even from a small island. It was about this time that Mr Hall, Editor of the *Sydney Monitor*, a fearless, sometimes unscrupulous champion of the underdog in the colony, wrote to Lord Goderich, Principal Secretary of State for the Colonies, regarding affairs on Norfolk Island. The letter is today in the Mitchell Library. Scribbled on the margin is written 'Is this from Mr Hall?' and marked 'No Answer'.

My Lord,

I beg to call your Lordship's attention to the trial of John McDonald and Francis Mullins, two Convicts, for an attempt to murder at Norfolk Island, under peculiar circumstances, a fellow prisoner . . . In my Journal of the following dates . . . I gave details of the various severities practised towards the Convicts . . . My Lord, I did expect the British Government would, on the bare recital of such atrocities . . . have directed enquiry! But I have been disappointed. I am however, still prepared to prove the whole of the allegations . . . in those Journals provided the eye-witnesses should not be dead . . . I trust, my Lord . . . it is not because men have been twice convicted and are distant from home half the circumference of the Globe, that they are to be made the prey of hunger and nakedness at the caprice of monsters in human form . . . and cut to pieces by the scourge . . . and to have no redress or the least enquiry made into their suffering? If the wretches at Norfolk Island . . . were fiends instead of men they could not have been worse treated, there is no parallel to the cruelties practised on them . . . I beg to observe, my Lord . . . that in the report of Mr Commissioner Bigge . . . that he examined the backs of the prisoners at Newcastle and found them furrowed and knotted in consequence of severe scourging. That scourging was inflicted by Colonel Morisset the present Commandant at Norfolk Island . . . this officer . . . of all officers who was ever employed to take charge of a settlement (where power unlimited and irresponsible is committed to him) is . . . one of the most improper that could have been selected by H.M. Government . . .[17]

Mr Hall was to have support for his views on the severity of punishment in the penal out-stations such as Norfolk Island, though it was indirectly given. Sir Francis Forbes, Chief Justice of New South Wales, told the Committee of the House of Commons, when he was in England shortly after the time Mr Hall's letter was sent, '. . . the experience furnished by these Penal Settlements, including Norfolk Island, has proved that transportation is capable of being carried to an extent of suffering such as to render death desirable, and induce many prisoners to seek it under most appalling aspects.'[18] He said he had known of many cases where prisoners on Norfolk Island had committed Capital crimes for which the penalty was Death, for the mere purpose of being sent to Sydney for trial, and the cause of their desiring to be sent was to avoid the state of endurance under which they lived on the Island. He also declared that if he were asked, he would not hesitate to choose death, under any form it could be presented to him, rather than endure the life of a convict at the Island. Another Judge, Sir Roger Therry, wrote in his *Reminiscences* of a party of witnesses brought from Norfolk Island to give evidence in a trial of another convict:

Their sunken glazed eyes, deadly pale faces, hollow fleshless cheeks and once manly limbs shrivelled and withered up as if by premature old age, created horror among those in court. There was not one of the six who had not undergone from time to time, a thousand lashes each and more. They looked less like human beings than the shadows of gnomes who had risen from their sepulchral abode. What man was or ever could be reclaimed under such a system as this?[19]

In June 1831, in a letter to Governor Darling which he requested should be sent on to Lord Goderich, Secretary of State for the Colonies, Morisset asked to be moved from Norfolk Island and be appointed to a Civil situation in New South Wales. The letter is not available in the Records, but in Darling's despatch of 26 August 1831 he states:

> I have the honor to transmit to your Lordship, at the desire of Lieut-Col. Morisset, the accompanying letter . . . requesting that he may be placed in some Civil Situation in this Colony, finding that the expectations, which he had formed on soliciting the appointment which he holds at Norfolk Island, have been totally disappointed. It is my duty to State, though I do not presume to offer any recommendation to your Lordship, that Lt. Col. Morisset is a very Zealous Officer, whose duties for some time past have been of a most arduous nature. The Conduct of the Prisoners has of late been outrageous in the extreme, having repeatedly avowed . . . to Murder every one employed at the Settlement, and it is only by the utmost vigilance that they have been prevented accomplishing their object . . . I have lately increased the Garrison from 80 to 120 rank and file, and have appointed additional Constables and overseers . . . The Prisoners at Norfolk Island . . . 554 in number, are Men of the most desperate Character. They are totally regardless of all consequences, and Commit Crimes, as was lately declared in the Supreme Court, with a view to their being brought to Sydney for trial and thus have an opportunity to make their escape . . .[20]

In Lord Goderich's reply received the following February, there was no comfort for Morisset — no change could be contemplated:

> . . . however much I may regret the disappointment of any expectations entertained by Col. Morisset in regard to the appointment he now fills, I have no means at present of complying with his request . . . Col. Morisset should be reminded that it was at his own solicitations that he was appointed to his present command, and convicts of the descriptions of those placed at Norfolk Island, was he chief ground for accepting his services as Commandant . . .[21]

This was indeed cold comfort for the now diminished Lieutenant-Governor of Norfolk Island.

It was about this time that Morisset ordered the cutting down of all orange trees on the island. Since the beginning of the First Settlement when King had planted seeds from the orange trees of Rio de Janeiro, the fruit had flourished there. Groves of them grew in the Governor's garden at Orange Vale and wherever else they had been allowed to grow. Morisset, it is said, maintained oranges were too great a luxury to be allowed the convicts, who were able to pick and eat them during the time they should be at hard labour, and in addition, absconders would be denied such fruit for, once lopped, the trees would not regenerate themselves. It seems a petty gesture, and one which was bound to increase the hate and simmering revolt, but there is little indication of Morisset's state of health at this time. He was then in his early fifties, clearly frustrated that his system of discipline brought, not orderliness but a continuing atmosphere of defiance and fear, fear which ran like a fire through the whole population. Morisset, like Foveaux, seems to have suffered from some undetermined illness during his term of office on Norfolk Island; whether the illness was a form of asthma as has been suggested, or a purely nervous disorder, has not been recorded. It is tempting to conclude that the atmosphere of hate directed towards them from many of the convicts under their charge, combined with the frustrations that beset them daily, was the prime reason for their ill-health. Neither Foveaux nor Morisset had any system of control over the convicts but the one of severity, yet it seems that to 'beat the Devil out' was the surest way to beat the Devil *in*.

Of Morisset's home life on the Island, little is known. Emily Morisset could have had little time to ponder the behaviour of the men confined in gaol only a few hundred metres from Government House, and little contact with them otherwise. She had brought her own female servant with her, thus obviating the need for a personal servant from the better-behaved convicts who were allowed to work as officers' servants. There were other women for her to meet, wives of the civil or military officers; their children would play together on the small, sandy-beached bay close by Government House; and it is most likely from Morisset's time that the bay was given the name Emily Bay, by which it is still known today. The Morisset family grew yearly, Emily had five children at the time she left Norfolk Island in 1834.

In June 1830 Mr Allan Cunningham, a botanist, arrived on the Island to study and record the native plant life. Afterwards he wrote a small pamphlet *Flora of Norfolk Island*, which is today a very rare item of Australiana.[22] Cunningham found himself with little to do once he had finished his work on Norfolk, and was advised to go to Philip Island where different species of plants might be found. Aaron Price's diary has a small item on this: 'Mr Cunningham proceeded to Philip Island in a whale boat, taking an overseer and two men. Landed. Boat returned to Settlement. The same night 11 prisoners escaped from camp'.

Cunningham had planned to spend two or three days on Philip Island, and return to Sydney when the Government vessel arrived with Stores, but his plans were rudely interrupted before his excursion really got under way. His visit to Philip Island was a heaven-sent chance for an escape. When the whale boat returned to the Settlement it was already dark, and for the men who were always on the look-out for a 'chance', it was a simple matter to let their mates know an escape was possible, if indeed it had not been planned earlier. By dawn the next morning the escapees had rowed across to Philip Island, where they awakened Cunningham with the news that there had been a mutiny on Norfolk Island and the Commandant and garrison were captured. They seized his belongings, his watch, telescope, gun, pistols, clothing, bedding, food and water, and pulled down his tent to use as a sail; some of the convicts piled their loot into the whale boat while three of them guarded Cunningham and his two servants. When they had cleared his camp of everything useful to them they set off on their voyage to freedom, well provided with enough supplies to keep them until they reached land, which would in all probability be New Zealand or New Caledonia. Within hours of their departure, a boat arrived from the settlement in search of the runaways, but found no trace except the distraught Cunningham and his two men. The runaways were never found.

Not long after Cunningham's disastrous visit to Philip Island, Aaron Price writes: 'September 25th. . . . three men, John Cook, Wm. Bubb, and James Murphy killed Adam Oliver their overseer . . . Cook knocked him down, the others beat him with spades till dead. It was the wrong overseer. Wm. Jacuerman was intended but was working elsewhere.[23] Violence was always in the air at this time. An atmosphere of insuppressible violence pervaded the gaol, and violence was met with violence—the floggings increased to match the crimes and as the lashings increased, so did the crimes. Planning crime was easy. In the new prison barracks, completed in 1830, the hammocks were slung in tiers, each hammock no more than twenty inches (50 centimetres) from the next, and up to 120 men were placed in a dormitory. Even the weather became violent. On 29 May 1832 Price wrote in his diary:

> . . . about 5 p.m. a violent shock resembling an earthquake was felt on
> the Island. Several prisoners thrown down. Many of the officers said
> the hills shook so violently they expected them to be thrown down
> also. Military barracks shaken, men took refuge outside. A huge mass
> of rock at Dry Quarry was observed to move. Bells at Government
> House rang for several minutes, and inmates ran for safety. Mrs
> Morisset fainted at the door. The breakfast bell at the prison rang
> several times, six or seven minutes, and everyone on the Island
> became uneasy for their safety.[24]

It was in June 1833 that Morisset, when reporting two murders on Norfolk Island, suggested the men should be tried on the Island instead of being sent to Sydney. The Attorney-General concurred with the suggestion and in August when a further murder was reported the Governor, Sir Richard

Bourke, gave orders for a vessel to be readied to take a Judge of the Supreme Court to conduct the trial.

On 3 September Judge Dowling and five officers embarked on the *Esther* of 300 tons, for Norfolk Island. Judge Dowling's son, Vincent, accompanied him, as did the Crown Prosecutor, a Court crier, and a hangman. Mr Plaistowe, an Attorney, was sent at Government's expense, as Counsel for the prisoners.[25] There were several cases for trial: one for murder; one for robbery and assault, and stealing a boat; and one for stealing wearing apparel. Three prisoners were executed on 23 September, for murder; six others sentenced to death for stealing a boat were recommended for mercy—as no lives had been lost their execution was delayed until the Governor's pleasure should be known; and Patrick Gogarty who had stolen the wearing apparel was sentenced to work in irons for three years from the expiration of his secondary sentence which he was then serving. 'I have reason to believe that this unusual expedition . . . has been attended with the desired effect, and I have no doubt that it will tend to keep down the lawless spirit of insubordination which has so frequently disturbed the quiet of the island', said Judge Dowling on his return to Sydney.[26] This was the first Criminal Court held on Norfolk Island. There was only one other while the Island was under the rule of the New South Wales Government—it was held by Mr Justice Burton in 1834, when 134 capital charges were heard. At this trial, one of the witnesses was John Knatchbull alias John Fitch, Labourer, who had been on Norfolk Island for two years of his seven-year sentence for forgery, an additional sentence to his original sentence of fourteen years for pickpocketing. In 1834 he was an informer-witness. Ten years later he was to meet Judge Burton again, this time, not as a witness, but from the dock.

The 1834 trial was for the abortive mutiny which had taken place on 15 January that year, resulting in nine deaths and many wounded, and which is described in the despatch sent by the Governor, Sir Richard Bourke to the Right Hon. T. Spring Rice in January 1835, but there is a more detailed and subjective one in the autobiography written by John Knatchbull in 1844.[27] It was this mutiny which ended Morisset's period of office as Commandant of Norfolk Island and brought Captain Foster Fyans to the fore as Acting-Commandant. This, too, is fully described in Knatchbull's story.

John Knatchbull

14

JOHN KNATCHBULL WAS 40 YEARS OLD WHEN HE ARRIVED ON NORFOLK ISLAND TO SERVE A SEVEN-YEAR SENTENCE FOR FORGERY, IN 1832. HE was already serving a fourteen-year sentence for pickpocketing, having been transported in 1824 despite his protestations of innocence. The crimes were not unusual for those times, but the fact of Knatchbull being the son of an English baronet was.

Sir Edward Knatchbull had twenty children by his three wives; John Knatchbull was the third son, by Frances, his second wife. John was sent to Winchester School and in 1804 he entered the navy as a volunteer, passing his examination as Lieutenant in 1810. He was commissioned to his own ship as commander in 1813 and saw action in several sea-battles.[1] In 1815 he was retired on full pay, a usual event when men-of-war were not urgently required, and it was from that time that his troubles began. His auto-biography, written in the death-cell at Darlinghurst Gaol in 1844, and inserted in full in Professor Colin Roderick's biography of Knatchbull, gives the details of his fall from grace and characteristically places most of the blame on everyone but himself.[2] This was his attitude throughout his life; all his troubles were of others' making, his own actions and intentions being blameless.

The years between being retired on half pay in 1818 and being arraigned as a pickpocket are neatly side-stepped in his autobiography, but he makes it clear that the whole thing was a dastardly plot on the part of his elder half-brother, heir to the baronetcy. Pickpocketing merited the death sentence, but the Judge, who knew Knatchbull's family, gave him a fourteen-year trans-portation to New South Wales.[3]

In the colony, where he arrived in April 1825, he made good after his fashion, earning a ticket-of-leave after four years for having captured eight 'runaways', during his time at Bathurst where he was employed at the Government establishment. His detractors maintained that his captures were plotted beforehand, Knatchbull having given the runaways directions on the best road to take and once the break was made, setting off in pursuit to

K

make the recapture.[4] There is no proof of this and any convict who swore it was the truth would not have been believed and would most probably have earned himself a further two dozen lashes.

But money, or the lack of it, bedevilled Knatchbull as it had done before. On 22 February 1832 he was indicted for forging a signature on an order for the payment of money to a Matthew Long or bearer. The amount was for £6 10s and, unfortunately for Knatchbull, the signature of James Dowling which he was alleged to have forged, was that of Mr Justice James Dowling of the Supreme Court. He was found guilty and sentenced to death, but respited to Norfolk Island for seven years. His ticket-of-leave was cancelled, he was put in double irons, and taken to the prison hulk *Phoenix* to await his second transportation. 'Sentenced to transportation to a penal settlement where the height of tyranny was carried on by Colonel Morisset. Was it not enough to harrow up the soul of a man that had never done wrong?' is the plaintive cry in Knatchbull's autobiography.[5]

He had several months of waiting before he arrived at the Island, however, months of complaints and accusations against various of his fellows, but chiefly against the Superintendent of the hulk, Thomas Makeig who in turn brought a list of charges against Knatchbull. Yet throughout those months he managed to avoid a flogging or any punishment worse than confinement in irons.

On 7 October he, with seventy other prisoners and a detachment of the 4th Regiment (King's Own), set sail for Norfolk Island. No sooner was the vessel afloat than rumours of a plot to poison the soldiers and such of the prisoners who weren't 'with them', was uncovered or betrayed by one of the prisoners. Knatchbull was the reputed leader, which he strenuously denied. The poison was found, the ringleaders hoisted on deck and chained to the main-stay where they were left for the rest of the voyage, says Knatchbull. On arrival at Norfolk Island he, with the others, was searched:

> On the beach without the least regard to any kind of delicacy . . . we
> were ordered to strip stark naked, our hair cut close off, and then
> what place had we for concealment of any weapon? But this state of
> nudity did not suffice their brutal propensities. A brute named Shaw
> thrust his finger up a part I need not name of many. Oh what a sight
> for a man who had not been brought up to such disgusting scenes . . .[6]

The poison-powder which the crew had taken from the prisoners during the voyage was handed to the two surgeons of the settlement. They tried it on a rabbit and a fowl both of which died within hours. But a cat, the next victim, though violently ill did not die then, and the powder was sent back to Sydney for analysis, and declared 'insufficient as evidence of intent to murder'. The Governor, Sir Richard Bourke, said he did not think it expedient to bring the men to Sydney to be tried for a mere misdemeanour and had therefore decided to overlook the offence.

In 1832 there were about 700 convicts on the Island, some at Longridge, and a few (the better behaved) in huts at various points, working as shepherds, gardeners, bullock-tenders or stockmen, but the majority at the Kingston settlement. Continual attempts were made to escape but most ended in failure; the standard punishment was 300 lashes apiece and work in heavy irons. Knatchbull was not in on any of these. For him, if escape was to be contemplated, it would be on a grand scale, the seizure of a ship maybe, which he would sail to freedom, and take with him those who were game to follow him as leader. Then, on the morning of 15 January 1834 came the Island-wide mutiny and the end of Morisset as Commandant. Rumours had been rife for some time, the military had remained ready night and day for a month, yet when the anticipated time arrived they were taken by surprise. It had all the overtones of a planned rising, and is fully detailed in the Report sent to London by Governor Bourke:

In the morning of that day [15 January] between 5 and 6 o'clock a rush was made on the guard which then received over as usual the Gaol Gang, consisting of about 30 convicts, generally of the worst character, to be escorted to work. About an equal number, under false pretences of ill-health had before this been taken to the hospital behind the gaol . . . but breaking out of the lock-up . . . they had overpowered and confined the attendants and some of the patients. Having knocked off each other's irons and armed themselves with such implements as the hospital afforded, and being joined by other convicts from the sawpits and neighbouring places, they rushed on the guard at the moment of their taking in charge the gaol gang . . . and a scuffle ensued in which the guard were for a time nearly overpowered. This scuffle lasted some time, when the soldiers obtaining free use of their firearms and being reinforced from the Barracks, dispersed the convicts, killing two and wounding eleven of whom seven died of wounds. In the meantime a party of convicts at Longridge . . . had . . . broken into the toolhouse, and armed with implements found there were running to join their confederates. They arrived in time only to increase the number of fugitives scattered before the fire of the military, who captured great numbers of both . . . parties. 162 convicts were charged as being more or less implicated . . . The Attorney General regarded the evidence warranting the trial of 55 . . . The trials commenced on 10th July when 29 were capitally convicted . . . 13 of the criminals were ordered for execution, the sentence of the remainder being commuted for various terms of additional servitude on the Island. The executions took place on the 22nd and 23rd September in the presence of the other convicts on the Settlement . . .[7]

That is the account as recorded in the official documents; there are others written from personal, involved viewpoints, including Knatchbull's account in his autobiography when he was under sentence of death himself, ten years later: 'I was in the lime shed before breakfast . . . When a firing of musketry was heard in the direction of the gaol . . . It was the custom for all working gangs to go to work before the gaol gang . . .', and he goes on to say that these men of the gaol-gang were 'the first projectors of the plan' though it had all the marks of having been planned like a military manoeuvre by someone with experience. 'Upon the commencement of firing', Knatchbull says, 'the overseer . . . came to me where I was breaking stones and said "What had I best do?" . . . I advised him to fall his men in and take them to the barracks . . . We were the first gang in.'[8]

It was the Acting-Commandant, Foster Fyans (Morisset was indisposed at the time), who effectively put down the revolt. When the noise from the shots and yells of soldiers and convicts aroused him some time before six he seized his arms, called out his men and, half-dressed though they were, brought them on the run just in time to fire into the rabble of Longridge men pouring over the hill to join their mates from the gaol. They had been told to listen for the first shot, rush to the toolsheds, grab any tool or weapon they could find and race down to the settlement. This they did, yelling 'Death or Liberty!' as they came, to be met by a line of soldiers armed with muskets or bayonets which they used to good effect, killing some, wounding others, while the rest of the men turned and fled into the forest.[9] The unequal fight was soon over, the toll seven dead and a number wounded, many of them of bayonet wounds. The dead were really the better off, for the punishments facing the survivors were fearful. Foster Fyans had his own way of dealing with men whose insurrection had threatened his own life. Knatchbull wrote:

> . . . Daily he would have a ward at a time paraded before him in the
> barrack yard with the triangles rigged and some six or seven floggers
> with a bag full of 'cats' attending him, when, without rhyme or reason
> he would call anyone that his eye met out and give him a hundred.
> One man, because he would not cry out, he ordered the flogger where
> to strike him, saying 'Now a little higher! A little lower! That's the
> place; now he feels it!' and such brutal language until the man was
> flogged from the back of his neck to the calf of his legs and upon the
> calves of his legs, until the blood ran in streams from him . . . Would
> it not have been better to have shot the man at once?[10]

At times during this horrific period, the men were flogged by candle-light, as Fyans himself says in his own autobiography written when he was an old man.

That Knatchbull was involved is clear; several informers claimed that he had planned it and was to command the ship in which the prisoners were to make their escape after killing all the officers: 'he [Knatchbull] would put the Colonel and Captain Fyans to a lingering death, and take the vessels or boats to any part of the world afterwards', said John Toms, a convict.[11] Jackson, another informer, when asked if Knatchbull had had any part in the mutiny, said, 'Certainly. He was to have commanded the Island until the arrival of a vessel, when he was to proceed on board, take her, and convey the prisoners off the Island'—a statement which drove Fyans into a fury. Fyans's fury sprang from the rebuke he had been given by Judge Dowling, for allowing Knatchbull to turn informer, before he had been called into the dock with other prisoners:

Most improperly, Sir, did you act as a magistrate, in accepting a confession from Knatchbull; neither should any deposition have been taken from him. Throughout the trials his name has been connected in every case he was the chief of the mutineers, the man you should have named first in the Calendar. You saved his life, or prolonged it. He never can do good.[12]

Prophetic words which proved true when, in January 1844, Knatchbull faced Judge Burton, this time from the dock.

Knatchbull was put in a cell, ringbolted to the floor, with a 48 lb (22 kg) iron fastened round his one good leg. At this time he was on crutches because he had suffered a slight stroke, which paralysed his left leg for a time, the previous year.

The following depositions of prisoners after the Mutiny of 15 January 1834 are of interest:

Sworn statement of Jeremiah Leary. February 15th 1834.

On 27th October 1833 Jeremiah Leary was told by three prisoners that 250 men were going to take the Island on Slop day. [This was the day when prisoners were issued with a certain amount of new clothing, which took place in January and June.] They were going to 'rush' the Guard, he was asked . . . if he would be one and they wanted to swear him in. I told Price [Aaron Price, then a police runner] that I wanted to see the Commandant, on the next morning Mr Macleod came to him at Longridge and then he gave the information to him. Knatchbull was to be Captain of the large Launch, Pat Glenny was to be Commandant—Butler to have Captn Fyans situation . . . Walter Burke was to be Superintendent of Convicts, Archd. McFarlane was to be Superintendent of Agriculture, Thomas Taylor was to be Commandant's Clerk. The Colonel (Morisset) was to be cut up into four pieces and to be divided about the Island, and the same to be done to Captain Fyans. Price and Ledgwick were to be burned alive, and all the rest that had a stain on their characters to be served the same. The men that had fought the best were to have the Women and do just as they liked with them— . . . When the Signal was given they armed themselves with Pitchforks, Hoes, and many other weapon they came across and when they had armed themselves they shouted out 'Death or Glory'. . . . I took particular notice of the men and directly afterwards ran to Orange Vale to alarm Ledgwick and Price . . . The Ringleaders were to go into the Garrison and live there, and if the Colonel and Captain did not promise them he would put up the right signal—to the vessel approaching the Island—they would kill him immediately, and if he did tell them they would spare his life till the Ship came, and then before they left the island they would put them to the most cruel death that a human being could possibly be put to, and they were to burn all the buildings on the Settlement. All the Gaol Gang were to be in the Mutiny.—52 men.

[This statement was signed by] Jeremiah Leary, X, His Mark. [and checked later by] Foster Fyans, J.P. Capt. 4th Regt. (the Kings Own).[13]

A second sworn statement was from John Toms.

. . . deponent asked them how many men were to be in it (meaning prisoners) they said the best part of the Gaol Gang and about 50 LongRidgers, with what tools they could procure at LongRidge . . . that about 30 or 40 men were to go to the Hospital on Monday morning for the express purpose of joining the Respite Gang who were jointly to attack the Guard in rere and the Gaol Gang in front, that many more prisoners were to come to their assistance from the Camp; . . . that on Tuesday the 14th ult the Respite Gang went to the Quarry to cart stones . . . that on Tuesday night Jno. Butler, Mich. Anderson, McCulloch, Robt. Knox, Jno. Haydon and Pat. Glenny came to him in his hammock and told him that everything was ready for attacking the Guard on the following morning . . . that they were to appoint an overseer, who was to conduct the Sham sick as far as the Saw-pits for attacking the Guard which took over accordingly on Wednesday morning.

[Toms then gives a list of names of men who attacked the Guard in the rear, and the names of 'such who ran away as soon as they came as far as the Gaol corner'] . . . that Patrick Glenny had a Soldier under him on the ground, and forcing his Musket from him, that Jno. Butler strove to force a Musket and Bayonet from a Soldier, who shot Butler and that Butler ran away wounded, that Freshwater was stabbed in the mouth, that Burns received a blow in the arm with the Butt end of a Musket . . . that deponent saw James Brady armed with a poker, or a piece of Iron . . . who made a blow at a Soldier with the same . . . that on Friday the 12th January Jno. Fitch or Knatchbull was sitting down in the Camp conversing with Jno. Jackson, Geo. Wright and Wm. Smith on the plot in contemplation which was to take place the following morning. Fitch said he was sorry he was lame, for in consequence he could not be at the engagement, but if they succeeded in taking the Settlement he would take it upon himself to conduct the first vessel or Boats, to any part of the world they thought proper . . . and that if the Ringleader would leave everything to him, he would put Colonel Morisset and Captain Fyans to a lingering death if they did not deliver up the Signal to them: but under any circumstances Captain Fyans should be put to death in consequence of what he said to them at the Church Parade on Sunday morning prior to the 12th, with which they felt much aggrieved; there is Aaron Price also, who has been the cause of hindering many a man from making his escape from the island and it was high time to stop him, so he would hinder no other man. Other men — said that if they succeeded in capturing the Island, they would march the Soldiers into the Commissariat under-ground cellar where they were to remain in heavy irons and should be fed on Corn as they had been . . . On Tuesday evening Butler came to deponent and told him that the men were all ready to attack the Gaol Guard on the following morning . . . John Toms signed his deposition himself, in a very legible hand.][14]

Throughout the days of the uprising Morisset had been confined to bed in Government House and Foster Fyans was Acting-Commandant. The 162 convicts seized were heavily ironed and put in cells. At various times they had to undergo Fyans's 'discipline', which consisted in making them strip, then dress themselves within seconds, then do exercises, then strip, dress, exercise and continue without pause; any who were slow or fumbling received a lashing or a prod with a bayonet. Talking in cells was also summarily punished. Once, when eight men were found to have cut almost through their irons, they were brought out and given a hundred each with the new 'cats' Fyans had requested from Headquarters.[15] At this time a sad event occurred, one which has not reached the history books; it concerns Emily Morisset's brother. It is reported in Aaron Price's diary for March 22nd:

D. A. C. G. Vaux, Mrs Morisset's brother in charge of Commissary Stores went fishing with Lt Fortescue and 1 prisoner. Being venturesome they proceeded to a rock which seemed safe. The prisoner cautioned them, the sea rose suddenly over the rock. Vaux was washed away and seen struggling for some time then turned and went down as though seized by a shark. Prisoner sprang on the rock and secured Lt. Fortescue. Vaux's three dogs . . . swam after him and were also swept away. Morisset was by this time off the Island. Fyans told Mrs Morisset who was then ill for several weeks.[16]

Poor Emily. Alone, perhaps afraid, and now bereft and ill herself. In mid-April she, with her five children, left Norfolk Island on the *Governor Phillip*, and five days later, the schooner *Isabella* brought Major Anderson of the 50th Regiment to take over the command.

At Sydney, Morisset had applied for leave of absence owing to the state of his health, a request which the Governor granted. In his despatch to the Colonial Secretary he wrote:

> Sir, I have the honour to inform you that upon application from Lt. Col. Morisset Commandant of Norfolk Island, representing his very dangerous state of health and the necessity of his immediate removal from the Island, I have given him one year's leave of absence from the 20th February last, which period he proposes to pass in this Colony, taking the benefit of medical assistance he can procure near Sydney.[17]

To this the Earl of Aberdeen, Secretary of State for the Colonies replied, with some asperity:

> . . . I regret that I cannot conclude this despatch without observing upon the unusual indulgence which you have extended to Col. Morisset in respect to his leave of absence . . . I cannot perceive any circumstances in his case which justified the extensive leave . . . you granted him, a leave which only the necessity of a voyage to Europe . . . for the recovery of his health would have been warranted . . . more particularly that it appears from the letter Col. Morisset addressed to this Department on 8th January 1834 that it was his intention to retire altogether from his situation at Norfolk Island, and that circumstances connected with his domestic concerns rather than the alarming state of his health, were his chief motives for such a step . . .[18]

On the mainland, Morisset attended one or more sales of cattle and horses, and in 1835 bought himself a fine estate near Bathurst.[19] Luck was not with him, however, for the money crisis which swept New South Wales around that time affected his financial position sufficiently for him to accept the post of Police Magistrate at Bathurst at a salary of £300 a year. He seems never to have been a financial wizard, for his savings were also lost in the failure of the Bank of Australia. With a family of ten children, five sons and five daughters, life was not the easiest for Emily.

After Morisset's death in August 1852, she petitioned Governor Fitzroy, telling him of her impoverished circumstances and asking if it was possible, that she be granted a pension. Emily died in 1892, and is buried at St. Thomas's, in North Sydney. Morisset is buried in Kelso churchyard.

'Potato Joe' Anderson and Major Thomas Bunbury

15

MAJOR JOSEPH ANDERSON WAS AN IMPRESSIVE-LOOKING MAN WITH PIERCING, DARK EYES, BRISTLING BEARD AND MOUSTACHE, A COMmanding air and was, he said, the shortest of twelve brothers, at six feet two (188 centimetres). He was born 1 July 1790 in Keoldale, Sutherland, Scotland, and made the Army his career, entering as ensign when 15 years old. He was a Major in the 50th Regiment when he arrived at Sydney, from where he was sent, almost at once, to Norfolk Island as Commandant in 1834.[1]

Opinions differ regarding his administration there from 1834 to 1839. John Knatchbull, who had cause to know him well, writes of him: '. . . a dark, morose evil-minded looking man . . . who, under the cloak of religion shewed his duplicity, villainous conduct and black heart'.[2] The Reverend Thomas Atkins, an Independent minister, who resigned as chaplain after a bitter dispute with Anderson on Norfolk Island, wrote; 'He could fawn and threaten, embrace as a brother and hate as a fiend',[3] while Father Ullathorne, who visited the Island in 1834 to bring spiritual comfort to the wretched men about to be executed for the January 1834 mutiny, said he was 'a man whose minute personal knowledge of the desperate men under his charge, and the discrimination with which he encourages the well-disposed while he strikes terror into the obstinate, has been attended with the most salutary consequences'.[4]

Anderson was a rigid disciplinarian and had the iron will to enforce his discipline, but he seems singularly short on humanity in some instances. He was receptive to 'informers' among the prisoners, Ullathorne notes, in the autobiography he wrote many years later '. . . I was walking with the Commandant in a wood; he was conversing with secret spies he had among the convicts, when suddenly a shot was heard from a distance . . .'. The shot, however, was not a signal for further revolt, but fired at a bird by a newly-arrived young officer, who received a good dressing-down from Anderson.

Like every newcomer, excepting the prisoners, Major Anderson considered

Norfolk Island a beautiful place, 'the most beautiful Island in the Pacific if not the world', and the Island served him well during his five years in command. He writes:

> The Island abounds in valleys . . . and in each of these is a stream of most pure crystal water. Lemons and citrus of the very best kind grow here . . . and at one time oranges were in abundance but my predecessor had all the trees destroyed as affording too great a luxury to the prisoners. By convict labour excellent roads have been made everywhere. The climate is the best in the world, never too hot or too cold . . . There were many hundreds of cattle and thousands of sheep . . . so all the free population had fresh meat daily and the officers were allowed to buy as much more as they wished, and flour also at a nominal price never exceeding twopence a pound . . . My garden at Orange Vale was a splendid one abounding with everything one could desire. We made about 400 lb of the best coffee annually . . . my pigs and poultry were kept near Government House, together with dozens of turkeys, geese, guinea-fowls and ducks. All our stock was fed on the refuse from the prisoners' breakfasts and from damaged corn, so we incurred no expense from such numbers. We made the best bacon that ever was known but could not succeed in making hams . . . there was something in the air which caused them to decay . . . We were allowed to have our boots and clothing made for us. The woods of the Island were very beautiful and supplied material for handsome furniture of every kind.
>
> All these advantages I had as Commandant . . . the public dairy was near my house and every officer, soldier and free person on the Island got a daily allowance of milk and butter. With all these advantages we lived most comfortably and almost for nothing.[5]

The convicts, 500 yards (450 metres) to the west of Government House, ate the food that was good refuse for the pigs and poultry; and the fifty-five men reefed to a cable-chain in the gaol, waited in their low-ceilinged cells for the day of trial. They were confined from the time of the mutiny in mid-January, to the beginning of July, when H.M.S. *Alligator* brought Judge Burton and the Crown Solicitor to conduct the trials, and carpenters were set to work to construct a room, attached to the prisoners' barracks, that would be used as the court-house.[6]

On 11 July the trials began. Day after day for the next two weeks the men were brought in one by one to give their testimony. Emaciated, grey-faced, shuffling as they came chained hand and foot, they stood before the Judge, as evidence was given against them, and informers' statements read. They were allowed to speak in their own defence, and Mr Plaistowe, their Counsel, added his plea, but the end was a foregone conclusion.

Judge Burton, humane after his fashion, and a man of deep religious conviction said of the prisoners as they shuffled in turn before him: 'The picture presented on that occasion was a Cage full of Unclean Birds, full of crime against God and man, murders and blasphemies and all uncleanness . . .' He deplored the fact that many of the convicts were 'Evil men with men more evil . . . who appear to gather no heartening effect from the beauties of Creation around them, but to make a hell of what might be a Heaven . . .' But unceasing hard labour was not very conducive to the heartening of man, even in a Heaven. After sentence was passed, with thirteen men having been sentenced to Death, one of them said:

> Sentence has been passed upon us before, and we thought we should
> have been executed, and prepared to die, and wish we had been
> executed then. It was no mercy to send us to this place. I do not ask
> life. I do not want to be spared on condition of remaining here, life is
> not worth having on such terms.[7]

In all Judge Burton passed sentence of death on twenty-nine of the men brought before him, and he had the power to order the sentence carried out before he left Norfolk Island. But in a last speech from the dock, one prisoner burst into an impassioned plea, not for clemency, but for a chance to see a priest. 'Your Honor, I have committed many crimes for which I ought to die,' he pleaded, 'but do not send me out of the world without my seeing my Priest.' His voice was not above a hoarse whisper, his face as grey and drawn as that of an old man, though he was not more than 30 years old. 'To appeals like these, the human heart could not be insensible,'[8] said Judge Burton, and after conferring with Major Anderson—whose responsibility the safety of the prisoners was, even though they be kept safe for the hangman only—he left for Sydney. Upon his arrival there he decided to lay the cases of all twenty-nine men before the Governor.

For two more months the convicted men festered in their cells. Knatchbull, who had had a narrow escape from the death sentence, an escape owed solely to his having turned informer, kept out of the limelight. Anderson, however, watched him closely, convinced that of all the prisoners, he was one who should most certainly have stood trial.

The prisoner's plea for his priest points to the degree of callousness and inertia on the part of the authorities. Each Commandant in turn, strict disciplinarian or lash-happy sadist, had asked, even pleaded, for a chaplain and a priest to be sent to Norfolk Island; but from the beginning of the Second Settlement in 1825, no chaplain had been found willing to take on the task, and the convicts in ever-growing numbers were left to their own devices. It could be argued that a Churchman would not have been heeded in such a 'Cage full of Unclean Birds', but this can be countered by letters written to parents and families in England at this time. Two Quaker missionaries visited Norfolk Island in 1835 as part of their tour through the Australian colonies and were allowed to carry back with them such letters as the prisoners were able to write.[9] Here are two examples:

Affectionate Parents,   April, Norfolk Island 1835.
                              An unfortunate Son, now embraces the afforded
opportunity of imparting to you in the strongest terms, his fervent
desire for your welfare, etc. Since the receipt of your last letter I have
through the want of a friend, and which I shall long feel the need of,
become convicted to Norfolk Island [Here there is a row of dots,
intimating censorship of the next sentence or two] . . . Dear Father
and Mother, mine is a bitter lot in life; but I, myself, am alone to
blame. My present situation . . . is such that nothing but pure
conduct, and the help of God alone, can afford me again the
opportunity of meeting with you in this world . . . bid my sister M. to
be careful over her son, lest he meet with my present unfortunate
situation. [A second omission here] And may every blessing that God
can impart, attend you all through life, is the prayer of your
unfortunate though affectionate Son.

*   *   *

My dear Wife and beloved Children,   Norfolk Island, April 1835.
        . . . I never had a task so painful . . . as the present one, of
addressing you from this doleful spot—my sea-girt prison, on the
beach of which I stand, a monument of destruction; driven by the
adverse winds of fate, to the confines of black despair . . . I am
wearing the garb of degradation and the badge or brand of infamy,
N.I. which being interpreted is Norfolk Island, the 'Villain's Home'.
My present circumstances and picture, you will find truly drawn, in
the 88th Psalm, and the 102nd commencing with the 3rd verse to the
11th inclusive; which you and my dear children I request will read
attentively . . . I am exceedingly anxious that my dear children should
have the cause of my present privations and humiliating and
degrading situation constantly pressed upon their attention, that they
may never be exposed to the same fate as that which has overtaken
me . . . you will expect to hear an account of the cruelty and tyranny
which is supposed to be inflicted, and in existence here; but to be
candid this is not that 'earthly hell' which it has been represented by
vindictive writers . . . there has been a very great degree of severity
exercised by the authorities . . . I have no hesitation in that the
insubordinate state of the prisoners fully warranted the exercise of
such rigorous discipline. But our present Commandant . . . has given
humanity a fair trial; and it has had a very good effect . . . and . . . he
could not, and did not, let his private feelings step between himself
and his duty . . .
                              I remain,
                              Your ill-fated Husband.[10]

The missionaries, James Backhouse and George Washington Walker, both

Englishmen, wrote a detailed report of their visit to the penal settlements of Australia, an undertaking which lasted two years or more. Backhouse made many suggestions to the British Government on improvements that could be made to the system in force at that time; he was a keen-eyed and unsentimental man, judging from his comments on conditions on Norfolk Island, where the two men stayed for a month. In one part of his Report Backhouse wrote:

> A man spoke to us of the defective quality of their provisions and complained of the dryness of the maize bread and the hardness of the salt meat. To be restricted to such a diet is felt to be a privation, but the state of the health of the prisoners shews that it is not unwholesome; and they are not designed to be pampered by indulgence. The supply of vegetables and wild fruits, keeps off scurvy, at this settlement.[11]

A month as a visitor, and a month as prisoner were clearly very different situations.

At the time of the convicted prisoner's plea for a priestly visit before execution, some months before Backhouse and Walker arrived on the Island, Governor Bourke arranged for a Roman Catholic priest and an Anglican minister to go to Norfolk Island. To the Reverend H. T. Stiles, Rector of Windsor parish, he wrote: 'I know well your disposition to do good whenever opportunity offers . . . to prepare some of the unhappy men for meeting that sentence which Mr Burton passed on them', and went on to say that as some of the prisoners were Roman Catholic, 'a priest of that religion will be sent . . . also'.[12] Early in September, Reverend Stiles, and Father Ullathorne left Sydney on the *Isabella* and arrived within a week of the time fixed for the executions. Both went immediately to the cells, and both left a graphic description of what they found. Father Ullathorne's memoirs give the pitiful picture:

> . . . a soldier was appointed to guide me to the prison . . . And now I have to record the most heartrending scene that I ever witnessed. The prison was in the form of a square, on one side of which stood a row of low cells, covered with a roof of shingles. The turnkey unlocked the first door and said 'Stand aside, Sir'. Then came forth a yellow exhalation, the produce of the bodies of the men confined therein. The exhalation cleared off, and I entered and found five men chained to a traversing-bar. I spoke to them from my heart, and after preparing them and obtaining their names I announced to them who were reprieved from death and which of them were to die after five days had passed. I thus went from cell to cell until I had seen them all. It is a literal fact that each man who heard his reprieve wept bitterly, and that each man who heard of his condemnation to death went down on his knees with dry eyes, and thanked God.[13]

From this place of utter despair Father Ullathorne went on to Government House where he and the Reverend Stiles were to stay. 'I found a brilliant assembly there,' he wrote, 'in strange contrast to the human miseries in which my soul had just been steeped.'

The executions were carried out on the 22nd and 23rd of September, and Major Anderson gave orders that every convict must attend. The gallows, a permanent death-machine built beside the great gate of the gaol, was on the outside of the prison barrack-yard. A strong stockade was erected in front of it, large enough to take half the number of convicts; the other half were to watch from the yard. On 22 September, the men who were to watch from the stockade were formed up in close columns and addressed by the Major: 'If any of you attempt to move or show any signs of resistance, the officer in the stockade has my positive order to open fire at once'.[14] Nobody moved.

When all was ready the first seven men were led from the low cells where they had spent the previous eight months. They were composed, each one dressed in white, each murmuring the prayers they had been taught within the past five days. 'Among them was a man so young that it was surprising to find him among such doubly and trebly-convicted criminals. He begged the chaplain as a favour, to write to his mother in England and tell her how his life had ended, but that he was sincerely penitent and begged forgiveness', wrote the Reverend Stiles.

The hangman, himself a Capital Respite from a mainland prison, recognised one of the condemned men as they mounted the scaffold, and said 'Why Jack, is that you?' The pinioned man turned, 'Why Bill! is that you?' for the hangman had suffered a fearful gash across his face in some earlier affray which had distorted his features. The hangman touched Jack's arm and said 'Well, old friend, it can't be helped', and within seconds the lever was pulled to launch the seven men into Eternity.[15] Next day the other six men were hanged, the same process carried out, the silence, the prayers, the frightening jerk as the 'drop' came. Anderson, in his *Reminiscences*, wrote: '. . . all passed over as before. From that time order reigned on the Island during the whole of my government, from March 1834 to April 1839'—a statement just a little at variance with the facts.

This dreadful happening, which had been triggered off before Anderson arrived on the Island, made him doubly aware of the need for some sort of religious teaching for the convicts. But neither his nor Governor Bourke's petitions were successful, and when no chaplain could be found, Anderson searched his convict records and found he had two men, one Catholic, the other Anglican, who had been trained in theology before they had committed crimes that finally brought them to Norfolk Island. He sent for them, put to each the proposition that they should be moved from the gaol to a hut of their own, with a man to attend to their wants, plain clothes to wear and a temporary church in which to hold services. In this place, they were to place a pew for the Major and the civil officers, 'that I might have an opportunity of hearing him occasionally and judging for myself'.[16] The two men were promised a commutation of their sentences if their work proved satisfactory, and a salary of one shilling a day. Each group, one Catholic, one Protestant, held services each Sunday at different hours, and when Backhouse and Walker heard of the experiment they advised Major Anderson to allow the men to have school for the convicts after work was finished for the day.

The room built for the January mutiny trial was used as the school. At first, lessons were on Sundays from 8 a.m. to 10 a.m. and from 12.30 p.m. to 2 p.m., each group of men with their teacher seated at opposite ends of the room. Their lessons were mainly learning how to read; and the Quakers suggested they might also learn to write, saying 'Hitherto, the materials for enabling the prisoners to acquire the art of writing and ciphering have, for the most part been withheld lest they should be appropriated to other purposes than those designed . . .' adding that such privileges would give a new impulse to the idea of going to school.[17]

Backhouse had austere views on what was good for convicts. He described corporal punishment as less necessary than solitary confinement, for flogging was treated with contempt by the most hardened men, he said, who vied with each other as to which of them could endure the most without flinching. He also advised a Treadmill, as a means of punishing the unruly and at the same time a means of grinding corn for the establishment. He deplored the commission of 'a crime most revolting to nature', which might be prevented in some measure by providing solitary sleeping cells instead of the wards where hammocks were slung with a '20-inch' space between them. 'The island . . . comparable to the Garden of Eden, is rendered a torment to these men not so much by the punishments of the law as by their conduct to one another', he wrote.[18] It was no secret that at this time Norfolk Island was known as 'Sodom Isle' in Sydney. When referring to the ever-increasing cost of maintenance Backhouse wrote:

Much benefit would accrue . . . from the use of more bullocks as beasts of burden. There would still be abundance of labour for the convicts. At present the earth is broken up by means of hoes, no manure is applied, and crops are consequently defective . . . Were bullocks to be used there would be no scarcity of work for the prisoners, but it would be effected to much better purpose . . . the waste of labour is very great . . .[19]

This piece of sound common sense, the 'muck-spreading' known to every English farmer, had no place on Norfolk Island where ground turned by human effort was the only method of agriculture approved by the authorities; and this was strange, when considering the huge amount of 'muck' provided daily by Major Anderson's milking cattle, horses, pigs and poultry. This, presumably, was used only for the officers' gardens, not for the growing of maize, the main crop grown for the daily allowance of bread for convicts.

It was during Major Anderson's time that many of the Georgian buildings still standing on Norfolk Island were erected. The largest of these, the three-storey Commissariat building, used today as the Anglican church of All Saints, has Anderson's name carved in bold letters on the pediment. The military barracks and the house for the Roman Catholic priests were also built, and the pentagonal gaol planned and begun, though not finished until ten or more years later.[20] The row of elegant cement-clad stone houses for civil officers, built along Military Road (known today as Quality Row) were not completed until about 1840. All the labour and materials, except nails and windows, were from the Island. One convict, when laying the flagstones of a verandah, cracked one by accident, and for this he was ordered a severe lashing. All Major Anderson's buildings had to be perfect.

Major Anderson earned himself the nickname of 'Potato Joe' when, in 1835 he asked whether Government potatoes might be issued daily to prisoners 'when the quantity will admit, in addition to their full ration: and whether in cases of certain supplies running short, potatoes may be issued as an equivalent: 'I make this last enquiry in consequence of Prisoners refusing to receive 1 lb Potatoes each daily in lieu of 1 oz Sugar, of which none remained in store'.[21] Governor Bourke replied that potatoes might be so used; Anderson then wrote a further letter on the matter, which the Governor's Chief Secretary answered, informing Anderson that if there was a surplus of potatoes on the Island they could be issued instead of an issue of maize meal. The convicts, in turn, refused the issue of a pound and a half of potatoes in lieu of one half pound of maize meal, and the correspondence on this subject continued for some months, with Anderson winning the final round, as was almost inevitable. After that 'Potato Joe' was the name by which the Commandant was known throughout the gaol, and probably farther afield also. In February 1836 Governor Bourke had good news for Anderson:

> Mr Atkins will proceed to the Colony under the arrangement . . .
> stated in my despatch . . . and from the high testimony . . . borne to
> his character and qualifications for the peculiar duty which will
> devolve upon him, I trust the best results may be anticipated from his
> exertions . . . He is a clergyman of the Established Church, at the
> recommendations of the London Missionary Society, the Reverend
> Thomas Atkins, an Independent Minister, to perform the duties of
> Chaplain at Norfolk Island.[22]

The Reverend Thomas Atkins arrived in November 1836, at the same time as Dr Harnett, who had come in response to a request from Major Anderson that a Government doctor should be sent to replace Dr Gamack, Chief Surgeon on the Island, who was, according to Anderson, too lenient with supposedly sick convicts.

Aaron Price writes of Thomas Atkins: 'This gentleman was an able clergyman. His principles as a Christian gentleman were not to be purchased, and he left the Island 'the prisoners' friend'. But Atkins's enthusiasm outran his discretion, and his righteous anger spilled over before he had learned the waiting game—to watch, listen, and stay silent until he had proof of the allegations he made. He was a new recruit, Major Anderson an old campaigner, and the odds were, as they so often are, with the astute veteran rather than the novice.

At the time Atkins arrived on Norfolk Island an epidemic of dysentery raged among the 'New Hands', the prisoners recently sent from the mainland colony. It was endemic on the Island, but the old hands had weathered its onslaught earlier, and were mostly immune. The disease was caused, it was claimed, by the quality of the food supplied and the continual diet of maize-meal and salt meat. The settlement's surgeon, Dr Gamack, a man of independent mind, laid off work those men he considered unfit or incapable through illness, and Major Anderson strongly disapproved his diagnosis, saying that the true cause of the convict's complaints was nothing more than malingering. The number of men off work must be reduced, he said; convicts laid off from hard labour produced nothing, neither crops in the field nor stone for the buildings. Gamack continued to hospitalise the men he considered unfit to work, and at one time had more than a hundred sick on his list.

With the arrival of Dr Harnett, the ranks of the 'work-shy' were thus cut in half, and the men returned to work in their gangs. One man, a New Hand, complained of 'bowel trouble', and was sent back to work.[23] He came again the next day, and the next. 'I shall report you to the Commandant if I see you here again', said Dr Harnett. The man, William Castleton, returned the next day, with a cell-mate who testified to 'seeing the blood run down his legs'. Dr Harnett promptly sent in his report. Castleton was brought to court on 9 December and sentenced to receive fifty lashes, the surgeon standing by. He was strapped to the triangle, and received thirty-seven strokes before the doctor ordered him to be taken down and removed to the hospital. On 13 December William Castleton died, and Atkins, when he heard of it, confronted Major Anderson in a fury, calling him 'a murderer'. Yet strangely enough, as was proved, Atkins had been on the bench at the time Castleton's case was heard and had signed the record of the verdict. After reflection he realised he had been wrong to sign and asked that his name be erased from the record, but this, said Anderson, could not be done.

Atkins then wrote to Governor Bourke, giving his views on Anderson and on conditions generally on Norfolk Island. Anderson also wrote to the Governor, putting his case, and Bourke upheld him. In April, after receiving the Governor's letter, Atkins wrote again:

Sir,
    As, during my residence at Norfolk Island several cases occurred
which I conscientiously believed required my interposition; as for the

part which I took in regard to those cases, I received insult from Dr Harnett, and both insult and persecution from Major Anderson; as the general conduct of the Commandant . . . induced me to solicit his leave to enable me in person to state the case to the Government of New South Wales; as the view which your Excellency has been pleased to take of my part of the case is very unsatisfactory . . . as the principles of Government adopted at Norfolk Island appear to . . . be diametrically opposed to the professed principles of the Government . . . and more especially to the Principles of the British Government from which my appointment was received . . . and the influence of the Government of Norfolk Island . . . is calculated to encourage vice and discountenance virtue: I therefore beg of your Excellency to accept my resignation of a situation which, in my opinion, I cannot hold without degrading the Character of a Briton . . . of a Christian, and of a Clergyman.[24]

Atkins had, at the time of writing this letter, betaken himself to Sydney to put his case personally to the Governor and to hand him the above letter. Within two days he received the Governor's answer which was sent to him through Deas Thompson, the Colonial Secretary; which gave him permission, if he so wished, 'to peruse and take copies of any part of the Official Communication from the Commandant on the several matters herein referred to'. But the bitterness Atkins felt for Anderson was not diminished by this offer, and he replied:

I have received your letter . . . and in reply beg to say that I have no wish to peruse the despatches of Major Anderson: further, it appears to me that from the position which Your Excellency occupies, Your Excellency is disqualified to form an impartial judgement between Major Anderson and myself: and therefore though it appeared to be my duty in the first instance to lay the case before Your Excellency, I presumed that Your Excellency would not incur the responsibility to sit to be judge on so important a business. But when a suitable time arrives, and a satisfactory Inquiry be instituted, I shall be prepared to state the facts upon which my Opinion of the influence of the Government of Norfolk Island is formed.[25]

The Reverend Thomas Atkins, 'the prisoner's friend', resigned his commission as chaplain of Norfolk Island, after he was told that his return was conditional on his acceptance of Anderson's authority. Righteous anger was not a strong enough weapon against the rigid regulations of the iron-bound settlement, and his resignation paved the way for the arrival of the Reverend Thomas Sharpe, who was sent from his parish in New South Wales, and two Roman Catholic priests Fathers McEncroe and Walsh, who came for the salary of one, saying that 'two priests can live as cheaply as one Anglican with a wife and family to maintain'.[26]

Thomas Atkins rates no mention in Major Anderson's *Reminiscences*, but Anderson does give a vivid description of the kind of life a young officer could expect to live on Norfolk Island:

> There was not a pretty spot at any distance beyond the settlement without a nice bower with tables and seats for our accommodation; and in one or other of these paradises we used to . . . pass many hours. We had also frequent dinner-parties and dances, and as I had then finished building the new military barracks and hospital, the latter (for we had no sick) made a most excellent and commodious ballroom . . . In a word, we all agreed well together . . .
> They also had other amusements—fishing, shooting, etc. Phillip [*sic*] Island . . . abounded with wild pigs, wild fowl, and a variety of birds, the most remarkable being the Phillip Island parrots, which were never seen in any other part of Australia. Whenever any of the officers wished for a day's sport there, they had a boat at their command for the day . . . and generally brought back with them some half-dozen or more pigs, besides other game . . . By this time I had an open carriage (made on the Island) and as we had many Government horses doing nothing . . . the Governor had no objection to my making use of them as much as I liked . . . and from that time we had our carriage and a first-rate (convict) coachman.[27]

In these years the cost of maintaining Norfolk Island as a penal settlement increased beyond the Government's expectations, and the ability of the convicts to maintain themselves diminished. There were no experienced farmer-superintendents to bring well-tried methods of agriculture to the Island, as Backhouse and Walker had suggested, no training for the men at hard labour who had only hoes to cultivate the soil with, and no settlers to provide extra supplies as there had been in the First Settlement. There had been correspondence between the Home Government and New South Wales since 1835 on the reduction of some of the penal out-stations because of the costs of maintenance, and it had been suggested that the prisoners at Moreton Bay should be progressively moved to Norfolk Island to reduce costs. Some had already been moved from Port Macquarie.

Sir Richard Bourke, in a despatch to Lord Glenelg in November 1837 stated he 'desired to retain but one Penal Establishment for the whole Colony, with a view to diminish expenses of management, to lessen the dispersion of troops, and to place the convicts in greater security on Norfolk Island than I found them at Moreton Bay . . .'[28] But here again came the seemingly insoluble problem of providing a chaplain for Norfolk, and the matter of keeping moral order on such a small Island where so many depraved men were herded together. Bourke was genuinely disturbed by the lack of any system for reform but the one of severity, but the urgent need of men sentenced by the law to long years of confinement won no priority at the seat of Government. However, in this same despatch, Bourke could write:

In the last four years indeed, the conduct of the criminals on Norfolk Island (now above one thousand in number) has been remarkably quiet and orderly, whilst considerably increased labor has been exacted. I attribute the tranquillity chiefly to the humane but firm and vigilant superintendence of the present Commandant, Major Anderson of the 50th Regiment, but in a great measure also to the power obtained about three years ago of trying capital offences on the Island . . . The chance of escaping on leaving the Island for the place of trial . . . led to many enormities. They have been almost entirely stopped by the measure in question.[29]

Yet the question of the closure of Norfolk Island survived, and Bourke recommended the number of prisoners held there be 'much reduced', and a system of religious and moral instruction introduced. In this he was well before his time, though it was not to be long before another and more outspoken man came to the same conclusion. Unfortunately for the convicts, neither Richard Bourke nor Alexander Maconochie could claim the necessary support for their theories from the hidebound authorities of the day.

In 1837 the cost of maintaining Norfolk Island, with 1200 prisoners, amounted to £11,166 9s 6d, though crops had been good that year and grain exported to the value of £863 15s. The cost for each convict amounted to nearly £13 and for a prisoner in a chain gang, £17 a year 'whilst the toil of the transport at a Penal Settlement at best serves but to diminish the cost of his maintenance'.[30]

The question of closure of Moreton Bay and Norfolk Island as penal settlements met a good deal of opposition in the New South Wales Council:

. . . from an apprehension that under it, Cattle stealers might be brought back, who are now at Norfolk Island under sentence for Life. The act must on the same account be carried into execution with great caution, Cattle stealers being a class of Offenders extremely obnoxious to the wealthy Graziers of the Colony.[31]

So wrote Sir George Gipps, Governor of New South Wales, in January 1839. The wealthy graziers were, in these years, powerful influences on policy-making, and at times a thorn in the side of Governor Gipps. Norfolk Island was to retain its thousand or so prisoners for a decade longer.

Major Anderson left the Island in April 1839, though he had been replaced as Commandant in January of that year. His replacement was Major Thomas Bunbury of the 80th Regiment, but Anderson was reluctant to leave, as Mrs Anderson's confinement was near and it was considered imprudent for her to undertake the sea-journey until after the birth, which took place on 9 February. It was not until 5 April that the Andersons left and young Lieutenant A. D. W. Best, of the 80th, who had been on Norfolk Island since the previous August, wrote in his Journal 'At two, called on

Major and Mrs Anderson. I never in my life saw so great a change as in the former; he used to be cheerful and confident and is now melancholy and desponding'.[32] Major Bunbury, in his *Reminiscences of a Veteran* says shortly, 'Anderson, from the force of long habit had brought himself to believe that he was necessary to the well-being of the establishment . . . and had contrived to make the authorities at Sydney think so too'.[33]

Anderson left the Island with all due honours paid him by the new Commandant and his men. It was a strange twist of Fate that on the same vessel was John Knatchbull, the only name Anderson mentions in his *Reminiscences* with dislike. Knatchbull had earned his probation, against Anderson's advice, and was soon to be released. It was not a long freedom however, for in January 1844 Knatchbull was arrested at the scene of the murder of Mrs Ellen Jamieson, a widow with two young children. He had been seen entering her small shop late at night, then her screams had been heard across the street and the police were called. Knatchbull was seized as he hid behind the door of the shop, with the money allegedly taken from Mrs Jamieson on him. This was one situation he could not talk himself out of. After a lengthy trial which drew crowds of spectators and much publicity, he was executed in Darlinghurst gaol on 13 February 1844; having written and signed a confession, and an autobiography, while in the death cell.[34]

Major Anderson returned to his Regiment from Norfolk Island and was posted to India. His military service ended in 1848 when he returned to England, sold his commission for £6,000, and afterwards brought his family back to Australia where he settled in Melbourne with his family of six, two sons and four daughters. He died in July 1877. His biographer writes of him as 'A firm disciplinarian, . . . a courageous soldier, but limited in outlook and with a well-developed acquisitive sense'.[35]

The most memorable quote on Major Anderson is, however, to be found in Knatchbull's own autobiography when he writes, in his death-cell 'Fifteen hundred lashes was I eye-witness to, ere the stars were off the sky'. There is little reason to doubt the accuracy of Knatchbull's statement on this occasion, for a 'three hundred' was a common sentence, and corporal punishment began with the dawn.

*　　*　　*

Anderson's successor, Major Thomas Bunbury, was a thoroughly professional soldier who had joined the 90th Regiment as ensign in 1807 at the age of 16. He, like Anderson, had been engaged in battle during the Peninsula wars, where he had his moment of glory when he carried the regimental colours into battle. He gained mentions in Despatches, and wounds, with equal frequency, and was twice promoted in the Field to the rank of Brevet-Major, finally being gazetted in November 1839 on his appointment as Commandant to Norfolk Island.[36]

He was confident of his ability to manage the doubly and trebly-convicted men in his charge, and he succeeded up to a point. He was a practical man who had no wish to impress by his benevolence, as he makes clear in his *Reminiscences* when writing of his time on Norfolk Island, 'I was not so imbued with the maudlin spirit of modern sentimentality as to be able to comprehend why a villain who had been guilty of every enormity, should feel shame at having his back scratched with the cat-o-nine-tails when he felt none for his atrocious crimes . . .', and in another part, '. . . if a man is too sick to work he is too sick to eat . . .'[37] After this pronouncement the line of would-be patients at the hospital diminished by 50 per cent, he says.

But he rewarded good behaviour with improvement in job, and took the oldest of the convicts off the hardest labour, giving them other and more suitable work to do. He seems to have preferred practice to precept, a welcome change after the previous five years' pietism. Better-behaved men were allowed gardens of their own, and in each working-gang one man was sent out daily to gather wild fruit for the rest of the gang; but when punishment was meted out it was as severe as the crime warranted, 300 lashes being the one ordered summarily on the party of convicts who attempted their escape in full view of the settlement and in broad daylight. The officers, who had spent a pleasant day's fishing in the bay just beyond the coral reef outside the settlement, were hauling the seine to the beach, excited at their catch, when a batch of prisoners on shore rushed through the surf to the boat, lying just off the reef with the prisoner-crew holding her steady. They threw out the crew, clambered into the boat themselves and set to steering the boat over the shoals and out into the bay. Ensign Best writes:

> The alarm was instantly given and two of the fastest boats started in pursuit, four soldiers in each . . . they soon overhauled the runaways and as soon as they were within range opened their fire; the runaways finding no chance of escape threw down their oars . . . they were brought back, tried, found guilty, and in a very few minutes each had received three hundred lashes.[38]

Best's *Journal* contains a few more items of life on the Island, during his short stay; items which show how pleasant life could be, depending on which barracks the writer lived in. He sounds a pleasant, uncritical young man with few worries and plenty of time for amusements, in spite of routine duties.

> Bathed at eight, there was a good deal of swell in the bay. Mrs Anderson gave us a picnic in Orange Vale . . . The gardens are truly beautiful, situated in a gully with a small stream running through it. Here . . . you may see the English oak, the N.I. pine, coffee, bananas, loquats, guavas, peaches, strawberries, pineapples, melons, the cabbage palm, the different fern trees in all their beautiful shapes, and every kind of vegetable I know except yams . . . After walking about the gardens we found a tent spread under the oak, covering a table loaded with the different productions of all parts of the world . . .[39]

Later that same week, the young bachelor officers gave a ball to the civil and military officers and their ladies, doing the honours in great style and providing a wonderful spread, in the military hospital building where no sick had needed to be admitted. The music was provided by a group of convicts, who played the violin and trumpet; and a backdrop was painted by the same party of convicts who produced the scenery for the military 'Corps Dramatique', as Major Anderson had styled the play-acting soldiers who regularly put on plays for their own amusement.

During Major Bunbury's first months of command on Norfolk Island, the gaol was comparatively free of planned disturbances. He was respected and had no need of undue punishments to enforce discipline. It was his own men of the 80th who brought his term of office to an abrupt and unexpected end before his first year was out; and the cause was the apparently innocuous one of soldiers' gardens. Soldiers had been allowed gardens of their own since Morisset's time. That shrewd officer realised that a garden was not only a form of recreation when a man had time on his hands, but would cut down the amount of convict labour needed to supply a large number of men with fresh vegetables; labour that could be used for Government supplies, under the eyes of vigilant overseers. At the time Morisset's men were withdrawn and the men of Anderson's 50th took over in 1834, bad feeling was created when the incoming troops discovered that the departing soldiers had dug the potato crop and taken it with them for what they called 'sea-stores', especially as the men of the 50th had paid good money when they took over the gardens. When Major Anderson heard of this quarrel, he issued stern orders:

The gardens are public property and granted to men only during good conduct. The produce of them is not to be sold or removed at pleasure of detachments ordered to return to Sydney. They are to be handed over from one detachment to another as relief takes place.

This was a reasonable order, as detachments changed frequently during the one Commandant's period of office. But there were also the convicts' gardens and the little matter of 'trafficking' between soldiers and convicts — some of the latter had been soldiers themselves, before being sentenced to Norfolk Island as prisoners. Trafficking went on wherever an accommodating soldier found an equally co-operative convict. Fruit, fowls, eggs, might be removed from an officer's garden by the convict employed as gardener and be hidden in the shanty where a soldier kept his tools or surplus vegetables. Payment for such goods might be left at that place; a fig of tobacco, or sugar, or soap for the convict. The shanties were clustered together, built out of public view; no one but the owners saw a man come and go. Trouble was bound to flare up sooner or later. In September 1839, Governor Gipps, in his despatch to Lord Normanby noted:

It is with very great regret I have to report to your Lordship that . . . on the 5th instt. serious insubordination having manifested itself, or indeed to speak more properly, mutiny among the Soldiers of the 80th Regt. at Norfolk Island in the beginning of . . . July last . . . nearly every man of the detachment was in possession of a small separate garden . . . in size from a sixteenth to an eighth of an acre. In many of these gardens small huts had been erected . . .

Major Bunbury, after he had been about three months in the command, thinking these huts to be the cause of many improper practices among the soldiers, ordered them to be taken down; it was in resistance of this order that a large number of the soldiers armed themselves on 1st July last, and joined in the Mutiny described by Major Bunbury . . .

There being at Norfolk Island about 1,200 doubly convicted and desperate Felons, kept in order only by a detachment of 180 soldiers, it is impossible without some degree of alarm, to know that these soldiers are themselves in a state of Mutiny . . .

The orders sent by Sir Maurice O'Connell [Major General Commanding] are for Major Bunbury to enforce the execution of the one given by himself and having done this (that is to say, having destroyed the huts) immediately embark his whole detachment.[40]

Gipps sent the *Alligator*, a sloop of war, and the *Cornwall* with a detachment of 180 men under the command of Major Ryan immediately on receiving the news from Norfolk Island, but by the time the vessels arrived there, the 'mutiny' had been quelled. Best, in his *Journal*, writes:

With regard to the propriety of this change I am not in a position to give an opinion . . . but in justice to our misguided men I must say that after their return to duty, which was immediate, I never saw duty so actively performed and they all appeared to be fully sensible of the rash act which they had committed . . .[41]

There had been a tense few hours on Norfolk Island when, on the morning of 1 July, a party of prisoners with their overseer arrived at the soldiers' gardens to demolish the huts. At 8 o'clock in the morning Captain Gulston and Captain Lockart of the 80th came hurriedly to Major Bunbury and told him their men 'had assembled in a very riotous manner', and had driven away the party come to raze the huts and build new ones in a more exposed place. Bunbury then gathered a fatigue party of loyal men who either had no gardens or wanted no part in the mutiny, and marched them to the shanty-town; when they arrived there, between forty and fifty men with loaded muskets rushed from the barracks towards him. Providentially, at that moment it began to rain heavily, the armed soldiers rushed back to shelter as quickly as they had come out, and it seemed as if the fracas was over, for the time being at least.

Not for long. Presently the men formed up again, this time under the shelter of the verandah, still armed and at the ready. In his Report of the incident, Major Bunbury wrote, 'I addressed them, not in very flattering terms', but he allowed them to voice their complaints, one of which was their right to retain the huts, since they had paid for them. The huts would stay, or they would take over the Island, the dissidents claimed. It was stalemate. The armed soldiers were obdurate, the officers and the rest of the detachment stood by the Commandant; and in the gaol, the prisoners were aware of all that was going on. To avoid a confrontation which would inevitably lead to some kind of flare-up and might, indeed, come to an uncontrollable situation, Major Bunbury did the wisest thing and agreed to let the huts remain 'for the time being'.[42]

Within an hour everything was back to normal, but Bunbury's report of the happening brought swift retaliation and Bunbury's recall. Best, in his account of the affair, said:

> Immediately on our arrival at Sydney a Court of Inquiry was instituted
> at which I, as in duty bound, gave the fullest evidence in my power.
> One result of the Inquiry was that Major Bunbury was ordered to
> frame charges against the Ringleaders and a General Court Martial
> assembled to try them. Eight were sentenced to be transported for life,
> and in pursuance of this sentence, conveyed to Port Arthur in Van
> Diemen's Land. A ninth, who was sentenced to fourteen years
> Transportation was pardoned by the General . . . Major Ryan
> remained in command some seven months during which time Captain
> Best, 50th Regiment, was lost in crossing the Bar on his return from
> a shooting party at Philip Island.[43]

Captain the Hon. Charles Best, son of a former Lord Chief Justice of England, was no relation of Ensign Best though the two men had met and become friends in Sydney. Charles Best was a man of 'gigantic size' according to his contemporaries and popular with everybody, convicts as well as soldiers under him, a man as generous as his size. Thomas Cook, an 'educated prisoner' serving his sentence on Norfolk Island at the time of the accident, tells of the happening in his *The Exile's Lamentations*, an account of his many troubles after transportation:

> A more terrific scene than it presented can scarcely be conceived. It
> happened on 14th February . . . the day was remarkably fine until
> within an hour of the boat nearing the land . . . but by the time the
> Coxswain brought her convenient to the Bar the seas rose and with a
> fury seldom witnessed . . . a race of them followed . . . In attempting
> to cross, the boat was caught . . . and thrown up perpendicular . . .
> she was again struck and thrown completely over . . . no sooner was
> the boat struck than all capable of doing so faced the mountainous
> waves . . . fighting with death to rescue their fellow countrymen. We
> succeeded in saving an officer and two privates of the 50th . . . the

coxswain and eight prisoners but lamentable to relate the Honourable
Charles Best and Mr McLean, Supt. of Agriculture, and a soldier
were drowned.[44]

Captain Best was not dead when lifted from the water, but died later. Cook
continues:

> . . . this generous gentleman expired in a few minutes. The linin [*sic*]
> frock he wore had . . . worked its way half over his head, and from the
> tightness of the collars of his flannel and linin shirts . . . his death
> may be ascribed to strangulation.

The great tombstone in memory of Captain Charles Best is in the old
cemetery at Norfolk Island, as is Mr McLean's; though few mourned the
death of the Superintendent of Agriculture, at least, among the convicts.

Major Ryan, the new commanding officer of the Garrison was only a 'stop-
gap' Commandant, for great changes were in the air regarding the Island's
future. Since 1837 a Select Committee under the direction of Sir William
Molesworth had been in session in London and returning Governors,
Commandants of penal settlements, clerics home from colonial service,
emancipists and even an unnamed former convict who had received a
pardon, were called to give evidence or to testify before it. Doubts about the
methods of discipline, of assignment of convicts to settlers, of the efficacy of
transportation itself, had been raised, and consciences awakened.

One man in particular had aroused interest and stirred many consciences
in parliamentary circles by his writings on the Convict System, and also in
the Report he had sent to the Society for the Improvement of Prison Discipline,
a report written at the Society's request. His article had been published in a
Parliamentary Paper, and an outcry from the public was the result. In a
despatch to Governor Gipps, in May 1839, Lord Normanby stated:

> With respect to Norfolk Island, it is the intention of Her Majesty's
> Government that an essential alteration should be made in the system
> of punishment there . . . In order to carry the new system fully into
> effect, the superintendence of it should be entrusted to an officer on
> whose qualifications the best reliance can be placed . . . who should
> feel a deep interest in the moral improvement of the convicts, and be
> disposed to devote his whole energies to this important object . . . I
> leave the selection of the officer in the first instance, in your hands
> subject to my confirmation . . .

The despatch had an enclosure, which read:

> It had been the intention of H.M. Government to have directed you
> to offer the appointment to Captain Maconochie . . . whose attention,
> as you are aware, has been much directed to the subject of Convict
> Discipline . . .[45]

For Norfolk Island, great changes were planned, and a foretaste of them was felt at the time Major Ryan, a 49-year-old Irishman, took over command of the Island in the interim between Major Bunbury's recall to Sydney, and the arrival of Alexander Maconochie early in 1840.[46] Ryan was an Army man as all the officers had been since the start of the Second Settlement on Norfolk, but his streak of humanity was better developed than some. He approached his task as Commandant in much the same way Maconochie was to do, regarding convicted felons as men sent for punishment on the Island, but still with hope of release at some time in the future. 'Punishment short of Death' was not his motto, and he gained early respect from a proportion of the men.

Rations were increased and, more to the point, he made a habit of inspecting the meal served out as breakfast in the prisoners' barracks; he allowed the full hour for meals, and returned prisoners' gardens to those who had behaved well and were willing to work in them in their free time. To many convicts, of course, a garden was useless, they had neither the skills nor the desire to work in one, though as unwilling captives they had perforce to do their hard labour in clearing and hoeing already depleted soil on the hillside terraces and plateaux.

Mr McLean the Superintendent of Agriculture (who was shortly to drown) strenuously opposed Ryan's lenity, and pointed out that only severe measures ensured any work from the men in his charge; and in severe measures McLean was expert. Thomas Cook, in his *Lamentations* relates how he heard McLean call one of the chain-gang field workers '"a Crawling scoundrel", and after ordering him to gaol, added "and throw yourself into the Blow-hole!". I expressed surprise to a gangmate . . . who remarked "You'll be a lucky man if he does not so express himself to *you* before long . . ."'.

Within a few months of taking command, Major Ryan fell ill, and his second-in-command took over, much to Cook's disgust, for he was, says Cook, 'a man who carried as severe an aspect towards the prisoners as any of his predecessors had done . . . I think more men were brought to the Triangles . . . than had been so sentenced during any of their reigns'.

It was at this time however, that changes were in the air. News flies fast, even though it was carried by sailing-ship only. Word was spread that a new man was coming, a man with a new method of governing convicts; a man who was going to try his system of 'Reformation by Moral Suasion', of all things. The Old Hands listened with deep suspicion and disbelief, the only reform they had been aware of was the lash and chain, coupled with solitary, and bread and water. The 'flash men' were sceptical. This new bloke, Captain Maconochie, was a Navy man. How would he manage the soldiers? How would he manage the refuse of the Colonies, the scum who were worth less than the officers' dogs? It was a question of Wait and See.

Alexander Maconochie

16

FOURTEEN HUNDRED DOUBLY-CONVICTED CONVICTS, THE REFUSE OF BOTH PENAL COLONIES, WERE RIGOROUSLY COERCED ALL DAY and cooped up at night in barracks which could not decently accommodate half the number. In every way their feelings were outraged and their self-respect destroyed. They were required to cap each private soldier whom they met and even each empty sentry-box they passed. If they met a superior officer they were to take their caps off altogether and stand aside, bare-headed, in a ditch if necessary and whatever the weather, till he had passed, in most cases without taking the smallest notice of them.

For the merest trifles they were flogged, ironed, or confined in gaol for successive days on bread and water . . . They were fed more like hogs than men. Neither knives nor forks . . . were allowed at their tables. They tore their food with their fingers and teeth, and drank for the most part out of water-buckets . . . The Island had been a penal settlement for 15 years when I landed on it, yet not a single place of worship was erected on it . . . There were no schools, no books, and the mens' countenances reflected faithfully this treatment. A more demoniacal looking assemblage could not be imagined, and nearly the most formidable sight I ever beheld was the sea of faces upheld to me when I first addressed them.[1]

The foregoing is an excerpt from Captain Maconochie's pamphlet *Norfolk Island*, published in London in 1847. Alexander Maconochie was born in Edinburgh, Scotland on 11 February 1787. His father was a legal officer, and agent for the Duke of Douglas; he was later a landowner in Scotland. He died when Alexander was 9 years old, when the boy was sent to live with his kinsman Allan Maconochie, a brilliant lawyer who was later appointed a judge of the Court of Session. He was created Lord Meadowbank in 1796. It was in this educated and intellectual atmosphere that the young Alexander grew up and was, for a time, prepared for the profession of Law himself. At 16, however, he entered the Navy as volunteer, being promoted to midshipman in 1804. In 1810 he was taken prisoner by the French for a period of three years, then rejoined the Navy on his release. In 1815 he was paid off, with the rank of Lieutenant-Commander, and put on the Reserve List.[2] In 1822 he married Mary Hutton-Browne, an Edinburgh girl, and in 1828 the family moved to London. Maconochie was obviously restless during those years. He tried farming before moving to London, and also wrote a number of pamphlets on subjects as varied as Steam Navigation; commerce with the Islands of the Pacific; establishing a Free Port in that region; it is an interesting exercise to imagine what original suggestions he might have brought forward had he gone into politics, and what position he might have attained.[3]

Maconochie was a founder and the first Secretary of the Royal Geographical Society, a post he retained until 1836 when his old friend of naval days, Sir John Franklin, offered him the post of Private Secretary when Sir John was appointed Lieutenant-Governor of Van Diemen's Land.[4] By this time there were six Maconochie children, two girls and four boys, who were described by Lady Franklin as 'of the modern rather than the Victorian type, with a liberality of principle in the parents which leaves their children's faults unchecked, and they are allowed to read any books they please . . . except alone the Bible'.[5]

The party left England in August 1836 and arrived at Hobart Town in January 1837. The Franklins were soon surrounded by the inevitable press of position-seekers, the colonial social set, and Government officers 'who read him in a moment and were delighted to find the measure of his foot so easily taken', as Maconochie wrote to his friend Sir George Back.[6] Van Diemen's Land had been opened to settlers for some years, and at the time Sir John Franklin arrived there were about 26 000 settlers and 17 000 convicts, most of them assigned to settler-masters. The ultra-rigid penal settlement at Port Arthur, on the Tasman Peninsula, had been formed as a separate or model prison, with Point Puer the prison for boys.

Before leaving London, Maconochie had been asked by the English Society for the Improvement of Prison Discipline to carry out investigations into the convict system in Van Diemen's Land and report back. This investigation was not part of his official duties for Franklin, but it seems logical to suppose that they were the catalyst which launched him into his great effort for the moral reform of convicts, in opposition to the methods then used, of reform by punishment, often interpreted by the authorities as corporal punishment.

Fletcher, in his *Colonial Australia before 1850* writes:

His [Maconochie's] report was so condemnatory of official policy that
Franklin dismissed him in 1838. In contrast to many English
reformers he regarded assignment as a severe punishment which
uniformly degraded and demoralised convicts by making them slaves.

He accepted the need for transportation but recommended that those sent to the colonies should be subject to treatment that 'would return them to society honest, useful and trustworthy members of it' . . .[7]

He reported that at the time of his arrival in Van Diemen's Land one in every 17 convicts was flogged, average number of strokes 30. At Port Arthur the number was one in four, average strokes 26. At the boys' prison, one in two boys was beaten with a cane, average strokes 20 and often the number exceeded the average in all cases.[8] He looked further and found that in New South Wales 2 000 000 lashes had been given between 1830 and 1837 and that this, in all probability, did not include Norfolk Island which could have added half as many again to the score.

Assigned convicts were in many cases little more than household slaves, said Maconochie in his report; they were creatures liable to be punished or brought to court for punishment, for any misdemeanour whatever. He wrote his report with no thought of the effect it might have on his own prospects and future; fired as he was with the crusader's zeal for reformation of what he saw as evil.

> Degraded servants make suspicious masters, and the habit of
> suspicion being once given, masters soon learn to suspect their equals
> and superiors as well as their inferiors, whence, among other
> symptoms, impatience and irritability under Government regulations
> and judicial decisions however just or well-founded . . . the habit of
> enforcing obedience by mere compulsion give a harsh and peremptory
> bearing in all transactions . . . The Convict System is cruel, uncertain
> and prodigal, ineffectual either for reform or example, can only be
> maintained . . . by extreme severity . . . It defeats in consequence, its
> own most important objects, instead of reforming, it degrades
> humanity, vitiates all under its influence . . . retards improvement and
> is, in many instances . . . the direct occasion of vice and crime . . ?[9]

In a second report he wrote what might be called his philosophy of reform:

> Punishment may avenge and restraint may, to a certain limited
> extent, prevent crime; but neither separately nor together will they
> teach virtue. This is the province of moral training alone, (including
> under this term everything which appeals to the mind, not to the
> body, as moral, religious and intellectual instruction, progressive
> degrees of freedom according to conduct, and the abuse of them
> checked by motives drawn from self-interest, and other principles
> producing mental impulse, not by mere force or the infliction of
> immediate punishment).[10]

He sent his report to London, after first showing it to Sir John Franklin. The Lieutenant-Governor was astounded, and disinclined to send it, as requested, to the English authorities, but, as Mrs Maconochie wrote in her letter to Sir George Back, a mutual friend of the Maconochies and the Franklins 'Alexander insisted, and with much difficulty, they were sent'.[11]

Although Maconochie's published *Report* caused trouble between himself and Sir John Franklin and the 'Government set', he gained much support from those settlers who admired his courage and candour, and 'his unassuming demeanour to all classes, and his readiness to oblige and advise the humblest supplicant to the Government for justice, or on other business', as the editor of the *True Colonist*, Gilbert Robertson, said.[12] Robertson was a man who knew the cost of speaking out. He had faced the magistrate in court more than once, when defending his own views of the treatment of assigned convicts; he had also served time in a debtors' prison after he was haled before the court again on a charge of publishing libellous statements about the Lieutenant-Governor, Sir George Arthur, and Mr Rowlands an attorney.

In London the Select Committee on Transportation, under the chairmanship of Sir William Molesworth, had been set up some time after Maconochie's departure for Van Diemen's Land, and when he sent his *Report* to the Society for the Improvement of Prison Discipline, he asked only that it be sent on to Sir George Grey, Under-Secretary to Lord John Russell, Secretary of State for Home Affairs. Lord Russell, on reading the report, sent it to the Select Committee — it was the kind of material they had been looking for. Russell was a member of the Committee and in such circumstances it was not surprising that the report, after being read, was ordered to be published by the Stationery Office.[13] After publication there was a great outcry among the thinking public of Great Britain and the report was written up in the newspapers, bringing Maconochie's name into prominence. When word of this reached Hobart Town there was uproar in Government circles, from the pro's and con's alike.

Maconochie himself refused to be drawn into any argument. Mary Maconochie, in a letter to Sir George Back, wrote: 'We see few, and go nowhere, your friend Alexander is like a lion at bay, deafened by the barking and yelping of the curs about him but in no way stirred from his steady honesty of purpose. He must bide his time, and pay the penalty for so noble an animal uniting himself with an . . . (fill up as you like, you can't go wrong.)'[14]

Like many other reformers Maconochie found the Cause he had taken up had taken him over:

> The Cause has now got me completely . . . I will go the 'whole hog' on
> it. If not successful in it from here . . . I return home . . . I will
> neither acquiesce in the moral destruction of so many of my fellow-
> beings nor in misrepresentation . . . of myself . . . I have hitherto been
> known for a quiet judicious person enough; and if I now appear

extravagant do not at once pronounce that I have sniffed Gas . . . but examine the case—read, mark, learn and become excited yourself . . .[15]

He spent his now ample leisure time in writing more pamphlets for publication, and during 1838 and 1839 several papers were published in Hobart and London. This enforced time of 'unemployment' was of great benefit, for as he wrote and studied and learned more of the complexities of the Convict System of Management, his thoughts matured and his exuberance, or perhaps rather his disgust at his early findings, settled into firm resolve on his future course.

In 1838 the Select Committee on Transportation recommended that transportation be abolished, though it was to be at least two years before this happened, and then only in New South Wales. They agreed with Maconochie's argument that 'A system of punishment which relies for its efficacy solely on the infliction of pain . . . hardens and brutalizes the culprit, renders him mentally incapable of looking beyond the moment . . .'[16] In May 1839 Lord Normanby, Secretary of State for the Colonies, intimated in a despatch to Sir George Gipps, Governor of New South Wales, that a new system should be used on Norfolk Island and its superintendence be given to an officer deeply concerned with the moral welfare of the convicts.[17] He did not actually mention Maconochie by name, but in an enclosure he recommended that Maconochie was the man who might put the new system into practice. This was the chance Maconochie had looked for, and Gipps sent the letter on to Sir John Franklin who in turn showed it to his former friend. Maconochie accepted the appointment with joy, and at the same time, the two men healed the wide rift that had grown between them.

With high hopes and a sense of fulfilment, the Maconochies left Hobart Town in January 1840. There were four long weeks to wait in Sydney, and during this time Maconochie met a staunch supporter of his proposed methods for convict reform by moral suasion, in the Reverend Dr William Ullathorne, who had visited Norfolk Island on more than one heart-rending mission. The two men found much to discuss, though Ullathorne warned Maconochie that he could find insuperable difficulties ahead of him:

. . . in Norfolk Island you will have the worst and most inveterate criminals, the scum of the Penal Settlements to deal with . . . and hard and unfit intruments [*sic*] in your co-operators. They, and not you, will be in hourly contact with the men and yet what you want is to carry your own spirit with you everywhere. Could you be your own overseers and wardens you might succeed . . .[18]

Ullathorne knew, as Maconochie did not, that it was those men holding responsibility under him, men accustomed to the despotic rule of master over slave, obedience or the lash, who could make or break the idealistic Maconochie by working with, or against him.

M

Governor Gipps, who waited the outcome of the experimental system of convict management with keen interest, showed his support by allowing the unexpected requests asked of him by the new Commandant-Superintendent of Norfolk Island. 'I need books', said Maconochie, 'there is no library on the Island, nothing but a few tracts, pamphlets, and a few bibles for the prisoners to read. Books are a solace and can be an immense power for good. Have I your permission to buy a small library of books to take with me?' Gipps agreed, and in his despatch to Lord Russell, wrote: 'As Captain Maconochie attaches great importance to the early formation of a Library, I have authorised him to expend £50 in the purchase of such Books as he may be able to select at Sydney. I fixed at first the sum of £20, but at his very earnest request I subsequently raised it to £50.'[19]

Maconochie next asked for permission to purchase some musical instruments, and Gipps agreed to this, too, allowing £100 for the musical instruments and a further £43 15s for the entire stock of Mr Ellard, a music seller who was leaving the colony for England. Maconochie said he intended to employ 'the old, lame, sick or other infirm prisoners in copying music, and such others as may be willing to gain marks of approbation by so employing their hours of rest from more severe labours'.[20] Gipps's thoughts on this have not been recorded, though his comments on Maconochie's further request that women and children should also be sent to Norfolk Island, were short and to the point.

> Women have never yet been sent to Norfolk Island, and the universal impression is that it would be highly dangerous to have them there (not less on account of the Male Convicts than of the Troops who guard them).[21]

In his biography of Alexander Maconochie, Sir John Barry maintains that Governor Gipps was 'an able and conscientious administrator and one of the great Governors of New South Wales'. In the days when 'justice' was more often considered in terms of retribution than of reform, it would require courage as well as good administration from the 'man at the top of the heap' to accede to what must have seemed revolutionary requests for indulgences for convicts. But at the same time, Gipps warned Maconochie very firmly that on no account were the 'Old Hands', the doubly-convicted prisoners, to be allowed any of the indulgences of Maconochie's new System of Moral Reform. Only those first-convicted men sent direct from England to the Island, were to be part of his Marks System. For the Old Hands it was discipline as usual, and for this purpose a Convict Superintendent and Deputy-Commandant, Mr Charles Ormsby, who had been a Chief Constable in Ireland before coming to Sydney, was sent out. Maconochie was given five other civil officers, men of his own choice: an assistant surgeon, James Reid; an overseer of works, John Sims; one chief officer; and two sergeants of police. These men sailed with him on the *Nautilus* from Sydney on 23

February 1840, together with his family and 300 convicts direct from England—the 'New Hands'.[22]

The *Nautilus* reached Norfolk Island on the 6th of March. The Old Hands were forbidden to share in the 'Marks System', and they were the reason Mr Ormsby had been sent, a man well-versed in disciplining prisoners. He had been given magisterial powers of punishment for any and every crime except capital offences. For the Old Hands the coming of Maconochie was nothing more than a change of Commandant. None of Maconochie's indulgences were to reach into the cells or over the gaol walls.

The newly-arrived 'guinea-pigs', the New Hands, were housed in wooden barracks at Longridge, the agricultural station two and a half kilometres from the main settlement. It was to Longridge that Maconochie went first, in order to explain his Marks System to the men who were to participate. These, of course, were not first offenders or men untried in the ways of crime, they were just the first shipment of prisoners sent direct to the Island instead of to the mainland colony. In 1840 an Act had been passed by the Home Government which ended the assignment of convicts to New South Wales, sending them instead to Van Diemen's Land or Norfolk Island and, many years later, to Western Australia. Lord Normanby, in a despatch to Gipps in 1839, wrote:

> With respect to Norfolk Island, it is the intention of Her Majesty's Government that an essential alteration should be made in the system of punishment pursued there. The healthiness of the climate, the fertility of the soil, and its entire separation from intercourse with ordinary emigrants render it peculiarly fit for the reception of a large number of convicts, subject to careful superintendence and discipline, and for whom regular means of employment must be provided . . . and whose superintendence should be entrusted to an officer who . . . feels a deep interest in the moral improvement of the convicts, and be disposed to devote his whole energies to this important object'.[23]

It was ironical that Governor Gipps, sympathetic as he was to Maconochie's aims for the reformation of convicts, should have insisted on himself rather than Maconochie choosing the man who was to oppose Maconochie's methods more than any other, namely, the Superintendent of Agriculture at Longridge where the experiment at reform was to be tried.

The Marks System was, in essence, Maconochie's philosophy for the reform of the then Penal System of punishment, a method which came to be called Reform by moral suasion rather than corporal punishment. As Barry says, 'He was a deeply religious man, of generous and compassionate temperament, and convinced of the dignity of man'.[24] His System rested on the principle that brutality (as corporal punishment) debased all who were associated with it, both the flogger and the flogged; and punishment should be designed to strengthen the wrongdoer's ability to resist further temptation once his sentence was served. Corporal punishment was not ruled out, but it should, he maintained, be inflicted if so ordered, in seclusion, 'its sight being morally as injurious to the one, as the being indiscriminately seen when under it, is to the other class'. A summary of his Marks System, which in full would occupy many pages, runs like this:

1   Good behaviour and good work was to be rewarded by a certain number of marks each day, for work well done, for good behaviour, for cleanliness, for punctuality etc.
2   Marks subtracted for bad language, dirtiness, insolence and similar offences.
3   Marks earned—or lost—would be entered into a record book every day by the Superintendent. When a certain total was reached, a total which would vary according to the length of sentence passed on the convict at the time of his trial, the convict would have earned himself a ticket-of-leave *valid on the Island only.*
4   Each man was to have a share in a garden, where, after his Government labour was done each day, he could grow vegetables or keep stock for his own use. Surplus produce could be sold to others, for marks only, not money; the marks thus earned being added to the daily tally of the seller, and removed from the tally of the buyer.
5   Each man in the Marks System was to do his full share of Government labour every day, and do it well.
6   Punishment, when ordered for disciplinary offences, would consist of the removal of marks from the prisoner's total, the amount removed depending on the offence.[25]

There was much more to the Marks System than the bare outline, but the foregoing gives the basis of it. However, it had a flaw. Maconochie insisted that the men must work their garden plots in groups of six or eight; they might choose the men with whom they would work, but once chosen they must stay together, no change from group to group being allowed, and if one member of the group lost marks for an offence, those marks were lost by all in the group. He hoped in this way to teach them the value of communal living in harmony, forgetting, if he had ever known, that almost every man under his charge was, or had been, a loner, whose strongest instinct was always his own survival; that each had lived largely by his wits and cared little or nothing for the other man. Maconochie firmly believed that goodness could be taught by example, and that men could learn that brutality debased a human being—both he who practised it and he who received it. To instil such precepts would need far longer training than the time he had at his disposal, more especially as the men he aimed to reform were also under the dominance of Ormsby, the former Police Superintendent, whose ideas on discipline were diametrically opposed to Maconochie's.

But the Marks System was begun with high hopes for its success. 'The object of the New System of Prison Discipline is, besides the inflicting a suitable punishment on men for their past offences, to train them to return to society honest, useful and trustworthy members of it, and care must be taken . . . that this object be kept strictly in view'.[26] Maconochie made no secret of the fact that his inspiration for the Marks System for Penal Reform was brought about by the conversations he had had with James Backhouse and George Washington Walker, who had been in Van Diemen's Land and spoken to him regarding conditions there. It was Backhouse who had suggested giving probationary tickets-of-leave for good conduct, and their removal for disciplinary offences, a suggestion Maconochie received with enthusiasm. He decided 6000 marks would discharge a seven-year sentence, 7000 a ten-year sentence, and 8000 marks for a 'lifer'. The daily tally was to be 11 marks, when fully earned. The New Hands listened, and took to the scheme except for the insistence that each group must stay together, once chosen; but even this could be endured if good behaviour really brought good marks as the Commandant said. The thoughts of Charles Ormsby at that time have not been recorded.

It was inevitable that a crusader like Alexander Maconochie would find it hard, if not impossible, to work with two systems of management so diametrically opposed. He petitioned Governor Gipps, before his departure from Sydney, to allow him to include the whole settlement in his Marks System; or to give him a completely separate Island, remote from all contact with doubly-convicted men, where his System could be given a fair trial. Gipps refused both requests. The Old Hands were to be rigidly excluded from the possible indulgences of Maconochie's system of Reform by Moral Suasion.[27]

A short time after his visit to Longridge, Maconochie visited the gaol at the Kingston settlement. He assembled all the Old Hands in the gaol-yard and spoke to them earnestly, telling them what the future might hold for them, one way or the other. He knew he had been expressly forbidden to do this, knew also that ears and eyes were listening and watching, and that his words would be reported. He was fired with the zeal of the reformer and his great concern was for the moral improvement of these men before him, 1200 of them; men with the marks of desperation, cynicism, depravity, and hopelessness variously written on their faces. He was certain they could be reached in some way.

He went alone, and unarmed, and spoke from his heart. The men stood silent before him, in groups or singly, lounging along the gaol-yard walls, men hardened from pitting their wits against those in authority; men scarred from countless punishments, men whose only hope of freedom was through death; rapists, murderers, thieves, forgers, outcasts all, condemned to carry the marks of the outcast for life, the 'demoniacal assemblage'. But for each of them his philosophy was that no man was utterly incorrigible. 'Treat him as a man and not as a dog. You cannot recover a man except by doing justice to the manly qualities which he may have about him, and giving him an interest in developing them. I conceive that none are incorrigible where there is sanity; there may be some proportion, but very small'.[28] The men listened and watched, their cunning eyes sizing him up. The 'flash men' turned away. A number of them had been on Norfolk Island a dozen years or more, had seen Commandants come and go, seen their mates die under the lash, go mad from solitary, could count their own number of lashes in thousands; and now this man came babbling about marks for good conduct, and tickets-of-leave and such. It was gammon. All gammon. He'd be gone soon enough.

Maconochie knew, when he spoke to the Old Hands about the prospects of a better system, and a better life on the Island if they behaved well, that he had been expressly forbidden by Gipps to do this, but he made no delay in sending his despatch to the Governor. Gipps at once wrote back an angry reply, but despatches took time to reach their destination, and by the time the reply reached Maconochie, his experiment had gone further.

It was customary in all the British dominions, to celebrate the monarch's birthday in true gala style among the free peoples, and Britain's Queen, the newly crowned Victoria, had her birthday on the 24th of May. Maconochie had, at that time, in 1840, been Superintendent and Commandant of Norfolk Island for three months; and he intended the Royal birthday to be commemorated in style. A General Order of the Day was issued on 20 May that on Monday 25 May 'Her Gracious Majesty Queen Victoria's birthday would be celebrated by a Public Holiday'. The holiday was for everybody. The gaol gates were to be opened, the prisoners would be given a ration of fresh pork, and he himself would be present at the midday dinner to be held in the prison yard. He invited the officers to be present also. A Variety show was to be given in the afternoon by the prisoners at the settlement, and later at Longridge also. In the evening there would be a display of fireworks, and during the daylight hours those men who wished to, could go where they pleased around the settlement, though not into the forest.

'Never was Norfolk Island so gay,' wrote the Rev. John West in his *History of Tasmania*, 'or its inhabitants so joyful, as on 25th May 1840.'[29] But it is safe to say that never were the administration staff so outraged. This made not a scrap of difference to Maconochie, the man with a mission. 'They too, are the Queen's subjects', he said; they should also share in the Birthday celebrations. It was a brave move, made by a man with faith in his fellow man, a move which he knew could well bring swift retribution for him, but worth a try.

A 21-gun salute was fired in the morning, the gaol gates opened, and the waiting men poured through on their first day of freedom for years. They were unfettered, free to wander or to play the village games they had almost forgotten how to play, free to wrestle, to walk along on the shore so close to the walled prison, or just to sit and dream of freedom or Home. At midday they ate and Maconochie ate with them. After the meal he mixed a Loyal toast, a concoction of rum well watered with lemonade made from the wild lemon of the Island. He called for 'Three cheers for our young Queen!' and the men cheered to the echo. Someone shouted 'and Three cheers for the Captain!' The roar was louder than before, and Maconochie knew then that he had been right, that each man no matter how hardened and bitter, could be reached in some way if treated as a man rather than a brute.

Then, the watered rum drunk, the dinner over, the afternoon's entertainment began. A set of Play-bills, carefully penned, had been nailed to posts throughout the settlement, announcing the programme to be presented at The Royal Victoria Theatre, Norfolk Island, giving the names of those taking part. All of them were Old Hands from the gaol. The costumes, scenery, and the music were all done by the convicts and the varied items must have surprised many of the civil and military officers and their ladies.

Two Acts of the admired comic opera, *The Castle of Andalusia* began the show, with ten principal parts and a chorus; then came a series of glees, and comic songs, and ballads. There was the 'Tent Scene from Richard II' played by H. Witton (whose original crime is lost in the mist of the past) and another playlet, 'Purse, or The Benelovent Tar'.[30] There were single turns by unexpected talent, such as the Dance Tyroleze, waltzed by Thomas Barry, and the Sailor's Hornpipe, light-footed by Michael Burns—his furrowed back which had felt over 2000 lashes upon it, decently covered for the occasion.

The show ended with a Grand National Anthem; only to be repeated later that day for the New Hands at Longridge, who, as orders required, were not allowed to mix with the men from the settlement. Maconochie sat it out there also, and he reported later, 'Not one case of misbehaviour or petty crime resulted from the indulgence. Some of the Old Hands even turned in early, at the end of the day'. When word reached the mainland it was as if a revolution had taken place on Norfolk Island. Convicts, scum of the earth, allowed to enjoy the Queen's Birthday! Drinking rum on the Island of the Damned! Cartoons lampooned Maconochie in the Press, outraged citizens loudly protested at such indulgences, anguished settlers saw hordes of murdering villains advancing on them, and Governor Gipps sent a resounding rebuke. He wrote to Lord Russell also:

> In all the conversations I had with Captn. Maconochie . . . I proceeded on the well understood assumption that the establishment of the doubly convicted was to be kept . . . entirely separate from the new establishment . . . Your Lordship will therefore, I am sure, readily imagine what must have been my surprise when I learned that Captn. Maconochie had, within a week after his arrival in Norfolk Island, abolished all distinctions between the two classes; that he had extended equally to all a system of extreme indulgence, and held out hopes, almost indiscriminately, to them of being speedily returned to freedom . . . Your Lordship will perceive . . . that though my disapproval of Captn. Maconochie's proceedings was notified to him on 28th of April 1840, and received by him on the 20th May, no

attention whatever was paid by him to my communications, but that, on the contrary, within a few days after the receipt of them the whole Convict population of the Island was regaled with Punch, and entertained with the performance of a Play . . .[31]

In his reply to that missive, Lord Russell suggested that Maconochie should be recalled from Norfolk Island and a severe disciplinarian installed in his stead. On Norfolk Island, the day after the Queen's Birthday celebrations, Maconochie pinned up a message of congratulation to all the prisoners on their good behaviour throughout the Birthday.

Within a short time of taking command, Maconochie had 1800 convicts on Norfolk Island, over 600 of them New Hands. More buildings were erected at Longridge, erected to the plans of Lieutenant Lugard of the Engineers, who had earlier been sent to the Island to estimate how many convicts could be accommodated there and what buildings would be needed. Lugard reported that the Island would not hold more than 4000 convicts; Gipps had considered sending 10 000. He was told, however, that the acreage was not above 9000, 'whereas before it had been estimated at 14 000'.[32] As it happened, there were never more than 2000 convicts on Norfolk Island at any time, during either penal settlement.

Lord Russell's suggestion of recalling Maconochie was ignored by Governor Gipps, who, however much he differed with him, held Maconochie in high regard and wanted to see if the new methods would be successful, if only in small measure. But he repeated his stern warning that 'Only the newly-arrived men, the New Hands, were to be subjected to the Maconochie System of Convict Management', and Maconochie, by then deeply enmeshed in the working of it, continued his methods with both Old Hands and New.

He removed one thorn in his side when he dismissed Charles Ormsby in August 1841. From the outset, the two men had been at odds, the one a Traditionalist, the other a Reformer. The dismissal came about when Maconochie found that Ormsby had brought charges against a convict known and trusted by Maconochie, for stealing or destroying sheep which were in his charge. A Board of Inquiry was appointed on the Island. Evidence given produced little, except more confusion, and in Maconochie's opinion pointed more to Ormsby's guilt; to him it seemed that Ormsby had deliberately planned the whole affair in order to rid himself of a 'Maconochie man'. Charges and counter-charges were made, Ormsby was sent back to Sydney, where Governor Gipps found the whole situation too difficult to unravel, as he wrote in yet another exasperated despatch to Lord Russell.[33] For Maconochie, it was fast becoming clear that those of his civil officers who disapproved of his Marks System, could and did make his administration an uphill task.

The man who took Ormsby's place was the Hon. W. H. C. T. Pery, who had been on the Island since Morisset's time as Clerk to the Commandant. Pery was a protégé of Lord Russell, and had gone to New South Wales with the recommendation that 'he should be advanced whenever an occasion might present itself'. In 1838 he married Mary Susannah Sheaffe, who died in August 1841 a few days after the birth of her second child. She and her child are buried on Norfolk Island. Pery married a year later, the daughter of Captain Horsley, an officer then serving on the Island, and two years later, through the unexpected deaths of several male relatives in Ireland, inherited the title of Lord Glentworth, and heir to the Earl of Limerick. He was then 36.[34] No doubt he found Ireland, even in the 'Hungry Forties' a calmer place than the turbulent Island where he had been for so long.

In spite of Maconochie's change from the former vindictive punishments to a just, though strict, method of discipline, he found that crimes of many kinds still took place. It was not possible for a mass of humanity already steeped in depravity to change except by the long and slow process of moral reform, and this he came to realise by degrees. His training, and much of his earlier life, had been spent among men bred to discipline, men who responded to encouragement, men who had chosen the life they lived, the life of a seaman. The principles by which he lived were barely known, let alone shared by the mass of convicts under his charge.

Maconochie found, in time, that he had to bring back the lash for one crime at least, the one he most abhorred, the 'unnatural offences' which were, on Norfolk Island, only too prevalent. To prevent this, he had lights set in formerly darkened dormitories, encouraged groups of men in reading aloud, during the evenings, tried a system which allowed trustworthy men to camp out in huts close to their work and their garden plots. Yet his Reports showed more cases of unnatural offences than those of his predecessors had done, and his detractors seized on this. He admitted there were more cases reported, but said 'When I heard of it, I followed it right to a conclusion either of guilt, or false accusation. When a man was found guilty he was punished with the lash. Before my time, few cases of this nature were brought to justice, it being considered more important to punish for crimes such as insolence to an overseer, neglect of work, failing to cap an officer and so on . . .'[35]

Thomas Cook's 'An Exile's Lamentations'

Although Maconochie had his detractors, as does any man who stands head and shoulders above the crowd in his manner of living, he also had his staunch supporters on Norfolk Island, some of them untutored, and some among the 'educated prisoners'. One such was Thomas Cook, an Old Hand who wrote of his life as a convict, including his period on Norfolk, while he was still there.[36] When he was discharged in October 1841 he gave his manuscript, 'An Exile's Lamentations', to Maconochie to read. Maconochie tried to get it published without success. The manuscript is now in the Mitchell Library, Sydney. Although most of Cook's 'Lamentations' were kept for his time in New South Wales, his recording of his time on Norfolk Island merits a place in that Island's history.

Cook had been transported to New South Wales when he was 19 for writing a threatening letter to one John Ruscoe of Whitchurch, in Shropshire, England; in which he said he would 'kill and murder him'. He was, at that time, an attorney's clerk, the son of good hard-working parents, and was also an astute and ambitious young man; too astute, for his letter-writing earned him a sentence of 14 years' transportation to New South Wales. 'The offence itself was the mere act of a youth bearing no malice, nor possessing the least cause for any against the prosecutor, but in reality done for the sport to entail alarm upon him without the most remote intention of injuring . . .' he writes, and this is his attitude throughout 'Lamentations'. He came to bitterly regret the 'sport' of writing a threatening letter.

In Sydney, where he arrived in 1831 or early 1832, he was sent as clerk to the Storekeeper at Hyde Park Barracks, where convicts were held before being distributed to the many road-gangs or similar works. Here he settled in well, until his 'astute' faculty surfaced once more, and he and the Storekeeper became embroiled in court proceedings. His lamentations now became loud and long—the accusations against him were all unmerited, especially the one of 'insubordinate conduct' towards Mr Ernest Augustus Slade, Keeper of the Prison Barracks, who lost no time in having Cook sentenced to work 'in the most distant Road Party in the Blue Mountain District, for the Governor's pleasure'. Cook writes, 'The inclemency of the weather, the haggard countenances of the men, the severity of the cold and the want of a second blanket to save half the frozen men from perishing, the cruelty of the overseers who robbed us of our rations; a sheet of bark for my head, the half of a threadbare blanket for my covering; many a tear did I shed when contemplating my hard fare, and this slight offence for which I had been doomed . . .' He was truly shocked by the 'horrible propensities' of his work-mates; '. . . the coarse and brutish language . . . coupled with their assignations towards one another . . . So far were these wretched men in depravity, that they appeared to have lost the feelings of men, and to have imbibed those that would render them execrable to all mankind.'

Cook had lost his privileges as an 'educated prisoner' long before this, and was to receive the lash several times while he was with various road-gangs. But a man who could read and write well was sure of an easier time than a labourer, and before long he went as book-keeper to an overseer some thirty kilometres down the road, only to fall again on his return when his gang-mates were arrested for killing and eating two fine young bullocks who had, unluckily, strayed too near the convicts' camp. Cook was scooped up by the police with all the others, protesting his innocence and swearing that the meat found in his tent had been given him by the overseer for whom he had worked. The gang was marched 30 kilometres to the stockade, where they were tried, and sentenced to 14 days, chained together and left with no covering of any kind to keep out the bitter frost, then returned to the road-gang.

Still wayward, Cook stirred up more trouble for himself when he was accused of forging the names of four men who wanted to go to Sydney. He did this by inserting their names on a list of witnesses already written, and was discovered though he denied the crime. This brought a spell in the Bathurst road-gang, a region where the Commandant of the prison settlement there had little time for men he considered loiterers at work. 'He enforced a system of running us to work at the point of a bayonet, five miles an hour. This continued for 14 days until some of the men offered resistance which led to much traffic in human flesh and blood, by the soldiers with their bayonets and the scourgers with their cat o'nine tails . . . at times, the officer riding past on his horse, would sentence the whole gang to 50 and 100 lashes each . . .' Cook, now a doubly-convicted felon, knew well what a lacerated back felt like.

It was at this time, in 1833, that a Circular was issued to the Justices of the Peace, by Governor Richard Bourke, requiring them to forward their returns of corporal punishment to the Colonial Secretary's office, and advising that '. . . the Instruments to be used for corporal punishment are to be the same throughout the Colony . . .' This Circular had been issued because some of the larger landholders had sent their 'humble petition' to the Governor, complaining of the inadequacy of the punishments given to their convict servants when they had been sent to the Magistrates Court. The floggings, they said, had been administered by incompetent scourgers whose 'cats' were threadbare and of no use, in most instances, as deterrents against repeated offences. Many of these colonists gave details of the best way to manufacture scourges which would inflict pain 'from the first blow', and thus give satisfaction to the convicts' employers. A second Circular was issued in August 1833 which gave instructions as to the method to be used when wielding these 'Intruments', for example 'by Counting for each lash, and taking care that the executioner administers each stripe with due force . . . has been observed in inflicting punishment . . . and report in the Column of Remarks . . . the amount of bodily suffering in each case . . . whether evinced by the effusion of blood, or by laceration, or other symptoms of bodily injury . . .'[37] This insistence that to be effective, punishment should be painful—and the more pain, the more good it would do—was the attitude taken by Government and other authorities. In his Returns for September 1833, Ernest Augustus Slade of Hyde Park Barracks, known for his unfailing severity, and in whose presence that month eighty-one men received 2250 lashes among them, drew attention to five cases who had been 'severely punished', adding 'in my opinion, the scourgers should be picked men of bodily height and power' so to administer the maximum amount of laceration and pain. But even in the lists sent in by magistrates and Justices of the Peace, there were men who refused to flinch under 100 lashes though the blood flowed 'copiously'.[38]

There were of course, scores of colonists whose assigned convict servants were well treated and content, clothed and fed far better than they would have been at home; men and women who served out their sentences in comparatively comfortable circumstances, though always under the shadow of summary punishment or a visit to the magistrate's court. The well-contented ones were not, however, the subject of government circulars or magistrates' returns, and they rate no mention in the records.

Cook, occasionally engaged in forging passes, writing letters under an assumed name, adding witnesses' names to already-written lists—though he strenuously denies any such involvement—as well as making plans to abscond, was as big a villain as any other. In his 'Lamentations' he wraps his supposed offences in such fancy verbiage that his meaning is often difficult to detect, but it seems that his final downfall was due to one of his many attempts at escape into the bush. He had fled and been recaptured often and his final fling ended in May 1836, when he was recaptured for the last time and sentenced at the Quarter Sessions at Maitland, to Norfolk Island for life. He was sent to await transportation, and was for a short time imprisoned on the hulk *Phoenix* which he records as '. . . that floating den of Infamy, in which scenes of human depravity nature shudders to contemplate, were exhibited with apparent delight'.[39] With ninety-nine other prisoners he sailed for Norfolk Island a month later and, having prayed to the Almighty during the voyage to 'suffer the vessel to sink'—a request which was not answered—he and the others arrived on Norfolk Island safely.

Major Anderson was Commandant and Cook was in such dread of him that he managed to escape punishment throughout the two and a half years that elapsed before the Major was transferred from the Island.

> Of those prisoners who defied the rules, the sentence of 300 lashes was the certain result . . . Insolence in many cases was construed into a threat of bodily injury and thus called forth a further infliction of 300 lashes. As an instance I would mention the case of two men named Moran and Smith, who were charged by a fellow-prisoner with wilfully passing over a portion of land without planting the corn given for that purpose. They were found guilty of 'Robbing the Earth of its seed', and each received 300 lashes. That much, for neglect of work.[40]

Cook's 'Lamentations' contain a horrifying account of the 1834 Mutiny, passed on to him by various eyewitnesses and, possibly, by some of the participants. The terrors wreaked by Foster Fyans exceed any reported at the time, and lose no colour in the telling.

> For a period of 5 successive months were the pitiable and already lacerated objects disciplined in a state of nudity for four hours each day with their Arms up and fingers extended, and such of them as betrayed the Slightest emotion of pain, were either stabbed by the Military or flogged on the spot. [These 'pitiable and lacerated objects' were, presumably, the 55 men chained together in cells, awaiting the result of their depositions, before the trial.]

In addition to the many sufferings under which they laboured . . .
the Irons rivetted upon them were as much as they could well drag,
and had been jagged purposely to lacerate their flesh. In the Gaol they
were literally naked, and so crowded that not one third of their
number could sit at one time. Mr Marshall, Chaplain and Surgeon of
Her Majesty's Sloop *Alligator*, upon visiting the Gaol, shed tears at
the moving sight which presented itself . . . he openly said it was by
no means surprising that Mutiny should take place, as even the Word
of God was scarcely to be found on the Island . . . They were also
compelled to brighten their chains, at all times to take off their Caps
to the Military, and even to the Guard House as they passed it.[41]

One of the truly shocking sections of Cook's 'Lamentations' deals with
punishments administered under various Commandants, figures which, as a
book-keeper, he must have had access to. Those of Michael Burns are the
most horrifying, and all occurred during Anderson's time and in little over
two years. This is the same Michael Burns who danced the hornpipe and
sang in the glees on the Birthday festivities of 25 May 1840.

NAME. MICHAEL BURNS.

14 days bread and water. Insolence.
14 days bread and water. Neglect of work 1 month gaol gang on
  suspicion of robbing store at Longridge, charge grounded on his
  refusing to account for a little first-class tobacco found in his
  possession.
1 month bread and water. Neglect of work.
300 lashes and to be confined in gaol till further orders. Charged with
  conspiring to set fire to the agricultural produce at Longridge.
  After liberation from gaol was again confined for being 20 yards
  from the Lumber yard gate.
200 lashes. Striking a fellow prisoner.
300 lashes, 12 months confinement in the gaol and 12 months
  addition to his Colonial sentence. Taking to the bush and robbing
  shepherds hut at Cascades etc. etc.
20 days on bread and water.
2 months bread and water. Insolence to Gaoler.
50 lashes bread and water.
300 lashes bread and water. Insolence to a soldier.
3 months solitary confinement in a dark cell. Singing a song.
300 lashes for insolence and threatening language to the Gaoler who
  declared himself to be in bodily fear.
100 lashes. Singing a song.
2 months solitary confinement on bread and water. Sending for Doctor
  to a fellow prisoner in the gaol.

200 lashes and kept in a solitary cell on the chain night and day for
   7 weeks with a lacerated back and no person to dress it. Endeavouring
   to break out of gaol.
300 lashes and to be worked in heavy irons on a chain and sleep in
   gaol 'til he left the Island. Bushranging and robbery.
100 lashes. Refusing to work being unable from debility.
50 lashes. Not being able to work and to be kept on bread and water
   till fit.
50 lashes. Not being able to work and to be kept on bread and water
   till fit.
50 lashes. Not being able to work on chain.
10 days bread and water.[42]

Burns suffered a total of 2210 lashes and almost two years in confinement, much of it in 'solitary', three months of that in total darkness, and at least six months of those two years with a diet of bread and water only.

*   *   *

During Maconochie's four years on Norfolk Island, Governor Gipps, watching the experimental Marks System with interest if not approbation, was often angered by the seeming contempt with which his firm instructions were received. Maconochie, though aware of the almost superhuman difficulties confronting him, had set his feet firmly on the path of prison reform by moral suasion and, like a blinkered horse, could see only the way that lay ahead of him. He brushed protests aside and instead, wrote long letters in reply, giving his reasons for this move or that, and the result he hoped to achieve by so doing.

   The distance between Sydney and the Island was a further frustration, for often, by the time Gipps's letter of instructions arrived, Maconochie had taken action. Beset as the Governor was by all the diverse problems of his government, it was understandable that he became impatient and frustrated with Maconochie and his Marks System. Yet Gipps always saw Maconochie's side of the question; it was a matter of trying to carry out his strict instructions from London, where in fact nobody had a close view or real idea of what was going on on Norfolk Island, and giving Maconochie a chance to work out his new System. The letters Gipps wrote to Lord Russell brought the reply that if the Governor thought it proper, he should remove Maconochie and the convicts under his control should gradually be moved to Van Diemen's Land.

   A number of Civil officers on the Island wrote bitter complaints about Maconochie's methods. Commissariat officer Smith attacked his policy of allowing breeding sows to 'ticket-of-leave' men. 'It is a well-known fact that when a man has lost his character in Society, he needs the very reverse of Captain Maconochie's treatment to keep him in subjection', he wrote, 'Norfolk Island needs a most radical change immediately. It bears no more resemblance to a penal settlement than a playhouse does to a church'.[43] Although he knew of these revilings Maconochie continued his System, helped by the addition of an Anglican chaplain, a catechist, and two Roman Catholic priests. He had asked for more clergy but was satisfied to have at least these. For his Jewish prisoners, approximately ten in number, he provided a room where they could meet and worship in private, 'for they were deplorably sunk and demoralized' he said.[44]

With the musical instruments brought across from Sydney, he formed a band, and at each church, a choir; he gave each man a garden of his own, and established evening schools for the men, employing educated prisoners to teach those who wished to learn, schools which he regularly inspected himself and gave prizes, in the form of marks, for work well tried, but these things were not compulsory and it was not to be expected that every prisoner would want to join in such activities.

Escapes were still attempted and a few succeeded. An attempt to seize the *Governor Phillip* was made in June 1842 by twelve convicts who had been placed on board overnight, ready to start unloading at daybreak. It was a desperate plan which had been laid by the men when they had expected a much smaller vessel to arrive, but the smell of freedom is such that even the presence of armed soldiers on the *Governor Phillip* was not enough to deter them, and for a short time it seemed the plan might succeed.[45] But within half an hour of the first attack, the soldiers and crewmen who had been earlier taken unawares freed themselves, shot their way through the convicts, killing five and wounding two others, and regained the ship. The surviving ringleaders were sent to Sydney for trial; four were hanged, two sent back to the Island in chains for life, and one acquitted. It had been a bold bid, and a drastic punishment, but by human comparison, less of a crime than the ordering of 300 lashes for 'singing a song'.

Maconochie had one failure, however, and this concerned his beloved eldest daughter Minnie (Mary Ann). All the family loved music and each member could play one or more instruments, so when Minnie wished to learn the violin and a teacher was available, the matter was arranged. Her progress was rapid, in music and in love. According to Lady Franklin, who as a matter of course knew much of what went on at Norfolk Island, and wrote regularly to her sister Mrs Simkinson, the gossips had already spread the news. The music teacher who had been a musician and composer in England before being transported for forgery, was handsome, educated and of good address.[46] How far the affair had gone when it was discovered has been kept a family secret. Minnie was, however, sent home to her aunt. She was then nineteen, a gentle girl, deeply in love. The episode made titillating talk for the gossips of Sydney and Hobart Town and caused many a sly wink among Maconochie's detractors. It was seen as a family disaster in those moralistic Victorian days and sections of the Press seized on it and reported it in veiled language which could be interpreted at will. When Maconochie returned to England, Minnie acted as his secretary. She died, unmarried, at the age of 32.

In February 1843 Governor Gipps made a sudden decision to go and see for himself what was happening on Norfolk Island. No prior information was sent to Maconochie and only when H.M.S. *Hazard* was seen off the Island was anyone aware that a vessel was making for the settlement. 'Notwithstanding my arrival . . . was altogether unexpected', he wrote in his despatch to Lord Stanley later, 'I found good order everywhere to prevail, and the demeanour of the prisoners to be respectful and quiet, the first impression produced on me was therefore a favourable one.'[47] Maconochie received the Governor enthusiastically, took him through the settlement, then left him to his visit of inspection.

> I visited every part of it, minutely inspected every establishment, almost every house and separately questioned or examined every person having any charge or authority, however small, taking down in writing the substance of what each individual stated to me, whilst he was yet present, though I did not administer the Oath to anyone.[48]

He went to the Agricultural Station at Longridge where the New Hands were housed, found that from a total of 679 men sent, 6 had escaped, 4 had been sent to Van Diemen's Land for bad behaviour, 1 to Sydney, insane, and 75 had died from dysentery. Dysentery was endemic on Norfolk Island, a scourge which attacked newcomers with virulence, though Old Hands, those who had survived early attacks, were immune. Gipps gave his reason for the deaths as the diet of salt meat and maize-meal bread. 'Fresh meat is given only once or twice a year, wheaten bread they never taste,' he wrote in April 1843, 'On the whole I would say their diet is as good or better than what prisoners receive in Government service in New South Wales, though I would not dispute Captain Maconochie's opinion that deprivation of wheaten bread on their arrival might have been the primary cause of the malignity with which the disease fixed itself among them.'[49]

It was the Old Hands, however, who surprised the Governor most: 'They seem far superior mentally and morally to the New Hands, and strikingly superior to them in cleanliness.' He even approved of the results of the Marks System as it had been applied to them and began to realise he had been over-hasty in his earlier judgements, before he had seen for himself; he realised, too, how biased some of his informers had been. For six days he walked and talked with the men on the Island, listening to all but making his own judgements. He realised that Maconochie's System of Moral Reform would work if he could be left to pursue it to a conclusion, and Maconochie's heart must have been high when the Governor left to return to Sydney and make his Report.

But the earlier despatches written in frustration and anger had had their result. The decision to recall Maconochie had been made some months earlier in London, and the news was on its way to Sydney at the very time Governor Gipps was on Norfolk Island. A new and severe disciplinarian was to be sent as Commandant in Maconochie's stead, to reinstate harsh Government regulations and punishments at the penal settlement. Captain Joseph Childs, of the Royal Marines, would leave England later that year, to arrive on Norfolk Island early February 1844.[50]

His recall was a bitter blow to Maconochie, the more so when Gipps assured him that he himself had been mistaken in his assumptions and had written to that effect though too late to avert the recall. But Lord Stanley had said that before the new Commandant took over, all the men promised a discharge at the end of their sentences would get it, and all who had earned 'Island tickets-of-leave' would be given probation in Van Diemen's Land where, after one or at the most two years, with good behaviour, they would be issued with Government tickets-of-leave.[51]

Before Governor Gipps left the Island he addressed the men who stood ranked before him, 'I have seldom seen a better-looking set, quite equal to the new prisoners from England . . .' which might not sound like praise, until put alongside Bishop Ullathorne's remark of around the same time 'Old Australian (Colonial) convicts looked like a long-degraded race by the side of the newcomers from England, whilst the Old Norfolk Islanders bore the stamp of degradation lower still beyond comparison, than even the Old Hands of Australian settlements. Higher testimony could not have been borne, to the result of Captain Maconochie's exertions'.[52]

Nine hundred and twenty doubly-convicted men had been discharged over the four-year term of Maconochie's administration, and by the time he sailed, he had discharged 538 more. He had wrought great changes during that four years, and in some of the men those changes were life-long. But it was to take more than a century before his Prison Reform methods were put into practice in Britain's gaols and in those in other parts of the world.

From Australia, Maconochie returned to England and in 1849 was made Governor at Birmingham's new prison designed with his theories in mind.[53] Again he was well before his time, found himself ridiculed for his leniency, was removed, replaced by a disciplinarian who soon made the prison a miniature Norfolk Island Penitentiary.[54] He continually wrote articles and pamphlets on prison reform, Minnie acting as his secretary until her early death in 1855. Maconochie himself died in 1860, aged 73. A friend wrote of him after his death:

> . . . his hair snow-white, his general appearance betokened premature
> old age, the consequence, doubtless, of his hard and bitter service . . .
> In his bearing was the frank cordiality of the sailor . . . the refinement
> and courtesy of high breeding and the noble attributes of a sincere
> Christian. It was his genuineness . . . his gentleness of manner . . .
> combined with great mental powers and earnest piety [that] gave
> Captain Maconochie that ascendancy of the most abandoned of men
> which the narratives of his Norfolk Island residence reveal . . .[55]

Maconochie is, without doubt, the most interesting, historically, of all the Commandants sent to Norfolk Island over its 68 years of penal settlement.

John Price, the last of them, may be the best known, but his reign is remembered only for its bloodshed and terror and the somehow 'just' retribution which overtook him later. Maconochie, often mocked for his revolutionary theories on the treatment of criminals, laid the foundations, on Norfolk Island, for the penal reforms that came eventually, years after his death.

The British press gave him no obituary, only the mention of his death in the appropriate columns. Mary Maconochie was given a very small pension, some years after his death. She died in 1869 and is buried beside him in St. Lawrence's Parish Churchyard, Morden, Surrey, England.[56]

Major Joseph Childs

17

NOT MUCH IS KNOWN OF MAJOR CHILDS'S EARLY LIFE. BORN IN 1787, HE BECAME A SECOND-LIEUTENANT IN THE MARINES IN 1809, REACHED the rank of captain in 1837, and was given the rank of Brevet-Major in 1843 at the time he was appointed Superintendent and Commandant of Norfolk Island. He was then 56 years old. He was reputed to be a strict disciplinarian, which was probably the reason he was chosen for the task, but to that date he had had no experience of living in a penal settlement, his career having taken him to America and Canada, the Napoleonic wars, and the campaign in Syria.[1] He was to learn that men trained only to the discipline of the gaol-yard were a totally different proposition from a corps of marines.

The reasons for the removal of Captain Maconochie from Norfolk Island, were set forth in Lord Stanley's despatch to Governor Sir George Gipps, in April 1843.[2] One, an ever-recurring reason, was the increasing cost of maintenance; another, the depredation of crops by Maconochie's 'ticket-of-leave' men as reported by the civil officers to Gipps, and by him relayed to Lord Stanley. But the overriding reason was the reported increase of 'unnatural' crime, as sodomy was then called. Lord Stanley wrote:

> Crimes, unattended with violence . . . appear, unhappily, to have been
> on the increase . . . I find no proof . . . of that renovation of Religious
> and Moral character which was promised . . . On the contrary, I find
> that ministers of Religion who have resorted to that place, have
> brought from it most unfavourable impressions on this subject . . .[3]

It is ironical that Lord Stanley's letter was penned at the very time Governor Gipps paid his unheralded visit to Norfolk Island, a visit which gave him a new outlook on Maconochie's experiment. The decision for Maconochie's removal stemmed directly from the frequency and tone of Gipps's despatches during the previous three years; he had voiced his complaints with vigour, and by the time he realised these complaints were often based on unconfirmed reports of others, men antagonistic to the new Convict System practised by Maconochie, it was too late for the decision to be reversed.

One of the 'ministers of Religion' who had written of the prevalence of unnatural crime on the Island, was the Reverend Beagley Naylor, a high-minded though somewhat strait-laced man who was distressed at the tales he was told by others, during his period of service on the Island.[4] He stayed on Norfolk Island eighteen months longer than Maconochie, and much of his comment was of Childs's regime, though he also disapproved of the freedom allowed convicts during Maconochie's time; an opinion he was to regret, for later, in a letter to a friend, he freely admitted 'the insurmountable difficulties surrounding Maconochie'. He wrote, 'how slowly I admitted, step by step, the full force of his propositions—how almost reluctant I was to admit that we perfectly agreed—how essentially I thought with him'.[5]

His earlier letter, written to Earl Grey and forwarded to Lord Stanley was, however, a startling revelation to their Lordships in London, who expressed their horror and decided that the cure for such penal evils was a course of even more severe discipline. Compassion was not an item written into the Rules and Regulations at that time. The new System of Convict Discipline was to be put in force immediately on the arrival of Major Childs at Norfolk Island:

> . . . the universal and inflexible rule must be that every man capable
> of bodily labour must be constrained to the steady performance of it,
> not for his own personal advantage but as the Law has subjected him.
> Compulsory and unrequited toil must be the rule . . .
> *Discipline* Rules should be established defining the gradations of
> punishment to be inflicted, and of mitigations of punishment to be
> allowed . . . effectual securities to maintain cleanliness, sobriety and
> decency. The prevention of moral evils of another Class may, perhaps,
> be partly effected in the same way . . . nothing but constant vigilance
> and inflexible rigour in enforcing the appropriate Punishments will be
> sufficient to restrain the immoralities to which I refer . . .[6]

He also warned of the urgent necessity of maintaining the utmost economy in expenditure, and recommended a keen look at the number of civil officers employed. Unnecessary expense seemed as abhorrent as unnatural crime to their Lordships of the Treasury. Agriculture was as always of primary importance—'with so great a manual power at his command, the Super-intendent ought to be able to render his Establishment independent of any foreign supply of the ordinary articles of consumption'.[7]

Lord Stanley knew nothing of the vagaries of climate on the Island, that rains were not seasonal or even predictable, and that drought often occurred in cycles of two and three years in succession. James Backhouse's suggestion that more 'muck-spreading' might be beneficial to the growing of crops, had not been taken up at that time, but the omission was to be rectified before long, when a competent Superintendent of Agriculture was brought in.

Major Childs arrived on Norfolk Island 7 February 1844 on the *Maitland* and with him were 200 prisoners direct from England. Maconochie was there to greet him, and to hand him the lists of prisoners who had earned their probation to Van Diemen's Land. Many of his 'probationers' had already been sent, but the vessels in Government service were infrequent, and a large number remained, though all who were eligible had been promised their removal.[8] At this time, the transfer of Norfolk Island to the Government of Van Diemen's Land was in process of being finalised, but it did not take place until September 1844[9] and this, in effect, made his initial period of command difficult for Childs, who had his instructions handed to him by Governor Gipps when he reached Sydney in January 1844, and later, was commanded to report to the Governor of Van Diemen's Land, Sir E. Eardley-Wilmot.

Childs's first despatch to Gipps, sent on 2 March 1844, details a number of 'domestic' problems among the civil officers, one of which was the difficulty of finding servants for their households. New regulations prohibited the employment of convict servants, but the civil staff strongly protested at this deprivation, and Childs was 'induced to suspend it until his Excellency's further instructions can be obtained'. Thus early was his lack of firmness shown to the staff. Another point of dispute of Regulations was the use of gardeners. Every family, it seems, had a convict gardener and the staff based their arguments that this indulgence should not be taken from them by saying 'that the greatest difficulty will arise in inducing free servants to come here at all . . . the expense of wages would be much more than they would have to pay elsewhere . . . that other peculiar difficulties exist here and, in short, that at this remote and secluded station their position would be rendered excessively irksome'.

> This is . . . the substance of the complaints which have reached me . . .
> I have, as before stated, been induced to suspend it: The provisions
> respecting gardeners I have carried out, and henceforth no more than
> the regulations provide for will be allowed, nor without payment for
> each convict so employed, of 6d. per diem. I have, however, deferred
> enforcing their sleeping in barracks until the remainder of the
> prisoners destined for Van Diemen's Land, have embarked.[10]

It was clear that Major Childs was no Maconochie in his handling of civil officers. Maconochie, who knew well the opposition many of his staff had for his new Convict System, stood firm on any principle he considered right, as in the case of Charles Ormsby, whose opposition ended in his dismissal. Childs, on the other hand, could be overborne by feasible-sounding arguments; he was to find no surer way of losing control than to acquiesce for the sake of peace. His reputation as 'a strict disciplinarian' had been gained in the Marine Corps, where thoroughly disciplined men were trained to obey orders without question and at once, or be punished. His charges on Norfolk Island were to tear his reputation to shreds.

One almost insuperable drawback for Childs was the lack of a suitable gaol. It seems incredible that after a lapse of twenty years there was no gaol newer than the one erected on the site of a public-house of the first settlement. A description of the gaol is found in Stewart's Report, made in May 1846:

> The gaol is an old stone building standing near the sea, not far from the landing-place. It contains two wards, about 15 by 20 feet, one cell between them 5 by 14, and three cells 4½ by 9. Adjoining in another building are four cells 5 by 15. These buildings, connected by a wall about 7 feet high, form an enclosure: the wards and the cell between them . . . a very confined space, not exceeding 50 feet square; while in front of the cells is a space about 30 feet by 7 feet . . . within which space, covered overhead by stone framing, the prisoners are permitted to take excerise for about one hour daily.
>
> At the entrance stands, external to the gaol, the gallows; so placed that you cannot pass the doorway without coming almost in contact with this engine of death. It is never moved . . . The gaol is generally crowded, is badly ventilated, low, and damp; the prisoners have each a thick straw mat, and a blanket, which forms a bed on the stone floor. At some short distance to the eastward of the old gaol is the new, of pentagonal form, each radiant intended to contain eighteen cells, 9 by 9, back to back, and opening to their respective partitioned yards, the whole standing on an enclosed parallelogram of some extent; only one set of eighteen cells has yet been completed; they are light, well ventilated, and appear to be dry. . . . There are now confined in the old gaol, awaiting trial before the Criminal Court, twenty-one prisoners, some having been committed upwards of eleven months; they are confined in seven cells, three of smaller size, about 4½ by 9 feet, are allotted to three men, the remaining eighteen prisoners being distributed in the four larger cells about 5 by 15 feet, whereof two contains four, and two five men each. The two wards occupied by the gaol-gang, the cell between them, used as a lock-up for men awaiting trial before the magistrate, and the seven cells last described, with the eighteen used for solitary confinement at the new gaol, are all the prison accommodation available for the control of upwards of 1000 men at the settlement, more than 500 of whom are felons convicted twice and oftener, and of the worst character . . . In addition to this, twelve cells for solitary confinement at Longridge, where there are nearly 600 men, and three at Cascade, with upwards of 300 men, are all that the island affords, an amount fearfully inadequate to meet the urgent . . . necessities of this extreme penal establishment, at which are stationed 2000 men.[11]

Major Childs had complained of the unfinished new gaol in his earliest letters to Gipps, and received the reply 'that the gaol was not on a good plan, and that the work was badly executed . . . indeed, his Excellency finally decided, when on Norfolk Island, that it should be abandoned. The erection, however, of a new gaol on the plan approved by Her Majesty's Government, is one of the measures most urgently required at Norfolk Island . . .'[12]

To this reply Childs made no protest to the effect that a decent building was of primary importance, and that to wait for a new plan and the assent of Her Majesty would mean a delay of at least two years or more—instead he actually apologised:

> Referring to paragraph 5, respecting the gaol, I regret exceedingly not having been previously made acquainted with his Excellency's view of that subject, or I should not in the face of that opinion have recommended its completion. I consider it would not have been my duty on public grounds to forward what better judgement had decided against.[13]

In the same letter, Childs made reference to the prisoners who had arrived on the *Maitland* with him:

> It affords me much pleasure . . . to remark to his Excellency on the good conduct of the prisoners generally during the past two months, more especially . . . the English prisoners per *Maitland*, from this ship we landed 193 criminals, the character of whose offences were so enormous as to attract public notice before leaving England . . . rape, murder, wounding with intent, and burglary . . . yet notwithstanding the severe labour they were almost immediately set to and continued up to this moment, but three cases of petty irregularities requiring light punishment have occurred, and this over but a few days short of three months . . . The labour I enforce is undoubtedly severe, yet the paucity of offence and the tranquillity of the island is the theme of general talk and wonder . . .[14]

This encomium to himself was at variance with the opinion of John Mortlock, an 'educated convict' who had come out on the *Maitland* with Childs, and had been appointed schoolmaster to the other convicts during the voyage. On Norfolk, he had been appointed wardsman, sluicing out the dormitory every day, and controlling the men at night, 'a difficult task in a dark room with lights forbidden—what could one person do with a hundred?' he wrote, in his book *Experiences of a Convict* written in 1857 after his release and return to England. He told of the appalling food he and the others were given:

> At breakfast and supper . . . insipid hominy made of unsifted Indian corn flour . . . a morsel of salt junk served out for dinner, and nauseous coarse bread, tasting . . . of sawdust. The debility brought on by this diet caused many deaths. Within the first fortnight we carried to their graves eight famished wretches of our ship's company . . .[15]

And of his first few months, of which Childs claims 'but three cases of petty irregularities requiring light punishment' Mortlock writes:

> During our first few months, many of my shipmates were flogged daily in the barrack yard under my windows (of the ward) on complaints made with a wicked purpose by the overseers: although I could shut my eyes, the horrid sound of the 'cats' upon naked flesh, (like the crack of a cart whip) tortured my ears . . . Petty dogs in office, in order to strike terror, would commonly threaten 'to see the backbone.'[16]

Mortlock's book gives a rare description of what a convict looked like:

> . . . a properly shaped head, pleasant to regard from any point of view, being quite a rarity, as was an agreeable well-formed mouth . . . Great numbers had long thick upper lips; most Old Hands possessed large noses. Perhaps Napoleon did not err in supposing this to be a sign of superior animal energy . . . a Case of raving madness never fell under my personal observation . . . mental derangement occasionally took place among persons, two-thirds of whom had cerebral malformations, or, at any rate, a cerebellum disproportionately developed.[17]

His luck took an upward turn when, in December 1844, he became tutor to the young son of Gilbert Robertson, the new Superintendent of Agriculture. Robertson was a forthright character, who had farmed for some years in Scotland, then migrated to Van Diemen's Land where he had been granted 400 acres (162 hectares) by Governor Arthur. He failed there, and was unable to pay his debts so was transferred for a while to the debtor's prison. From there he was given the job of Superintendent of a Government farm, but was dismissed later for supplying his assigned servants with wine to celebrate a harvest thanksgiving—a celebration which ended in a fracas and the death of one of the participants. After that, he became editor and reporter of the Hobart newspaper *The Colonist*. Before long, he published his own paper, the *True Colonist*, which proved a popular daily.[18]

Robertson courted serious trouble when he published what were called 'libellous charges' against Lieutenant-Governor Arthur, and Mr Rowlands, a Hobart attorney. Not surprisingly, he was again sent to gaol but managed to continue publishing the *True Colonist* as a weekly until he was released. The last issue of the paper was out on 26 December 1844, when he left to take up the post of Superintendent of Agriculture on Norfolk Island.

As tutor, Mortlock thoroughly enjoyed his job. 'A comfortable dinner now became a diurnal occurrence. Sleeping in a hut not far from the house, I enjoyed many a pleasant ramble in the evenings and on half-holidays'. He admitted to some embarrassment though when Mrs Robertson and the four Robertson daughters arrived from Van Diemen's Land, 'because of the horrid clothing . . . a source of intense humiliation'. Certainly, he looked nothing like the dandified figure he had been in Cambridge, in his 'magnificent velvet-lined cloak'. His two years on Norfolk were up in February 1846, and he, with others, was moved to a probation gang in Van Diemen's Land. He left the Island with some regret, as 'stowed away more like pigs than human beings, in the prison ship', he began the second period of his 21-year sentence, which in fact ended in 1855 when he received a formal pardon, signed by Governor Sir William Denison.

Not everything on the Island was tainted with evil or given over to despair, nor was everyone living there aware of the malevolence that hung over the gaol. Some inhabitants knew that regular flogging went on, but in those somewhat brutal days, flogging was an accepted part of prison discipline, and few people, other than military officers ever saw a flogging administered. There were officers' wives and children whose daily lives were much as they would have been on any outstation, and among them, was Elizabeth Robertson, eldest daughter of Gilbert Robertson the Superintendent of Agriculture. She left a diary in the form of a letter written to another sister who was living in Hobart Town after her marriage, and short as the diary is, it gives a picture of life outside the gaol walls.

Elizabeth comes through as a rather 'proper' young woman, retiring, church-going, thoughtful, and delicate. She died on Norfolk Island in April 1847, of consumption. Her 'diary' was written for Fanny, another sister, who married before the rest of the family left Hobart Town to join Gilbert Robertson and young George on Norfolk Island.

She was an acute observer of the people around her. She mentions almost all the civil and military officers and their wives and children in one or other of the pages, and each one is either approved of or dismissed with gentle irony. From the tone of her remarks, the life as lived by the free people on Norfolk Island seems to be more of a working-holiday style, the brooding atmosphere of the *ne plus ultra* prison settlement barely impinges, and this might, of course, stem from the fact that the Robertsons had spent many years in Van Diemen's Land where prisoners were no unusual thing, and severe punishments were daily occurrences, even touching their own assigned servants at times. Her diary gives a closer look at the social situation of the civil and military personnel than any other document has done, though Elizabeth made no close friends among the other women from the settlement and her descriptions are only external. She often writes of 'feeling very ill', and having to retire from the room where the others were laughing and singing or playing cards (of which she also disapproved at times), and she suffered from homesickness for Hobart Town, which she was never to see again.

In spite of his close association with the family, Elizabeth mentions John Mortlock only once, when she writes of George and his tutor going out on a shooting expedition and staying rather late in the forest; but in his *Experiences of a Convict* he refers to her as 'the eldest, guardian angel of the family in a season of sharp distress, became my favourite; most deeply did I grieve at the tidings of her decease, some months after I had left the Island, conveyed to me by a *Maitland* man with whom they had entrusted a friendly message . . .'

The 'season of sharp distress' is not identified in her diary, though there could have been more than one occasion when misfortune came to this singularly united family. Some time after Mortlock was transferred to Van Diemen's Land, Robert Pringle Stewart, a barrister and Police Magistrate from Hobart Town arrived on Norfolk Island to investigate affairs in the settlement, both from the prison and the civil point of view and this visit certainly preceded distress for the Robertsons. But no indication of this appears in the only section of Elizabeth's diary which is available. She wrote on the first page (earlier pages have been lost):

Sunday was a most beautiful day, I never knew anything like it, we went to church in the morning to hear Mr Chapman and had a very poor sermon, we were only in church an hour and five minutes . . .
We had scarcely got in before in came Captain Hamilton, Harding, Cockroft, and Lieutenants Simmons, Edwards, and Garstone, and they had not been in many minutes before in came Messrs Rowlands and Padbury. I wished them all at France . . . I was fairly *sick* of visitors, and as soon as tea was over I went off to my bed and left them.[19]

Poor Elizabeth, so used to the company of her sisters she could have had no idea of the sensation it must have caused among the junior and unmarried officers when not just one, but four eligible young women appeared, and all of them from the one family. Paying calls was the fashion with Norfolk Island society as it was elsewhere in those Victorian days:

We went today to call on Mrs Farrell and Mrs Tomes, they seem homely sort of people, also on Mrs Major Arney, she is a very beautiful woman, I think, and very ladylike but too ceremonious. This is the first day we have been in the settlement; there are nice buildings there but I'm glad we don't live in it, I think Longridge much more pleasant . . . When we were coming home we met the Major on the hill. He got off his horse, and stopped and had a long chat.[20]

Elizabeth's diary is the only known account of the social life of the Island. Ensign Best, in his *Journal*, and Anderson, in his pompous *Recollections of a Peninsula Veteran*, intimate that there was the occasional ball, but of families they wrote little or nothing. Elizabeth Robertson's pages are sprinkled with the names of wives, and for children she seems to have had that feminine interest common to most young women of marriageable age, though nowhere does she show anything more than an ordinary interest in the constant stream of young officers who came to Longridge to see her or her sisters—

This evening we saw a picnic party returning . . . two carriages
crammed full as they could hold, and two gentlemen riding on the one
horse. I daresay we shall hear tomorrow who were all at it, as we
intend to return the calls of the officers' ladies. I would rather do
anything else, almost.[21]

This was written a short time before Samuel Barrow arrived on the Island as
Stipendiary Magistrate. Elizabeth writes of doings in the Police court which
almost certainly she heard from her father, whose position as Superintendent
of Agriculture included that of magistrate also.

There are some dreadful bad men at the settlement, you would
scarcely believe how some of them will speak to the magistrates while
they are trying them. They ask if they 'think they care for flogging'.
One hardened wretch who is always getting flogged has got some of
the prisoners to tattoo on his back 'Flog well and do your duty'.
Yesterday Dr. Graham and Rogers [the chaplain] were trying a man
for robbery and sentenced him to three months in gaol. A spade and
an axe that he had stolen were in the office, and he seized them and
threw them at Dr. Graham on the bench; and they will tell the Major
to his face that they will see him . . . before they will work. They say
they were not sent here for work, but for reformation.[22]

It was reports of conditions like this, that decided the Van Diemen's Land
Government to send a Stipendiary Magistrate to Norfolk Island. Although
Barrow was not given arbitrary power he at times assumed it, and from the
time he arrived, he overruled the other magistrates such as Robertson, the
doctor, and even Childs, if he considered their punishments too light for the
prisoner. But Elizabeth writes:

All the men at Longridge behave very well, indeed no set of men
could behave better. We do not feel the least fear, though many do . . .
I went over with father to see the men shearing sheep . . . as we were
coming back we met the Major and Mr Holman and had a long chat. I
like the Major better every time I see him . . .[23]

By the end of September 1845 Elizabeth's health had become worse. Her
illness was not an uncommon one for those days, and little seems to have
been made of it, except for an occasional visit from Dr Graham, who brought
some 'phisic' when she 'spit a little blood'. She herself was aware that a
shadow hung over her, for she writes:

I often think of you with the greatest pleasure and anticipate the joy
of meeting you again, but somehow when I begin to reflect on the
uncertainty of life, the thought comes into my mind that we may
never see each other again in this world . . . Few families have lived to
our age without ever having had a break among them . . .[24]

She finds time, however, to record some of the good times:

> There was a grand picnic party to Orange Vale on Thursday, given by
> Captain Cockroft. All the officers and their wives were there except
> Major and Mrs Arney. Dr and Mrs Graham, Mr Holman, Mr, Mrs
> and Miss Ison [the other Anglican chaplain, who had replaced
> Reverend Beagley Naylor] Mr Rogers, Mr Chapman . . . Captain and
> Mrs Hamilton and a Miss Wells . . . at about twelve o'clock they
> stopped by our gate and . . . came in and asked us to go with them . . .
> We went at two o'clock . . . it is a beautiful place for a picnic, we had
> dinner on a grass plot under an immense large oak, all were very
> attentive to us . . . but talk of noise! One of our Kangaroo-point
> picnics was nothing to it! And to finish it off, two of the gentlemen
> got drunk and one of them, a young officer, struck another gentleman
> in the mouth with his fist, he returned the blow and set the officer's
> nose bleeding, *before all the ladies*!
>
> One of the bushrangers was taken last night. Yesterday . . . a man
> at the settlement was stabbed by a wretch of the name of Logan, who
> had been sentenced to be hanged three times . . . There has been a
> Court Marshal [*sic*] sitting this two days, trying Sergeant Price for
> selling the rum he had to serve out to the soldiers, and making it up
> with water.
>
> On Saturday morning three men escaped from the settlement, and
> about ten at night a shepherd . . . took one in the scrub just at the
> back of our garden . . .[25]

Escapes into the bush were fairly common. A bold or desperate man would
find it fairly easy to dash away from a gang while working in the fields,
especially if he had companions who were in the know, and though he knew
it was only a temporary freedom, it was worth a try and there was always a
hope that this time Lady Luck would take a hand. One Monday morning a
break-out happened at the Kingston settlement, and Elizabeth writes:

> Mr Rowlands came running out of breath with a pistol in his hand, to
> tell us that five very desperate men had escaped from the gaol and had
> come towards Longridge. He ran on to protect his own house. We
> have only one gun which father gave to Mr Bolton, a free overseer, to
> go with a party of men in search of them, but not one of the prisoners
> would go with him. Dr Graham . . . succeeded in riding one down,
> but the other four escaped, which now makes seven men in the bush.
> The whole Island is in a state of excitement, police are scouring the
> bush in every direction, and several of the free people are out . . .[26]

Four were recaptured next evening in a gully about two hundred metres from
the Robertsons' house, and another of the seven was caught the next day, but

this event was not unusual enough to have been mentioned in any official document, except perhaps an official despatch of day-to-day happenings. Of the Longridge farm, we have one picture given in Elizabeth's diary:

> I got up early and went for a ride with father when he went round the field. I went several places where I have never been before, and was compelled to acknowledge that Norfolk Island is a most beautiful spot . . . the whole of the views were delightful, all the crops seem to be flourishing. There were about four hundred men at work, and twenty teams of bullocks, and three teams of horses . . . which would have pleased the Quakers Backhouse and Walker.
>
> I went down to father's office today and who should come up and speak to us but the celebrated Martin Cash. He is considered a very quiet, well-behaved man here. Mother and Meg wanted to ask him into the kitchen to get his dinner but I objected, for I do not think such a man ought to be countenanced, particularly by *Vandemonians . . .*[27]

Illness was taking its toll of Elizabeth and her gentle kindly nature. Her diary, which gives such a vivid picture of family life, its stresses and its joys, even on brutal Norfolk Island, does not continue after 1845. She writes nothing of the dramatic events of 1846, the removal of Major Childs, or the arrival of John Price in August, and the dismissal of her father soon afterwards.

The undercurrent of turbulence, barely perceived in the house of the Agriculture Superintendent, at least by his daughters, grew daily in the Kingston settlement. The stringent Rules laid down by Lord Stanley at the time Major Childs was given command of the Island, had added to the defiance of the prisoners.[28] There was an air of recklessness among the men of the Ring when word filtered through, as it inevitably did, of the punishments that could be meted out for the least infringement of those Rules.

It had been laid down that good conduct could not delete any time from the sentence to be served on Norfolk Island, but any slight offence might add time—from three months to three years—at the decision of the Commandant. When a man might not even be aware of what his 'infringement of the Rules' was, yet found himself condemned to spend months or years longer in the purgatory that was Norfolk, any remaining hope died.

> At this moment, one half of this hemisphere is morally ruined by the pest of neglected convicts; and very soon . . . from a thousand quarters the question will reach you, 'What is to be done with your convicts?' When that moment comes, my Lord, perhaps you may be induced to take a wiser course . . . At all events, my Lord, you must do something. Norfolk Island cannot remain the plague-spot it is much longer . . .[29]

This is part of the closing paragraph of Reverend Beagley Naylor's letter to Earl Grey, written in 1846. It was to lead to a number of things, among them, an Inquiry into the state of affairs on the Island.

But before that day came, the mutiny of July 1846 occurred. It was a flash-point mutiny, a sudden expression of hate that had been smouldering for a long time, and which led to the deaths of many men on Norfolk Island.

Men of the July Mutiny

18

THE JULY MUTINY WAS THE CULMINATION OF A LONG PERIOD OF MIS-
MANAGEMENT, THOUGH THE INCIDENT WHICH SPARKED IT OFF
seemed a minor one. The thought of revolt simmered perpetually among the
Old Hands, the incorrigibles who had not or could not benefit from
Maconochie's efforts at reformation by moral persuasion. For such men,
with a lifetime of crime and mismanagement behind them, reformation was
not possible within the short time Maconochie's System had been tried. He
knew total success was not possible without many years of trial and the added
strength of hope, when he wrote 'There is no man utterly incorrigible. Treat
him as a man and not as a dog. You cannot recover a man except by doing
justice to his manly qualities . . . none are incorrigible where there is
sanity . . .'[1] But he had not succeeded, on Norfolk Island, in recovering the
overlords of the lumber-yard, those men of the 'Ring' whose oath of
brotherhood was

> Hand in Hand, On Earth, in Hell
> Sick or Well, On Sea or Land
> On the Square, ever.
> Stiff or in Breath, Lag or Free,
> On Earth, in Hell, You and Me,
> In Life, in Death, On the Cross, never.

The Ring, by some regarded as a figment of writers' imagination, and
brought to life in Marcus Clarke's novel *For the Term of his Natural Life* and
Price Warung's *Tales of the Early Days*, was no imaginary notion but actual
fact. Robert Pringle Stewart witnessed it during his visit of inspection in May
1846, when one of the Old Hands, openly smoking a pipe when in the
Lumber-yard, refused to remove it after being ordered by an officer.[2] Instead,
his mates crowded round him, thus preventing him from being taken off to
the cells, and the officer had to withdraw hastily. These were the 'flash-men',

or gang-leaders of the settlement, all of them Capital Respites, former bush-rangers, cattle-thieves, robbers, pirates, men whose wits were sharpened by hostility against all authority, men who thought nothing of stabbing another convict who had given evidence against one of the Ring, or had assisted in a capture, or indeed anyone who behaved well. These men of the Ring were the toughest of them all, and showed it in the contemptuous manner they accepted whatever punishment was meted out to them.

Five officers were on the Bench at the Police court: Major Childs, the Military doctor, the Officer commanding the Garrison, the Chaplain some-times, and Gilbert Robertson as senior Superintendent though he did not always attend. The Major would order 'Fifty lashes', and the flash-man jeered 'Not enough t' take me coat off for!', and when the hundred was ordered instead '*That's better*'.[3] The lashing that followed was taken, as their Oath demanded, without flinching no matter the ferocity of the scourger or the amount of blood he made to flow. Backs were knotted with scars, bones beneath the crusted skin gleamed ivory-white, but no flash-man gave satisfaction by so much as a whimper.

This hard core of men was the reason Samuel Barrow had been sent to the Island in August 1845 as Stipendiary Magistrate, some eighteen months after Childs's arrival. Barrow was a barrister of the Middle Temple, London, before being appointed by the British Government as assistant Police Magistrate in Hobart Town, where, at that time, John Price was the Police Magistrate. When Barrow arrived, the post had been filled, and he was given a lesser appointment at Bothwell. He was 28 at the time he came to Norfolk Island, 'a bumptious brutal fellow whose arbitrary assertions of authority . . . caused great resentment among the free officials . . . Rogers and others ascribed much of the discontent among the convicts to his harsh punishments and brutal methods of his convict police . . .'[4] Rogers was the Anglican chaplain at the time, and he has a significant part in the later period of the Island's history.

Despite Barrow's bumptiousness and brutality, the men of the Ring were to best him eventually, as they bested everyone and everything except Death itself. Barrow, in turn, was possibly the major cause of Childs's dismissal from his post as Commandant of Norfolk Island, by the revelations he gave to his friend Pringle Stewart whom he had known well, in Van Diemen's Land—of Childs's vacillating decisions and lack of firmness. It was this that Barrow exploited, overriding decisions made by the Commandant on punishments and at times, rather than dispute a sentence handed down by himself, Childs would not dissent when Barrow doubled or added to it. 'The Christ-killer' was Barrow's name among the men of the Ring, and Barrow was to be the first victim of their hate if the opportunity came; Childs, the second, and the prison constables along with them.

But Barrow's arbitrary assumption of power was not a valid reason for Childs's 'vacillating', as Pringle Stewart described it. As Commandant he would have been aware of much that went on in the Kingston Prison settlement; he, as well as Barrow, had his informers among the men and it is hard to believe that he knew nothing of the tortures that took place in the gaol, the barracks, or the lumber-yard. Prisoners brought before the court would have physical evidence of 'tobacco-track', the 'tube-gag' and other sadistic cruelties perpetrated by vengeful overseers, turnkeys or gaolers; but it needed more courage than many of the pitiful wretches in court possessed, to state openly what went on out of sight of authority; inevitably, such telling would bring a repeat or worse.[5]

No man was safe from 'tobacco track'. Tobacco, forbidden to all but a few of the best-behaved men, was prized beyond food by the convicts. Only the overlords of the Ring dared to smoke openly, challenging the constables to seize them, and the men could be searched anywhere, in the fields, the quarry, the open privy behind the lumber-yard, even in a hammock at night. The victim was seized by the throat, his head forced back and his mouth opened, with the end of a bludgeon between his teeth if necessary, while the searcher grouted with filthy fingers inside the mouth, for traces of tobacco or a shred caught on tongue or teeth. The punishment was twenty-five lashes on the spot, more if resistance was offered. Talking in the cell brought the 'tube-gag', a small round tube of hard-wood with a hole bored through the middle, a leather strap fixed to each end. The victim's hands were tied, the gag thrust into his mouth often with such force that his teeth were knocked out, the strap winched tight and fastened at the back of the head. A low spasmodic whistle, a froth of blood, were evidence the gag was working well. Men who proved difficult customers were taken outside and chained to a lamp post, hands fastened behind it and feet chained together, and there left for several hours, in all weathers. These were but two of the tortures, and each must have left physical evidence.

'Scavenger's daughter' was another refinement practised in the gaol. The offender's head was forced to his knees as he sat on the floor of his cell. He was then trussed like a fowl readied for the oven, and sometimes the gag was applied for good measure. 'Spread-eagle' was another method of testing a man. Two strong ring-bolts were affixed to the cell wall six feet (183 centimetres) apart and five and a half feet (168 centimetres) from the floor, a third bolt fixed to the floor. The victim was fastened facing the wall, his outstretched arms tied to the wall-bolts, his feet fastened to the floor, and if he called out or made any protest his mouth was closed by the gag. None of these obscenities was court-ordered, but no one, it seems, was inclined to forbid them.

There was the 'water-pit' as well. This was a cell below ground level, where salt water came up to a man's waist, and he was left there for days. There was the strait-jacket, the strapping-down, and the solitary cell in which a man could be imprisoned for weeks underground in total darkness, his food pushed through to him as if to a savage beast, his only company the swarming rats. Those men who did not succumb, and there were a few, became more defiant, harder and more cunning, and they bided their time,

o

waiting for the day which would inevitably come, when they would find either freedom or death, preferably by force.

This vengeful and determined hatred grew ever stronger in the prison at Kingston. The men knew, by some weird bond of brotherhood intelligence, that there was to be no remission of sentence for them no matter how well they behaved, and so the ones with nothing to expect but punishment and more punishment, chose their incorrigible way to eventual death.

In May 1846 Commissioner Robert Pringle Stewart, a Police Magistrate in Van Diemen's Land, arrived on Norfolk Island to conduct as thorough an investigation into every aspect of administration on the Island, and the conditions under which all classes of inhabitants lived, as could be made in a two week stay.

Stewart, whose *Report* reads like that of a man without humour, but with an eagle eye for breaches of the Rules, was a man also without sympathy for criminals, and certainly a man with little compassion and small understanding of the common man. He visited every department of the Island administration and inspected all the records, made instant judgements and copious notes. He seems to have missed nothing, his *Report* is comprehensive, a horrifying document filled with substantiated facts; the administration of the Island seems to have had as much worth in it as a rotten apple. His findings have little that is good, he exposes every evil from the quality and scarcity of food supplied to the convicts, along with the inferior quality of their clothing; to the horrors of torture and incessant flogging and the inadequacy of their housing and the crudity of their privies.

There were almost 2000 convicts on Norfolk Island at the time of Pringle Stewart's visit, 1064 at the Kingston settlement, 556 at Longridge, and 328 at Cascades.[6] Only at Longridge did he find the men properly worked and fed, indeed, his sharp eyes discovered some of the men were given privileges they were not entitled to, such as fresh meat when the issue should have been salt beef, gardens where they could grow vegetables, and in some cases, the privilege of sleeping out, near their daily work. Such indulgences were uncalled for, and were the subject of much jealousy by others, he reported.

Mr Champ, the Comptroller-General of Convicts, who had sent Pringle Stewart to Norfolk Island to make his *Report*, was deeply disturbed at the findings, and in his letter to the Governor, Sir E. Eardley-Wilmot, gave his opinion of Major Childs's administration:

> Making every allowance for the difficulties with which Major Childs
> had to contend, from the want of buildings sufficiently extensive, and
> adapted for the proper coercion of the number of convicts on the
> island, still, the conclusion remains, in my opinion inevitable, that
> either from want of experience or from an absence in his own
> character, of the qualifications necessary for the control of criminals,
> he is totally unfitted for the peculiar situation in which he is
> placed . . . It is impossible indeed to conceive that an officer endued

with sufficient degree of firmness would have tolerated, supported as
he was at all events, by a sufficient military force, the insolent
insubordination of the convicts, and allowed it to pass uninquired and
unpunished . . . unless an officer of more experience, energy and
decision be placed at the head of the establishment at Norfolk Island,
all the other remedies which may be resorted to will be found to be of
but comparatively small avail.[7]

The Executive Council which deliberated Stewart's *Report* decided that
Major Childs should be immediately recalled and a new Commandant, Mr
John Price, be sent in his place. But on the day the decision was made, 1 July
1846, the mutiny burst over the Island like a flow of molten hate.

I submit that proper and secure means of coercing such men should
have been afforded me before they were sent to this island, and not to
have left me powerless . . . to seek for means to restrain the worst
passions of the worst men that the annals of criminal jurisprudence
can hold forth to the world as an example of all combined evil . . .[8]

This is part of Major Childs's letter to Colonel Champ, the Comptroller-
General in Van Diemen's Land, in explanation of 'the most serious, disastrous
and fatal outbreak' which occurred on the morning of 1 July 1846. It was a
valid observation, but it could make no difference to the decision, already
taken, of the Executive Council to send John Giles Price to Norfolk Island as
Civil Commandant in Childs's place, as soon as possible.

The morning of 1 July was much the same as any other morning in that
cold month of mid-winter. The 'turn-out' bell rang as usual, the men tumbled
out of their frowsty wards as usual, and assembled in the prison barrack-yard
for the token prayers before breakfast as usual. There was a certain amount
of muttering among the crowd of Old Hands, but the prisoners were
mustered and marched to the usual place of worship, where prayers were
read and the murmuring still went on. After prayers they were marched back
to the lumber-yard where they were to take breakfast. With them was
Patrick Hiney, assistant Superintendent of Convicts, who took the muster;
and after prayers a group of the men of the Ring gathered in the middle of the
yard, surrounded Hiney and complained that the kettles and pans in which
they cooked their food, had been taken away.[9] The maize-meal they saved
from the previous day's ration was also gone, taken from the boxes where
some of the men kept their own belongings. Hiney left them, went into the
Cookhouse and told the overseer there that it looked like trouble brewing.
The overseer, Stephen Smith, a former convict, was alarmed at this, for he
was not a member of the powerful Ring and knew he could expect little
mercy from any of them if things turned nasty.

When Hiney came out of the Cookhouse he found a great body of the
prisoners stirring around like a hive of disturbed bees, and suddenly a yell

went up 'Come on, you *** '. Hiney walked over to one of the men, William Westwood a former bushranger from Van Diemen's Land, whose nickname was 'Jackey-Jackey', and said 'What's the matter, Westwood?' 'There's something the matter, I don't know what', Jackey-Jackey answered, and as he said it, the whole body of prisoners surrounding Hiney made a rush out of the lumber-yard gate, Jackey-Jackey with them. They made for the convict barrack stores, which had been locked after the cooking utensils had been placed in there the night before, and brought the confiscated vessels out.

The shouts died down while the men cooked their breakfasts over the wood fires in the lumber-yard and things simmered down for about fifteen minutes. Hiney left them and went off to tell the other overseers and constables gathered outside the gates in preparation for marching the convicts to work. Suddenly a shrill voice cried 'Come on—we will kill the *** ', and the men, led by Jackey-Jackey came pouring out of the gates, each man grabbing a billet of wood as a bludgeon, or a pole or an axe, anything that was handy to use as a weapon. John Morris, a police constable stationed by his hut at the gate, was felled with a blow, two of the other overseers standing by were knocked over by men following Jackey-Jackey and the mob rushed on towards the Cookhouse. Stephen Smith had hidden himself behind the door, and it was the work of seconds for Jackey-Jackey to raise his bludgeon and smash it down on Smith's head with the force of a madman.

'Come on, you *** ' he yelled, 'Follow me and you follow to the gallows!' The men followed, more than fifty of them, while the rest of the prisoners in the yard held back, fearful of the outcome of this explosion of hate and killing. Jackey-Jackey and his mob, crazy for blood, reached the first of the row of huts where the constables were housed near the Lime-kiln, a few hundred yards from the gate and rushed inside. The two constables, Saxton and Quion, were asleep and Jackey-Jackey split the first man's head from forehead to chin with a blow. The second man, wakened from sleep, shouted 'I saw who did that!' They were the last words he spoke. In seconds he too was bludgeoned into a bloody pulp about the head and the mob rushed, shouting like maniacs, towards the Stipendiary Magistrate's house. Barrow was the man they wanted, Barrow 'the tyrant', the 'Christ-killer' as he was known among them, from his use of the scourge.[10]

But by this time the military had been alerted, and Barrow, who had risen early that morning in preparation for a journey into the interior of the Island for some other purpose, was already alerted by overseer Price who had given the alarm and informed the Commandant and the commanding officer of the garrison. The sight of Major Harold and his men, their muskets at the ready, advancing towards the mob, caused them to turn and rush back to the lumber-yard. There had been no formulated plan for the mutiny, it was an eruption as unexpected by themselves as by the officials and the military; an eruption as inevitable as death, the end result of petty deprivations which acted like a rasp on a long-opened wound. In his despatch to Sir E. Eardley-Wilmot, Childs wrote:

The details of this lamentable affair are contained in the depositions
sent herewith, and in a Report from the Board of Officers, which I
caused to be assembled . . . the horrible murders were perpetrated
with so much rapidity that their prevention was impracticable, and
the savage ferocity exhibited by the leaders in the tragedy was only
allayed by the arrival of the military under the command of Major
Harold.[11]

The Commission to investigate the mutiny consisted of Major Harold,
Captain Hamilton Royal Engineers, and Samuel Barrow the Stipendiary
Magistrate, who met on the afternoon of 1 July. They took evidence from
the officers who had either witnessed the affair, or had been on duty at the
time. Their first witness was Mr William Foster, Superintendent of Colonial
Prisoners, whose job it had been to order the collection of the cooking
utensils, the spark which lit the fuse of violence.

The usual half-yearly Board of Survey was ordered to be held this day
upon all stores in my charge. I was, in consequence yesterday
preparing for the said Board. At three in the afternoon I went
through the Lumber Yard to ascertain what cooking utensils,
serviceable or otherwise, were there. I found a great deficiency of tin
dishes and mess kits; numbers of the dishes had been converted into
small cooking apparatus. I missed several saucepans. I consulted with
Free Overseer Smith, in charge of the Lumber Yard, Cook House &c.
whether it would be advisable . . . to search the Lumber Yard
premises in the evening after the prisoners were locked up in their
barracks. He said he wished to be excused that duty as he was all the
day amongst the prisoners in the Lumber Yard . . . and Mr Baldock,
Acting Chief Constable and the other free constables would do that
duty . . . Mr Baldock reported this to Mr Stipendiary Magistrate
Barrow, who sanctioned the proceeding . . . The search in question
took place, and all the articles that were seized, a great numer of all
descriptions, were placed in the Convict Barracks Store . . . This
morning, about a quarter before seven o'clock, after public prayers, I
was in my office . . . when my attention was suddenly attracted by a
vast mass of prisoners (about 500) coming into the Barrack Yard . . .
I saw this mass go up to the Barrack Stores . . . the mass shortly . . .
returned and left the yard. I went to see what they had been about and
found they had taken away all the seized articles.[12]

The march of events is told as it actually took place. It is clear that the
prisoners knew their utensils were going to be removed. What they had not
known was *when*. Mr Foster, preparing to make a written report to the Civil
Commandant about this insubordination, decided that discretion was the
better part of valour when, on his way from his office to his home, he saw a

rush of prisoners towards their barracks; he went to look for Childs himself. In the short space of time it had taken him to go from his office, which was at the gate of the prisoners' barracks, to the Old Gaol some hundred metres away, the mutiny had taken place, the men had been murdered, and the military had arrived on the scene. The eruption was only a matter of minutes from start to finish. Hiney then gave his evidence as already described, and Alfred Baldock, Acting Chief Constable repeated much of what the others had said about the seizure of the cooking pots and kettles. In addition, he seized a large quantity of knives.

> Next morning the men at muster seemed to be in their ordinary state.
> After muster I had occasion to go to my quarters to get some
> blanketting for Mr Superintendent Foster, which had been previously
> seized . . . A constable . . . came running down to me and reported a
> great mass of prisoners . . . had rushed the stores and taken out all the
> utensils deposited there. I . . . went to the convict barracks to inspect
> the store and on coming out I saw several constables jumping from
> the upper storey out of the windows of the police hut which overlooks
> the prisoners barrack yard. A prisoner named Douglas said to me
> 'Save yourself, or else you will be murdered;' at the same moment
> both sashes of the windows of the police hut were smashed. Free
> overseer Dwyer told me that some of the prisoners were looking out
> for me and that Overseer Price had gone for the military.[13]

Baldock's evidence corroborated Patrick Hiney's. He was ordered by Barrow to seize every prisoner on whose clothes were any spots or marks of blood, and reported that he took six prisoners in charge for blood-stained clothing, and forty-five others under strong suspicion of having been concerned in the murders. Nine of the men were probation prisoners direct from England, the others were doubly convicted colonial prisoners.

When asked what he thought was the immediate cause of the outbreak he said 'I attribute it to the seizure of the pots and kettles', and went on to give his reasons the men at the core of the mutiny had sway over the rest of the prisoners:

> There are some forty or fifty prisoners leagued together in the lumber
> yard, all these men are doubly convicted colonial prisoners; they
> exercise a fearful sway over the whole body of prisoners. These men
> were in league with the cooks, who supplied them with the best of the
> food, abstracted from their fellow prisoners' rations, thereby enabling
> the cooks to derive advantage from the mal-appropriation of the
> victuals by them abstracted . . .
>   The cooks gave the provisions gratuitously to these forty or fifty
> men, who kept the body of the prisoners down, and in awe, from
> bringing these extensive pilferings and frauds under the notice of the

authorities; in fact this system of plunder was only clearly brought to light very recently. Some short time back Overseer Smith had been placed in charge of the cookhouse, in consequence of the rumours then rife respecting the before-stated malpractices . . . I do not hesitate to affirm that no officer, overseer or constable is at any time safe in his life, when in the lumber yard in the exercise of his duty . . . I have every reason to believe that had not the military arrived at the moment they did . . . a body of fifty or sixty prisoners had determined to take to the bush and commit every atrocity against the free inhabitants . . .[14]

Dr Everett however, took a different view of the outbreak. He had been on Norfolk Island for some time and was called Doctor 'Bluestone' by the convicts from his habit of prescribing bluestone to rub on their backs after a flogging.

On the 1st of July, in the morning at eight o'clock, four bodies, dead and dying, were brought to the convict hospital — of these one was dead when brought in, and two died a few minutes after, the fourth, at this moment, July 3rd, 11 o'clock a.m. is in a dying state.
These deaths were caused by violent injuries sustained from axes and other deadly weapons; the wounds had been chiefly inflicted on the head and face; another man was also brought in . . . with a fracture of his skull likewise caused by violence, and two other persons were brought in with severe contusions.[15]

He was asked what he considered the cause of such violence, and replied that it was the removal of the pots, kettles and other cooking utensils. He was then asked:

Q. Do you think in your medical opinion, that there is any necessity for the prisoners cooking their own maize meal?
A. I certainly do think it necessary; . . . had I been aware of the change made in the cooking of the prisoners' food I should most decidedly have written to the Civil Commandant on the subject . . . I think they should be allowed to cook their maize meal themselves as by so doing, they constitute it a nutritious and wholesome diet, which is of the greatest importance at this moment, under the prevailing fatal form of dysentery . . . they also burn or roast some part of the maize meal and mix it with hot water, thus making a warm drink which . . . in this climate, is a wholesome and desirable beverage.[16]

The next witness was Aaron Price, Principal Overseer of Public Works, and his evidence was much the same as Baldock's and Hiney's. Aaron Price was a tough and unemotional man who had been through every mutiny and near-mutiny that had occurred on Norfolk Island since the start of the Second Settlement, a man who seemed content to remain on the Island long after his sentence was remitted and his freedom regained. He was one of the men the Ring wanted to kill, for some of them, too, had been on Norfolk for many a long year and would have known him when, as Police-runner, he had informed on them and brought them untold punishments.

I saw a great number of prisoners rush out of the lumber-yard towards the spot where I was standing along with two other free officers; the foremost of the men, who had a large bludgeon in his hands, said aloud *'Let us begin with these *** wretches*, we will *settle* them *first*;'—thus saying, he made a tremendous blow at me, which I happily evaded and the blow struck free officer Pinkney with much force on the shoulders; the man . . . is Westwood, commonly called Jackey-Jackey.

Q.   What do you think was the cause of . . . the atrocities committed . . .?

A.   In my opinion the cause was the prisoners having been latterly prevented from having their fling, which they had formerly . . . had not the military come up, the prisoners would have slaughtered every free officer on the island.[17]

Price was closely questioned on why, in his opinion, things had come to such a pass, and replied that the 'very vicious prisoners ought to be selected and separated in a strong place from the general body of prisoners', and added his advice on the best way to separate, and keep separated, the two classes. He was asked how long he had been on the Island:

I have been twenty years and four months on this island. I was the Police Runner for many years, which gave me immense opportunities of getting acquainted most thoroughly with all the ins and outs of prison life, and as Principal Overseer of the Works these last nine years, I have added considerably to my knowledge of the men, and the best means of working and employing them.[18]

Gilbert Robertson, the Superintendent of Agriculture, and Captain Blackford, Superintendent of the Longridge Station, both gave evidence after Price, and it seems that undercurrents of revolt were apparent at Longridge as well, though no outbreak had occurred on 1 July.

After the evidence was given, the Commission deliberated, then set down their findings, which were that Norfolk Island was totally unfit for accommodating the

. . . abandoned and blood-thirsty characters that had been sent there . . . the gaols were unfit for the confinement of so large a body of desperate assassins, and the present prisoners under charge for the recent barbarous murders . . . should be immediately removed to Van Diemen's Land . . . in order that they might meet with speedy and condign punishment . . .[19]

Along with the Commission's Report was a letter written by Samuel Barrow addressed to Colonel Champ, the Comptroller-General. In it he told of his having been 'incessantly engaged in bringing the offenders in the tragical events . . . to justice' and in thus doing, felt himself 'perfectly justified in omitting many minor points of duty, although . . . not to overlook any matters of absolute importance'. He corroborated all the evidence given to the Commission, and gave his own description of the carnage of that gruesome morning:

. . . on going through the gates [of the lumber-yard] borne on the shoulders of six men, I met the murdered, horribly mangled, mutilated corpse of the unhappy victim Smith. I was then going into gate-keeper Morris's hut, which adjoins the lumber yard . . . when a cry reached me that two more men were nearly murdered and dying at the Lime Kiln police hut . . . I speedily hastened there and one of the most frightful bloody spectacles met my sight as I opened the door. On one stretcher opposite me lay a sub-constable named Saxton, with his forehead completely laid open so that I could see into the cavity of the head. Another frightful gash, from the eye down the cheek, gaped so fearfully as to render the roof of the mouth quite perceptible . . . and another horrible wound in the back of the head. This poor fellow was still alive and my first impulse was . . . to obtain some particulars of the manner in which he had been nearly murdered, but he was too weak to articulate anything distinctly and under the advice of the medical officer I caused his immediate removal to the hospital . . . My attention was arrested by the groan of another man . . . I went into the room and a more terrifying sickening sight I never witnessed; There lay the almost lifeless body of this unhappy victim, with one side of his face completely smashed in from the temple to the mouth; his face presented a ghastly and bloodless hue; he appeared to me to be quite dead, but he was not so, although senseless; he was conveyed . . . to the hospital and almost immediately afterwards expired.

The first direction I issued by the Civil Commandant's authority was, that all the prisoners should be mustered and that those upon whom any marks of blood or other suspicious circumstances appeared, should be apprehended and confined . . . upwards of fifty were lodged in the Gaol . . . About twenty-five to thirty I have tried summarily for the tumult and riot, and inflicted in most instances, the punishment of twelve months imprisonment with hard labour in chains; and purpose, with the Civil Commandant's sanction, to submit them as soon as there is sufficient gaol accommodation, to a rigid system of separate confinement.

. . . To attribute the recent painful exhibitions of a thirst for blood to the mere depriving the prisoners of an unsanctioned indulgence is, in my opinion a perfect fallacy . . .[20]

Barrow's views on the circumstances which had led to the bloody mutiny were that '. . . prisoners who had been allowed every indulgence, and not taught or made to feel the humiliation their crimes and offences had reduced them to, being unfortunately allowed to remain on the island'. He ended on an ominous note:

Whilst I am not prepared to yield unnecessarily to alarm, I will not shrink from that solemn duty which I feel imposed upon me, of telling you . . . that I believe the motive that superinduced these horrible murders . . . and a latent thirst for blood . . . which I now forewarn you, in my conscience I do not believe is quenched. I believe there is still a smouldering flame that will again burst out with a yet more frightful and devastating fury, unless strong remedial measures are speedily adopted . . .[21]

Even as he wrote, the 'strong remedial measures' he advocated had been put in train. Barrow was to find those measures would affect himself, along with other officers.

Within ten days of the mutiny the brig *Governor Phillip* arrived from Van Diemen's Land, bringing despatches and stores. The vessel had left Hobart Town long before any news of the outbreak could have reached the colony, but among the Governor's despatches was one informing Major Childs that his replacement, already appointed as Civil Commandant of Norfolk Island, was to arrive shortly. News of the uprising horrified those on board, and when the vessel had unloaded its stores and cargo of prisoners the Captain hastened back with the Report of the Commission, and other despatches giving news of the bloody mutiny. Before the *Governor Phillip* arrived at Hobart Town, the *Lady Franklin* had sailed for Norfolk Island with Judge Burgess who was to conduct the trial of nine convicts already gaoled for some months on capital charges. Also on board was John Giles Price. When they arrived at the Island, both Price and Judge Burgess were shocked to find that not nine, but possibly half a hundred men must be tried.

Within a few days of their arrival the trials began, but Judge Burgess was taken seriously ill and was unable to continue his duties. He returned to Hobart Town on the *Lady Franklin* which had not then left, and the gaol prisoners were left to fester in the cramped Old Gaol until a new judge arrived. Barrow conducted preliminary trials which reduced the number of men of the mutiny to twenty-seven. Within days, two more were added to the criminal list for the murder of their overseer, Adam Clarke.

The new judge was Mr Fielding Browne, who left Hobart Town on the *Lady Franklin* on 3 September.[22] On 23 September the fourteen men considered the ringleaders in the mutiny were put on trial. They were, William Westwood, John Davies, Samuel Kenyon, Dennis Pendergrast, Owen Commuskey, Henry Whiting, William Pearson, James Cairnes, William Pickthorne, Lawrence Kavanagh, John Morton, William Lloyd, William Scrimshaw, and Edward McGinnis; there were five counts of murder and aiding and abetting in murder, and all the prisoners pleaded Not Guilty.

The schoolroom was used as the court, and for the first two days, twelve witnesses were called to give evidence for the Crown, while the prisoners at the bar stood listening, jeering at times as the free officers answered Pringle Stewart's questions with their own predictable answers. The result was, as they knew, a foregone conclusion; of the fourteen, twelve were sentenced to death, only John Morton and William Lloyd escaping the noose. Sentence was pronounced on 5 October as the prisoners shouted, jeered, or yelled obscenities, while John Price looked on coldly, sizing up the now diminished 'flash-men' of the lumber-yard, those men of the Ring who would no more hold sway over the mass.[23]

Little time was given for the men to prepare themselves for death. The Reverend Thomas Rogers, who had been the prisoners' chaplain, together with the Roman Catholic priest Father Bond, attended them each day in their cells, and walked with them to the foot of the gallows, where they were to be hanged in two batches of six.

On Tuesday 13 October, in the clear spring morning, the first six men emerged from their cells, led by their pastor. A strong force of the military stood by, armed and ready to move at any sign of restlessness. The men, Jackey-Jackey among them, mounted the gallow steps, were pinioned and 'turned off'. There was no sound above that of the sea, as it washed over the rocky foreshore, and the sigh of the men's breath as they watched the six in their last struggles. It was soon over, the bodies cut down, the next six brought to the gallows and the same procedure gone through, the drop, the struggles, the stillness.

When it was done, the bodies were piled into rough wooden coffins and loaded on three bullock carts, then hauled off to a disused saw-pit outside the cemetery where they were to be buried. The Reverend Rogers, unaccountably late at the scene though he had been with the men at the moment of their deaths, came hurrying along in his vestments, ready for the burial. He was told the bodies were already covered, in the communal grave. He ran, but by the time he reached the saw-pit all was over and the constables ready to leave. He asked 'Who ordered this?' and he was told 'The Civil Commandant'.[24] Bodies of murderers were human refuse, rubbish to be put out of sight as soon as possible, for Price. Rogers had already crossed swords with the Civil Commandant, and was to do so again, many times.

On 19 October William Brown was executed for aiding and abetting in the murders of 1 July; on 3 November two men were hanged for the murder of sub-overseer Clarke, who had been dubbed an 'informer' by the men. A month later, on 3 December, two more men were hanged—a total of seventeen in seven weeks.

The Hon. the Comptroller-General,   Norfolk Island
                    Civil Commandant's Office, October 6, 1846
Sir,
    I have the honour to acquaint you that the prisoners named in the margin were yesterday found guilty of the murder of Crown prisoner John Morris . . . and the extreme sentence of the law was accordingly passed upon them; the trial has extended over the lengthened period of eight days and one conducted with greater fairness or consideration towards the prisoners I never witnessed. These unhappy men will suffer on Monday next, the 12th instant, as it is neither prudent or safe under present circumstances to delay beyond that time.

                                                    John Price.[25]

The Hon. the Comptroller-General,   Norfolk Island
                    Civil Commandant's Office, October 13, 1846
Sir,
    I have the honor to inform you that the sentence of the law upon the prisoners named in the margin, for the wilful murder of John Morris . . . was carried into effect this morning.
Many of these unhappy men persisted in their declaration of innocence to the last moment, notwithstanding the weight of evidence against them left little room for doubts of their guilt.
In consequence of the number it became necessary to employ two executioners . . . After the execution of others under sentence of death, I would submit to you whether it would not be desirable to remove these men to Van Diemen's Land.

                                                    John Price.[26]

    The Ring was broken, Norfolk Island was rid of its prison-yard overlords. Their place was to be taken by the strongest overlord of them all, John Giles Price, Civil Commandant.
    The Reverend Thomas Rogers was a man of rare courage and somewhat hasty temper, and one of the few officers on the Island to stand up to John Price. He had been on Norfolk Island since August 1845, arriving on the same vessel that brought Gilbert Robertson's family from Hobart Town. It was his duty to visit the men in the condemned cells. There were a few of Anglican faith, a few Roman Catholics, and others who had long since abandoned all religious observances. Jackey-Jackey was one of Rogers's charges, and after the trial he, with the others, was confined in the cells of the new pentagonal gaol. The cells were of stone blocks, with tiny, barred

windows too close to the wall dividing it from the next one to permit more than a hint of sky to show through.

With a small steel file smuggled to him by an unnamed person—though Price hinted that the person was Rogers—Jackey-Jackey began filing away at the two-inch thick ceiling beam. He worked throughout the night and was within a fraction of success when someone, alerted by the soft rasping, called the turnkey who came running, dragged Jackey-Jackey out and pushed him into another cell with a ring-bolt centred in the floor. Manacled and heavily ironed, he was left fastened to the floor, able to move only as the chains permitted. He cried aloud for death to come and take him, he beat his head against the stone walls, and was for a time unmanageable.

Rogers found him so, calmed him down, then suggested that if he was given pen and paper he might be able to write down the story of his life from childhood, or as much as he could remember. There were not many days left to wait—the trial ended 5 October, the execution was to be on the 13th—so Jackey-Jackey wrote. He left his manuscript with Rogers, and also wrote a 'confession' and a letter to a Hobart newspaper for publication. At the time of his death, Jackey-Jackey Westwood was 27 years old.[27] Here follow some excerpts from Westwood's account.

I was born and bred in Maunden, Essex, and had good parents to give me a good education but at 16 I was taken up for highway robbery and committed to Chelmsford gail in 1835. I got off with twelve months through the intercession of my parents and because of my youth. I resolved to live well, but soon forgot and on January 3 1837 I was tried for robbery, and being an 'old' offender got 14 years transportation. I was sent to Australia on board *Mangles* with 300 other prisoners.

I had a hard settler as my assigned employer, who gave me not enough food or clothing, and I took to the bush after awhile. I was taken by the police, brought back and given fifty lashes. Again I took to the bush, was recaptured and given 6 months in the chain-gang. After 6 months was done I was sent back to my old master. I went out at night with another man to rob, with arms, and get enough food and clothing . . . We robbed the first traveller we met of money and good clothes which I exchanged for my own rags. I took his horse and galloped off. I quarrelled with my companion who tried to take liberties with the mistress of the next house we robbed, then rode off alone. Next I robbed a mailman in the bush. He had saddlebags full of money and cheques, this was just before Christmas. Then I visited a friend who gave me away to the police. I ran off, robbed two men on horseback, stole one horse and their money. I robbed a settler's house, took a pack-horse loaded with necessities and made for the mountains. I stayed in ambush for some time, after that I robbed a mailman on a coach, and this time I hooked £200 . . .

I robbed a rich settler's place, Cardoe by name, and tackled his Superintendent who I knew as a great wretch, tied him to a verandah post. When I untied him I made him kneel down. 'Don't shoot me' he begged, 'I'll never get another man flogged if you forgive me this time.' So like a fool I let him up and took off, leaving that part of the country.

Went on a visit to a pub, was taken by police when I was drunk but not quite drunk enough. Four men were put to guard me but I escaped again, was caught again and this time I was trussed like a faggot. I was tried at Berrima in 1841 and transported to Norfolk Island . . .[28]

But Jackey-Jackey escaped yet again before he could be transported, and went bushranging through the countryside 'robbing as I went'; 'I allowed a parson to go by, out of respect for the cloth and the fact that he probably had no money anyway and I didn't want his clothes.' By this time the troopers were out looking for him, saw him and gave chase, but lost him again, so he went to a settler's house 'where I tied the man and robbed him as his convict servant beat him for having had him flogged not long before . . . he gave me a suit of his master's best clothes and I rode off accompanied by a servant-woman who refused to go back.'

His freedom couldn't last, and Jackey-Jackey was finally caught, taken to Sydney and sentenced to Van Diemen's Land for life. But once there he escaped again, was caught, given 100 lashes and put in irons:

Our daily work was to carry a 100 lb log of wood up and down the settlement room every day for nine weeks, then we were sent to the chain-gang. I absconded again, with three others. On the beach we saw a large dead whale, ate the flesh for several days while we built a canoe. Constables came up just as we finished . . . we were given another 100 lashes by Captain Booth, and heavy irons and chained to ringbolts while we were stone-breaking. This went on for about twelve months. After that we were sent out to hard labour. After four months I absconded again . . .[29]

And so it went on—escapes, recapture and more punishments, 90 days' solitary, hard labour in chains, in the name of reformation. Then Booth left and William Champ took his place.

He was a kindlier man, took off my irons and placed me as servant . . . in Port Arthur, then I was promoted to boat crew and did well . . . but after six months I took again to bushranging with two men, we were robbing as we went . . . I was taken by police as I slept, then sentenced to 10 years on Norfolk Island . . .[30]

Such was the record of his life, written by Jackey-Jackey William Westwood in the few days before he was to die. It calmed him to write it and when it was finished, he asked Mr Rogers to baptise him into the Anglican church. The testament of his life he gave to Rogers, who said that 'every page bore the imprint of truth'.[31]

During these tense weeks when every man at the prison settlement was aware of the undercurrents of fear and hate, one of them, Principal Overseer Aaron Price found time to record the day-to-day events as he had done for many years past. It is through his eyes that we see some of the happenings in 'this Lazar house of crime' as it was named by John Price, Civil Commandant.

Aaron Price's Diary for the Period of September & October 1846.

August 16. 1846   The Bugle is sounded every morning when the men come out of Barracks to muster, as a notice to the Military and Civil authorities.

September 3. 1846   There was found upon Westwood this day committed for the murders of July 1, 2 Springsaws and the lead of the Night Tub fastened in his belt to form a weapon of attack on the first person that might enter his cell.

4th.   Edward Mooney charged with leaving his Gang and going into the Lumber garden in Government time. 14 days in cells.

4th   Joseph Kaye charged with leaving gang and going to the West Gang. Hard labour at Cascades for 2 months, in irons.

5th   Wm. Ayton struck Matthew Reid on head with stone-breaker's hammer while at work in stockade. Reid in hospital.

6th Sept.   R.C's at Longridge attended Service at Settlement, first time since Childs's departure. Protestants in the afternoon.

10th   Ayton brought to trial.

11th   Mr Ewing married to Miss Ison, sister of Reverend Ison (now on leave having been suspended from duty for alleged negligence of duty.)

Sept. 12th   Jackey-Jackey made attempt to break out of cell by cutting a hole in the ceiling, 15 inches by 14 inches, and had also cut his irons partially. Consequence was immediate dismissal of Cole for neglect of duty as Gaoler, and removal of Westwood to another cell, and ringbolted to walls by the hands, and chained to floor by leg irons. Intention was to escape, set fire to Aaron Price's house (Principal overseer) and in the confusion thus afforded, to let out as many of the prisoners as possible, and all to have absconded to the Bush. His further intentions have not transpired, believed to have been of deadly and more desperate character.

13th September.   The Reverend Mr Rogers by order of Mr Price the Civil Commandant, is not to appear in the Settlement in consequence of some alleged misconduct not publicly known.

Flagging taken up from Westwood's former cell by Price and workmen, found a steel spring-saw and two or three made of tin. He is now handcuffed and door open, and policeman patrols day and night. His daring and desperation seems unbounded.

16th   Thomas Bowring overseer, got 1 month in irons for working for Reverend Mr Murray (R.C.) without authority. James Ford to 18 months in irons and to separate treatment in cells for insolence to and assault upon Mr Turnham, Acting Superintendent of New Hands.

11 men 4 days solitary for neglect of work. Harry Jenkins 4 months in irons for having money and jewellery in his possession. Wm. Smith 4 months hard labour in irons for insolence to Captain Hamilton R.E.

17th   Thomas Stacey nine months separate treatment in cells for having spring-saw in possession and attempting to pass a bible with some information to Jackey-Jackey.

Sept. 21   Arrived Judge Browne (and Mrs) on *Lady Franklin* and Rev. Bond R.C. on a visit to Mr Murray (R.C.) and 199 more prisoners from Millbank, England, on the *John Calvin.*

Sept. 22.   Bell at 5.a.m. for all hands to go to work.

23 Sept.   Jackson under sentence of death for stabbing with intent to murder Aaron Price, overseer, took lead from night-tub, stood behind door, to murder first person who entered. Gaol Police beat him about the head with truncheons to bring him to submission.

Court opened Sept 23. Summing up on Oct. 3. Verdict returned Oct. 5th on the Jackey-Jackey murder. 2 acquitted on charge but attained on others.

Oct. 6.   Richard Boardman, Wm. Trueluck and Wm. Brown tried for murder of Stephen Smith.

Oct. 9   Brown sentenced to Death, requested to be executed with the others, request refused.

Men to be executed on a new drop in one of the yards of the new Pentagonal Gaol, erected during the previous week. All are said to be very penitent and prepared to meet their fate with fortitude based on repentance.

Mr Robertson Superintendent of Agriculture was this day suspended on account of some charge of Impropriety as was also Mr Fraser, Assistant Superintendent at Longridge. Mr Wade directed to take Robertson's place and commenced duty accordingly.

12th   Mr Fraser brought before court today charged with using Government leather for making of shoes for himself. Fined £10.

Oct. 12th   A.E.Baldock Chief Constable, married by Reverend Rogers at Longridge to Miss [name undecipherable].

Oct.13th   Day of execution. None of the hands was allowed to leave Barracks at 8. First six men brought out, led to New Drop in Gaol yard. In charge of police who accompanied them to foot of scaffold which they ascended without particular emotion. Immediately placed under beam, 3 under each, ropes adjusted by the two executioners, White and Hammond. Two R.C. priests present, and Mr Rogers in attendance on them, having been up the whole night preceding. Burial service was read by Mr Rogers, also a service by Rev. Murray after which they had close communication with each of a very affecting character applicable to the awful situation to which they had brought themselves. All united in singing a hymn, and after it finished Kenyon sang one alone. Last moment at quarter past eight. Drop fell, and they were no longer part of the dwellers upon earth.

Price, his deputy Captain Blackford, military officers and a few of the officials were present. Strong body of military in Gaol yard, guards at other suitable places. Police outside and in front of Drop.

Prisoners irons were struck before they ascended scaffold but arms severely pinioned. Drop was 6 ft. One or two severely convulsed for a few minutes but all appeared to die almost at once. Their conduct was becoming the dreadful change which awaited them. After hanging there for the usual time they were put into shells ready for interment in the burial ground and there buried. Kavanagh and 3 others asserted their innocence of the crime, (unaware that to be present at the act was also to assist in it). The barbarous ferocity which characterized the expressions of these men gradually left them after their condemnation, from efforts of the clergy (unceasing) to humanize them, a task at first hopeless but in the end successful. At 1 o'clock, all hands rung out to work.

Oct. 14th   Today at 2 o'clock sailed the *Lady Franklin* from Cascade. Mr Barrow, Mr Robertson, Mr Fraser, wife and children; Mr Lawler, wife and children; Mr Smithies, G. Mohring (boatman) Miss Burgess, Mr Kelly, Thos. Hatchett, Lt-Hunter and 5 prisoners.

Oct. 19th   Wm. Brown executed for murder of John Dinon on 1st July. Trueluck found guilty of murder of Stephen Smith, sentenced to death.

20th.   Eaton guilty of assault of M. Reid.

21st   B. McCarthy and John Liddle sentenced to death for murder of Henry Clarke, sub-overseer August 27th. Eaton got 3 years in heavy irons.

28th October.   This morning the Gaol gang sent to work for the first time on the reef to carry the Pier further out.

30 November   21 prisoners from Van Diemen's Land arrived. Rev. Mr Ison returned also. Death warrant for Jackson and Taverner in 7 days.

Dec. 2.   Gaol gang of 37 working in Quarry behind the new Gaol. 2 sent to Gaol by overseer for neglect of duty. Wm. Roberton said 'We'll all go to gaol' and lifted his pick, 'I'm longing for the life of some bloody wretch'. George Briton followed him, lifted a large stone. Military sent for, all marched to gaol. Price (J) tried them, gave 4 corporal punishment, rest in solitary on bread and water.

Dec.3rd   Sub-overseer Price (Charles) charged with sitting down in front of his gang during Government hours. 6 months in gaol-gang.

Dec.9th   Jackson and Gardiner executed for murder.

Dec.9th   New windmill finished. performed well.

10th   *Lady Franklin* lost anchor and thirty fathoms of chain.

12th.   Judge Browne and Mr Stewart, Crown Prosecutor left Norfolk. Old Gallows pulled down by order of Price (J).

13th   Michael Burns and Dennis Dogherty severely kicked and beat Michael Croker and Thomas Hampton. All men of very bad character. A remarkable fact that the same day the Judge left the Island they again commenced their old career. Burn and Dogherty got 30 days solitary and 6 months in irons.[32]

John Price, Civil Commandant 19

JOHN PRICE, ARISTOCRAT BORN AND 'FAVOURITE SON' OF THE COLONIAL GOVERNMENT OF VAN DIEMEN'S LAND, WAS WITHOUT DOUBT, THE most notorious of Norfolk Island's Commandants. He was a legend in his own lifetime; he knew it and gloried in it, in the adulation he inspired in upper-class colonials who admired his implacable rule over the convicts under his charge, and in the terror he wrought in the vast majority of those prisoners.

He was a fine-looking man, six feet (183 centimetres) tall and of immense physical strength. He had a charming manner, when he chose to exert himself to use it. His curling hair was thick and of a reddish hue, his eyes a steely grey, his voice soft and cultured when he was with friends, his sense of humour at times macabre.[1] He was a rock of a man against whom some might lean with confidence; others he might crush without pity. He had a haughty, arrogant manner when dealing with inferior officers, unless they happened to be his toadies, and few if any of those who knew him, knew the whole man. Possibly not even Mary Price, his wife.

Price was born 20 October 1808, the fourth son of Sir Rose Price of Trengwainton, Cornwall, England. 'Rose' was from a maternal ancestor. The Prices were of ancient lineage, and Sir Rose Price inherited great estates in Jamaica, his will disclosing that 237 Negro slaves were part of his Jamaican property.[2] However, at his death there was little to inherit for any of the fourteen sons and daughters, and in 1836 John Price sailed to Van Diemen's Land, armed with letters of introduction from influential friends and relatives, to the Lieutenant-Governor Colonel George Arthur. He was warmly received, granted good farming land in the Huon River District, and the services of several assigned convicts, to begin his life as a gentleman-farmer.[3]

Not very much is known of Price's early life. He was educated at Charterhouse, an English Public School, entered Brasenose College, Oxford, where there is no record of his having obtained a degree; and from the time he matriculated at Brasenose in 1827 to the time he left England in 1836 the years are shrouded in mystery and therefore the source of rumour. In later years, it was said among the convicts that he had been 'inside', as he knew the 'cant', the peculiar tongue of criminals and the flash men of the underworld. It was also said, in Hobart Town, that while there he frequently visited the dens where such people gathered, mingling with them as one of themselves. He did not deny this. He seemed to know, with terrifying accuracy, the way a criminal's mind worked, and this, coupled with his merciless administering of the Law, gave him an almost hypnotic power over them, though some of his victims declared it was the basilisk stare of his steely eye behind the monocle that 'got them'.

He ran his farm well, and according to report he had been 'assigned convict labour of a better class than generally fell to settlers newly arrived in the Colony', though credit for this must be given to Price also, coming as he did from a long line of land-owners and having an inborn sense of order and good husbandry. His farm at Risdon was said to be 'a regular English establishment . . . managed in the best style'.[4]

In June 1838 Price married Mary Franklin, niece of the Lieutenant-Governor Sir John Franklin, who replaced Governor Arthur in 1837.[5] Price was then 29, Mary Franklin about 24. In the next year he was appointed Muster-Master in the Convict Department of Van Diemen's Land, and was also appointed Assistant Police Magistrate, a position which could point to the fact of his having had some training in Law.[6] His new appointments required that he live in Hobart Town and in this move, it seems he found his career. He had power, great responsibility, the approbation of the 'Government Set', and also an outlet for the streak of cruelty which seemed to surface from time to time when dealing with the underdog.

In his authoritative study of John Price, Barry says:

> He was strangely fascinated by their viciousness and attracted by the evil in them even as he was repelled by it. It was a psychopathological love-hate relationship. He regarded them as less than human, with no claim to justice in a civilised sense, but his vanity nevertheless demanded that they should move in submissive terror of him. At the same time a peculiar warped strain in his nature made it necessary for him to have their reluctant regard and grudging respect as a 'fly' man . . . one who but for the accident of circumstance might have been a king among them.[7]

In April 1846 Price applied for leave of absence for health reasons. What his complaint was is not known, but his doctor warned 'it is very desirable that he should absent himself from business or else he will be laid up seriously'.[8] The leave was approved, but before he could take advantage of it, he was appointed to Norfolk Island as Civil Commandant. Norfolk Island came under the Government of Van Diemen's Land in 1844, and the Executive Council decided to recall Major Childs immediately and appoint an 'iron-fisted' Commandant in his stead. John Price was their obvious choice; in his duties as Police Magistrate he had controlled the men who came before him, his reputation as a disciplinarian was such that when word was put about that he was about to leave Van Diemen's Land, strong appeals came from the inhabitants of Hobart Town for him to stay.[9]

His leave was put aside, he was offered a big increase in salary to go to Norfolk Island, but it is said he was loath to go. There can be little doubt that Mary Price would have preferred to stay in Hobart Town. The five children in the Price's family were all under seven, the youngest barely six months old, but in July, Price and his family sailed on the *Lady Franklin* arriving on Norfolk Island 6 August.[10] Neither Price nor Judge Burgess, who also travelled on the *Lady Franklin*, had any inkling of the situation that was to greet them on arrival; for the *Governor Phillip*, which carried news of the mutiny to Hobart Town, had passed the *Lady Franklin* during her voyage. In a despatch to the Secretary of State Mr W. E. Gladstone, Sir E. Eardley-Wilmot wrote:

I have sent Mr Price, the Police Magistrate of Hobart Town, to Norfolk Island as Civil Commandant . . . I have perfect confidence in his prudence, zeal, and knowledge of the duties and the trust reposed in him, to be assured that very few weeks—I had almost said days—cannot elapse after his arrival before everything will be restored to order and regularity.[11]

He enumerated Price's duties in the despatch, the first of which was:

to disarm the prisoners of the knives which each of them possesses . . . to make them wear convict dress . . . to make them attend muster regularly and in silence . . . to institute messes with a given number in each mess . . . and one person to cook and prepare the meat.
To ensure punctuality and attention to the hour and time for which each duty is specifically marked . . . and above all, to attend to that separation at night, and that continued surveillance and watch without which nameless horrors are perpetrated and . . . cannot always be prevented.[12]

Sodomy was as endemic as dysentery on Norfolk Island, and as much feared. The despatch was written on 6 July, before news of the mutiny had reached Hobart Town.

Judge Burgess, who was suddenly taken ill within two or three days of commencing the trials, returned to Hobart on the *Lady Franklin*. When Mr Fielding Browne arrived on Norfolk Island six weeks later, he found still more murder cases were to be tried.

On 19 August the *Mary* sailed from Norfolk Island. The *Mary* had called in on her way to Port Jackson, and when she had taken on provisions and water, she also took on board Major Childs, who was to return to duty with the Royal Marines. There had been little communication between Childs and Price. The new Civil Commandant preferred to make his inspection of the Island on his own or with men of his own choice. He knew some of the officials, a number of whom had come from Government service in Van Diemen's Land, and many of the prisoners had been despatched by him from Hobart Town as doubly-convicted colonial prisoners. The acting Chief Constable, Alfred Essex Baldock, was a former convict who had served his sentence in Port Arthur and had arrived as a 'free' official on Norfolk Island six months before Price's arrival.

It was when Price visited the old boatshed to inspect the mutiny prisoners, chained together and reeved by a cable-chain running the length of the cells, that he came upon the Reverend Thomas Rogers the Anglican chaplain who had been on Norfolk Island since August 1845.[13] Rogers, tall as Price but spare in build, was a man of rare courage and high principles, but he had an easily-bruised pride; a difficult trait to counter with an opponent like John Price. Rogers had gone to the boatshed to return the prisoners' depositions to Baldock. Until mid-July Rogers had been a Justice of the Peace and a Magistrate, and as a matter of course had considered it his duty to help the prisoners with their defence—there was no one else competent or willing to do so. No advocate had been deputed to attend the trials and prepare the prisoners' depositions, and Rogers had taken the men's statements some time before his magisterial powers had been abolished, probably a result of the Pringle Stewart *Report* which had been caustic in the comments on the second Anglican pastor Reverend John Ison.

By malevolent Fate, Price happened to arrive at the boatshed at the precise moment Rogers handed the papers to Baldock. He demanded to know 'What have you there?', in his imperious manner. Rogers explained, made it clear that he had done this as part of his duty many times. Price reminded him he was no longer a Justice of the Peace, nor a Magistrate, and dressed him down smartly, before the listening prisoners, Alfred Baldock, and the constables and turnkeys present.[14] Though Rogers fumed there was nothing he could do. Price himself took the papers. From then on, the two men spoke to each other only when absolute necessity made it unavoidable; Price made it clear that there was to be only one man in command on the Island, himself. He was no incompetent to be overborne as Major Childs had been. Each civil officer and Superintendent in turn came under his scrutiny, and one by one he weeded them out, dismissing those who were manifestly unfit, and those who were likely to stand out against him.

It was clear that drastic measures needed to be taken on Norfolk Island, if order and discipline was to be absolute. The insubordination among the men of the Ring, their overt admission by dress and behaviour that they had no regard for the regulations and that sodomy was indeed rife among them had to be checked. So, too, had the constant breaches of discipline. Price had no intention of suffering insubordination, and no intention of retaining any officer who showed opposition to his orders.

Within a few weeks of his arrival Price suspended Gilbert Robertson, the Superintendent of Agriculture. Price had known of Robertson during his time in Van Diemen's Land, and was aware of his reputation as a spirited man who spoke his mind, a man who had, however, spent two periods in prison, if not as a criminal then as a disturber of the peace in one fashion or another. There were informers among the free officers and police who were not loath to speak against a man of whom the convicts thought well — a non-conformist type who got his work done without the constant goading of the scourge.[15] Price was aware that Robertson was a spirited man who feared no one and would speak his mind. His work was good, Longridge Farm had greatly improved under his guidance, as Pringle Stewart had commented in his *Report*, though he had also found a number of things to carp at, as well.[16]

From the greatly improved state of Longridge Farm, and the thriving state of agriculture there which Pringle Stewart had commented on in his *Report*, there could have been no reason of importance to the running of the place, which would have resulted in removing so useful an officer as Robertson. But on the 25th August, less than three weeks after his arrival on Norfolk Island, Price sent a letter from his office to the Superintendent of Agriculture:

Sir, I have perceived at many of the Huts occupied by the Shepherds and Stockmen, Gardens in cultivation and in some instances larger pieces of ground under their occupation apparently. I learnt from my predecessor that he had directed you to discontinue the practice of allowing these Gardens and I can only express my surprise that you should have permitted them to continue. You will now, however, immediately cause all these gardens to be destroyed, and you will also warn the Shepherds and Stockmen to discontinue the practice of keeping Birds or other animals, to permit such indulgences as these is in direct violation of the rules laid down for the management of Convicts undergoing a Probationary term, and an adherence to the Regulations as far as practicable I must expect may be carried out as being of paramount importance. I have the honor to be, Sir,

Your Obt. Servant

John Price.[17]

The customary formal ending to the letter no doubt brought a wry smile from Gilbert Robertson as he read it. His reply to this order, and John Price's subsequent letter are not available, but presumably Robertson's explanation and appeal that the men retain their gardens as necessary for their health and well-being, brought about his dismissal, for a further letter has been preserved:

To John Price.   Longridge, ½ past nine P.M.
                                       Sept. 19 1846.

Sir,
   I write to appeal to your humanity against the repeated revolution
of my rights as a British Subject by the Police seizing the opportunity
of the severe calamity under which my family are suffering, to annoy
us and disturb my poor dying child by coming at night into premises
which have always been held to be the property of the Officer holding
my situation—viz—the Garden Hut of the Superintendent of
Agriculture, which I have allowed to be occupied in part for the
convenience of the public service.
   The effect of the Police in coming into my office, and asserting
their right of search there, has been to through [*sic*] my eldest
daughter into a state of illness from which there is hardly a hope of
recovery.
   Surely this might have satisfied the deepest animosity and desire to
annoy me and my family, for I have been warned that this persecution
is intended to compel me to abandon an office in which I have
endeavoured to discharge my duties faithfully, and I flatter myself the
result will shew, not uselessly, to the Government. The hour chosen
for the perpetration of this second outrage was nearly nine o'clock at
night—without any notice to me except the furious barking of the
Dogs which I keep for the protection of my own Poultry and of the
Government property which is exposed in my own Garden and
Stockyard for the convenience of the Public Service. The
consequence is the throwing of my family, who are worn out with
watching the dying bed of a suffering child and sister—into a state of
terror and excitement—and the probability is that another victim will
be added.
   I bring this under your notice in the hope that it is done without
your knowledge and approval, and to ask from you, as the Chief
Authority, protection for my family and the premises which we
occupy. The Constables have chosen the same unseasonable hour for
searching the Lumber yard, and have imprisoned the overseers on a
charge of having in his Hut some eggs—which I believe were given to
him by my Wife, although she is in deep distress and suffering for
me to enquire of her—also some tea and sugar—this is a matter
which does not concern me personally—but it will certainly very
seriously affect the public Service if the services of this man are lost
for a day—at a season when they are wanted every hour, and when
there is not one man in the Island to supply his place.
   Myself and all my family are in too deep distress of mind, and I am
too anxious to have this put into your hands tonight to admit of my
taking a copy, which it may be important for me to be able hereafter

to produce, of this letter—I must therefore trust to your generosity to allow me to have one.

> I have the honor to be,
> Sir
> Your very obedient Servant,
> Signed, Gilbert Robertson, Supt. of Agriculture.

P.S.   In my agitation I forgot to state that the Constable told me when I asked him by what authority he came to my premises at that hour of the night—that he was acting under orders, and when I asked him whose orders—he answered me in the most insulting and threatening tone—'You will know that on Monday morning'. G.R.[18]

And below this letter is written 'A true copy, W. Belstead'. Within a few days, Robertson received a reply to his plea.

> Civil Commandant's Office
> September 24 1846.

Sir,

I have the honor to acknowledge the receipt of your communication of the 19th instant, and to acquaint you that in my opinion the Constable only acted in accordance with the Strict, proper, and efficient exercise of his duty.

I regret to learn that you have given a license to the Sub Overseer of the Longridge Lumber Yard to employ himself in making articles of traffic—such a course of proceedings and such an assumption of improper authority on your part requires me to demand of you a most satisfactory explanation, which I desire you will immediately furnish me with.

I have also to observe that Mrs Robertson appears to have given the Prisoner named in the Margin some Tea and Eggs, any interference with the Convicts by the female portion of an officers family can only be viewed as highly improper, and will undoubtedly cause the removal from the Island of any Officer who for one moment permits or sanctions such a Gross violation of the Regulations.

I am willing, from the momentary excitement under which you appear to have written your letter of the date referred to, to pass over without remark your unwarranted observation on the conduct of the Constables, but I consider it necessary to inform you that all the Buildings except your private dwelling houses, are open, where Convicts are placed, to the inspection and surveillance of the Police, and that I do not recognise the Building alluded to by you as forming any portion of your Quarter.

> I have the honor to be
> Sir
> Your Obedient Servant.
> John Price.[19] [the signature only is in
> Price's own handwriting]

Here is inescapable evidence of Price's attitude to those who were under his domination, or whose nature demanded a modicum of sympathy for the underdog—and who were able to perform their duties without the assistance of the lash or the solitary cell.

Nowhere in the Regulations is there any mention of the removal of an officer whose wife has given food to a prisoner of the Crown; this statement by the Commandant was merely a convenient handle on which to hang his decision to remove a man who might become a thorn in his side. Robertson's eventual removal from Norfolk Island during the term of Price's Commandancy was inevitable in any case for the two men, opposites in nature as they were, for both had choleric tempers and both were stubborn. It was the Island's loss that Robertson's dismissal came when it did, for the seasons following his departure were drought and more drought, and his replacement was a man who knew little of farming on Norfolk Island.

Price himself had not observed the defalcations he complained of, they had been related to him by petty-minded officials retaliating for considered slights. Informers were encouraged, especially those men who had been sent from Van Diemen's Land by Price during his time as Police Magistrate at Hobart Town. Such a man was Baldock, who already had the ear of Price. In a deposition he gave to Price in December 1846 he said, among many other statements:

> . . . a system of searching was commenced . . . many of the officers . . . were averse to it, in particular the Superintendent of Agriculture who, on two or three occasions publicly complained of it. On the 21st of June he complained of a prisoner of the Crown being searched, and wished to be informed by what authority it was done; and on the 29th of the same month, when a prisoner named White, employed as sub-overseer, was found in an indecorous position with one of his gang by the free police, he refused to go to gaol, producing a pass and exciting the minds of his men by saying he had orders from his master the Superintendent of Agriculture that the police were in no way to interfere with him or his gang . . .[20]

Gilbert Robertson was not an easy man to deal with when his authority was questioned, as it was most certainly questioned by Price, who knew of Robertson's imprisonment on 'libellous charges' in Van Diemen's Land in the paper the *True Colonist*. Price knew also of the charges against Robertson while he was farming, charges which accused him of 'indulgences' to his assigned servants. Whatever the reason, Robertson was removed from his post as Agricultural Superintendent and he, with other officials, left Norfolk Island in 1846.[21] It was more than likely this harsh decision and the turmoil resulting from it that hastened Elizabeth Robertson's early death. She died in January 1847, within weeks of her father's dismissal, and was buried on 11 January in the Old Cemetery on the Island, where a handsome gravestone keeps her memory fresh.

On 7 December 1846 Price, in his despatch to the Comptroller-General in Van Diemen's Land, wrote:

In the removal of the cooking utensils from the prisoners I cannot see a sufficient reason for the murderous outbreak of July last, except in what I gathered from the lips of some of the murderers prior to their deaths. Horrible though it be I consider I am bound to make known to you what I learnt from them shortly before their execution. Many of these wretched beings acknowledged to me that for years . . . they had been given to unnatural practices, declaring that the crime prevailed to a great extent, both in Van Diemen's Land and in this Island; and from one I learnt that those who pandered to their passions were paid in tobacco, extra provisions, fancy articles made for them and any indulgence they could obtain to induce them to yield to their brutal desires. That by their being deprived of their cooking utensils they would have been unable to prepare the food they might surreptitiously obtain for the objects of their lusts, and that this aroused their savage and ferocious passions to a pitch of madness. This is the tale of a man about to die; the relations of these abominable practices came from the men who in a few days knew they must be numbered with the dead; and I have no reason to doubt the disgusting and horrible confessions . . .

The address of another to myself on entering his cell was to this effect: 'Sir, as you value your soul, separate both here and at Van Diemen's Land as much as possible, my class of people, we are nearly all given over to unnatural practices. I have witnessed scenes that you would not believe were I to recount them, and which are not fit to be related; the flash men you see with made over clothes and fancy articles, are all given over to these practices; no check can be given to it but by separating the men as much as possible, and I beseech you to use your best endeavours to let the men sleep in cells . . .

John Price.[22]

Price mentions no name, and as this letter was written on 7 December it must refer to the men of the mutiny. Yet from Price's attitude towards Rogers on their first meeting, it seems unlikely that the Commandant would adopt such a confidential pose towards the condemned men unless he had an ulterior motive. That motive might well have been to enhance his own standing in the eyes of his immediate superior when he reported it, or simply to gain enough information to enable him to pick out the miscreants who had not before been identified as 'given over to unnatural practices'. In actual fact there were many other factors besides sodomy which had sparked off the July mutiny. The removal of the cooking pots was the last in a series of petty deprivations put in train after Stewart's visit in May.

There were other reasons for the unrest and insubordination, and one was simply hunger. The prison diet of maize-meal slush and greyed salt beef made the gorge rise, and could be tolerated only by the strongest stomachs day after day. When served out uncooked, the meal could be mixed with sweet-potato flour, for bread, or burnt to a tolerable coffee substitute and the beef could be cooked in other ways than boiling to a tattered lump; vegetables (stolen or given on the sly) could be added, portions of fresh meat from a sheep 'knocked off' could be substituted for the ration. These were the pay-offs for the men of the Ring.

New Regulations had come into force since Stewart's visit. No man could wander beyond the boundary markers set around the settlement after he left. Messes were to be formed for meals, all meals to be served out by the cooks. There were no more unauthorised visits to gardens or the stock-yard, unless a man was willing to run the risk of being seen, and reported by a 'dog'. Here is part of a dissertation on convict discipline given by Maconochie some years after he left Norfolk Island:

> In a large, distributed community like that of Norfolk Island, where there can be little principle to begin with, and these aids and stimulants refused, the disposition to rapine, plunder and the destruction of property will be found as naturally to arise . . . The effect on the men of my giving them all gardens and allowing those quartered in the Bush to raise stock on them, was most excellent . . . I also allowed the men to grow and use tobacco. It is a weed on the island and no severity or regulation will ever prevent its being largely used . . . The possession of knives by prisoners, as by lunatics, is only dangerous when they are mismanaged. Where men are viciously inclined, everything is a weapon as well as a knife.[23]

Price was wrong, wilfully or obtusely, in attributing the July outbreak solely to 'lust' or 'abominable practices'. A human being has many desires and needs, and a full belly is, for most, the prime need. He had seen this for himself when, within three weeks of his arrival in August 1846, he increased the meal ration from 1 lb to eighteen ounces (454 g to 510 g); yet strangely he seems to have forgotten this at the time his letter was written. Price began his rule on Norfolk Island as he intended to go on. Not for him the timidity or vacillation shown by Major Childs to Barrow's overbearing manner and handing down of summary punishments; there was room for only one Commandant. In April 1847 the post of Stipendiary Magistrate was abolished, and Samuel Barrow with it.

One by one the men dismissed by Price were replaced by others who were pliant, or were sent up from Van Diemen's Land. He invigorated the system of 'informing'. Informers could bring reports to him at any time in his office; overseers, constables and other minor officials could approach him with petty breaches of discipline, or with items as trivial as the loss of a pair of bootlaces, or being late at muster. No man in the gaol or in the field felt safe from the pounce of a sub-constable with authority to haul him to the Police court for summary punishment, a twenty-five or a fifty, solitary confinement or maybe extra chains or all of them, in some cases; many of the less hardened went in terror day and night.

In October 1846, two months after his first brush with Price, the Reverend Rogers wrote to the Superintendent of Convict Chaplains Archdeacon Marriott, in Van Diemen's Land, to fiercely protest against Price's arrogant behaviour towards himself, and his manner of disciplining the convicts under his charge.

> ... no language of mine can ever convey an adequate notion of his
> barbarous inhumanity ... towards the prisoners. It can not be realised
> by description, it is sickening to think of, and it can be practised with
> impunity ... My Lord, I believe that the condition of the lost in a
> world of endless woe may best be imagined from what I have seen
> suffered by human beings in your diocese, by prisoners at Norfolk
> Island. Why should Price in his ferocious severity cause such cries of
> ineffable wretchedness from the captives under his sway? 'They never
> pardon, who have done the wrong'.[24]

It was a long letter and gave many details of Price's 'ferocious severity'. The Archdeacon sent it on to the Administrator C. J. LaTrobe, probably because in it Rogers had asked that the Archdeacon come to Norfolk Island to see for himself. LaTrobe, however, after reading it, sent several pages of the letter to Price, for his comments. The result was a foregone conclusion. Price firmly rebutted Rogers's allegations, and after his reply was received, the administrator wrote to Archdeacon Marriott, giving it as his opinion that Rogers should be moved from Norfolk Island. The Archdeacon informed Rogers of this decision, which '. . . is made on account of your communications in writing on various subjects, from the whole tone of which the Administrator of the Government thinks you are not well qualified to meet the peculiar difficulties of your position'.

These letters took several months to reach each destination and it was not until February 1847 that Rogers left Norfolk Island for Van Diemen's Land, and on arrival began his protests over again. Sir William Denison was the new Governor, and he made short work of Rogers and his protestations at his dismissal, by having him dismissed altogether from further employment as a Convict Chaplain 'because of a deficiency in temper and discretion'.[25] The Archdeacon and the Archbishop both declared Rogers was unjustly dismissed but their protests were, as often, too late and his return to the service could not be arranged. Price, at this time, was too valuable to the Government to be disrupted in his work of subduing the convicts on Norfolk Island.

Rogers was appointed to the parish of Windermere, near Launceston instead, and there he found many staunch supporters of his cause among his parishioners. He filled in his spare time by writing a lengthy document *Correspondence relating to the Dismissal of the Reverend T. Rogers from his Chaplaincy of Norfolk Island*, which was published in Launceston in 1849. To this he added *The Review of Dr. Hampton's First Report on Norfolk Island* which exposed the Comptroller-General's cover-up of many facts relating to the cruelties perpetrated on Norfolk Island. The document is a damning indictment of Price and his System. It is written with passion and truth, in an effort to put a stop to the atrocities committed in the name of 'justice' on the Island, and as well, to vindicate himself from the charge that he was 'not well qualified to meet the peculiar difficulties of his position there'.

Thomas Rogers was born in England in 1803 and lived to 1901, his 99th year. To the last he was tall, upright and in full possession of all his faculties except for failing eyesight. He is recognised as the man on whom Marcus Clarke based his Reverend North, in *For the Term of his Natural Life*, though the character is obviously overdrawn.

Rogers died at Malvern, Victoria, after having been for many years a journalist and a writer of many pamphlets. He had turned to the Catholic faith—as distinct from Roman Catholic—some years before he left Tasmania, as Van Diemen's Land was known from the 1850s on. The British Government gave him a Civil pension for 'distinguished Service in bringing about Reform of the English Prison System'.[26]

*   *   *

Excerpts from the Correspondence of the Reverend Thomas Rogers

On several of the mornings the ground on which the men stood at the triangles was saturated with human gore as if a bucket of blood had been spilled on it covering a space three feet in diameter and running out in various directions in little streams of two or three feet long. I have seen this.[27]

Thomas Rogers wrote this in Major Childs's time. He had expected such terrible practices might have ended to some extent when Price took over, as suggested in the letter from Archdeacon Marriott, which told him of the imminent arrival of John Price, the Archdeacon had written: 'You will find in Mr Price a manly and able Commandant and one who will, I am sure, gladly attend to any plan you may form for the spiritual benefit of the convicts . . .'[28]

But there was to be no change for the better, only a more repressive system of administration, of which fear was the chief agent; fear of the vigilant spy, of the informer, who might be anyone, even the man chained to a mate in the gaol-gang, so widespread was the system of informing under Price's rule. There was also fear of the extended sentence, a favourite form of punishment which could add months or years to a man's time on Norfolk Island. Men feared the living death that was 'solitary', or the tortures newly devised in that place where every known torture was thought to be already practised.

In his *Correspondence* Rogers set down those practices he saw and those of which he was given incontrovertible proof or evidence. He must often have wished his wrath could turn into a sword to smite the supercilious face of the Commandant as he listened to complaints, rather than have to oppose him with words only. In that battle, Rogers was always bested, but in defeat he persisted in attack, and later his *Correspondence* proved to be a powerful weapon. The following is part of his *Correspondence*, written at first-hand and published by Rogers in 1849:

A man whose age prevented his employment at heavier occupation than that of gate-keeper, was one day eating his dinner; he had a mouthful of salt beef and maize bread left. A fellow-prisoner happened at that moment to pass by, and was asked if he would have the morsel of bread and meat, it was instantly accepted. While he was eating, a constable who had been watching the giving and eating, rushed up and took the two men into custody. Mr Price sentenced them, the one for giving, the other for eating the morsel of food, to a month's detention on the Island, which detention might prolong their sentence for several months.

*   *   *

Prisoner named Dytton was chained down to the floor and gagged, for getting up to the window in the hospital cell for air. He had been ill at the hospital for six or seven weeks, has never been well since a beating he received whilst in the chain gang. He had abused a constable for removing pegs on which he hung his clothes and rations, so was gagged, taken to the New gaol, chained down and dreadfully beaten by several constables. He lay in a puddle of blood. Next day a constable came in and jumped on his chest. Elliott, (the catechist) went to his cell and asked him when the beating was done. 'I received a portion yesterday' he said, 'and a portion today'.

*   *   *

Visited the gaol. Found Waters strapped down on suspicion of having prevented his eyes from recovering. [This refers to the habit some convicts had of rubbing their eyes with the leaves of the manchineel tree, causing them to blister and produce temporary blindness, and thus get off work.] His back was bad, having been flogged, and the cord which laced the straitjacket placed on him pained him much. His eye was very bad. He was laid on his back, bound and unable to stir hand or foot, in an agony of pain from the pressure of the lacing cord on his lacerated back. When his back was stinking, the turnkey went to Price who allowed him to remove the cord but had his hands tied to the foot of the bed instead. He was kept thus for many days. He afterwards received a sentence of eighteen months on the reef in chains, some of them 36 lbs in weight.

*   *   *

Feeling of pity or compassion were also repressed. It was customary in my time on the island to return any men of the gaol-gang to their cells for the remainder of the day on which they were flogged. The man who happened to be flogged was washed by his companions with cold water, the mangled skin pressed down, and a wet cloth applied to the wounded parts. Subsequently the cooling leaf of the banana was applied. One Sunday I was told that an officer's servant was in gaol. On making enquiry I found that he was sent to gaol for having given a few banana leaves out of his master's garden for the use of the gaol-gang in dressing each other's backs. A constable saw him and took him to gaol . . .

*   *   *

Graham, a cart driver at Longridge, found a young bird in the bush. He brought it home to the stable and tamed it. He was brought before Mr Price charged with 'having a tamed bird'. He got thirty-six lashes for having a tame bird!

*   *   *

Higson, a stock man, was passing along his run. Mr Ison's gardener said 'Give this tree a push, I want to roll it down the hill to mend the garden fence where your bullocks come in'. Higson put his foot to the tree; one push sent it to the bottom of the hill. A constable saw him and charged him with 'pushing a tree with his foot'. For this *crime* he got thirty-six lashes on his back and thirty-six on his breech. Six days later he was flogged for having tobacco. Four or five days after this last flogging he was reported for not having the bullocks in by bell ring. He hid in the bush—was taken—and received one hundred lashes!

*   *   *

Clayton was flogged four times within a month for trifling breaches of discipline.

*   *   *

Launder was charged with having government paper improperly in his possession. He had once been a very respectable man at home, and felt the charge keenly. The government paper was three or four small slips which the commissariat officer had torn and thrown down to the floor to be swept out. Launder wished to explain this to Mr Price at

Kingston Settlement about the late 1850s. Note the unroofed prison barracks, also the civil hospital near the jetty. (La Trobe Collection, State Library of Victoria)

Prison Settlement some time early in the 1900s. (La Trobe Collection, State Library of Victoria)

Kingston Settlement 1848, before the arrival of the Pitcairn settlers June 1856. (La Trobe Collection, State Library of Victoria)

The Cemetery, Norfolk Island, about 1920. The Old Cemetery is in foreground. Graves of the Pitcairners on the right of the Old Cemetery. (La Trobe Collection, State Library of Victoria)

Kingston Jetty about 1926. Today's ship still anchors in the Bay, and supplies are still ferried in to land. Cars have replaced horses. (La Trobe Collection, State Library of Victoria)

the police office. Mr Price bid him hold his tongue. He begged a
second time to be heard in his defence. Mr Price then cried out 'Give
him the gag!'

*   *   *

The constable seized, and dragged him to the gaol; he was in a very
feeble state of health and nearly blind with opthalmia; yet the gaoler
forced the gag into his mouth with so much violence as to dash out
two of the man's teeth—cut his gums—and caused such distension of
the jaw that it was supposed for a time to be dislocated. Next day, on
another false or frivolous charge, Launder was brought before
Mr Price again and sentenced to four months extension.

*   *   *

Lloyd, a young man 27 years of age, was transported when a boy. He
was again transported in the colony, and sent to Norfolk Island. In
October 1845 he joined in robbing an officer's house. I was one of the
sitting magistrates who committed him for the robbery. He remained
in gaol nearly ten months before he was tried. He was sentenced at
the assizes in 1846 to three years further imprisonment, with three
months in each year in solitary. After he had gone through a year of
his sentence he was charged with indecency in the gaol yard, and
sentenced by Mr Price to nine months extension in gaol. He became
so despondent that he hung himself in his cell: the turnkey discovered
him before life was extinct. Mr Price was informed of what had taken
place. He went down to the gaol and sentenced him to receive fifty
lashes for attempting to hang himself. The medical officer, however,
would not answer for the man's life, and the lashes were not inflicted.
But what does Mr Price gain on the score of humanity from the
surgeon's intervention? Instead . . . of being flogged, he was strapped
down and kept in that exhausting posture on his back for six weeks.
The chaplain who visited him, told me that he looked more like a pale
distended corpse than a living being, and his voice so weak it could
hardly be heard. One day, the chaplain, seeing his lips moving, leaned
down to put his ear to the man's mouth, and at length distinguished
the words 'Loose me—oh loose me'. The chaplain replied 'No Lloyd, I
dare not do that'. A deep sigh followed the refusal, and the tears
trickled down the culprit's emaciated face . . .

    I have not picked out a few rare cases. They were of daily
occurrence, I have given a fair specimen of what was frequent and
usual . . . My authority is either personal knowledge or information
from credible parties who had personal knowledge. Finally, no
contradiction of the charges against Mr Price has ever been openly
and fearlessly put forth in the colony.

*   *   *

August 6—Visited the general hospital; found a man named Lemon dreadfully beaten, and having his arm broken. It appears that constable Baldock was taking a man to gaol, charged with either having or using a towel irregularly. He threw his shirt to Lemon, and asked him to get it washed. Baldock would not allow him (Lemon) to have it. Upon this, the man Lemon gave Baldock either a blow or, as he says, a push, when a number of constables fell upon him and beat him with their clubs. It was just as divine service was commencing yesterday evening. All the officers and constables left the church, except Mr Duncan, and the 'old hands' made a general rush towards the windows to see what was going on. Mr Bott told me he interfered to cause the constables to desist after the man was down, but Baldock said 'lay it into him—lay it into him'. While down he was handcuffed with his hands behind him; after this he was taken to gaol and gagged two hours with his hands chained behind him, to the lamp post, *having all this time his arm broken.* He was then taken to the new gaol, and Stephens sent for the doctor who received him into hospital.

*   *   *

Spread-eagle torture. Two ringbolts about 6 feet apart and 5 and a half feet up are securely fastened in the walls of the cells, and a third in the floor. Prisoner is placed with his back to the wall or sometimes facing it, with arms outstretched and fastened to the bolts, feet close together fastened to the one in the floor. Bridle and ironwood bit are sometimes added to increase the torture. I have several times seen the floor and walls of the cells spattered and streaked with blood after prisoners have been beaten by the turnkeys. I have known C—to remove a man from the cell where he was beaten, to have the floor and walls whitewashed to obliterate all traces . . .

I came into the gaol while a cell was being whitened. A jet of blood from a prisoner's head reached, in one instance I recollect, as high on the wall as I could reach with my extended arms. The man had been struck by the bludgeon of one of the wardsmen.

*   *   *

One hundred and nine men were in solitary in the old gaol within a period of six days. There are ten cells in all. Seven of these were only large enough to hold one inmate with anything like due regard to health and decency. In one day eighty men were packed into two cells seventeen foot square. I have known thirteen men locked in a cell commonly called the 'Nunnery', a room of six feet by twelve feet, when the thermometer was at one hundred; their only vessel a night-bucket. I had to step out into the yard at first, to save myself from fainting.

*   *   *

Some of the crimes for which 'solitary' was the sentence were:
Not walking fast enough when going out to work. 14 days.
Not being in rank when the bell rang. 14 days.
Being at the privy when the bell rang. 14 days.
Getting a drink of water after dinner. 10 days.
Having some ravelling from an old pair of trousers. 14 days.
Having some fat in his possession. 14 days.
Walking across the prison yard to make an enquiry. 14 days.
Refusing work. This man was ordered to lift a stone back into a cart going uphill. Two men lifted it. 14 days.
When the charge sheet was considered not full enough, extra cases were made out, the informers getting remissions or other indulgences for this service to justice.

Rogers's *Journal* is a book of sorrows, one piled upon another in grim sequence. While the lot of newly-convicted men in other parts of the Colony were marginally improving, on Norfolk Island it grew steadily worse. In Van Diemen's Land tobacco was allowed in small quantities to well-behaved men. Price was reluctant to allow the issue to prisoners on Norfolk, but a notice tacked to the barrack gates giving the men leave to use tobacco if they got it honestly, was signed by the Commandant. One prisoner, given a morsel, not more than a quarter-inch, by one of the chaplains, was charged with 'having tobacco improperly in his possession'. He protested, but was given thirty-six lashes.

Rogers used these cases in his arguments to his Bishop as well as to the Governor, in his protests against his dismissal by Price and his further dismissal from the list of Convict Chaplains by Denison. He wrote:

It is because I know that such merciless inflictions are wholly
unnecessary that I am constrained to speak. Omitting some twenty or
thirty villains from the convict population in my time on Norfolk
Island, all the rest were as manageable by the common methods of
just and firm and rational government as the peasantry of Kent or
Devon . . . If your Lordship asks 'What, then, could have been the
reason why, as Chaplain, you . . . were so much the object of aversion
to the authorities at Norfolk Island?' the answer is obvious. The
Chaplains were acquainted with everything that was done . . . we had
constant opportunity of witnessing the harsh and unfair measures
dealt out to the men. We were the prisoners' clergymen . . . we knew
their character . . . to us they avowed their most secret motives . . .
because we conversed with men often unjustly punished we were
supposed to sympathise unduly with them . . . our presence on the
Island was . . . an embarrassment, and the next step was to impute
some unfitness or feign some malicious accusation and get us taken
away.[29]

But no argument or pleading by Rogers could bring Governor Denison to change his mind and restore the chaplain to his duties on Norfolk Island. John Price had the Governor's full confidence, he was doing the duty he had been sent to do, and he had refuted all the charges made by Rogers who was, he said 'too emotional . . .. to work at Norfolk Island'.[30]

It was to take a more powerful voice than Thomas Rogers's to drive home the actual state of Norfolk Island to Denison, and to the authorities in the British Government. There were almost 2000 convicts on the Island at this time, 1846 to 47, more than half of them at the Kingston settlement. There had been three Protestant 'instructors', Rogers and Mr Ison, an Anglican clergyman, and Mr Elliott, the catechist; two Roman Catholic priests; no schoolmaster; two doctors; five superintendents and eight assistant superintendents; one chief constable; and twelve constables and signal men. The Garrison was under the command of Major Harold. Price had no jurisdiction there except to ask for help when it was necessary. Among the convicts however, his power was absolute.

The Last Days of the Settlement

20

IN 1847 THE BRITISH PARLIAMENT DISCUSSED THE OFTEN-RECURRING QUESTION OF THE BREAK-UP OF THE CONVICT ESTABLISHMENT ON Norfolk Island.[1] Earl Grey had received the impassioned plea from the Reverend Beagley Naylor that something be done about conditions on the Island; information from Bishop Willson had also been given to a Select Committee of the House of Lords, that year. Both reports referred to the time of Major Childs's Commandantcy, but by 1847 John Price had been appointed Civil Commandant and despatches from Van Diemen's Land intimated that his firm and unyielding rule had brought some kind of order to the settlement, and had also gained the Lieutenant-Governor's highest approval.

Work on the formerly abandoned pentagonal gaol on the Island had been recommenced. When completed, the large number of solitary cells would prove a fitting place for the subjugation of men who derided 'corporal'. Three months or so in 'solitary' on a diet of bread and water tamed many an incorrigible, for a while at least. Instead of the break-up of the settlement and transfer of all the prisoners to Van Diemen's Land, it was decided that only New Hands, or first-sentenced prisoners, would be shipped out; in their place the worst of the doubly-convicted men would be sent.[2]

This plan had been first suggested in 1844 by Governor Gipps, at the time of the proposed transfer of the Island to Van Diemen's Land government in September of that year:

> Recently . . . some men of the very worst description have been removed by the government of Van Diemen's Land from Tasman's Peninsula to Norfolk Island; and if Norfolk Island is thus to be the place of punishment for the very worst offenders from Van Diemen's Land, there is no reason why persons of the same class should not be sent to it from New South Wales . . .[3]

And in September 1844 Sir E. Eardley-Wilmot seized on the idea, 'I propose that Norfolk Island should be dedicated to the reception of doubly-convicted prisoners, and for all such as have been convicted of very heinous crimes in the first instance'.[4] It was small wonder Bishop Willson found such degradation and brutality rampant on his visit to Norfolk Island in 1846, and that Beagley Naylor could write:

> An amount of Crime inconceivably enormous, is produced by herding together so large a body of men in such a place. I do not intend to pollute these pages with the abundant evidence of this awful fact, which in the discharge of my duties . . . has been forced upon me. I would gladly escape from the horrible recollection, nor would I have referred to it had I, in fulfilling the task I have undertaken, dared to be silent. As a clergyman and a magistrate I feel bound to tell your Lordship that the curse of Almighty God must sooner or later fall in scorching anger upon a nation which can tolerate the continuance of a state of things so demoniacal and unnatural . . .[5]

This was written after Beagley Naylor left Norfolk Island in 1845, and conditions grew steadily worse, as Bishop Willson found in 1846.[6] In 1849, however, the Bishop on his second visit found much to encourage him:

> I cannot omit to mention . . . the improvement I found in the quality of, and the method of issuing, the rations to the convicts . . . the satisfaction I experienced in finding the perfect unanimity which existed among the whole staff of officers on the island, whether civil or military, lay or clerical. How different in 1846! And this pleasing fact I must, in great measure, attribute to the judicious conduct of Mr Price, the Commandant.[7]

But his final word was to warn of the danger of power entrusted to one man so far from the seat of government:

> Now, it is under the superintendence of a Civil Commandant who possesses a master mind for carrying out the work entrusted to him— one who possesses such a combination of qualifications so important and peculiar as are rarely to be found in one man. As long as he has charge of this penal settlement, there is little reason to fear that abuses to any extent could exist; yet from its immense distance from the seat of government and comparatively unfrequent and irregular visitation, it is not difficult to imagine circumstances occurring from which evils of a fearful description might arise and exist for a considerable time before a remedy could be applied.[8]

It is evident that the good Bishop saw none of the instruments of torture that had formerly been in constant use; nor the weighted chains that were riveted on recalcitrant men as punishment for crimes such as insolence (which could be failure to remove the pipe from the mouth when spoken to by an officer, or not removing the cap when passing a superior), or blasphemy, which could be affirmed if a man shouted 'Oh my God' when under duress. But his visit was a comfort to those of his Roman Catholic prisoners who maintained belief in their religion.

Price impressed the Lieutenant-Governor Sir William Denison by his methods of control on Norfolk Island, and Denison supported him when complaints were made by civil officers. Mr Mclean the Deputy Commissary-General of Agriculture claimed that the maize crop of 1848 failed not only through drought, but from an insufficient number of men being allotted to the task of planting;[9] in his reply Denison wrote:

It must be borne in mind that Mr Price's first and most arduous duty in taking charge in July 1846 was to make arrangements for the supervision of the convicts so as to put a stop to the vices and crimes which hitherto had been perpetrated . . . I am satisfied that Mr Price has done all that could have been done for the attainment of this object, consistently with other more important interests . . .[10]

It was clear that Lord Stanley's earlier instructions to Childs, that 'self-sufficiency in supplies was to be of paramount importance', was not considered as urgent a duty as subjection to discipline.

An interesting item in the Mitchell Library, describing Norfolk Island at this time, is an article by someone who signed himself 'Officer on the Spot', 1848. He could have been a military man stationed there for a tour of duty, or more likely a civil officer, probably a Commissariat officer, from his knowledge of domestic details.

On Phillip Island a few wild goats, sickly-looking rabbits, some fowls originally domesticated. A weatherboard hut erected by Captain Best, the Hon. John Charles Best of the 50th or Queen's Own Regiment, who was drowned in 1840. The timber on Phillip Island is small and numerous, rabbits live on shrubs.

On Norfolk Island in 1836 16,000 bushels of maize were raised on less than 400 acres. Maximum in 1840, 27,000 bushels on 800 acres. 1843 crop had dwindled to 8000 bushels on 600 acres. The annual consumption about that time was 20,000 bushels, made up of imports from Sydney. Wheat, oats, rye and barley grown, but unprofitable owing to want of skilful agriculturists. Tobacco was grown with success but not persevered with, owing to prisoners indulging in this forbidden luxury. Balatea, or sweet potato, peas, beans, artichokes, common potatoes and other vegetables, Cape gooseberries, figs, loquats, love-apples, strawberries, pineapples, peaches, guavas, grapes, bananas, apples, lemons and limes all grow. Oranges were plentiful but were extirpated by Colonel Morisset. Common pigeons abound. Fish was excluded before Price arrived, because of supposed danger of having boats afloat except in emergency or urgent necessity. A crew of free men were there to man the boat. Latterly the boat has been sent twice a week to fish, sometimes 1½ tons has been taken in a few hours. Snapper 5–50 lbs. Travalli, Trumpeter, 5–20 lbs, Kingfish up to 70–80 lbs, . . . likewise sharks but not large, they frequently carry off the fishermen's hooks.

Breakfast is hominy, maize-meal boiled in water and salt, eaten with a small quantity of fat or slush, the skimmings of the flesh-pot. Old Hands eat it but New Hands find it distasteful. Dinner is salt beef with fresh pork issued about 10 times a year. The lumber-yard is dirty and out of repair, with the roof leaking . . . Many overseers are ticket-of-leave men but are sometimes beaten or stabbed for want of protection. Cascade is a neat and cheerful place . . . A Superintendent and one Chaplain live here, and about 240 men. There are Bank of England clerks, Spanish legionnaires, rich and poor, high and low, Hindu, Chinese, Malay, Aborigines of Australia, Africans, English, French, German, Poles, Swedish all represented in this congress of ruffians and rogues.

At Longridge, weatherboard barracks can house 700 prisoners, 400 are there. A room for prayers and a small school where about 70 attend in the evenings. There are 25 horses, 755 horned cattle, 5228 sheep, 533 swine, and the only demand on supplies are for the hospital and free residents.[11]

'Officer on the Spot' says nothing about the lighter side of life on the Island, if such there was during Price's rule; he also says, '. . . the Island police are selected from the most active and trustworthy convicts', a situation with which both the Reverend Thomas Rogers, and Bishop Willson disagreed. It is in his list of the variety of nationalities that he makes his most interesting comment. With such a variety of miscreants the question arises 'Who was there to interpret the rigid rules to the Chinese, Malay or Hindu prisoners?' Or was Fear the universal tongue?

One other man who met John Price at this time has left a brief personal description of him. Mr Bartley, passenger on the *Harriet Rockwell* which called at the Island for water and supplies on her voyage to India, writes:

We were supplied with butter, milk and produce, and invited to come ashore. Price was said to be a martinet. All I saw of him was a mild-faced, mild-spoken gentleman with a big head, curly fair hair and pleasing voice and gentle manner, and sadly seasick on our moving decks.

But never shall I forget the monkey-like eagerness of the convict boatmen, their working brows and wrinkled foreheads under leathern caps, and the mute appealing looks they cast at the many hands grouped along our bulwarks, which meant, the tars said, 'Tobacco, for the love of God'. And while Price drank a glass of wine in the cabin to stave off the seasickness, our pitying tars threw down figs of Barrett's Twist into the rocking surf-boat, treasures which were caught by the Norfolk Island crew as famished tigers might catch flying legs of mutton, and were swiftly hid away under the blue serge recesses of their shirts.[12]

At this time, the number of first-sentenced prisoners on the Island was being shipped out to Van Diemen's Land thus leaving room for the incorrigibles who were to be disciplined into submission by John Price. This decision, seen in retrospect, seems like a trick of malevolent Fate. Price, who was suffering with some unspecified malady at the time he took command on Norfolk Island, a malady for which he had asked leave of absence from duty, was to be given an even heavier load than heretofore. Though the numbers diminished, the power increased. He was, literally, deemed capable of doing what could not be done by any other Commandant or Governor of any prison, tame the wildest and most incorrigible men the System had produced.

One of these men shipped from England to Norfolk Island wrote of his three years under John Price from 1850 to 1853. His name was Mark Jeffrey, 'Big Mark' to Price, for he was one of the few convicts bigger and taller than the Commandant. Jeffrey's book, written many years later when he was 68 years old and living, still a prisoner, in Hobart Town, was most probably 'ghosted' for him by J. Lester Burke who also ghosted Martin Cash's life story, and though the narrative loses something because of this, many if not all the facts it contains can be confirmed by the records.[13]

Mark Jeffrey was a country boy, with good parents and a good home, but he began his career of crime when, in his teens, he ran away from home and inevitably fell in with bad company. One escapade led to another; he discovered the thrill and the profit to be got from burgling; was eventually caught, sentenced, and shipped off to Norfolk Island on the *Eliza*, with fifty-nine other prisoners. He was then 25, six-feet-one (185 cm), and weighed, he says, a good 15 stone (95 kg). His besetting sin was an ungovernable temper, and this, coupled with a huge appetite, was to land him in deep trouble on Norfolk Island.

Brash, and something of a braggart as a big man sometimes is when surrounded by smaller men, it was his size that brought him to Price's special attention in the Police court on the Island. It was his admission that the rations were not sufficient to keep him at his heavy work, that gave Price the one weapon he could use to bring the big man to his knees.

For an attack on the overseer of his gang he was given ten days in solitary and a ration of 1 lb (454 g) of 'corncracker', or maize meal mush a day. This tamed him for a while but not for long. Time after time his appetite or his temper got him into trouble, the lash made no difference to his constant appearances in the Police court, and finally he was put in the quarry-gang where the worst men were put, and here he gives a picture of the torment faced by the prisoners:

> . . . it is difficult, in these enlightened days [1890] to picture the abject misery into which prisoners were thrown; to imagine the humiliation, indignities and persecutions which were heaped upon us . . . though my passionate protests had dragged me into the vilest cells and placed me on the brink of the gallows . . . my heart sickened and my senses revolted at the inhuman tyranny which surrounded us on every side . . .[14]

In the quarry-gang, Jeffrey had to work with 36 lbs (16 kg) of iron chain to drag around as well as the quarried rocks. His overseer abused him for being slow, and up flared his temper again. 'I told him I would "do" for him, and for this threat I was given more solitary'.

His diet was reduced to the corncracker and water again, and his overseer was in charge of this. His water was allowed to grow filthy, only when desperate could he drink it. When Price came round on his visit of inspection Jeffrey told him of the stinking water. 'He made a thorough investigation . . . and found the water was as I had described it. The casks were filthy and the liquid they contained was horrible'. The overseer was reprimanded and the water changed. Jeffrey says of Price, 'He was tyrannical, it is true; but he was, to a certain extent, fair and impartial. He never swerved from his course of tyranny—a hard cruel system carried out to the bitter end'.

Jeffrey's 'bitter end' came when, again in solitary, he was left until he broke down, was then given fifty lashes and put in irons weighing 36 lbs (16 kg). He was taken from his solitary cell and put in a 'refractory' cell with scarcely room to sit, let alone lie down. Price came occasionally to see him, sometimes 'foppishly putting his eyeglass to his eye, and regard me with contemptuous insolence saying "How do you like it by this time, Big Mark?"'

After six weeks, Jeffrey was skin and bone, and one day, as Price stood waiting for the admission of defeat, Big Mark grabbed the bars of his cell door, shook them in a fury and yelled 'You unnatural monster! Come . . . take my place . . . and learn how a man can enjoy such punishment!', as Price sauntered away.

Within a few days of the visit Jeffrey was on the point of death, and was moved to the hospital, little more than a living skeleton. He was there three months, and '. . . much to the surprise of the doctor I recovered my health and grew fat and strong as ever'. He was later given a job as sub-constable in the lumber yard. While there he met up with Martin Cash, the bushranger from Van Diemen's Land, but he had little liking for him. Cash had been on Norfolk Island since 1845 and kept himself out of trouble all the time. Jeffrey says of him:

Martin Cash, whose life many people in Hobart Town have read with interest—was one of those who gave information concerning his fellow-prisoners. When I was warder in the lumber-yard he often came in from the plaiters shop where he was overseer, in order to give information to the petty constable, which was surely followed by severe punishment. My curiosity being aroused by the frequent visits he made, I asked one of the constables the nature of Cash's business and he informed me to the effect I have just mentioned.[15]

In the years from 1850 onwards Price's rule grew steadily more harsh. Eventually Governor Denison, his staunch supporter, showed disquiet at the increasing amount of corporal punishment ordered, as entered on the punishment lists. On 2 February 1852 the Deputy Comptroller-General wrote, as directed by the Lieutenant-Governor, querying the reasons for this:

I have been directed to acquaint you that the 'special returns of convicts whose periods of detention at Norfolk Island are recommended to be extended', for the months of June, July, and August last, have been submitted to the Lieutenant Governor and that his Excellency has approved of your recommendation in each case being carried into effect. I am to observe, however, that his Excellency's attention has been drawn to the increasing amount of corporal punishment which these returns show to have been inflicted on the island, and that he regrets very much that you should have considered such punishment necessary to so great an extent; and that his Excellency, while he is aware that the character of the convicts with whom you have to deal may occasionally require resort to severe methods of punishment and restraint, and is disposed to place full confidence in your judgement in the exercise of the discretion necessarily placed in your hands in this respect, trusts that you may find it in your power to adopt for the future effective means of enforcing proper discipline without recourse to such frequent infliction of this mode of punishment.[16]

Price's reply merits quoting:

. . . Implying as this communication does, a censure on the course I have pursued for some months past, I feel it due to myself to point out . . . the cause of my deviating from my former course in the allotting of punishments for offences by convicts on this settlement . . . I assure you that it has been only the absolute necessity arising from . . . causes which I shall presently detail, which has compelled me to resort to the lash more frequently than for some years past . . .

I have received the cullings of the convict department in Van Diemen's Land; men who . . . had rejected the inducements—utterly neglected the advantages which are held out to the convict by that system. English incorrigibles also, the worst that could be selected from Gibraltar and Bermuda, from Millbank, the Hulks, Pentonville, Portland and Parkhurst, and convicts from India, represented as most dangerous characters, most of these too young men of vicious characters, have been landed here; . . . influenced by desperadoes remaining on the island under sentence from all the adjacent colonies . . .

These convicts for the greater part are reckless of future consequences, regardless of any sentence in chains which may be passed upon them . . . Stringent the regulations are, and stringent they must be but they are not more so than those imposed on soldiers, indeed on boys at public schools in England . . . Persuasion is useless, advice is thrown away; they will not listen to me who have turned a deaf ear to the appeals of a parent, a wife a brother or a friend. Ere they reached Norfolk Island they had chosen their paths in life, and they doggedly pursue them until driven from them . . . They laugh at sentences in irons, and I have no sufficient means of carrying out sentences of solitary confinement; I have not cells enough. What then remains but to have recourse to the scourge? . . . I was at length driven to corporal punishment. That it has had a beneficial effect I have no hesitation in asserting . . . the magisterial returns . . . show a very material reduction in the number of offences . . . more especially at Longridge. The number of cases there ranged from one hundred to one hundred and fifty weekly until scourging commenced, but is now reduced to an average of forty . . .

Were I asked what punishment I consider most effective I would reply, that of isolated cells . . . and I may here observe that in no case has it been found necessary here to sentence a prisoner to corporal punishment while imprisoned in the isolated cells . . .

John Price.[17]

This letter was written in March 1852, from the Commandant's office. Yet, in February of that year the Anglican Bishop of Van Diemen's Land wrote to the Comptroller-General Dr Hampton:

. . . You are aware that I have serious misgivings as to the expediency even of a penal system which can only reform externally . . . while it leaves the heart, probably, more hardened than before . . . They have to deal with large masses of men, a large proportion of whom have grown grey in crime, become hardened and brutalized by familiarity . . . with every form of punishment . . . it is then, I fear, a stern necessity that superinduces another and more rigid mode of treatment . . .
Mr Price had a more difficult work to accomplish. When he arrived at Norfolk Island all was anarchy . . . crimes of the most revolting kind

were matters of constant commission and even of notoriety. No man
could walk about the settlement or mix amongst the prisoners with
any degree of safety unless armed.

At the present moment no prison in England can be more orderly,
quiet, peaceable or safe than every portion of Norfolk Island. I went
from cell to cell, spoke freely to men who, before Mr Price came,
were regarded more as wild mischievous animals . . . I . . . rambled
alone through the greater part of the island . . . in perfect safety . . . It
has been my duty to preach before . . . all classes and in many
countries. I may truly say that I never ministered to a more orderly or
more attentive congregation than the hundreds of prisoners in the
chapel at Norfolk Island . . .

J. R. Tasmania.[18]

One month later, in March 1852 the Roman Catholic Bishop Willson,
uneasy from increasing rumours of the terrible conditions on Norfolk Island,
made his third visit. Dr Hampton, the Comptroller-General was there also,
and this time no amount of personal friendship between Hampton and Price
could cover up the findings of the Bishop.

On Sunday 14 March he held a service for his 'parishioners'. His congregation trudged in slowly, silent except for the clanking of chains, which
they wore 'crossed':

. . . the exact number of men in chains I am not able to state, but . . .
out of 270 convicts who attended the church when I officiated, only
52 were without them. Complaints regarding the frequency of the
lash were great indeed. It was stated . . . that on the Monday previous
to our arrival . . . thirty-nine men belonging to the settlement had
been flogged, and fourteen from Longridge Station next day . . . and . . .
the state of the yard, from the blood running down men's backs,
mingled with the water used in washing them when taken down from
the triangle—the degrading scene of a large number of men . . .
waiting their turn to be tortured, and the more humiliating spectacle
presented by those who had undergone the scourging . . . were painful
to listen to . . .[19]

This is from a thirty-page letter Bishop Willson sent to the Lieutenant-
Governor on 22 May 1852 after his return from Norfolk Island shocked and
saddened at the deterioration he had found since his last visit in 1849. Every
one of the 130 cells had an occupant, many in heavy irons which were placed
on them, not to prevent escape, but as extra punishment. 'The image of one
of these living skeletons . . . is so strongly impressed on my mind that no day
passes without having it many times vividly before me . . .', Willson says, and
he goes on to tell of men who were in cells, with 36 lb (16 kg) weights
attached to their leg-chains, hands manacled 'in fact with their bodies placed

in a frame of iron work', of the grey faces and shrunken bodies and the fetid conditions in many of the cells.

Hampton, the Comptroller-General, when called upon to explain how it was he had not mentioned these things in his report to the Lieutenant-Governor, explained that some of the Bishop's findings were inaccurate, only twenty-nine, not thirty-nine men from the settlement had been flogged—he himself had seen no blood in the yard, the men were washed in the cells—no prisoner was sentenced without evidence from a free constable, etc. etc. 'It was as evasive and unconvincing as most official explanations', says Barry.[20] Hampton also maintained that the reason Price used the summary punishment of flogging was because he was overworked; many of his junior officers had tendered their resignations, they intended to leave the Island and go to the newly-discovered goldfields in New South Wales and Victoria—the former Port Phillip District where gold could literally be picked up, or found a metre below the surface. Hampton wrote:

> . . . unless the Government is enabled to meet the views of most in respect of increased remuneration, the greater portion will quit the establishment on the first opportunity; indeed I have learnt that it has been and is the determination of some, should the Government not meet their views, to insist upon their resignations being accepted without notice, and if not provided with immediate means of transport to Van Diemen's Land to sue the Government for damages for illegal detention.[21]

There were 950 convicts on Norfolk Island at the time Hampton wrote this letter, on 15 March 1852, and Price had only fifteen overseers to supervise them, most of these men former convicts who had been employed as turnkeys or constables, 'the present strength is wholly inadequate'. It was indeed a parlous state of affairs and one which left Price little alternative but to order summary corporal punishment rather than task-work or supervised hard labour; an alternative which inevitably led to the abandonment of any attempt to reclaim a single one. Price ended his letter: '. . . I wish it to be most distinctly understood that I regard it as perfectly impossible to work this island with convict overseers. I for one would be unwilling to undertake the responsibility'.

Aaron Price, the Principal Overseer and recorder of events (though only spasmodically) gives his view of Price, in some of his diary entries:

Christmas 1846   This day being Christmas Eve, the Civil Commandant issued an order for the gangs to leave work at 4 o'clock, the same privilege allowed them on Saturdays. A great many went to the R. C. chaplain for spiritual advice.

25th. Served with 1 lb fresh beef. Men got up a play among themselves in the lumberyard, and made themselves as merry as possible. Military had high jinks on Boxing Day. Sports, running and jumping, greasy pole with a silver watch atop, every sport that could be named. Watch taken down at 7.30. Nobody reached it.

13th December. 1850. Died this day the infant son of Lt. de Winton, and buried on the 14th at 5 o'clock in the morning.

April 4. 1851. 10 prisoners acting as sub-overseers are this day sworn in as sub-police, a step taken to give them somewhat more power and to encourage them in the performance of their duty. They will not be required to perform the ordinary duties of constables.

May 1851 55 more prisoners and passengers arrive on island.

23 June 1851 *Franklin* delayed at Sydney, most of the crew having deserted to go to the diggings at Bathurst. Something unusual, not a Police report this day.

1853. We now commence a New Year and with it a fresh administration of local affairs. Civil Commandant and Captain Blachford proceed on board to arrange passage to Van Diemen's Land. Sale by auction of Captain Blachford's chattels.

18th Jan Civil Commandant gives over command to Rupert Deering Esq. Captain of 99th Regiment. Civil Commandant leaves Norfolk Island this day at 5.p.m. per *Franklin* for Hobart Town. I think from the appearance of the officers assembled on the jetty to witness the departure and bid him farewell that a kind of melancholy dejection is apparent. He is good and I must mark the general marked opinion of the gentlemanly deportment in his public and private life.[22]

This is not the last entry in Aaron Price's diary, but it is the only one so far found, written by a former convict and a man who had been on Norfolk Island during the whole of John Price's term of office, in which the Commandant is spoken of as 'good'. Aaron Price was a shrewd man. His opinion should be at least considered if not agreed with.

John Price had applied for leave of absence in 1850 'from this Lazar House of crime', and had asked to be employed 'in a place other than Australia'.[23] He gave as his reason the necessity of having his children educated away from the influence of a penal settlement. Instead of leave he was given an increase of salary. Not until January 1853 did he leave the Island and, in the Old Cemetery, the grave of Emma Julia Price, who died in 1849 aged sixteen months. The de Wintons too, left the grave of their infant son George, who died in 1850, six days before his first birthday.[24] The two children lie side by side in the cemetery among the graves of soldiers, soldiers' wives, officers, convicts, children, and men from passing ships who had died and been buried on the Island. On Norfolk Island death exacted its toll from free and bond without partiality.

The Prices lived for one year in Hobart Town after their return from Norfolk Island, and during this time a second child, young Gustavus Lambart, died from scarlet fever. In January 1854, Price was appointed Inspector-General of Penal Establishments in Victoria, where 'mountains of gold' had been found, and diggers from all over the world flocked in their thousands, to seek their fortune.[25] Convict escapees, ticket-of-leave men, reprobates and regular prospectors joined in the rush. The colonists in Victoria were alarmed, in some measure, for their own safety, for their property or, in some instances, for their lives. 'Greed, and its misshapen bodyguard, aggression, stalked the land . . . the proportion of the vicious and the irretrievably corrupted was dangerously high . . . fear and insecurity became general'.[26] A strong man was needed, and in January 1854 John Price was installed in the Inspector-General's house at the Pentridge Gaol. Once again Mary Price and her children were surrounded by the stockade and the grim walls of a prison. But this time was the last. Price's iron grip on the 'incorrigible rogues' in the gaol and the men festering in the hulks off Williamstown, was prised loose by death on 27 March 1857. In a sudden attack, sparked off, probably, by a word or a gesture of Price's—in much the same way as the mutiny of July 1846 had erupted—he was stoned, battered unconscious when he fell to the ground, and left beyond help.[27] Hunger was the primary cause—hunger and hatred. Seven men were hanged for the crime, but two others, who had crept from their hiding places after the mob had fled, were commended for their compassion in tending the unconscious Price, bathing his blood-matted head and carrying him to the doctor's house nearby the quarry where the murder took place. John Price was 48 years old at the time of his death.

On Norfolk Island after Price's departure, the command was taken over by the senior military officer Captain Deering, who soon had a taste of convict audacity when, on 11 March, nine men seized a Government launch, put out the military guard aboard her, and rowed off to freedom.[28] Deering and a party of soldiers set off in pursuit, but Aaron Price, in his diary, writes: '. . . arrived at 4.p.m. a very much exhausted Commandant—no intelligence of the launch, 6.p.m. and nothing heard of Coxswain Forsyth and Boardmore, (Government men) who it is supposed, are drowned.' One prisoner left behind, who was found at the launching site feigning sleep, was given nine months' hard labour in chains, put back into cells, and had his Norfolk Island sentence lengthened by 18 months. The incorrigibles were still incorrigible.

At this time the settlement was being 'wound down' and on her official voyages the *Lady Franklin* took a number of civil officers and their families, and a number of prisoners, usually about 68, and a military guard, to Van Diemen's Land where they were put under the strict discipline enforced at the Port Arthur settlement.

Captain Deering had little liking for Norfolk Island, and sent in his resignation within months of becoming Commandant. He was replaced by Captain Day, the next-senior officer. In these days when the Island was manifestly 'winding-down', the occasional batch of prisoners was still sent

*This is probably a remnant of the first settlement, and used as
a guard-house.* (Photograph by the author)

All that remains in the gaol of a row of cells. (Photograph by
the author)

Norfolk Island children and adults, on their annual procession on Anniversary Day, 8 June, to celebrate the arrival of their forebears from Pitcairn's Island on 8 June 1856. (Photograph by courtesy of the Norfolk Islander Gazette)

from Van Diemen's Land or from England. In July 1853 Aaron Price records: 'Twenty-one prisoners, two R.C. priests, three boatmen, one free coxswain, wife and family; two Military officers, twenty rank and file'. These were sent to fill the gaps left by those inhabitants who had gone to the goldfields. By the same vessel came news of the capture of the stolen launch on the coast of New South Wales, and the safety of Forsyth and Boardmore: 'Two of the nine runaways are in custody'.

A number of American ships called in at this time for fresh water and provisions. All, except the whalers, carried a full load of passengers bound for Victoria, where gold was to be had for the picking up, they had been told. Aaron Price does not record whether any stowaways were taken on from Norfolk Island, but it seems unlikely that any ship would sail away without at least one on board. On 18 September Captain Day arrived to take over as Commandant. With him was his wife and family, 10 rank and file of the 99th Regiment, and 11 prisoners 'sent to be employed as servants, etc.'

Slowly the settlement was reduced. Sixty-eight prisoners and a detachment of the military sailed on the *Lady Franklin* each time it brought provisions and replacement detachments to Norfolk Island, and on one of these trips, news came of the capture of the last of the runaways 'with the exception of James Clegg, commonly known as Ginger Clegg'.[29]

In this final period, conditions were very much eased on Norfolk Island. Captain Day was a humane man whose treatment of the convicts seems like a shaft of light after years of darkness. Aaron Price, not given to rhapsodising, reports:

Christmas Day falling on a Sunday this year, the Civil Commandant Captain Day of the 99th Regt. was so kind as to allow the prisoners the indulgence of half a day on Monday to keep Xmas—and also allowed the officers to invite the men to their quarters, which they did in a most liberal manner. The few not asked out, (20) and the Gaol men (15), the Captain provided for himself, making all hearts glad with his kindness, and sending all to bed in good humour and with full bellies'.

24th May, Queen's Birthday
This being the anniversary of Her Majesty's Birthday—was kept as a holiday. The Civil Commandant allowed such prisoners out to dine at officers' quarters by whom they were asked. The few left in the Lumber Yard were plentifully supplied with tobacco and provisions by the C.C. A discharge of Fire Works in the evening. The Civil Commandant with his usual liberality in the evening made a present of a bottle of grog to each officer—and I am happy to be able to record as an act of grace, he reinstated Timothy Ford in his situation of turnkey at the gaol.

R

On 30 May 1854 Captain Day's sixteen-year-old daughter Catherine married Ensign Joseph Dinham Mablon of the 99th. 'The Civil Commandant gave a splendid entertainment to the Principal Officers of the Island, both Civil and Military—As also displayed his liberality to all on the Island not invited to Government House'.[30]

This is almost the last entry in Aaron Price's diary. It was a fitfully-kept book, of immense value, from the length of time it covers, and the little incidents given which are not to be found in any other document. He left the Island later in 1854, presumably to follow his young son to the Victorian goldfields, though he makes no mention of this except on his 'title-page' which mentions that he 'recovered his freedom' in 1854.

His last entry is 1 August 1854. It tells of the marriage of Mr Samuel Padbury, Storekeeper, to Miss Helen Belstead, daughter of Captain Belstead. 'Little Padbury' is the same one that Elizabeth White Robertson wrote of in her *Diary* in 1845, when he was a constant visitor at the Robertsons' house at Longridge. He had been one of the few civil officers who stayed on the Island throughout John Price's period of office, and Price spoke well of him in his letters to the Comptroller-General.

In July 1854 the *Lady Franklin* took a batch of prisoners and their military guard to Van Diemen's Land. She had brought despatches to the Commandant, stating that Norfolk Island was to be abandoned as a penal settlement by January 1855, but this proved impossible, from the number of men and provisions which had to be moved. In December, Captain Willett of the *Franklin*, wrote, in a letter to his friend Lukin, 'I am now engaged in breaking up Norfolk Island as fast as possible and should finish it in about six months'. His estimate was optimistic. Not until January 1856 was he able to write: 'Just returned from last trip to Norfolk Island, and completed the breaking-up of the settlement and selling the *Franklin*', adding a lugubrious 'I have little faith in the justice of the Convict Board re pension entitlement . . .'[31]

Norfolk Island, with its sixty-eight years as a penal settlement, was at last free of its miasma of human sorrow and brutality. The buildings, and the quiet graveyard with its record of mutiny, execution, heroism and accident, were the only evidence of its past. It was soon to return to serenity, with the coming of the Pitcairners, whose home it was destined to be.

The New Arrivals on Norfolk Island

WHEN THE *LADY FRANKLIN* SAILED FROM NORFOLK ISLAND IN MAY 1855 IT CARRIED THE FEW REMAINING CONVICTS—TICKET-OF-LEAVE MEN, and those emancipated—leaving only five of the best-behaved to maintain essential services and act as caretakers. Mr Stewart the Commissariat Storekeeper was to be in charge until the new settlers from Pitcairn's Island arrived—which would not be until mid-1856.

The days passed in a peaceful silence. The newly-built pentagonal prison, its cells whitewashed for the last time, stood as a malevolent monument to John Price. The neat Georgian houses in their pretty, untended gardens, the large Administration buildings, the military barracks, the prison dormitories and the lumber-yard were all eerily silent, their gates standing open.

It was a strange twist of Fate that the newcomers were the descendants of men who would—had they been caught in the widespread search made by *Pandora* in 1791, and lived through the fearful voyage back to England—been retransported to New South Wales in chains, and maybe from there to Norfolk Island.[1] It is more than likely that some of them at least, would not have lived to reach England. Captain Edwards of the *Pandora* was a man so brutal that beside him Captain Bligh would seem a ministering angel.

The history of the Pitcairners begins in 1787 and is an enthralling and bloody story. Books have been written about it, both fiction and purported fact; films have been made, all of them wildly imaginative; the essence of the story eludes all but a few of the accounts set down at the time of the mutiny.

The H.M.S. *Bounty* left England in December 1787 on its way to Tahiti where Captain Bligh had orders to take aboard a cargo of bread-fruit plants to be carried to the West Indies, where they were to grow into trees whose fruit would provide a cheap and nourishing food for the slaves—who had also been carried from their homelands to the sugar-plantations of Jamaica and other islands in the West Indies.[2]

Bligh arrived at Matavai Bay in Tahiti too late in the year to gather the young trees, so he was forced to wait from October 1788 to April 1789, the time needed for newly-planted seedling trees to grow strong enough for the long voyage of transportation. Bligh had been to Tahiti before, with Captain Cook; he and his crew were made welcome, and for those five or six months the *Bounty* men lived the kind of life sailors might dream of.[3] Many close associations were made between the pliant and handsome Tahitian women and the sailors, and when, in April, the plants were stowed and the ship readied for the long haul, the partings were sad indeed.

Three weeks out of Tahiti, on the evening of 27 April 1789, the *Bounty* anchored off Tofua Island.[4] On that night the mutiny was hatched—a sudden explosive hatching which had been unforeseen by Bligh or, for that matter, by any of his officers other than Fletcher Christian.[5] Christian and Bligh had been on bad terms on several occasions after the *Bounty* arrived in Matavai Bay, mostly on points of discipline, but that would have been no unusual thing between a captain of a vessel and his master's Mate, which was the position Christian held. Bligh's short-tempered abuse and intolerance would also have been a common characteristic in the sailing ships of those days, when men of such varying dispositions were closely confined in a small and crowded vessel. This was not Christian's first voyage with Bligh; he had sailed twice before, as midshipman, with Bligh to the West Indies in the merchant-ship *Britannia*.[6]

At daybreak on 28 April, Bligh was seized in his cabin by Christian and Churchill (the Master-at-Arms), his hands bound with cord, his nightshirt his only garment, and forced on deck—Alexander Smith (alias John Adams), and Thomas Burkitt marching behind him—and tied to the mizzen-mast.[7]

With eighteen loyal members of his crew he was later set adrift in the *Bounty*'s launch, after being given enough food and water, with a little wine and rum, to last the nineteen men about two weeks with care, to find his way across uncharted seas to safety—or to perish.[8] It had been Christian's plan to send Bligh and his men away in the ship's cutter, but the remonstrances of the master, boatswain and carpenter prevailed on him to allow the launch to be hoisted out instead. Even with the larger boat the castaways were within a few centimetres of the water.

On Sunday 4 June 1789 Bligh and his men reached Coupang, in Timor.[9] A sorrier lot of men had surely never been landed on that shore before—they were in rags, emaciated almost to skeletons, full of sores, and with tears of joy and relief in every eye. They had come more than twelve hundred leagues (6670 kilometres) in an open boat, with no charts—and no deaths; a voyage which has never been acclaimed as the magnificent achievement it was. His *Journal*, kept even in that awesome period of his life, is a better indication of the man than are any of the acrimonious judgements passed on him in later years.

From Tofua, the mutineers sailed the *Bounty* to Tahiti, where they rejoined their Tahitian 'wives'—and with four Tahitian men and two men from a nearby island sailed away to find a secluded island where they might live in safety from discovery.[10] Christian was well aware that if Bligh succeeded in reaching England, the long arm of the British Navy would reach out and pluck them all back to face trial, with its inevitable verdict of death by the hangman's rope. Sixteen of the mutineers chose to stay on Tahiti rather than go with the others.[11] It was two years before the *Pandora* (Captain Edwards) caught up with them and carried them back to face trial. On the *Pandora* they were manacled and pushed into a large 'cage' on deck; four of them drowned when the ship was wrecked on the Great Barrier Reef on her voyage home.[12] At the subsequent Court-Martial held at Portsmouth three men were hanged for the mutiny, on board H.M.S. *Brunswick* in Portsmouth Harbour on 29 October 1792.[13]

Fletcher Christian and his shipmates made one or two abortive attempts to find a safe place to settle, before finding tiny Pitcairn's Island, far from normal shipping lanes and with only one possible landing-place, which in itself was dangerous. Here the nine mutineers, twelve Tahitian women, six Polynesian men, and one baby girl belonging to one of the women, went ashore. They found signs of an earlier settlement; fruit trees, coconut palms, tumbledown huts, and a burial ground but no inhabitants. Here was the place where they could be safely hidden, Christian decided, and within days everything useful had been removed from the *Bounty* and carried ashore. On 23 January the *Bounty* was burnt to the water-line lest a passing ship should see her masts and investigate the island.[14] So began the Elysium for which so much had been dared.

But the fragile fabric of their lives was torn when one of the women fell to her death while gathering eggs on the cliffs. She was Pashotu, Williams's wife and it was October 1790. Williams brooded, and in time demanded one of the three women who belonged to the Polynesian men. This was not allowed, but in 1792 he took Toofaity, who belonged to Tararo, and so began the dark days of revenge and murder. Tararo and a second Polynesian plotted to kill the white men — but were killed themselves after their plot had been whispered to the mutineers by one of the women.[15]

Bad feeling flowed between the two races, and in September 1793 the Polynesians plotted to kill all the white men who, by this time, were no longer the friends but the masters. Williams was the first to be killed as he worked repairing his fences broken down by hogs who had trampled and eaten his crop of yams. He was shot through the back of the head and the shot was heard by Christian and others; they thought it only the shot of a hunter after pigs. The next victim was Christian, who was also busy in his garden, bent over a pile of yams he had been digging. The same man, Tetaheite, shot him and mutilated his face with blows from an axe. Still nobody seemed unduly alarmed, only McCoy ran for cover, calling out as he ran 'They are murdering us all — hide yourself.'[16]

In turn, Mills, Brown, and Martin were shot or clubbed to death on that day. The 'beautiful life' was ended, fear lay heavy on every soul — none knew who would be the next victim. It was Alexander Smith, the small nuggety man who had been friendly to everyone and who drank as hard as the next.

He was shot in the shoulder, but the ball passed through and came out at his neck without killing him. He was attacked again, this time with a club, but he struggled to his feet and succeeded in getting away. By this time the first frenzy was over, Smith was spared, Quintal and McCoy fled to the mountain for safety. Ned Young, beloved of the women, seems not to have been involved in the uproar.

Of the twenty-eight people who arrived on Pitcairn's Island in January 1790, only fifteen were left by September 1794, and several children born during those years.

Blood had not yet ceased to flow. McCoy, using the old Bounty kettle as a still, experimented and made potent spirits from the ti-tree; he, and the others began drinking heavily, McCoy and Quintal reaching the point where they were suspected of losing their reason. Quintal's wife Sarah, subject to her husband's insane rages, beaten and dreadfully abused, was found dead at the foot of the cliffs in 1799; McCoy had died in 1797 also from a fall from the cliff-top, though when he was found his feet and hands were bound and a weight was tied about his neck.[17] When Quintal found his wife dead he immediately demanded one of the women, threatening to kill Young and Smith if his demands were not met.

At this threat, Young and Smith knew there was only one way out—they must kill Mat Quintal first. It was not difficult to invite him to drink with them, and, when he was in a drunken stupor attack him with an axe.[18] This was probably done in Ned Young's house—the blood-spattered walls were the evidence of the ferocity of the attack. It must have been a fearful moment when the two survivors of the bold party which had mutinied in April 1789 realised the terrible happenings of the past few years, and the plight they were in. Young already had his death sentence hanging over him—he had severe asthma and was to die within a year of Quintal's death. In a book written some years after these events, is described what happened during that last year of Ned Young's life:

These two men were now the sole survivors of the nine Englishmen (and of all the coloured men) who, nine years previously, had sought concealment and safety in the island. Happily their minds had not been irremediably seared by crime. They desired to change the tenor of their evil lives, and to turn to those paths of virtue which lead to tranquillity and peace. A Bible and a Prayer-book, which Christian had constantly studied, but which had not been used since his death, were diligently sought for. The observance of daily morning and evening prayer was established, as well as a system of regular instruction for the children and young people, Smith zealously assisting Young, and improving his own slender acquirements by associating with a man of superior education. Edward Young however, did not long survive this improved state of mind and feeling. An asthmatic complaint with which he had been afflicted for several

years, proved fatal to him at the age of thirty-six, and consequently in
the early part of the year 1800, Alexander Smith [John Adams] found
himself the sole surviving man on the island and the only guardian
and teacher of a community of helpless women and young children.[19]

'Helpless' was scarcely the right word for the Tahitian women but it suited
the Victorian times in which the book was written. It is a fairer picture of
what probably took place than is the dramatic tale of the vision appearing to
Alexander Smith one night, with dire threats of what would befall him if he
did not repent his evil ways and turn to teaching the Bible to the little
community on Pitcairn's Island. No doubt his 'visions' were nightmares
brought on by excesses—but the end result was the same.

Alexander Smith, or John Adams as he now becomes—was described by
Bligh as of April 1789 (the last time he saw him) 'aged 22 years; 5 feet
5 inches high; brown complexion; brown hair; slender made; pitted with the
small pox; very much tatowed; scar on his right foot.'[20]

Adams was the son of a poor family in London's dockside area; he had little
if any schooling and less religious learning, his only contact with the Bible or
prayer-book would have been from the services mandatory on all His Majesty's
ships, but he was intelligent and quick to learn from Young as much as he
could in the short time they were together. Reading and writing came easily
to him, and after Young's death he took on the teaching of the whole
community, with only the aid of the *Bounty* bible and prayer-book. As self-
appointed pastor, he married Thursday October Christian—Fletcher
Christian's first-born son and so called for the obvious reason he was born
on a Thursday in October 1790—to Sarah, Edward Young's widow. The
groom was 16, the bride 31, and the wedding ring was one that had belonged
to Young. So began the second generation of Pitcairn-born islanders.

The community was discovered when, in 1808, Captain Matthew Folger,
captain of the *Topaz*, an American whaler, anchored off the island to go
ashore for wood and water.[21] Adams told the story of the unexpected
settlement—his own version naturally—and gratefully accepting what
provisions the *Topaz* could spare in return for wood, water and island
produce. It was a further six years before the British Navy arrived—not to
hale the last mutineer back to England but to take a closer look at the small
island jutting out in the ocean where no island was marked on their charts.
H.M.S. *Briton* and H.M.S. *Tagus* were in search of an American ship at the
time, and as John Adams saw the flag of His Majesty's Navy at the masthead,
he felt certain his hour had come.

But when Sir Thomas Staines, captain of the *Briton* and Captain Pipon of
the *Tagus* requested him, as the senior man on the island, to come aboard, he
went, with Thursday October Christian and Edward Young, son of Ned
Young.[22] He was received at first with caution, once the position was known,
but in remarkably short time the air was cleared as the young men showed
their great affection for their leader, and on shore the whole community

clung around him beseeching the officers not to take him away from them. Sir Thomas Staines wrote of this occasion:

> The greatest harmony prevailed in this little community . . . They are
> honest in their dealings . . . Their habitations are extremely neat . . .
> In their houses, a good deal of furniture . . . tables and chests to
> contain their valuables, and clothing which is made from the bark of a
> certain tree, prepared by Otaheitan females . . . The woods abound
> with a species of wild hog, and the coasts of the island with several
> kinds of good fish . . .[23]

From this time on the Pitcairners were visited occasionally by ships of the British Navy to ascertain their progress. In 1823 two young men, John Buffett and his friend John Evans came ashore from the British whaling-ship *Cyrus*, and on request, were given leave to stay. John Buffett a cabinet-maker by profession and a man of some education, took over as schoolteacher, and before long he married a daughter of Young. Evans married soon after, and new blood-lines were begun on Pitcairn.

Two more seafarers arrived to stay in 1828, Noah Bunker an American, and George Hunn Nobbs his friend and shipmate. Noah Bunker, already seriously ill, died within days of reaching Pitcairn; Nobbs was to become John Adams successor. George Hunn Nobbs, a mysterious figure whose background is not clear-cut, had come at an opportune time, for John Adams died in March 1829 and Nobbs, a man of wide experience of the world, took on himself the role of leader, pastor and doctor.[24]

Apart from an emigration *en masse* to Tahiti in 1830—a visit which proved disastrous to many Pitcairners who died from influenza and other ills while there—and from which they were only too glad to return—the Pitcairner's lives were peaceful; with one disruption. In 1832 Joshua Hill, an Englishman came to Pitcairn who was, to say the least, eccentric. He declared he had come as President of the Commonwealth, his first act was to exile Buffett, Evans and Nobbs to the Gambier Islands, nearly 500 kilometres from Pitcairn. Claiming kinship to the Dukes of Bedford, Hill was exposed for the fraud he was, when H.M.S. *Actaeon* arrived offshore, its Captain none other than a son of the Duke, Lord Edward Russell.[25] In short order Hill was removed and the three exiles brought back to Pitcairn.

During the years of peaceful progress on Pitcairn's Island the men on Norfolk Island sweated under their several Commandants—the four years of Maconochie's Superintendency the only alleviation. These men would, and sometimes did, give their lives to escape from its vicious cruelty, brutality, and hunger. They were, for the most part, devoid of hope. Thousands of prisoners passed through the gates of the prison barracks—many of them never to leave. New punishments were devised, new prisons built, and until January 1853 when John Price left Norfolk Island, that once beautiful spot seemed doomed to become nothing more than a purgatory through which thousands more men must pass.

But unknown to the mass of men on Norfolk Island, plans had been made for its complete transformation. In May 1853 the Pitcairners agreed with the suggestion of the British Government that they transfer in a body from their small and now over-crowded island, to the larger Norfolk Island which would, said the Government spokesman, soon be abandoned as a penal settlement. Pitcairn's Chief Magistrate Arthur Quintal, wrote to their friend and advisor, Rear-Admiral Fairfax Moresby C.B.:

> We, the undersigned . . . having according to your request convened a
> public meeting of the inhabitants of the island . . . do unanimously
> and fully acquiesce in your opinion . . . It is very evident that the time
> is not far distant when Pitcairn's Island will be altogether inadequate
> to the rapidly increasing population; and the inhabitants do
> unanimously agree in soliciting the aid of the British Government in
> transferring them to Norfolk Island or some other appropriate
> place . . .[26]

1854 was the year first decided upon but the Government found that a removal was not a simple matter of moving a number of people from one place to another. The ships available for taking prisoners from Norfolk Island to Van Diemen's Land could take, at the most, sixty-eight men and their guards; and with the length of time it took to sail from Norfolk to Hobart Town, then turn around and sail back for a second and a third and fourth load, a matter of 2250 kilometres each way, only four trips a year could be managed. Governor Denison needed more time to arrange matters. He had to ensure all convicts were safely lodged at Port Arthur or Hobart Town or other places where the necessary supervision was available. The date of the Pitcairners' transfer was delayed, it would now be mid-1856.

On 5 May 1855 the *Lady Franklin* carried the remaining officers and some prisoners from Norfolk Island, leaving only the skeleton staff to act as caretakers.

On 18 September, Mr William Bishop, Commissary-General in Van Diemen's Land—or Tasmania as it was generally to be known—replied to Denison's enquiry regarding stores to be left on the island for the Pitcairners. He wrote:

> Instructions were left with Mr Stewart the Commissariat Storekeeper
> in charge . . . to make a careful selection of the most valuable of the
> stores remaining there, for shipment to Hobart Town—and also to
> ship the mare Diamond and her filly if possible . . . the number of
> livestock to be left at Norfolk Island for the Pitcairners are, about
> 1,300 sheep, 250 horned cattle milch cows heifers steers etc. 8 horses
> including 1 young colt. The swine are running wild in the bush, and
> their numbers may be estimated at from 40 to 50. At Philip Island
> there is . . . a flock of wild goats, also swarms of rabbits. Pigeons and
> parrots abound . . . Fish is very plentiful around the Coast, a ton

weight having occasionally been caught in a few hours . . .

At the last sowing season, 1854, the only grain sown was Oats and Rye for forage—and as vegetables, vines for sweet potatoes. The wild pigs destroyed nearly the whole of the former—and the cattle all the latter, the fencing having gone generally to decay from the want of convict labour.[27]

It continued with a list of things which grew well and those which should only be planted at certain times if they were to crop well. A crop of maize could not be expected before 1857, he wrote, and suggested that an extensive supply of bread-stuffs and groceries should be provided before the Pitcairners arrived. Then followed five lists of goods and materials to be left on the island, some of the lists filling eight closely-written pages. At Kingston settlement were, 12 Officers houses, 10 of them stone buildings of four to eight rooms each and outbuildings of stone, stone-flagged verandahs 'all complete'. There were 33 buildings for 'Inferior persons quarters' [constables, overseers etc.], 27 of them stone, 6 weatherboarded. A windmill and hut, a Water-mill and hut, and 24 other buildings of stone. A Protestant Chapel and Vestry, fitted with pews and seats, Pulpit and Reading Desk, Communion table and rail, a Gallery and Vestry, the ten Commandments written over the Communion table and on the Walls. Also a Catholic Chapel and Sacristy, with Altar and Altar railing, Altar window and pulpit, and with paintings on the walls.

Longridge had one stone house and five weatherboarded ones, three large Barracks for the prisoners, 2 Stone barns, a 12-stall stable, 1 tool-house, bake-house, cook-house with cooking apparatus, a fowl-house and a 12-cell Gaol.

Cascades station was 'in a dilapidated condition' (it was the first one to be vacated by the prisoners), but it had a stone Gaol with 3 cells, a cook-house and Bake-house and two wells, and at Cascade Landing-place, other buildings and 'a Strong Crane secured to the Rock, used for hoisting goods out of Boats alongside'.[28] All in all, it was a fair exchange for the 194 Pitcairners whose island was too small to accommodate them all.

After the 'stock-taking' was done, all but five of the convicts were shipped away with the civil officers, leaving only Mr Stewart who was to greet the newcomers. Early in June, Captain Denham of H.M.S. *Herald* came ashore with his surveyors to prepare plans for the subdivision of the island among the Pitcairn families.

On 8 June 1856, which was a cold, rainy morning, the *Morayshire* dropped anchor in Sydney Bay.[29] The first boatload of weary travellers were greeted by Mr and Mrs Stewart, Captain Denham and his senior officers, and taken to Government House for warmth and a comforting cup of tea. Boatload by boatload the Pitcairners were brought ashore; it took a week to bring all their goods and chattels from the ship but it was done at last, and the new Norfolk Islanders could begin their new life. All of them felt strange, some were disappointed—they had built their hopes so high, and expectation had been greater than the reality, especially on a cold wet winter's day with a keen wind blowing.

In December 1858 sixteen of the Pitcairners returned to their island, pining for their former homes; but the rest, under Pastor Nobbs, remained and were happy. A school-teacher, Thomas Rossiter, was sent from England; James Darve, a miller, wheelwright, and smith, along with H. J. Blinman, a mason and plasterer were also sent to familiarise the Pitcairners with the totally new tools and conditions on Norfolk. None of them had seen stone buildings before, except Buffett, Evans and Nobbs. At the first, the children were frightened of the horse which drew a small cart; but that didn't last long, soon they were vying with each other for 'first go'.

In September 1856, within weeks of the Pitcairners' arrival, Bishop Selwyn, Bishop of New Zealand, came to the island which was part of his diocese, and confirmed eighty-six people, the oldest 66 (the daughter of John Mills, one of the mutineers) the youngest, a great-grandson of Fletcher Christian, a boy of 15. The service was held in the former prison Chapel, and later, Bishop Selwyn wrote:

> The Chapel opens into the prison yard, set round with every kind of cell . . . in every corner heaps of rusty fetters or cast-off garments marked with the broad arrow and numbered on the back as if the owners were no longer worthy of a name; and all . . . made more striking by the horrid silence of the solitary cells . . . Close to this visible type of everything which is the most hateful . . . might be heard the song of praise in which every voice is joined . . [30]

The 'Great Hulk or Penitentiary from which there is no escape' was now a place of which Pastor Nobbs wrote 'The land is a goodly land and needs nothing but a contented mind . . . and a grateful heart to render it pleasant . . .'

Yet the 'goodly land' still holds the bodies or remains of hundreds, if not thousands of men whose lives were forfeited to the Government of their day. Cattle may wander freely over the places where the flogging-yards were; no longer do gates bar the entrance to the Lumber-yard or prison barracks, but the blood spilt, the 'punishment short of Death' still, at times, pervades the darker, unvisited corners of the Old Cemetery.

References

Abbreviations

ADB	*Australian Dictionary of Biography*
HRA	*Historical Records of Australia*
HRNSW	*Historical Records of New South Wales*
JRAHS	*Royal Australian Historical Society, Journal and Proceedings*
PP (HL, HC)	*Parliamentary Papers, House of Lords, House of Commons*

Chapter 1: A Paradise Discovered

1 James Cook, *Journal*, vol. 2.
2 Cook's opinion that the Island was part of an extended ridge from New Zealand to New Caledonia was proved correct recently in findings published as follows: (a) T. H. Green, 'Petrology and Geochemistry of Basalts from Norfolk Island', *Journal of the Geological Society of Australia*, vol. 20, part 3, 1973; (b) J. G. Jones & I. McDougall, 'Geological History of Norfolk and Philip Islands, South-West Pacific Ocean', *Journal of the Geological Society of Australia*, vol. 20, part 3, 1973; (c) G. B. Udentsev, 'Bathymetric Map of the Pacific Ocean', *Institute of Oceanology, Academy of Science*, Moscow, 1964.
3 Cook, *Journal*, vol. 2.
4 William Wales, Journal on H.M.S. *Resolution* Sept. 1773–Oct. 1774, Mitchell Library, Safe 1/84.
5 George Forster, *A Voyage Round the World Performed in His Britannic Majesty's Ships the Resolution and Adventure in the Years 1772, 1773, 1774 and 1775*, Dublin, 1777, vol. 4, pp. 378–80.
6 Lord Sydney to the Lords Commissioners of the Treasury, 18 August 1786, *HRNSW*, vol. 1, part 2, pp. 14–19.
7 *HRA*, series 1, vol. 2, p. 25.
8 *HRNSW*, vol. 1, part 2, p. 25.
9 Captain John Hunter, *An Historical Journal of the Transactions at Port Jackson and Norfolk Island*, London, 1793.
10 Hunter, *Journal*, pp. 2–3.
11 Charles Bateson, *The Convict Ships 1788–1868*, Glasgow, 1959, p. 86.
12 Hunter, *Journal*, pp. 3–4.
13 Lieutenant Ralph Clark, *Journal and Letters 1787–1792*, Australian Documents Library, 1981, p. 24.
14 Phillip to Lord Sydney, 15 May 1788, *HRNSW*, vol. 1, part 2, p. 122.
15 *HRNSW*, vol. 2, pp. 513–44, 660; also John Cobley, *Sydney Cove 1788*, 1962, p. 40.
16 Captain Watkin Tench, *A Narrative of the Expedition to Botany Bay*, 3rd edn, London, 1789.
17 *HRNSW*, vol. 1, part 2, p. 89; *HRA*, series 1, vol. 2, p. 89.
18 *HRNSW*, vol. 1, part 2, 12 Feb. 1788; *HRA*, series 1, vol. 2, p. 136.
19 *HRNSW*, vol. 1, part 2, pp. 137–8; *HRA*, series 1, vol. 2, pp. 137–8.

Chapter 2: Philip Gidley King and the First Settlement

1 Philip Gidley King, *Journal of Philip Gidley King R.N., 1787–1790*, Australian Documents Library, 1980, p. 383.
2 Charles Bateson, *The Convict Ships 1787–1868*, p. 96.
3 King, *Journal*, p. 40; *HRA*, series 1, vol. 1, pp. 33–4.

4 *HRA*, series 1, vol. 1, p. 13.
5 J. J. Auchmuty (ed.), *The Voyage of Governor Phillip to Botany Bay*, Sydney, 1970, p. 28.
6 Arthur Bowes Smyth, *The Journal of Arthur Bowes Smyth: Surgeon, Lady Penrhyn 1787–1789*, (ed. Fidlon & Ryan), Australian Documents Library, 1979, p. 65.
7 John Cobley, *Sydney Cove 1788*, 1962, p. 75; also David Collins, *An Account of the English Colony in New South Wales*, A. H. & A. W. Reed, Sydney, 1975, p. 11.
8 Cobley, p. 75; all names given with the exception of 2 males—the latter are mentioned in the following pages of this volume.
9 Captain John Hunter, *An Historical Journal of the Transactions at Port Jackson and Norfolk Island* (ed. J. P. Bach), Sydney, 1968, p. 299; also King, *Journal*, pp. 45–6.
10 King, *Journal*, pp. 46–7.
11 King in Hunter's *Journal*, p. 301.
12 King in Hunter's *Journal*, pp. 307–9.
13 King in Hunter's *Journal*, p. 304; also Collins, *An Account of the English Colony in New South Wales*, p. 31; and King, *Journal*, p. 55.
14 King in Hunter's *Journal*, p. 311.
15 King, *Journal*, p. 67; King in Hunter's *Journal*, p. 311.
16 King in Hunter's *Journal*, p. 311; King, *Journal*, p. 69.
17 King, *Journal*, p. 75; King in Hunter's *Journal*, pp. 314–15.
18 King, *Journal*, p. 87.
19 King, *Journal*, pp. 103, 105; Collins, p. 31; Cobley, p. 217.
20 *HRA*, series 1, vol. 1, pp. 88, 97; Collins, p. 34; King, *Journal*, pp. 147–9.
21 *HRA*, series 1, vol. 1, p. 98 (report of this letter by Phillip to Lord Sydney); King, Letter-book, Mitchell Library, C. 189.
22 King in Hunter's *Journal*, p. 345; King, *Journal*, p. 177.
23 Norfolk Island Victualling Book, Mitchell Library A1958.
24 King in Hunter's *Journal*, pp. 346–53; *HRA*, series 1, vol. 1, pp. 140–1; King, Letter-book, Norfolk Island, 1788–89, pp. 38–9.
25 King in Hunter's *Journal*, pp. 356–8; *HRA*, series 1, vol. 1, p. 141.
26 Collins, pp. 50–1.
27 King, Letter-book, Mitchell Library, C. 189, pp. 41–2.
28 *ADB*, 1788–1850, vol. 2, p. 397.

Chapter 3: Major Robert Ross
1 *ADB*, 1788–1850, vol. 2, pp. 397–8.
2 *ADB*, 1788–1850, vol. 2, p. 397.
3 *HRA*, series 1, vol. 1, pp. 107–11.
4 *HRA*, series 1, vol. 1, pp. 134–6.
5 *HRA*, series 1, vol. 1, p. 135.
6 *ADB*, 1788–1850, vol. 2, p. 398.
7 *HRA*, series 1, vol. 1, p. 167.
8 Lieutenant Ralph Clark, *Letters and Journal 1787–1792* (ed. Fidlon & Ryan), Australian Documents Library, 1981, p. 119.
9 *HRA*, series 1, vol. 1, p. 142.
10 Captain John Hunter, *An Historical Journal of the Transactions at Port Jackson and Norfolk Island* (ed. J. P. Bach), Sydney, 1968, p. 175.
11 Hunter, p. 175.
12 King in Hunter's *Journal*, p. 384.
13 Hunter, p. 176.
14 King in Hunter's *Journal*, p. 386.
15 King in Hunter's *Journal*, p. 387; Clark, pp. 123, 124.
16 Clark, p. 122.
17 Clark, p. 124.
18 Hunter, p. 182; Clark, p. 187 ff.
19 Clark, p. 130.
20 Clark, p. 163.

21 *HRA*, series 1, vol. 1, p. 227.
22 *HRA*, series 1, vol. 1, pp. 241–5.
23 Clark, entries on various pages.
24 Clark, p. 185.
25 Clark, p. 229.

Chapter 4: D'Arcy Wentworth

 1 Norfolk Island Victualling Book, Mitchell Library A1958; David Collins, *An Account of the English Colony in New South Wales*, Sydney, 1975, p. 604; *ADB*, 1788–1850, vol. 2, pp. 579–80.
 2 *ADB*, 1788–1850, vol. 2, pp. 579–80.
 3 Arnold Kellet, *The Knaresborough Story*, Huddersfield, Yorkshire, 1972.
 4 *ADB*, 1788–1850, vol. 2, p. 580.
 5 Old Bailey Sessions, Papers, Dec. 1789–Oct. 1790; Collins, p. 604.
 6 Old Bailey Sessions, Papers, Dec. 1789–Oct. 1790.
 7 Charles Bateson, *The Convict Ships 1787–1868*, pp. 113, 126–30; G. Mackaness (ed.), 'Some Letters of Rev. Richard Johnson', *Australian Historical Monographs* (new series 1977), vol. 21, letter 9, pp. 30–4; Collins, pp. 99–101.
 8 Bateson, p. 129.
 9 *HRA*, series 1, vol. 1, pp. 334, 353, 379, 760 (note).
10 Bateson, p. 130, 323 (notes); *HRNSW*, vol. 2, pp. 802–6.
11 Captain John Hunter, *An Historical Journal of the Transactions at Port Jackson and Norfolk Island* (ed. J. P. Bach), Sydney, 1968, p. 188.
12 Lieutenant Ralph Clark, *Letters and Journal 1787–1792* (ed. Fidlon & Ryan), Australian Documents Library, 1981, pp. 187, 212, 216–7.
13 Philip Gidley King, *Journal* while Lieutenant-Governor of Norfolk Island, 1791–96, National Library MS70, p. 11.
14 Clark, p. 184.
15 Clark, p. 186.
16 King, p. 26.
17 King, p. 88.
18 Norfolk Island Victualling Book.
19 Joseph Holt, *Memoirs* (ed. T. Croker), Colburn, London, 1838.

Chapter 5: King Returns

 1 *ADB*, 1788–1850, vol. 1, p. 56.
 2 Chapman Papers, Mitchell Library A 1974; Letters of W. N. Chapman, Alexander Turnbull Library, Wellington, New Zealand.
 3 M. Bassett, *The Governor's Lady*, Oxford, 1940, Appendix 1, p. 114.
 4 *HRNSW*, vol. 1, part 2, p. 562.
 5 Philip Gidley King, Journal while Lieutenant-Governor of Norfolk Island, 1791–96, National Library MS70, p. 2; Bassett, p. 22.
 6 King, p. 19.
 7 Norfolk Island Victualling Book, Mitchell Library A1958.
 8 Letters of W. N. Chapman.
 9 Philip Gidley King, Letter-book, Mitchell Library A2015; *ADB*, 1788–1850, vol. 2, p. 56; Bassett, p. 33.
10 *HRA*, series 1 vol. 1, pp. 166–7.
11 *HRNSW*, vol. 2, pp. 87–8.
12 David Collins, *An Account of the English Colony in New South Wales*, Sydney, 1975, pp. 290, 429–40.
13 *HRA*, series 1, vol. 2, p. 87.
14 *HRNSW*, vol. 2, p. 125.
15 *HRNSW*, vol. 2, pp. 107–8.
16 *HRNSW*, vol. 2, p. 141.
17 *HRNSW*, vol. 2, pp. 135–70.
18 *HRNSW*, vol. 2, p. 105.
19 *HRNSW*, vol. 2, p. 106.
20 *HRNSW*, vol. 2, pp. 125–6.
21 *HRNSW*, vol. 2, p. 130.

22 *HRNSW*, vol. 2, pp. 126–7.
23 *HRNSW*, vol. 2, pp. 26–7.
24 G. Mackaness (ed.), 'Some Letters of Rev. Richard Johnson', *Australian Historical Monographs* (new series, 1977), vol. 21, letters 22, 26.
25 *ADB*, 1788–1850, vol. 1, pp. 57, 61.

Chapter 6: Foveaux
 1 *ADB*, 1788–1850, vol. 1, p. 407.
 2 *HRNSW*, vol. 2, p. 234; *HRA*, series 1, vol. 2, pp. 502, 505.
 3 *HRA*, series 1, vol. 2, p. 687; *ADB*, 1788–1850, vol. 1, pp. 536–7.
 4 I. A. Ramage, *A Cameo of Captain Thomas Rowley*, Australian Library of History, Sydney, 1981.
 5 *HRNSW*, (Hunter to King), vol. 2, p. 96; Ramage, part 2.
 6 John Turnbull, *A Voyage Round the World in the years 1800–1804*, London, 1805.
 7 Lieutenant Ralph Clark, *Letters and Journal 1787–1792* (ed. Fidlon & Ryan), 1981, p. 201.
 8 Turnbull, pp. 118–20.
 9 Joseph Foveaux, Letter-book, vol. 1, Mitchell Library A1444.
10 *HRNSW*, (Hunter to King), vol. 2, p. 98.
11 Foveaux, vol. 1, p. 46.
12 Foveaux, vol. 1, p. 39.
13 Foveaux, vol. 1, p. 16.
14 *HRA*, series 1, vol. 3, p. 15.
15 *HRNSW*, vol. 4, p. 266.
16 *HRNSW*, vol. 4, p. 267.
17 *HRA*, series 1, vol. 4, p. 86.
18 G. W. Rusden, *History of Australia*, vol. 1, pp. 284–5.
19 *HRA*, series 1, vol. 4, pp. 108–9.
20 *HRNSW*, vol. 2, pp. 157–8.
21 Mrs Eliza Kent, Letter written to her mother in May 1803 from H.M.S. *Buffalo* during the voyage from Sydney to Calcutta, Mitchell Library.
22 *ADB*, 1788–1850, vol. 1, pp. 407–9.
23 *HRA*, series 1, vol. 5, p. 331.
24 Robert Jones, Recollections of 13 Years Residence in Norfolk Island and Van Diemen's Land, 1823, Mitchell Library CY½D.

Chapter 7: Recollections of Robert 'Buckey' Jones
1 Robert Jones, Recollections of 13 Years Residence in Norfolk Island and Van Diemen's Land, 1823, Mitchell Library CY½D.
2 Norfolk Island Papers, Muster of Settlers, 1808, Mitchell Library 4/1167B.

Chapter 8: 'General' Joseph Holt
 1 Joseph Holt, *Memoirs* (ed. T. Croker), London, 1838.
 2 Holt, vol. 1, pp. 2–3.
 3 Holt, vol. 1; *Dublin Courier*, 19 November 1798.
 4 *HRNSW*, vol. 4, pp. 120–9, 235.
 5 Holt, vol. 2, pp. 118–23.
 6 R. W. Eastwick in Herbert Compton (ed.), *A Master Mariner, The Life of Captain R. W. Eastwick*, pp. 196–201.
 7 Holt, vol. 2, p. 379.
 8 Holt, vol. 2, p. 383.
 9 Holt, vol. 2, pp. 225 ff.
10 Holt, vol. 2, p. 230.
11 *HRNSW*, vol. 5, p. 404; *HRA*, series 1, vol. 5, p. 331.
12 Holt, vol. 2, p. 238.
13 Holt, vol. 2, pp. 239 ff.
14 Holt, vol. 2, p. 230; *HRNSW*, vol. 5, pp. 550–1.
15 Holt, vol. 2, pp. 225–6.

Chapter 9: John Piper
1 *ADB*, 1788–1850, vol. 2, pp. 334–5.
2 M. Barnard Eldershaw, *The Life and Times of John Piper*, Sydney, 1973, p. 27.
3 Eldershaw, p. 28; Piper Papers, Mitchell Library.
4 *HRA*, series 1, vol. 5, p. 331.
5 *HRA*, series 1, vol. 5, pp. 325–6.
6 *HRA*, series 1, vol. 5, p. 327.
7 *HRA*, series 1, vol. 5, p. 327.
8 *HRA*, series 1, vol. 4, p. 86.
9 *HRA*, series 1, vol. 5, p. 405.
10 Eldershaw, p. 76.
11 John Cobley, *Crimes of the First Fleet Convicts*, Sydney, 1970, p. 247.
12 John Cobley, *Sydney Cove 1791–92*, Sydney, 1965, p. 6.
13 *HRA*, series 1, vol. 5, p. 321.
14 W. S. Hill-Reid, *John Grant's Journey, A Convict's Story 1803–11*, Heinemann, 1957, p. 247.
15 H. V. Evatt, *Rum Rebellion*, Sydney, 1938, p. 120.

Chapter 10: John Grant
1 W. S. Hill-Reid, *John Grant's Journey, A Convict's Story 1803–11*, Heinemann, 1957, p. 1.
2 Hill-Reid, p. 2.
3 Hill-Reid, p. 8.
4 Sessions Records, Guildhall, London; the trial took place at the Old Bailey, London, on 15 April 1803.
5 Hill-Reid, pp. 15–16.
6 Evidence given to the Select Committee at a Parliamentary Enquiry, *Parliamentary Papers* (House of Commons), vol. 18, Sessions, 1847.
7 Hill-Reid, p. 24.
8 Hill-Reid, p. 36.
9 Hill-Reid, pp. 31–2.
10 Hill-Reid, p. 54.
11 *ADB*, 1788–1850, vol. 1, p. 526.
12 *HRA*, series 1, vol. 4, p. 86; Hill-Reid, p. 94.
13 Hill-Reid, p. 105.
14 Hill-Reid, p. 115.
15 Hill-Reid, p. 131.
16 Hill-Reid, p. 159.
17 Hill-Reid, p. 163.
18 Hill-Reid, p. 163.
19 Hill-Reid, p. 172.

Chapter 11: The End of the First Settlement
1 *HRA*, series 1, vol. 6, pp. 75–80.
2 *HRA*, series 1, vol. 5, pp. 328–9.
3 *HRA*, series 1, vol. 6, p. 74.
4 *HRA*, series 1, vol. 6, p. 421; H. V. Evatt, *Rum Rebellion*, Sydney, 1938, p. 218.
5 *HRA*, series 1, vol. 7, p. 257.
6 Norfolk Island Papers, Mitchell Library 4/1168B.
7 M. Barnard Eldershaw, *The Life and Times of Captain John Piper*, Sydney, 1973, p. 28.
8 Register of Births, Marriages and Deaths, St. Philip's, Sydney, Mitchell Library A2130.
9 *HRA*, series 1, vol. 7, p. 705.
10 Eldershaw, pp. 195–6.
11 Eldershaw, p. 120.
12 *HRA*, series 1, vol. 7, pp. 248, 259, 591–2.
13 *HRA*, series 1, vol. 7, pp. 591–2.
14 *HRA*, series 1, vol. 8, p. 143.
15 *HRA*, series 1, vol. 8, pp. 164–5.

Chapter 12: The Second Settlement, 1825 to 1855: 'Forever Excluded from all Hope of Return'

1 *HRA*, series 1, vol. 11, p. 322.
2 *HRA*, series 1, vol. 11, p. 604.
3 *HRA*, series 1, vol. 11, p. 553.
4 *HRA*, series 1, vol. 11, p. 698.
5 Rev. Thomas Sharpe, Papers, Mitchell Library MS. A1502.
6 *HRA*, series 1, vol. 13, p. 105.
7 Sharpe.
8 *HRA*, series 1, vol. 15, p. 595.
9 *HRA*, series 1, vol. 13, pp. 266–7.
10 *HRA*, series 1, vol. 15, p. 630.
11 Aaron Price, History of Norfolk Island from Period of Discovery in 1774 to the present day, Dixson Library, Sydney, MS. Q247, 248, 249.
12 *HRA*, series 1, vol. 15, pp. 596–7.
13 *HRA*, series 1, vol. 15, p. 597.
14 *HRA*, series 1, vol. 15, p. 597.
15 *HRA*, series 1, vol. 15, p. 594.
16 *HRA*, series 1, vol. 11, p. 665.

Chapter 13: James Thomas Morisset

1 *ADB*, 1788–1850, vol. 1, pp. 260–1.
2 Foster Fyans, Reminiscences, MS., La Trobe State Library, Melbourne.
3 *ADB*, 1788–1850, vol. 1, pp. 260–1.
4 John Bigge, *Report on the Colony of New South Wales*, 1822, C.O.201/114, p. 114.
5 B. W. Champion in *JRAHS*, vol. 20, part 4, p. 213.
6 Lachlan Macquarie, *Journals of his Tours in New South Wales and Van Diemen's Land*, Library of Australian History, 1979.
7 *HRA*, series 1, vol. 11, Brisbane to Bathurst, Dec. 1824, p. 430.
8 *HRA*, series 1, vol. 11, Darling to Bathurst, Dec. 1824, p. 431.
9 *HRA*, series 1, vol. 13, Darling to Bathurst, p. 112.
10 *HRA*, series 1, vol. 12, Bathurst to Darling, 24 Sept. 1826, p. 585.
11 *HRA*, series 1, vol. 14, Darling to Murray, Feb. 1829, p. 642.
12 *HRA*, series 1, vol. 13, Hay to Darling, 20 May 1827, p. 315.
13 *HRA*, series 1, vol. 16, Bourke to Goderich, Feb. 1832, p. 542.
14 *HRA*, series 1, vol. 15, p. 214.
15 Aaron Price, History of Norfolk Island from Period of Discovery in 1774 to the present day, Dixson Library, Sydney, MS. Q247, 248, 249, entry: 18 November 1829.
16 Mrs Napier George Sturt, *Charles Sturt, Sometime Captain 39th Regiment, and Australian Explorer*, London 1899, pp. 95–6.
17 E. S. Hall, Letter to Lord Goderich, 9 February 1832, Mitchell Library A2146.
18 Sir Francis Forbes, Chief Justice of New South Wales, to Committee of House of Commons, 1836.
19 Sir Roger Therry, 'Reminiscences of Thirty Years Residence in New South Wales' in Bill Beatty, *With Shame Remembered*, Melbourne, 1962, pp. 69–70.
20 *HRA*, series 1, vol. 16, Darling to Goderich, pp. 338–9.
21 *HRA*, series 1, vol. 16, Goderich to Darling, p. 530.
22 W. G. McMinn, *Allen Cunningham, Botanist and Explorer*, Melbourne, 1970, p. 97.
23 Price, History of Norfolk Island . . .
24 Price, entry: 29 May 1832.
25 J. A. Dowling, 'An Account of Norfolk Island', *JRAHS*, part 11, 1905, pp. 213–20.
26 Dowling, p. 220.
27 Colin Roderick, *John Knatchbull, From Quarterdeck to Gallows*, Sydney, 1963, pp. 186–91.

Chapter 14: John Knatchbull

1 *ADB*, 1788–1850, vol. 2, pp. 65–6.
2 Colin Roderick, *John Knatchbull, From Quarterdeck to Gallows*, Sydney, 1963.
3 Roderick, pp. 8–9.
4 Roderick, p. 13.
5 Roderick, p. 82.
6 Roderick, p. 13.
7 *HRA*, series 1, vol. 17, pp. 638–9.
8 Roderick, pp. 188–91.
9 Foster Fyans, Reminiscences, MS., La Trobe State Library, Melbourne.
10 Roderick, pp. 91–2.
11 Roderick, pp. 189–90.
12 *ADB*, 1788–1850, vol. 2, p. 66.
13 Dixson Library, MS. Add. 566.
14 Dixson Library, MS. Add. 566.
15 Roderick, pp. 192–3.
16 Aaron Price, History of Norfolk Island from Period of Discovery in 1774 to the present day, Dixson Library, Sydney, MS. Q247, 248, 249, entry: 22 March 1834.
17 *HRA*, series 1, vol. 17, pp. 456–7.
18 *HRA*, series 1, vol. 17, p. 614.
19 *ADB*, 1788–1850, vol. 2, p. 66; B. W. Champion in *JRAHS*, part 4, vol. 20, p. 224.

Chapter 15: 'Potato Joe' Anderson

1 *ADB*, 1788–1850, vol. 1, pp. 13–14.
2 Colin Roderick, *John Knatchbull, From Quarterdeck to Gallows*, Sydney, 1963, p. 93.
3 Rev. Thomas Atkins, *Reminiscences of Twelve Years' Residence in Tasmania and New South Wales; Norfolk Island and Moreton Bay; Calcutta, Madras and Cape Town; United States of America; and the Canadas*, London, 1869.
4 Rev. W. B. Ullathorne, *Autobiography of Bishop Ullathorne*, London, 1891, p. 101.
5 Joseph Anderson, *Recollections of a Peninsula Veteran*, London, 1913, pp. 152–4.
6 *HRA*, series 1, vol. 17, p. 639.
7 W. W. Burton, *The State of Religion and Education in New South Wales*, London, 1913, pp. 152–4.
8 Burton, pp. 259–60.
9 J. Backhouse, *Narrative of a Visit to the Australian Colonies*, London, 1843.
10 Backhouse, Appendix J, pp. lxxvi–lxxx.
11 J. Backhouse & G. W. Walker, Report of a Visit to the Penal Settlement of Norfolk Island by James Backhouse and George Washington Walker, written to Governor Sir Richard Bourke, June 1835, Royal Commonwealth Society Library, London.
12 B. W. Champion, 'James T. Morisset', *JRAHS*, part 4, vol. 20.
13 Ullathorne, p. 100.
14 Anderson, p. 157.
15 Ullathorne, p. 105.
16 Anderson, pp. 159–61.
17 Backhouse & Walker, Report.
18 Backhouse & Walker, Report.
19 Backhouse & Walker, Report.
20 P. Cox & W. Stacey, Building Norfolk Island, Sydney, 1971, p. 24.
21 Roderick, pp. 204–5.
22 *HRA*, series 1, vol. 18, p. 301.
23 *HRA*, series 1, vol. 18, pp. 766–72.
24 *HRA*, series 1, vol. 18, p. 768.
25 *HRA*, series 1, vol. 18, p. 772.

26 Rev. Thomas Sharpe, Papers, Mitchell Library A1502; *HRA*, series 1, vol. 18, p. 768.
27 Anderson, pp. 170–1.
28 *HRA*, series 1, vol. 19, Bourke to Glenelg, 5 Nov. 1837, pp. 150–1.
29 *HRA*, series 1, vol. 19, p. 152.
30 *HRA*, series 1, vol. 19, pp. 154–5.
31 *HRA*, series 1, vol. 19, Gipps to Glenelg, 26 Jan. 1839, p. 775.
32 Ensign A. D. W. Best, *The Journal of Ensign Best 1837–1843* (ed. Nancy M. Taylor), Turnbull Library Monograph, New Zealand, 1966, p. 31.
33 Major Thomas Bunbury, *Reminiscences of a Veteran*, vol. 2, p. 291.
34 *HRA*, series 1, vol. 23, pp. 448–53; Roderick, pp. 238–40.
35 *ADB*, 1788–1850, vol. 1, p. 14.
36 Bunbury, vol. 1.
37 Bunbury, vol. 2, p. 320; Best, p. 32.
38 Best, p. 215, Appendix II, pp. 403–4.
39 Best, p. 186.
40 *HRA*, series 1, vol. 20, pp. 352–3.
41 Best, pp. 32–4.
42 Best, p. 33
43 Best, p. 213.
44 Thomas Cook, *The Exile's Lamentations*, Library of Australian History, Sydney, 1978.
45 *HRA*, series 1, vol. 20, pp. 152, 155.
46 *ADB*, 1788–1850, vol. 2, pp. 412–13.

Chapter 16: Alexander Maconochie

1 Alexander Maconochie, *Norfolk Island 1840–1844*, Hobart, 1973, p. 8.
2 *ADB*, 1788–1850, vol. 2, pp. 184–6; Matthew Davenport Hill (ed.) *Our Exemplars Poor and Rich*, 2nd edn, London, 1861, pp. 213–41.
3 F. T. Boase, *Modern English Biography*, Truro, Cornwall, 1897.
4 J. V. Barry, *Alexander Maconochie of Norfolk Island*, London, 1958, pp. 9–11.
5 Barry, p. 12; H. R. Mill, *The Record of the Royal Geographical Society 1830–1930*, London, 1930, pp. 19–72.
6 G. Mackaness (ed.), The Franklin Correspondence, Review Publications, 1977, part 2, p. 55.
7 Barry, p. 20; Alexander Maconochie, Correspondence re Norfolk Island, 1846, p. 5; Alexander Maconochie, *Crime and Punishment*, London, 1846, pp. 31, 65.
8 B. Fletcher, *Colonial Australia before 1850*, p. 90–1.
9 Barry, p. 43; K. Fitzpatrick, *Sir John Franklin in Tasmania 1837–1843*, p. 90.
10 Barry, p. 47; Alexander Maconochie, *Report on the State of Prison Discipline in Van Diemen's Land, PP (HL)*, 1838, vol. 9, p. 445 ff.
11 Barry, p. 48.
12 Barry, p. 53.
13 *ADB*, 1788–1850, vol. 2, p. 185; Barry, p. 58 (*True Colonist*, 28 Sept. 1838).
14 Barry, pp. 54–5.
15 Barry, p. 58.
16 Barry, p. 59.
17 *(Report) 1838 Select Committee on Transportation, PP (HL)*, pp. xxi, xxxii–xxxiii; Barry, p. 62.
18 *HRA*, series 1, vol. 20, pp. 152–4.
19 Rt. Rev. W. B. Ullathorne, *On the Management of Criminals*, London, 1866, pp. 32–3.
20 *HRA*, series 1, vol. 20, p. 528.
21 *HRA*, series 1, vol. 20, pp. 530–46.
22 *HRA*, series 1, vol. 20, p. 525.
23 *HRA*, series 1, vol. 20, Normanby to Gipps, pp. 152–4.
24 Barry, p. 71.

25 Maconochie's outline of the Marks System is set out in his *Report on the State of Prison Discipline, PP (HL)*, vol. 9, pp. 453–5; it was later incorporated into his *The Mark System of Prison Discipline*, January, 1858.

26 Alexander Maconochie, *Secondary Punishment, the Marks System*, London, 1848, p. 8.

27 *HRA*, series 1, vol. 20, p. 690.

28 Barry, p. 217; *Second Report of Select Committee on Transportation, PP (HC)*, vol. 17, p. 8 ff.

29 Rev. J. West, *The History of Tasmania*, Launceston, 1852, vol. 2, p. 284.

30 Barry, p. 103; *the Castle of Andalusia* is described in the London magazine *Opera*, vol. 3, December 1852.

31 *HRA*, series 1, vol. 20, Gipps to Russell, pp. 689–90.

32 *HRA*, series 1, vol. 20, Gipps to Normanby, pp. 402–3.

33 *HRA*, series 1, vol. 21, Gipps to Russell, Aug. 1841, pp. 494–5.

34 J. F. Mortlock, *Experiences of a Convict* (G. A. Wilkes & A. G. Mitchell edd.), Sydney, 1965.

35 Maconochie, *Secondary Punishment*; Barry, pp. 112–17; Maconochie, *Norfolk Island 1840–1844*, p. 13.

36 Thomas Cook, An Exile's Lamentations, MS. Mitchell Library, published Australian Library of History, Sydney, 1975.

37 (Circular)—Colonial Secretary's Office, Sydney, No. 33. 48, 16 October 1833.

38 (Circular)—Colonial Secretary's Office, Sydney, No. 33. 48, 16 October 1833.

39 Cook, p. 43.

40 Cook, p. 55.

41 Cook, pp. 50–4.

42 Cook, pp. 56–7.

43 Barry, p. 131; *HRA*, series 1, vol. 22, Gipps to Stanley, Aug. 1842, p. 204.

44 Maconochie, *Secondary Punishment*, p. 9 ff.

45 *HRA*, series 1, vol. 22, pp. 200–1; 'A Chaplain', A Tale of Norfolk Island, MS. Mitchell Library.

46 Franklin Correspondence, part 2, letter 39, p. 53.

47 *HRA*, series 1, vol. 22, Gipps to Stanley, 1 April 1843, pp. 617–40.

48 *HRA*, series 1, vol. 22, Gipps to Stanley, April 1843; Barry, p. 140.

49 *HRA*, series 1, vol. 22, Gipps to Stanley, April 1843, p. 619.

50 *HRA*, series 1, vol. 22, Stanley to Gipps, 29 April 1843, p. 691.

51 *HRA*, series 1, vol. 22, Stanley to Gipps, 29 April 1843, p. 698.

52 Rev. W. B. Ullathorne, *Autobiography of Bishop Ullathorne*, London, 1891, p. 33.

53 Barry, p. 196; Report of Commissioners to inquire into condition and treatment of prisoners confined in Birmingham Prison, 1854, *PP*, vol. 31.

54 Barry, pp. 197–204; Birmingham Prison Report, Evidence, pp. 377, 429, 430.

55 Barry, p. 223; Florence Davenport Hill, 'The Friend of the People', 17 November 1860, p. 628.

56 Barry, p. 225.

Chapter 17: Major Joseph Childs

1 *ADB*, 1788–1850, vol. 1, pp. 220–1.

2 *HRA*, series 1, vol. 22, p. 693.

3 *HRA*, series 1, vol. 22, p. 692.

4 Rev. Beagley Naylor, letter to Rt. Hon. Lord Stanley, *c.* April 1846, in *Norfolk Island, Botany Bay of Botany Bay*, Sullivan's Press, Hobart, 1979. The letter was delivered to Maconochie by Naylor's wife, who was in England at that time, and by him sent on to Lord Stanley.

5 Naylor, letter 'received by a Friend', 3 February 1847, in A. Maconochie, *Secondary Punishment*, London, 1848.

6 *HRA*, series 1, vol. 22, pp. 695–6.

7 *HRA*, series 1, vol. 22, p. 697.

8 Alexander Maconochie, *Norfolk Island 1840–44*, London, 1847, pp. 10–14.

9 *HRA*, series 1, vol. 23, Stanley to Gipps, pp. 215–16.

10 Childs to Colonial Secretary, 16 April 1844 in *Correspondence and Papers Relating to Convict Ships, Convict Discipline and Transportation 1843–47*, PP *(HC)*, 1847, vol. 29, pp. 10–12.
11 Robert Pringle Stewart, *Report*, 20 June 1846, in *Correspondence on Convict Discipline and Transportation*, PP *(HL & HC)*, 16 February 1847, vol. 8.
12 Colonial Secretary to Childs, 16 April 1844, *PP (HL)*, vol. 8, 1846, p. 12.
13 Childs to Colonial Secretary, 1 May 1844, *PP (HL)*, vol. 8, 1847, p. 13.
14 Childs to Colonial Secretary, 1 May 1844, *PP (HL)*, vol. 8, 1847, p. 13.
15 J. F. Mortlock, *Experiences of a Convict* (G. A. Wilkes & A. G. Mitchell edd.), Sydney, 1965, p. 70.
16 Mortlock, p. 70.
17 Mortlock, p. 76
18 *ADB*, 1788–1850, vol. 2, pp. 384–5.
19 Elizabeth White Robertson, Diary, 1845, Dixson Library, Sydney, MS. 163.
20 Robertson.
21 Robertson.
22 Robertson.
23 Robertson.
24 Robertson.
25 Robertson.
26 Robertson.
27 Robertson.
28 *HRA*, series 1, vol. 22, Stanley to Gipps, p. 516; *Regulations, Instructions re Convict Discipline*, pp. 514–23.
29 Naylor, letter to Earl Grey, 1846.

Chapter 18: Men of the July Mutiny

1 Alexander Maconochie, evidence to second Report of Select Committee on Convict Transportation, 20 June 1856, *PP (HC)*, vol. 17.
2 Robert Pringle Stewart, *Report*, 20 June 1846, in *Correspondence on Convict Discipline and Transportation*, PP *(HL & HC)*, 16 February 1847, vol. 8.
3 Elizabeth White Robertson, Diary, 1845, Dixson Library, Sydney, MS. 163.
4 J. V. Barry, *The Life and Death of John Price*, Melbourne, 1963, p. 72.
5 These, and other forms of torture may be found in W. F. Rogers, 'Man's Inhumanity to Man', Typescript, Mitchell Library C 214.
6 Stewart, *Report*.
7 W. Champ, Comptroller-General of Convicts, Van Diemen's Land, to Lieutenant Governor Sir E. Eardley-Wilmot, 30 June 1846 in *Correspondence on Convict Discipline and Transportation, PP (HL)*, vol. 8, 1847, papers presented 16 February 1847.
8 Letter from Major Childs to Comptroller-General, Van Diemen's Land, 11 July 1846 in *Correspondence on Convict Discipline and Transportation*, PP *(HL & HC)*, 16 February 1847.
9 Patrick Hiney, evidence in Report of the Commission held on Norfolk Island, 1 July 1846.
10 Frank Clune, *Martin Cash, The Last of the Bush Rangers*, p. 297.
11 Childs to Comptroller-General.
12 William Foster, evidence in Report of Commission held on Norfolk Island.
13 A. E. Baldock, evidence in Report of Commission held on Norfolk Island.
14 Baldock.
15 Dr Graham, evidence in Report of Commission.
16 Dr Graham.
17 Aaron Price, evidence in Report of Commission.
18 Price.
19 Findings of Report of Commission.
20 Letter from Samuel Barrow to Colonel Champ, 27 July 1846.
21 Barrow.
22 Fielding Browne, Report in *Further Correspondence on Convict Discipline and Transportation*, PP *(HL)*, 1847, vol. 8.
23 W. H. Barber in *Household Words*, London, 1852, vol. 5; Rev. T. Rogers, *Correspondence*, p. 163.

24 Rogers, p. 164; Rev. John West, *The History of Tasmania*, 1852, vol. 2.
25 Price to Comptroller-General, 6 October 1846.
26 Price to Comptroller-General, 13 October 1846.
27 Rogers, *Correspondence*, pp. 41–3; Frank Clune, *The Norfolk Island Story*, Sydney, 1967, pp. 246–52.
28 Clune, pp. 246–52.
29 Clune, pp. 246–52.
30 Clune, pp. 246–52.
31 Rogers, *Correspondence*.
32 Aaron Price, History of Norfolk Island from period of Discovery in 1774 to the present day, Dixson Library, Sydney, MS. Q247, 248, 249.

Chapter 19: John Price, Civil Commandant
 1 Evidence, Report of Victorian Parliament Legislative Assembly, 1857.
 2 Burke's *Peerage and Baronetcy*, London, 1969, pp. 2042–4.
 3 Gunn Papers, Mitchell Library A316; *Hobart Town Gazette*, 3 March 1843.
 4 J. V. Barry, *The Life and Death of John Price*, Melbourne, 1964, p. 10.
 5 *Cornwall Chronicle*, Tasmania, 23 June 1838, p. 2.
 6 *Hobart Town Gazette*, 4 January 1839; Colonial Secretary's Office 50/2, Tasmanian State Archives.
 7 J. V. Barry, *The Life and Death of John Price*, Melbourne, 1963, p. 16.
 8 Colonial Secretary's Office, 20/29/637, Tasmanian State Archives.
 9 *Biographical Memoir of the late Mr John Price, Inspector-General of Penal Establishments for Victoria*, p. 7.
10 Barry, p. 24.
11 Despatch from Sir E. Eardley-Wilmot to Rt. Hon. W. E. Gladstone, 6 July 1846, in *Correspondence on Convict Discipline and Transportation*, *PP (HL & HC)*, 16 February 1847.
12 Eardley-Wilmot to Gladstone, 6 July 1846.
13 Rev. T. Rogers, *Correspondence*.
14 Rogers.
15 Rogers; Barry, p. 27.
16 Robert Pringle Stewart, *Report*, 20 June 1846, in *Correspondence on Convict Discipline and Transportation*, *PP (HL & HC)*, 16 February 1847.
17 Price to Robertson, 25 August 1846, Dixson Library, Add. 566.
18 Robertson to Price, 19 September 1846, Dixson Library, Add. 566.
19 Price to Robertson, 24 September 1846, Dixson Library, Add. 566.
20 A. E. Baldock, Chief Constable, to Civil Commandant, December 1846, in *Correspondence on Convict Discipline and Transportation*, *PP (HL & HC)*, 16 February 1847.
21 Aaron Price, History of Norfolk Island from period of Discovery in 1774 to the present day, Dixson Library, Sydney, MS. Q247, 248, 249.
22 John Price to Denison, 7 December 1846, in *Further Correspondence on Convict Discipline and Transportation*, *PP (HL)*, 14 May 1847.
23 Alexander Maconochie in *Correspondence on Convict Discipline and Transportation*, *PP (HL & HC)*, 16 February 1847.
24 Rogers, p. 196.
25 Rogers; quoted in W. Foster Rogers, Man's Inhumanity to Man, MS. Mitchell Library, C 214.
26 W. Foster Rogers, grandson of Rev. T. Rogers, in 'Man's Inhumanity', pp. 5, 181–2; obituary in the *Advocate*, Melbourne, 24 January 1903.
27 Barry, p. 22; Rogers, p. 144.
28 Rogers, pp. 96–100; Barry, pp. 45–53.
30 Rogers, p. 196.

Chapter 20: The Last Days of the Settlement
 1 Earl Grey to Sir Charles Fitzroy, 27 February 1847, *PP (HC)*, vol. 8, 1847, *Correspondence on Convict Discipline and Transportation*, p. 76; *HRA*, series 1, vol. 23, p. 685.
 2 Sir E. Eardley-Wilmot to Rt. Hon. W. E. Gladstone, Secretary of State, *PP (HL)*, vol. 8, 1847, p. 119.

3 *HRA*, series 1, vol. 23, 20 July 1844, p. 687, Gipps to Stanley; *PP (HC)*, 1846, vol. 29, p. 10.
4 Wilmot to Stanley, 21 September 1844, *PP (HC)*, 1846, vol. 29, p. 16.
5 Rev. T. Beagley Naylor to Earl Grey, 1846, *PP (HC)*, vol. 48, 1847, pp. 67–76.
6 Archbishop Ullathorne, *Memoir of Bishop Willson*, London, 1887, pp. 56–61.
7 *PP (HC)*, vol. 48, 1847.
8 Bishop R. W. Willson, *PP (HL)*, vol. 11, 1850, p. 114.
9 McLean's letter of 12 May 1848, *PP (HC)*, vol. 45, 1850, *Accounts and Papers*, pp. 61–2.
10 Denison to Grey, 12 November 1849, *PP (HC)*, vol. 45, 1850, p. 61.
11 'Officer on the Spot, and Twelve Months on Norfolk Island 1847–1848', Mitchell Library, 981.90. (The author was probably the Commissariat Officer.)
12 Nehemiah Bartley, a traveller who wrote three books on his travels, this account is in *Opals and Agates*, Brisbane, 1892, pp. 42–3.
13 Mark Jeffreys, *A Burglar's Life*, Hobart 1893. This work is presumed to have been 'ghosted' by J. Lester Burke.
14 Jeffreys, p. 90.
15 Jeffreys, p. 95.
16 W. Nairn to Price 2 February 1852, in *Further Correspondence on the Subject of Convict Discipline and Transportation*, *PP (HL)*, 1852–53, vol. 18, pp. 88–9.
17 Price to Comptroller-General, 15 March 1852, *PP (HL)*, 1852–53, vol. 18, pp. 89–90.
18 Bishop Nixon to Comptroller-General, February 1852, *PP (HL)*, vol. 18, 1852–53, Papers presented 4 February 1853, p. 9.
19 Bishop Willson to Denison, 22 May 1852, *PP (HL)*, 1852–53, vol. 18, p. 88; *Personal Recollections of the Right Reverend Robert William Willson D.D.*, Hobart, 1882, pp. 38–52; also, Ullathorne, *Memoirs of Bishop Willson*, pp. 57–61.
20 J. V. Barry, *The Life and Death of John Price*, p. 58.
21 Price to Hampton, 15 March 1852, *PP (HL)*, 1852–53, vol. 18, p. 92.
22 Aaron Price, History of Norfolk Island etc., Dixson Library Q 249.
23 Denison to Grey, 6 February 1851, no. 21 G.O. 1/81; Barry, p. 59.
24 R. N. Dalkin, *The Colonial Cemetary of Norfolk Island*, Sydney, 1975.
25 Barry, p. 67.
26 Barry, pp. 68–9.
27 Barry, pp. 107–8; *Report of Legislative Assembly*, Victoria, 1856–7; *Biographical Memoir of the late Mr John Price, Inspector-General of Penal Establishments for Victoria*, 1857, Melbourne, printed by W. Fairfax. This is a pamphlet of 97 pages, pencilled on cover is T. L. B. Ferguson 14384.
28 Aaron Price, Q 249.
29 Aaron Price, Q 249.
30 Aaron Price, Q 249.
31 *Lukin Papers*, ed. S. G. Demasson, *Lukin—A Soldier of Misfortune 1850–1864*, 1929, p. 108.

Chapter 21: The New Arrivals on Norfolk Island
1 Sir John Barrow, *The Eventful History of the Mutiny and Piratical Seizure of H.M.S. Bounty, its Causes and Consequences*, London, 1831 (reprinted 1977).
2 Barrow, pp. 49–51. This gives a complete description of the bread-fruit and its uses.
3 Barrow, p. 11. Bligh was appointed Sailing Master on Cook's ship *Resolution* in 1776.
4 William Bligh, *A Voyage to the South Sea* (1979 ed.), p. 150.
5 Lady Belcher, *The Mutineers of the Bounty*, New York, 1871, p. 56.
6 Barrow, p. 13.
7 Richard Hough, *Captain Bligh and Mr Christian*, New York, 1973, p. 21.
8 Bligh, p. 158; Hough, pp. 162–9.
9 Bligh, pp. 231–2; Belcher, p. 67; Hough, pp. 188–9.
10 Hough, p. 204.
11 Hough, p. 201; Barrow, p. 123; Belcher, p. 50.

12 Barrow, pp. 123–51; Hough, pp. 222–9.
13 Barrow, p. 208; Hough p. 282.
14 Robert Nicholson, *The Pitcairners*, Sydney, 1968, pp. 37–8; Hough, 237–9.
15 Nicholson, p. 40; Hough p. 247; Belcher, p. 158.
16 Hough, p. 257; Belcher, p. 158.
17 Belcher, p. 159; Hough, p. 267.
18 Rev. T. Murray, *Pitcairn, The Island, the People, and the Pastor*, 1860, p. 116; Nicholson, p. 50; Hough, p. 267.
19 Belcher, pp. 159–60.
20 *HRNSW*, vol. 1, part 2, p. 706. Pp. 704–6 give the List of Mutineers who stayed on the *Bounty*, 28 April 1789, given by Bligh to the Admiralty.
21 Murray, p. 125; Belcher, p. 161; Hough, pp. 273–5.
22 Barrow, pp. 216–7; Murray, pp. 127–9; Belcher, pp. 163–8; Hough, pp. 273–5.
23 Nicholson, pp. 56–7.
24 Murray, p. 176; Belcher, pp. 172–5.
25 Belcher, pp. 182–95; Murray, pp. 176–9; Nicholson, p. 87.
26 Nicholson, pp. 108–10.
27 William Bishop, Commissariat Van Diemen's Land, letter to Lieutenant-Governor Denison, 18 September 1855, Archives of New South Wales.
28 Bishop, list of 15 September 1855, Archives of New South Wales.
29 Merval Hoare, *Norfolk Island, An Outline of its History 1774–1968*, 1969, p. 69; Belcher, pp. 262–5; Murray, p. 385.
30 Murray, p. 396.

Bibliography

The Bibliography is set out in the following way:
1 *Standard Reference Works*
2 *Official Publications*
    (a) British Parliamentary Papers
    (b) Other
3 *Manuscript Sources*
    (a) Journals, Diaries, Papers
    (b) Correspondence
4 *General Published Material*
    (a) Books
    (b) Articles
5 *Newspapers and Journals*

1 STANDARD REFERENCE WORKS

Australian Dictionary of Biography.
Australian Encyclopaedia, 10 vols, Sydney, 1958.
Historical Records of Australia, vols 1–22.
Historical Records of New South Wales, vols 1–8.
Index of Parliamentary Papers, House of Commons.
Index of Parliamentary Papers, House of Lords.

2 OFFICIAL PUBLICATIONS

(a) British Parliamentary Papers (in chronological order):
Report from Select Committee on Transportation, July 1837, PP (HL), July 1837, vol. 36, p. 1.

Report on the State of Prison Discipline in Van Diemen's Land, by Captain Maconochie, presented by Command of Her Majesty, 1838, PP (HL), 1838, vol. 9, p. 445.

Report from Select Committee on Transportation, 3 August 1838, PP (HL), 1838, vol. 36, p. 1.

Correspondence Relative to Convict Discipline, PP (HC), 1846, vol. 29, concerning transfer of authority for Norfolk Island from New South Wales, to Van Diemen's Land, pp. 7–12. Also correspondence from Major Joseph Childs and Colonial Secretary, pp. 10–13, pp. 46–9.

Correspondence Relative to Convict Discipline and Transportation, PP (HL), 1847, vol. 8, pp. 1–250.

Report of Commission on Norfolk Island, 1 July 1846, in *PP (HL)*, 1847, vol. 8, pp. 181–90. Complete *Report* of the 1 July Mutiny on Norfolk Island can be found in *PP (HL)*, 1847, vol. 9, *Correspondence on the Subject of Convict Discipline and Transportation*, pp. 174–90.

Robert Pringle Stewart *Report* on Norfolk Island, June 1846, in *PP (HL)*, 1847, vol. 8, pp. 84–101. (This volume also has letter from Reverend T. Beagley Naylor re conditions on Norfolk Island, pp. 71–80.)

Correspondence on the subject of Convict Discipline and Transportation, PP (HC), 1847, vol. 48, letters from John Price to La Trobe, in Papers presented 16 February, and 15 April, pp. 3–4, 13–17. See also Judge Fielding Browne's *Report* on the 1 July 1846 mutiny trial on Norfolk Island, pp. 35–40.

Correspondence Relative to Convict Discipline and Transportation, PP (HL), 1850, vol. 11, pp. 1–282.

Further Correspondence on the Subject of Convict Discipline and Transportation, PP (HL), 1851, vol. 11.

Further Correspondence on the Subject of Convict Discipline and Transportation, PP (HL), 1852–53, vol. 18, pp. 88–95.

(b) Other
Archives of New South Wales.
Old Bailey Sessions, Papers, December 1789–October 1790.
Report of Legislative Assembly (Victoria), 1856–57, La Trobe Library.
Royal Commission into Matters Relating to Norfolk Island, Sir John Nimmo, Commissioner, 1975.
Tasmanian State Archives (including Records of Governor's Office and Colonial Secretary's Office).

3 MANUSCRIPT SOURCES

(a) Journals, Diaries, Papers
Backhouse, J. & Walker, G. W., Report of a visit to the Penal Settlement of Norfolk Island, for Major-General Richard Bourke, 4 March 1835 Bound MS., Royal Commonwealth Society Library, London.
Bishop, William, Memorandum Called for by Sir William Denison, 1855, Archives Office of New South Wales.
Chapman Papers, Mitchell Library, A1974.
Clark, Ralph, Diary, Mitchell Library, C.219.
Cook, Thomas, An Exile's Lamentations, MS., Mitchell Library.
Dillon, C., Norfolk Island, its History, Typescript, Mitchell Library, B1586.
Foveaux, J., Letter-book, 2 vols, Mitchell Library, A1444.
Fyans, Foster, Reminiscences, MS., La Trobe Library, Melbourne.
Gunn Papers, Mitchell Library, A316.
Jones, Robert, Recollections of 13 Years Residence on Norfolk Island and Van Diemen's Land, 1823, Mitchell Library C/Y½.
King, P. G., Journal while Lieutenant-Governor of Norfolk Island 1791–96, National Library, Canberra, MS. 70.
King, P. G., Letter-book A2015, Mitchell Library.
King, P. G., Letter-book C187, Mitchell Library.
Knatchbull, J., Autobiography, written while in Darlinghurst Gaol, January 1844, Mitchell Library.
List of Convicts to Norfolk Island in the *Maitland*, September 1843, Dixson Library, Microfilm Reel 2424.
Norfolk Island Papers, Mitchell Library, 4/1167B; 4/1168B.
Norfolk Island Victualling Book, Mitchell Library, 1958.
Price, Aaron, History of Norfolk Island from Period of Discovery in 1774 to the present day, Dixon Library, Sydney, MS. Q247, 248, 249.
Richards List of Convicts embarked on First Fleet transports, 1787, Archives Office of New South Wales, Microfilm Reel 61.
Robertson, Elizabeth White, Diary, 1845, Dixson Library, Sydney, MS. 163.
Rogers, W. F., 'Man's Inhumanity', Typescript, Mitchell Library, C214.
Sharpe, Rev. T., Papers, Mitchell Library, A1502.
Shipping Lists of Settlers and Convicts removed from Norfolk Island between 1806 and 1810, Tasmanian Archives, Hobart.
'A Tale of Norfolk Island', by A. Chaplain, MS. Mitchell Library.
Wales, William, Journal of H.M.S. *Resolution*, Sept. 1773–Oct. 1774, Mitchell Library, Safe 1/84.

(b) Correspondence

Chapman, W. N., Letters to his Mother and sisters, Alexander Turnbull Library, Wellington, New Zealand.

Franklin Correspondence: *see* part 4, Books, General Published Sources, under Mackaness, G.

Hall, E. S., Letter to Secretary of State 9 February 1832, Mitchell Library, A2146.

Kent, Mrs Eliza, Letter written to her mother in May 1803, while she was on H.M.S. *Buffalo*.

King, P. G., Letters re his two sons Norfolk and Sydney King (the children born to Ann Inett in 1789–90), King Papers, National Library, Canberra.

Price, John, Letters to Gilbert Robertson, August, September 1846, Dixson Library, Add.566.

Robertson, G., Letter to Price, September 1846, Dixson Library, Add.566.

Wroe, T., Letter to Captain Day, April 1854, Dixson Library, Add.566.

4 GENERAL PUBLISHED MATERIAL

(a) Books

Anon., *Biographical Memoir* (of John Price), 97 pp. with 'T.L.B.' inscribed on cover, printed by W. Fairfax & Co. (Ferguson 14384), Melbourne, 1857.

Anderson, Joseph, *Recollections of a Peninsula Veteran*, London, 1913.

Astley, W. [Price Warung], *Tales of the Early Days*, London, 1894.

Atkins, Rev. T., *Reminiscences of Twelve Years Residence on Tasmania and New South Wales, Norfolk Island and Moreton Bay, Calcutta Madras and Cape Town, The United States of America and the Canadas*, London, 1869.

Backhouse J., *A Narrative of a visit to the Australian Penal Colonies*, London, 1843.

Barnard, M., with Eldershaw, *A History of Australia*, Sydney, 1962.

Barrow, Sir John, *The Eventful History of the Mutiny and Piratical Seizure of HMS Bounty, its Causes and Consequences*, London, 1831.

Barry, J. V., *Alexander Maconochie of Norfolk Island, A Study of a Pioneer in Penal Reform*, Oxford University Press, 1958.

Barry, J. V., *The Life and Death of John Price*, Melbourne University Press, 1964.

Bartley, N., *Opals and Agates*, Brisbane, 1892.

Bassett, M., *The Governor's Lady*, Oxford University Press, 1940.

Bateson, C., *The Convict Ships 1787–1868*, Glasgow, 1959.

Beatty, B., *With Shame Remembered*, Cassell & Co., Melbourne, 1962.

Becke, L., *Wild Life in Southern Seas*, 1898.

Belcher, Lady, *The Mutineers of the Bounty and their Descendants in Pitcairn and Norfolk Islands*, New York, 1871.

Best, Ensign A. D. W., *see* Taylor, N.

Blainey, G., *The Tyranny of Distance*, Sun Books, Melbourne, 1966.

Bligh, William, *A Voyage to the South Sea undertaken by Command of Her Majesty for the purposes of Conveying the Bread-fruit Tree to the West Indies, in HMS Bounty, commanded by Lieutenant William Bligh Including an Account of the Mutiny on Board the Said Ship and the Subsequent voyage of Part of the Crew, in the Ship's Boat, from Tofua to Timor, a Dutch Settlement in the East Indies, the Whole Illustrated with Charts etc*, London, 1792 (republished by Hutchinson, Australia, 1979).

Boase, F. T., *Modern English Biography*, Truro, Cornwall, 1897.

Bradley, Lieutenant W., *A Voyage to New South Wales*, 1786–1792, Journal, reproduced in facsimile by the Trustees of the Public Library of New South Wales, Ure Smith, 1969.

Bunbury, T., *Reminiscences of a Veteran*, London, 1861.

Burton, W. W., *The State of Religion and Education in New South Wales*, London, 1913.

Clark, C. M. H., *Select Documents in Australian History 1788–1850*, Sydney, 1950.

Clark, C. M. H., *Sources of Australian History*, Oxford University Press, Melbourne, 1957.

Clarke, Marcus, *For the Term of his Natural Life* (published unabridged Sydney, 1929, having earlier been published in instalments).

Clark, Ralph, *Journal and Letters 1787–1792*, Australian Documents Library, 1981.

Clune, F., *The Norfolk Island Story*, Sydney, 1967.

Cobbe, H. (ed.), *Cook's Voyages and People of the Pacific*, London, British Museum and Library Board, printed for the Australian National University Press, 1979.

Cobley, J., *Crimes of the First Fleet Convicts*, Sydney, 1970.

Cobley, J., *Sydney Cove 1788*, London, 1962.

Cobley, J., *Sydney Cove 1789–1790*, Sydney, 1963.

Cobley, J., *Sydney Cove 1791–1792*, Sydney, 1965.

Collins, Lieutenant D., *An Account of the English Colony in New South Wales*, 2 vols, London, 1798 and 1802 (republished Sydney, 1975).

Compton, H. (ed.), *A Master Mariner, The Life of Captain R. W. Eastwick*, London, 1861.

Cook, Captain James (J. C. Beaglehole ed.), *The Journals of Captain James Cook on his Voyages of Discovery*, 3 vols, *The Voyage of the Resolution and Adventure*, Cambridge, 1961, for the Hakluyt Society.

Cook, T., *The Exile's Lamentations*, (limited edition of 1000), Library of Australian History, Sydney, 1978.

Cox, G. H. [attributed to], *Memoirs of William Cox, J.P.*, published 1901, reprinted by Library of Australian History, Sydney, 1979.

Demasson, S. G. (ed.), *Lukin, A Soldier of Misfortune*, 1929.

Denison, Sir W., *The Varieties of Vice-Regal Life*, London, 1870.

Derrincourt, W., *Old Convict Days* (Louis Becke ed.), New York, 1899.

Easty, John, Private Marine, *Memorandum of the Transactions of a Voyage from England to Botany Bay 1787–1793* (Fidlon & Ryan, edd.), Australian Documents Library, 1980.

Eldershaw, M. Barnard, *Phillip of Australia*, Sydney, 1938.

Eldershaw, M. Barnard, *The Life and Times of John Piper*, Sydney, 1973.

Ellis, M. H., *John Macarthur*, Sydney, 1955.

Evatt, H. V., *Rum Rebellion*, Sydney, 1938.

Fitzpatrick, K., *Sir John Franklin in Tasmania, 1837–1843*, Melbourne, 1949.

Fletcher, B., *Colonial Australia before 1850*, London, 1976.

Forster, G., *A Voyage Round the World Performed in His Britannic Majesty's Ships the Resolution and Adventure in the Years 1772–1773–1774 and 1975*, Whitestone, Dublin, 1777.

Forsyth, W. D., *Governor Arthur's Convict System*, 1955.

Franklin Correspondence: *see* Mackaness, G.

Harris, A. [attributed to], *Settlers and Convicts*, London, 1847 (reprinted with foreword by Manning Clark), 1964.

Hill, M. Davenport (ed), *Our Exemplars Poor and Rich*, London, 1861.

Hill-Reid, W. S., *John Grant's Journey, A Convict's Story 1803–11*, Heinemann, 1957.

Hoare, M. H., *Norfolk Island, An Outline of its History 1774–1968*, University of Queensland, 1969.

Hoare, M. H., *The Discovery of Norfolk Island* (pamphlet), Canberra, 1974.

Holt, J., *Memoirs*, (T. Croker ed.), London, 1838.

Hough, Richard, *Captain Bligh and Mr Christian, The Men and the Mutiny*, New York, 1973.

Hunter, Captain J., *An Historical Journal of the Transactions at Port Jackson and Norfolk Island etc. Including the Journals of Governors Phillip and King, and of Lieut. Ball, and the Voyages from the First Sailing of the Sirius in 1787, to the Return of that Ship's Company to England in 1792*, London, 1973, facsimile edition edited by John Percival Bach, Angus & Robertson, 1968.

Ingleton, G. C., *True Patriots All*, Sydney, 1952.

Jackson, T., (Tamati Tiakihana), *Norfolk Island*, United Publishing Printing Company Ltd, Rotorua, New Zealand, 1966.

Jeffrey, M., *A Burglar's Life*, Walsh, Hobart (no date, but *c.* 1893).

Johnson, K. A. & Sainty, M., *Gravestone Inscriptions N.S.W.*, Genealogical Publications of Australia, 1973.

Kellet, A., *The Knaresborough Story*, The Advertiser Press Ltd, Huddersfield, Yorkshire, 1977.

Kelsh, Rev. T., *Personal Recollections of the Right Reverend Robert William Willson D. D.*, Hobart, 1882.

Kennedy, G. (ed.), *The Mutiny of the Bounty*, an illustrated edition of Sir John Barrow's original account, Boston, 1980.

Levi, J. S. & Bergman, J. F. J., *Australian Genesis, Jewish Convicts and Settlers 1788–1850*, Rigby, 1974.

Lyte, C., *Sir Joseph Banks*, Reed, Sydney, 1980.

Macintosh, N. K., *Richard Johnson, Chaplain to the Colony of New South Wales*, limited edition, Library of Australian History, 1978.

Mackaness, G. (ed.), *Australian Historical Monographs* (these monographs, 44 in number, were originally privately published between 1935 and 1962, and include *The Franklin Correspondence*, 2 vols).

McMinn, W. G., *Allan Cunningham, Botanist and Explorer*, Melbourne University Press, 1965.

Maconochie, A., *Norfolk Island*, London, 1847 (reprinted as *Norfolk Island 1840–44*, limited edition, Hobart, 1973).

Maconochie, A., *Secondary Punishment, The Mark System*, London, 1848.

Macquarie, L., Governor of New South Wales 1810–1822, *Journals of his Tours in New South Wales and Van Diemen's Land 1810–1822*, Library of Australian History and Library Council of New South Wales, Sydney, 1979.

Maude, H. E., *Of Islands and Men*, Oxford University Press, 1968.

Mill, H. R., *The Record of the Royal Geographical Society*, 1830–1930, London, 1930 (*see* p. 13 of J. V. Barry's *Alexander Maconochie of Norfolk Island*).

Mortlock, J. F., *Experiences of a Convict*, London, 1864–5 (republished G. A. Wilkes & A. G. Mitchell, edd., Sydney University Press, 1965).

Murray, Rev. T. B., *Pitcairn, the Island the People and the Pastor*, London, 1860.

Neville, D., *Blackburn's Isle*, Lavenham, Suffolk, 1975.

Nicholson, R., *The Pitcairners*, Sydney, 1968.

Noah, W., *A Voyage to Sydney in New South Wales 1798–99*, Library of Australian History, 1978 (the Journal describes the voyage on a convict transport *Hillsborough*, and arrival at New South Wales).

Palmer, V., *National Portraits*, Sydney, 1940.

Park, Ruth, *The Companion Guide to Sydney*, Collins, 1973.

Phillip, Governor Arthur, *The Official Account of the Expedition to New South Wales and the Founding of the Australian Settlement*, London, 1789 (republished as *The Voyage of Governor Phillip*, J. J. Auchmuty (ed.), 1970).

Pike, E. R., *Human Documents of Adam Smith's Time*, London, 1974.

Radzinowicz, L., *History of English Criminal Law and its Administration from 1750*, 3 vols, 1948–1956.

Ralston, J. P., *Historical Records of Newcastle 1797–1897*, Newcastle, 1897 (facsimile by Library of Australian History, 1978).

Ramage, I. A., *A Cameo of Captain Thomas Rowley*, Library of Australian History, 1981.

Ritchie, J., *Punishment and Profit, Reports of Commissioner John Bigge, 1822–3*, Heinemann, Melbourne, 1970.

Robson, L. L., *The Convict Settlers of Australia*, Melbourne University Press, 1965.

Robson, L. L., *History of Tasmania*, vol. 1, Oxford University Press, Melbourne, 1983.

Roderick, C., *John Knatchbull, From Quarterdeck to Gallows*, Sydney, 1963.

Rogers, Rev. T., *Correspondence relating to the Dismissal of the Rev. T. Rogers from his Chaplaincy at Norfolk Island*, Launceston, 1849.

Rusden, G. W., *History of Australia*, 3 vols, London, 1883.

Shaw, A. G. L., *Convicts and the Colonies, A Study of Penal Transportation from Great Britain and Ireland to Australia and other parts of the British Empire*, Melbourne University Press, 1978.

Smythe, A. Bowes, *The Journal of Arthur Bowes Smythe, Surgeon, Lady Penrhyn 1787–1789*, Fidlon & Ryan (edd.), 1980, Australian Documents Library.

Sturt, Mrs Napier, *Charles Sturt, Sometime Captain 39th Regiment and Australian Explorer*, London, 1899.

Swan, R. A., *To Botany Bay*, Roebuck Society Publication, No. 8, Canberra, 1973.

274   *Punishment Short of Death*

Tamati Tiakihana, *see* Jackson, T.
Taylor, N. (ed.), *The Journal of Ensign Best 1837–1843*, Turnbull Library Monograph, New Zealand, 1966.
Tench, W., *A Complete Account of the Settlement at Port Jackson*, London, 1793 (republished 1961, L. F. Fitzhardinge (ed.), Library of Australian History in association with Royal Australian Historical Society, Sydney, 1979).
Tench, W., *A Narrative of the Expedition to Botany Bay*, London, 1789.
Tucker, J., *Ralph Rashleigh* (MS. written 1845, published by Jonathon Cape, 1929; republished with explanatory Introduction by Professor Colin Roderick, The Folio Society, London, 1977).
Turnbull, J., *A Voyage Round the World in the years 1800–1804*, London, 1805.
Ullathorne, Rt. Rev. W. B., *Autobiography of Bishop Ullathorne*, London, 1891.
Ullathorne, Rt. Rev., *On the Management of Criminals*, London, 1866.
Weidenhofer, M., *The Convict Years 1788–1868*, Lansdowne, 1973.
West, J., *The History of Tasmania*, 2 vols, Launceston, Tasmania, 1852 (reprinted, 2 vols, Public Library of South Australia, 1966, further printing, Angus & Robertson, Sydney, 1971).
Windross, J., *see* Ralston, J. P.
Worgan, G. B., *Journal of a First Fleet Surgeon*, 1788, Library of Australian History, 1978.

(b) Articles
'Bass's Land Explorations', *JRAHS*, vol. 37, part 4, pp. 244–50.
'Captain John Piper', *JRAHS*, vol. 26, part 6, pp. 479–98.
Currey, C. H., 'An Outline of the Story of Norfolk Island and Pitcairn's Island', *JRAHS*, vol. 44, part 6, pp. 325–74.
Dalkin, R. N., 'Norfolk Island—The First Settlement 1788–1814', *JRAHS*, vol. 57, part 3, pp. 189–212.
Dowling, J. A., 'An Account of Norfolk Island', *JAHS*, 1905, part 11, pp. 213–20.
Green, T. H., 'Petrology and Geochemistry of Basalts from Norfolk Island', *Journal of the Geological Society of Australia*, vol. 20, part 3, 1973.
Henry, E. R., 'A Tale of Two Islands', *Tasmanian Historical Research Association, Papers and Proceedings*, vol. 22, no. 4, 1976.
Jones, J. G. & McDougall, I., 'Geological History of Norfolk and Philip Islands, South-West Pacific Ocean', *Journal of the Geological Society of Australia*, vol. 20, part 3, 1973.
'Letters of David Blackburn', *JRAHS*, vol. 20, part 5, pp. 318–34.
Robson, L. L., 'The Historical Basis of *For the Term of His Natural Life*', Australian Literary Studies, vol. 1, 1963.
Sayers, S., 'Captain Foster Fyans of Portland Bay District', *Victorian Historical Magazine*, vol. 40, nos. 1 & 2, pp. 45–66.
Udentsev, G. B., 'Bathymetric Map of the Pacific Ocean', *Institute of Oceanology, Academy of Science*, Moscow, 1964.
'Vaucluse Estate from 1793–1829', *JRAHS*, vol. 6, part 1, pp. 36–68.

5   NEWSPAPERS AND JOURNALS

(a) Newspapers
Age, Melbourne, December quarter 1856, March quarter 1857.
Argus, Melbourne, December quarter 1856, March quarter 1857.
Collection of newspaper-cuttings, photographs, etc. of Norfolk Island, Mitchell Library 992.9 .
     M
Hobart Town Gazette and Southern Reporter, January–December 1818–19.
Port Phillip Gazette, no. 48, November 1850.
Sydney Gazette and New South Wales Advertiser, January–December 1810.
Victorian Government Gazette, 5 May 1857, vol. 1.

(b) Journals
Australian Historical Society, Journal and Proceedings, 1905, part 11.
Australian Literary Studies.
Gentleman's Magazine, vol. 43, New Series, 1855.
Royal Australian Historical Society, Journal and Proceedings, vol. 6, part 1, pp. 36–38.
Tasmanian Historical Research Association, Papers and Proceedings, vol. 12, no. 2, 1964; vol. 22, no. 4, 1976.
Victorian Historical Magazine, vol. 39, nos. 1 & 2; vol. 40, nos. 1 & 2.

T

Index

Abbreviations of place-names and rank as follows: NSW New South Wales;
NI Norfolk Island; VDL Van Diemen's Land; Lt.-Gov. Lieutenant-Governor;
Capt. Captain; Lt. Lieutenant; Asst. Assistant; Supt. Superintendent; Dr Doctor;
Rev Reverend.

277